Anxiety

Jacques Lacan

Anxiety

The Seminar of Jacques Lacan
Book X

Edited by Jacques-Alain Miller

Translated by A. R. Price

polity

First published in French as *Le Séminaire livre X - L'angoisse* © Éditions du Seuil, 2004

This English edition © Polity Press, 2014

Polity Press
65 Bridge Street
Cambridge CB2 1UR, UK

Polity Press
350 Main Street
Malden, MA 02148, USA

ISBN-13: 978-0-7456-6041-7

A catalogue record for this book is available from the British Library.

Typeset in 10.5 on 12 pt Times NR MT by
Servis Filmsetting Ltd, Stockport, Cheshire
Printed and bound in The United States of America

The publisher has used its best endeavours to ensure that the URLs for external websites referred to in this book are correct and active at the time of going to press. However, the publisher has no responsibility for the websites and can make no guarantee that a site will remain live or that the content is or will remain appropriate.

Every effort has been made to trace all copyright holders, but if any have been inadvertently overlooked the publisher will be pleased to include any necessary credits in any subsequent reprint or edition.

For further information on Polity, visit our website: www.politybooks.com

Contents

vi   Contents

Book X

Anxiety

1962–1963

INTRODUCTION TO THE STRUCTURE OF ANXIETY

I

ANXIETY IN THE NET OF SIGNIFIERS

The desire of the Other
Towards an orography of anxiety
Seriousness, care, expectation
Inhibition, impediment, embarrassment
Inhibition, emotion, turmoil

This year, I'm going to be speaking to you about anxiety.

Someone who's not at all remote from me in our circle neverthe-less let slip the other day some surprise at my having chosen this subject, which didn't strike him as having much on offer. I must say that I won't have any trouble proving to him the contrary. Amidst the mass of what is proposed to us on this subject in the form of questions, I shall have to choose and drastically so. This is why I shall be trying, as of today, to fling you into the thick of it.

But this surprise already seemed to me to harbour the trace of some unstemmed naivety, which consists in believing that each year I pick a subject just like that, a subject I would deem fit for teasing out some malarkey. Not so. Anxiety is very precisely the meeting point where everything from my previous disquisition is lying in wait for you. You're going to see how a certain number of terms, which until now may not have appeared adequately linked to one another, can now be connected up. You're going to see, I think, how in being knotted together more tightly on the ground of anxiety each one will fall into place even better.

I say *even better*, since it appeared to me, in what was said during our Society's recent meeting outside Paris, that something had effectively fallen into place in your minds concerning the structure which is so essential and which is called *the fantasy*. You'll see that the structure of anxiety is not far from it, for the reason that it's well and truly the same.

1

I've put a few brief signifiers here on the blackboard to serve as reference points or to jog your memory. It's not such a big blackboard and it might not include all those I'd have liked it to, but it's also better not to overdo it when simplification is at issue.

They form two groups. On the left, this one, which I'm going to be completing.

Que me veut-Il ?

Care ↘◯↗ *Seriousness*   *Inhibition*

                               Symptom

Expectation   *Anxiety*

On the right, this graph which I apologize for having pestered you with for such a long time, but which is all the same necessary, since its reference-value will appear to you, I think, ever more effective.

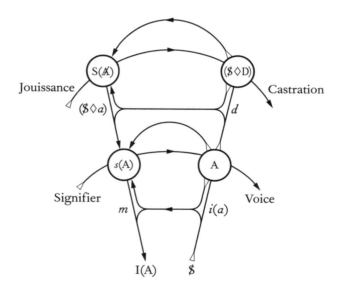

Likewise, might not its form ever have struck you as being akin to the shape of a *poire d'angoisse*, a choke pear? Perhaps it's not a chance evocation.

On the other hand, whilst the little topological surface to which I devoted so much of last year, that of the cross-cap, might have suggested to some of you the folding forms of the embryological germ layers, even the layers of the cortex, no one, in spite of the at once bilateral and woven arrangement of oriented intercommunications proper to the graph, has ever mentioned in this regard the solar plexus. Of course, I'm not claiming to be delivering up its secrets here, but this curious little similarity is perhaps not as far-fetched as might be thought and deserves to be brought up at the beginning of a disquisition on anxiety.

As the reflection with which I introduced my disquisition confirms to a certain degree, the reflection from one of my close associates here in our Society, anxiety doesn't seem to be the thing that stifles you, as psychoanalysts, I mean. And yet, it would not be going too far to say that it ought to. Indeed, it's part of the logic of things, that is to say, the logic of the relationship you have with your patient. Sensing what the subject can bear of anxiety puts you to the test at every moment. It has to be supposed therefore, at least for those of you who've been trained in technique, that the thing has finished up slipping into your way of regulating things, quite unperceived, it has to be said. But for the analyst starting out in his practice, it's not ruled out, thank goodness, much as he might show great aptitude for being an analyst, that he may feel some anxiety from his first dealings with the patient on the couch.

In this regard, the question of the communication of anxiety still needs to be touched on. Is the anxiety that you know, it seems, how to regulate and buffer so well in yourselves that it guides you, the same as the patient's? Why not? I'll leave the question open for the time being, perhaps not for very long. It's worthwhile raising it at the outset, even if we shall have to turn to our essential articulations to give it a valid answer and therefore wait until we've trodden for a while the first winding paths I'm about to propose.

These paths are not entirely beyond expectations for those who are regular members of my audience. Indeed, if you remember, during another series of our Society's so-called Provincial Study Days, which were far from giving me that much satisfaction, I thought it necessary, by way of an aside in my disquisition from last year, to launch, in advance, a formula indicating the essential relationship between anxiety and the desire of the Other.

For those who weren't there, I'll recall the fable, the apologue, the amusing image I briefly set out before you. Myself donning the animal mask with which the sorcerer in the Cave of the Three Brothers is covered, I pictured myself faced with another animal, a real one this time, taken to be gigantic for the sake of the story, a praying mantis. Since I didn't know which mask I was wearing, you can easily imagine that I had some reason not to feel reassured in the event that, by chance, this mask might have been just what it took to lead my partner into some error as to my identity. The whole thing was well underscored by the fact that, as I confessed, I couldn't see my own image in the enigmatic mirror of the insect's ocular globe.

This metaphor preserves its full worth today. It justifies my having placed at the centre of the signifiers on the board the question I introduced long ago as the hinge between the two storeys on the graph, inasmuch as they structure the subject's relationship with the signifier, which strikes me as having to be the key to what Freudian doctrine introduced regarding subjectivity, *Che vuoi?*, *Que veux-tu?*, *What wouldst thou?* Push the functioning, the insertion of the key, a little further and you have, *Que me veut-Il?* with the ambiguity that the French permits with respect to the *me* between the direct or indirect object. It's not simply, *What does the Other want with me?* but also a suspended questioning that directly concerns the ego, not *How does He want me?* but, *What does He want concerning this place of the ego?*

The question is held in abeyance between the two storeys and precisely between the two return routes that designate in each of them their characteristic effect. The distance between them, which it is so essential to construct and which will be at the root of everything we are going to be moving into, renders the relationship to desire at once homologous with and distinct from narcissistic identification.

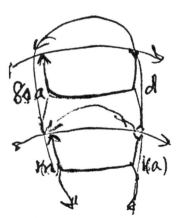

We're going to see the function of anxiety being introduced into the play of the dialectic that knots these two levels so tightly together. Not that this function is in itself the mainspring thereof, but it's what allows us to orient ourselves here in keeping with the moments at which it appears. So it is, therefore, that the question I've posed, as to your relation as analysts to anxiety, leaves this other question in abeyance – who are you sparing? The other party, no doubt, but also yourself. Sparing yourself and sparing the other, though they overlap, mustn't be confused. We even find here one of the aims that will be proposed to you at the end of this year's disquisition.

For the time being, I'll content myself with introducing an indication pertaining to method for the lessons we're going to have to draw from our research on anxiety. Seeing at what privileged points it emerges will allow us to shape a true orography of anxiety, which will lead us directly onto a terrain that is none other than that of the term-to-term relationships constituted by the particularly condensed structural attempt from which I believed I should fashion for you the guide of our disquisition, in the form of this graph.

If, therefore, you know how to manage with regard to anxiety, trying to see how will enable us to make some headway. And likewise, I couldn't produce anxiety myself without managing it in some way. Maybe that's a pitfall. I oughtn't to manage it too quickly. Nor does this mean, in any way, that, through some psychodramatic game, my goal should be to *vous jeter*, to cast you into anxiety – with the pun I've already made on the *je* in *jeter*.

Everyone knows that projecting the *I* onto the inroad to anxiety has for some time been the ambition of a philosophy that is termed *existentialist*. There's no shortage of references, from Kierkegaard to Gabriel Marcel, Shestov, Berdyaev and a few others. Not all of them have the same place, nor can they be used in the same way. But I insist on saying at the start of this disquisition that this philosophy – in so far as, from its patron saint, named first off, down to those whose names I've listed after him, it incontestably shows some decline – is marked, I feel, with some haste and even some disarray, I'd say, in relation to the reference in which, in the same era, the movement of thought has put its trust, namely, the reference to history. In relation to this reference, existentialist thought is born of and precipitated by a disarray, in the etymological sense of the term.

The horse of thought, I will say; to borrow the object of his phobia from Little Hans, that imagines itself for a while to be the one that pulls the stagecoach of history, all of a sudden rears up, runs wild, then falls down and gives itself over to that great *Krawallmachen* wherein Little Hans finds one of the images of the fear he holds dear. It's what I call a movement of haste, in the negative sense of the term, that of disarray. And it's precisely for this reason that this is far from being what interests us most in the line of thought I singled out just now, as does everyone else for that matter, with the term existentialism.

Also, it may be remarked that the last one to come along and not perhaps the lesser of them, Monsieur Sartre, expressly applies himself not only to putting this horse back on its hooves, but back between the shafts that pull the said coach of history. It's precisely on this account that Monsieur Sartre has been much occupied with the function of seriousness and has wondered about it a great deal.

There is also someone else whom I didn't put in the series and of whom I will say, since I'm simply venturing into some background details by touching on this at the beginning, that it's in reference to him that the philosophers who observe us, at the point we're coming to in this, can ask themselves – *will the analysts measure up to what we make of anxiety?* There stands Heidegger. With my play on the word *jeter*, it was precisely to him and his originative dereliction that I was closest.

Being-unto-death, to call it by its name, which is the inroad by which Heidegger, in his well-versed disquisition, leads us to his enigmatic examination of an entity's Being, doesn't really go via anxiety. The reference of Heidegger's question is a *lived* reference. He named it, it is fundamental, and it's to do with everyone, with *one*,[1] with the omnitude of everyday human life, it is *care*. Of course, in this capacity, this reference cannot, any more than care itself, be in the least bit foreign to us.

Since I've called on two witnesses here, Sartre and Heidegger, I won't hesitate to call on a third, in so far as I don't think him unworthy of representing those who are here, observing what he too is going to say, and that's me.

I'm going by some accounts I've received, once again in the last hours, concerning what I shall call expectation. But on this occasion I'm not only speaking about yours. It was in just such a way that a piece of work came to me yesterday evening which I'd told one of you I'd be waiting for before beginning my disquisition here today. I'd asked him whether I might have a copy of this text and even whether he might orient me with regard to a question he'd posed me. Even though I haven't yet been able to go through it, the fact that it was brought to me on time met my expectation, just as, after all, I've come here on time to meet yours. Is this an action of such a nature as to give rise in itself to anxiety? Without having questioned the fellow concerned, I don't think so. As for me, upon my word, I can answer that this expectation, albeit just what it takes to bring a certain weight down upon me, is not, I believe I can speak from experience, a dimension that in and of itself gives rise to anxiety. I would even say, quite the contrary.

I have insisted on making this last reference, which is so close to home that it might strike you as problematic, so as to indicate how I mean to put you to the question that has been mine from the start – at what distance is anxiety to be poised so as to speak to you about it without immediately shutting it away in a cupboard and without leaving it in a vague state either? Well, my goodness, at the right distance. I mean one that doesn't put us too close to anyone, at this familiar distance that I've evoked for you in picking up these recent references, the distance from my interlocutor who brings me his paper at the last minute, and the distance from myself who must take a risk here with my disquisition on anxiety.

We're going to try to take this anxiety under our wing. That won't make it any more conspicuous. Believe me, it's really going to leave us at the opaque distance that separates us from those who are closest to us.

So, between this care, this seriousness, and this expectation, are you going to think that this is how I wanted to encircle anxiety, to pin it down? Well, don't believe it. It isn't to be sought in the middle. If I've drawn a little circle in the midst of these three terms, with these splayed arrows,[2] it's to tell you that, if you're searching there, you will quickly see that, if ever there it was, the bird has taken flight.

2

Inhibitions, Symptoms and Anxiety, so runs the title, the slogan, under which the last word of what Freud articulated on the subject of anxiety is held in an analyst's memory and leaves its mark.

I won't be going into this text today, for the reason that I'm determined, as you've seen from the beginning, to go without a safety net, and because there's no topic for which the net of Freudian disquisition is more likely to give us a false sense of security. When we do go into this text, you shall see very well what there is to be seen as regards anxiety, namely, that there isn't any safety net. When anxiety is at issue, each piece of the mesh, so to speak, only carries any meaning in so far as it leaves empty the space where anxiety lies.

In the disquisition of *Inhibitions, Symptoms and Anxiety*, everything is spoken about, thank goodness, except anxiety. Does this mean that it may not be spoken about? Going without a safety net evokes the tightrope walker. My only rope is the title, *Inhibitions, Symptoms and Anxiety*. It leaps, if I may say so, to one's understanding that these three terms do not sit at the same level. This makes for something heteroclite, which is why I've written them on three staggered lines. In order for it to work, in order for them to be understood as a series, they really need to be seen as I've put them here, on a diagonal, which implies filling in the blanks.

I'm not going to take the time right now to demonstrate for you what's obvious, namely, the difference between the structure of these three terms, each of which absolutely does not have, if we want to situate them, the same terms as their context or surrounding.

So it is that inhibition lies within the dimension of movement, in the widest sense of the term. I won't go into the text, but you remember enough of it to see that Freud, with respect to inhibition, cannot help but speak solely of locomotion. Movement exists, at least metaphorically, in every function, even if it isn't a locomotive one.

In inhibition, it's the halting of movement that's involved. Does this mean that the word *inhibition* is designed only to suggest a halting? You would easily object with the notion of a keeping in check. Why not? I would grant you as much.

So, a matrix needs to be constructed which will allow us to distinguish the dimensions involved in a notion that is very familiar to us. I don't see why we shouldn't put the notion of difficulty on the horizontal axis and that of movement on the vertical axis of coordinates. This is what's going to allow us to see more clearly, because it's also what's going to allow us to come back down to earth, the earth of what isn't veiled over by the learned word, the notion, or even the concept, that people make do with.

Why not use the word *impede*? This is precisely what's at issue. Our subjects are inhibited when they speak to us about their inhibition and we ourselves are when we speak about inhibition at scientific congresses, but every day they are very much impeded. To be impeded is a symptom. To be inhibited is a symptom tucked away in a museum.

Looking up the etymology doesn't imply any superstition. I help myself to it when it's helpful to me. *Impedicare* means *to be ensnared* and it's an extremely precious notion all the same. Indeed, it implies the relationship between one dimension and something that comes to interfere with it and which, in what interests us, impedes not the function, a term of reference, not movement, which is rendered difficult, but truly and verily the subject. Here then is what brings us closer to what we're searching for, namely, what happens in what goes by the name of anxiety. Therefore, I'm putting *impediment* in the same column as *symptom*.

I'll tell you straight off that the snare in question is narcissistic capture. Following this we're going to be led to link up a great deal more to that, but with this point you're already no longer at the elementary stage, if you care to remember what I linked to the last term concerning the very precise limit that narcissistic capture introduces with regard to what can be invested in the object, in so far as the phallus, for its part, remains auto-erotically invested. The fracture that results from this in the specular image comes to be what specifically gives its support and its material to the signifying articulation that, on the other plane, the symbolic plane, is called castration. The impediment that arises is linked to this circle that makes for the fact that, with the same movement by which the subject advances towards jouissance, that is to say, towards what is furthest from him, he encounters this intimate fracture, right up close, by letting himself be caught, along the way, by his own image, the specular image. That's the snare.

Here, we're still at the level of the symptom. Let's try to go further. If we push forward the examination of the meaning of the word *inhibition*, which term is to be put in the third column? After *inhibition* and *impediment*, the third term I propose, still for the sake of leading you to the bottom of lived experience, to the derisory seriousness of the question, is the fine term *embarrassment*.[3]

It's going to be all the more precious to us given that today etymology is satisfying me to the full, the wind is clearly blowing my way. Embarrassment is quite precisely the subject S decked out with the bar, $, since *imbaricare* makes the most direct allusion to the bar, *bara*, as such. We've really got the most direct image of the lived experience of embarrassment here. When you don't know what to do with yourself any more, you look for something behind which to shield yourself. The experience of the bar is precisely what's at issue. If I've been well informed, this bar assumes more than one form in the numerous patois. But there's no need to resort to patois. There aren't any Spaniards here, are there? Too bad, because I've been told that in Spanish, the *embarazada, she who is embarrassed*, designates a pregnant woman, which is another form, a very significant one, of the bar in its place.

There you go then for the dimension of difficulty. The first horizontal row, which begins with inhibition and continues with impediment, ends up at this slight form of anxiety called embarrassment.

In the other dimension, that of movement, what terms are we going to see drawn up vertically after the term *inhibition*?

First off, there's *emotion*.

You'll forgive me if I continue to trust in an etymology that has so far been propitious. Emotion refers etymologically to movement, except that here we'll give a little nudge by putting forward Goldstein's sense of throwing off, *ex*, out of the line of movement – it's movement that disintegrates, it's the reaction that one calls catastrophic. My pointing out to you where to put that was useful, since, after all, some people told us that anxiety was just that, a catastrophic reaction. It's not unrelated, of course, but what wouldn't be related to anxiety? It's precisely a question of knowing where anxiety itself really lies. The fact that, for example, the same reference to the catastrophic reaction has been used, and without any misgivings, to designate hysterical fits, or even, in other cases, anger, proves well enough all the same that this isn't sufficient for distinguishing anxiety, nor for pointing out where it is.

Let's take the next step. We're still maintaining a respectful distance from anxiety, since here we're two squares away from it. In the dimension of movement, is there something that corresponds more precisely to the level of anxiety? I'm going to call it by a name that for a long time I've set aside with you in mind, as a delicacy. Maybe I made a fleeting allusion to it, but only those particularly prehensile ears will have retained it. It's the word *turmoil*.[4]

Etymology is favouring me here in the most fabulous way. It's delightful. This is why I'm not going to hesitate to take further advantage of it, once I've told you first of all everything it's furnished me with. I'm going to indicate to you expressly to refer to the entry in Messrs Bloch and von Wartburg, with apologies if it's surplus to requirement with regard to what I'm about to say to you now, all the more so given that what I'm going to say to you is a direct quote from the text. I borrow things wherever I find them, whether that upsets anyone or not.

These fellows tell me then that *linguistic sentiment*, as they express themselves, has moved this term closer to the word *émouvoir, to move emotionally*. Now, don't be fooled, it has nothing to do with that. Etymologically, as indeed for anyone who knows how to use words, *émoi* has nothing to do with *émotion*. At any rate, let me tell you that the term *esmayer* is already attested in the thirteenth century – that before it, *esmais* and even *esmoi-esmais*, should you care to know, only triumphed, to express myself as the authors do, in the sixteenth century – that *esmayer* has the sense of *to trouble, to frighten* and also *to become flustered* – that *esmayer* is indeed still commonly used in the various patois and leads us to the vulgar Latin *exmagare*, which means *to cause to lose one's might, one's strength* – and that this vulgar Latin is linked to a graft from a Western Germanic root which, when reconstructed, gives *magan*. Besides, there's no need to reconstruct it because it exists in this same form in High German and in Gothic. However much German you speak, you can look up the German *mögen*. In English, there is *may*.[5] Does *smagare* exist in Italian?

Not really. Going by Bloch and von Wartburg, it means *to become discouraged*. So, some doubt remains. As there aren't any

Portuguese here, I won't make any objection to accepting what, not I, but Bloch and von Wartburg advance by including *esmagar*, which purportedly means *to crush*, which, until further notice, I'm going to hold onto as having great interest for the next part. I'll spare you the Provençal variations.

Be that as it may, it's certain that the translation, which has been accepted, of *Triebregung* as *émoi pulsionnel* is absolutely incorrect and precisely because of all the distance that stands between *émotion* and *émoi*. *Émoi, turmoil*, is trouble, the fall of might, *Regung* is stimulation, a call to disorder, even to *émeute*, to riot. I shall also fortify myself with this etymological enquiry to tell you that, up to a certain era, more or less the same one that saw what is called in Bloch and von Wartburg the *triumph* of *émoi, émeute* itself carried precisely the meaning of emotion and only took on the meaning of collective public action from the seventeenth century onwards.

All this ought to make you feel that the linguistic nuances, the linguistic versions even, being evoked here, are being made to guide us into defining, with *turmoil*, the third place in the direction of what *inhibition* means on the axis of movement, just as, on the axis of difficulty, we singled out the corresponding reference as *embarrassment*. *Turmoil* is trouble, *to become troubled* as such, to be as deeply troubled as one can be in the dimension of movement. *Embarrassment* implies reaching the maximum level of difficulty.

Does this mean that we've reached anxiety? The boxes of this little table are there to show you that this is not what we are claiming.

Difficulty			
Movement	*Inhibition*	*Impediment*	*Embarrassment*
	Emotion	*Symptom*	*X*
	Turmoil	*X*	*Anxiety*

We have filled in the two boxes in the vertical direction with *emotion* and *turmoil*, and the two in the horizontal direction with *impediment* and *embarrassment*. This box marked with an *X* is still empty, as is this one here.

How can they be filled in? It's a subject of the greatest interest with regard to the handling of anxiety.

I'm going to leave it for you a while as a conundrum.

3

Having set out this little preamble in keeping with the Freudian triad of inhibition, symptom and anxiety, the ground has now been cleared, to speak of it in a doctrinal fashion.

After having brought it back, by way of these evocations, to the level of experience itself, let's try to situate it in a conceptual framework.

What is anxiety? We've ruled out the idea that it might be an emotion. To introduce it, I will say that it's an affect.

Those who follow the movements of affinity or aversion in my disquisition, often allowing themselves to be caught out by appearances, no doubt think that I'm less interested in affects than anything else. That's absurd. I've tried, on occasion, to say what affect is not. It is not Being given in its immediacy, nor is it the subject in a raw form either. It is in no respect protopathic. My occasional remarks on affect amount to nothing but that. And this is even the reason why it has a close structural relationship to what a subject is, even traditionally speaking. I hope to articulate this for you in an indelible fashion next time.

On the other hand, what I said about affect is that it isn't repressed. Freud says it just as I do. It's unfastened, it drifts about. It can be found displaced, maddened, inverted, or metabolized, but it isn't repressed. What are repressed are the signifiers that moor it.

The relationship between affect and the signifier would necessitate a whole year on the theory of affects. I've already hinted at how I understand it. I did so with regard to anger.

Anger, I told you, is what happens in subjects when the little pegs won't fit into the little holes. What does that mean? When at the level of the Other, of the signifier, that is to say, always, more or less, at the level of faith, of *bona fides*, the game isn't being played. Well, that's what sparks off anger.

To leave you with something that preoccupies you, I'll make a simple remark. Where does Aristotle deal best with the passions? I think that there are all the same a certain number of you who know. It's in the second book of his *Rhetoric*.

The best there is on the passions is caught in the net, the network, of rhetoric. This is not by chance. The signifiers on the blackboard are just that, the net. This is precisely why I spoke to you about a net in connection with the first linguistic bearings I tried to give you.

I haven't taken the dogmatic path of prefacing what I have to say to you about anxiety with a comprehensive theory of affects. Why not? Because we aren't psychologists here, we're psychoanalysts.

I'm not developing a *psycho-logy* for you, a disquisition on the unreal reality that is called the psyche, but a disquisition on a praxis that warrants a name, *erotology*. It's a question of desire. And the affect by which we are perhaps prompted to bring out everything that this disquisition entails as a consequence, not a general consequence but a universal one, on the theory of affects, is anxiety.

It's upon the cutting edge of anxiety that we have to hold fast and it's upon this edge that I hope to be able to lead you further next time.

14 November 1962

II

ANXIETY, SIGN OF DESIRE

> An ideal of straightforwardness
> Hegel and Lacan
> The desire of the Other in five formulae
> Division and its remainder
> I desire you, even if I know it not

At this stage of going a little more deeply into my disquisition on anxiety, I may legitimately pose the question as to what a teaching is here.

Since in this room we are, in principle, let's say, for the most part, analysts, and since the analytic experience is taken to be my essential reference when I address this audience that you comprise, the notion we may have of teaching must all the same be affected by the fact that the analyst is, we cannot forget this, if I may say so, an *interprétant*.

Indeed, the analyst plays on the tense, such an essential tense, that I've already accentuated for you on several occasions, using the various subjects of the verb – *he didn't know, I didn't know*. We shall leave this subject indeterminate then, by rounding it up under an *it wasn't known*.

Regarding this *it wasn't known*, the analyst is reckoned to know something. Why not even admit that he does know a thing or two? But can he teach what he knows? This isn't really the question, or at least, it would be premature. Up to a certain point, the sheer existence of somewhere like this and the role I've been playing here for a certain while is a way of settling this question – well or poorly – but of settling it.

No, the question is – what is it to teach what he knows?

1

What is it to teach, when what is to be taught has precisely to be taught not only to one who doesn't know, but to one who *can't* know? And it has to be admitted that up to a certain point all of us here are in this same boat, given what's at stake.

Watch carefully where, if I may say so, what is off-kilter is off to.

Were it not for what lies off-kilter, an analytic teaching, and this Seminar itself, could be conceived of as an extension of what takes place in supervision, for example, where you bring along what you might know and where I would only enter the fray to impart the analogue of interpretation, namely, that addition by means of which something appears, which gives some meaning to what you believe you know and makes that which it's possible to grasp beyond the limits of knowledge appear in a flash.

It's nevertheless to the extent that a piece of knowledge is constituted in a work of elaboration which we shall call communitarian rather than collective, a work of analysis, among those who have experience of it, the analysts, that a work of rounding up of knowledge is conceivable, which justifies the place that a teaching such as the one being put forward here can take up. If you will, it's because there's a whole literature, fostered by the analytic experience, called analytic theory, that I'm forced, often very much against my will, to give it so much consideration. And yet, this same analytic theory is what necessitates me doing something that has to move beyond this rounding-up, that has to move, by way of this rounding-up of analytic theory, in the direction of bringing us closer to what constitutes its wellspring, namely, the experience.

An ambiguity arises at this point, which isn't due simply to the fact that a few non-analysts mix with us here. There's nothing particularly inconvenient about that since even the analysts also roll up here with positions, stances and expectations that aren't necessarily analytic. They've already been conditioned quite well enough by the fact that all manner of references get introduced in the theory produced in analysis and in far greater number than would seem on first glance, references that may be qualified as extra-analytic, as psychologizing references, for example.

The simple fact that I deal with this material – my audience's material, the material of my object of teaching – means that I shall be led to refer to this common experience, thanks to which any teaching communication gets established. This means that I can't stay in the pure position that just now I called *interprétante*, but that I shall have to pass over to a broader communicative position and move onto the ground of *making-things-understood*, to appeal therefore to an experience in you that goes far beyond the strict analytic experience.

It's important to recall this because making-things-understood is and always has been the real stumbling block in psychology, in the widest sense. It's not so much that the emphasis has to be put on the theme which at one time appeared as the great originality of a work like Blondel's on pathological consciousness, *La Conscience morbide*, namely, that there are limits to understanding. For example, let's not imagine that we understand the real or authentic lived experience of the ill. But the question of this limit is not what's important for us. At this moment of speaking to you about anxiety, this is one of those questions we're putting on hold.

Indeed, the question is rather one of explaining how we can speak about anxiety when we subsume under this same category experiences as diverse as – the anxiety we can fall into following some such meditation guided by Kierkegaard – para-normal anxiety, or even frankly pathological anxiety, which can seize hold of us at such moments, we being ourselves subjects of an experience that is more or less psychopathologically locatable – the anxiety we're faced with in our neurotics, the everyday material of our experience – and also the anxiety we can describe and localize at the level of the principle of an experience that is more on the fringes for us, that of the pervert, for example, indeed that of the psychotic.

Although this apparent homogeneity finds itself justified by a structural kinship, this can only be at the expense of the original comprehension, which nevertheless will necessarily increase along with the danger of making us forget that this comprehension isn't the understanding of a lived experience but the comprehension of a mainspring. It also presumes too much about what we may assume of the experiences this comprehension refers to, specifically those of the pervert and the psychotic.

From this perspective, it is preferable to warn people that they aren't to believe too much of what they may comprehend.

It's precisely here that the signifying elements I'm introducing for you take on their importance. As bare of comprehensible content as I'm endeavouring to make them, through their notation in a structural relationship, they are the means by which I'm trying to keep up the level necessary for an understanding that will not be misleading, whilst leaving the variously significant terms through which we're moving out where they can be spotted. This is very much to be underlined at the point where affect is at issue, since I haven't denied myself this classificatory element. Anxiety is an affect.

From the teacher's point of view, the approach to this theme presents itself in keeping with three different paths that can be defined summarily, that is, by summing them up, under three headings.

First of all, there's the path of the catalogue. As concerns affect, this consists in exhausting not only what it means, but also what was meant in constituting this category. This path puts us in the position of teaching on the subject of teaching, in its widest sense, and would allow us to link up what's taught within analysis with what's brought to us from without. Why ever not? It's come down to us from quite considerable contributions and I'm a long way from stopping myself, as I told you, from putting anxiety in the catalogue of affects, as in the various theories that have been produced on affect.

To take things up in a kind of separating interpunct, there are in Saint Thomas Aquinas, to mention him by name, some very, very fine things concerning a division of affect, a division he didn't invent, into the *concupiscent* and the *irascible*. The long discussion, which proceeds in accordance with the format of scholastic debate, proposition–objection–reply, whereby he weighs up the question as to which of the two categories is first with respect to the other, and how he decides, and why, that, in spite of certain appearances and certain references, the irascible always gets inserted somewhere into the chain of the concupiscent, this concupiscent thus standing first in relation to it – all this won't fail to aid us, for, in truth, this theory would be quite admissible for us were it not, at its utmost term, hanging entirely upon the supposition of a Sovereign Good against which, as you know, we already have great objections to make. We're going to see what we can hold onto in this theory, what it clarifies for us. I ask you to consult it. I'll give you the references in due course. We can certainly find plenty of material there to feed our own reflections – much more, paradoxically, than in the modern developments, recent developments, let's call a spade a spade, nineteenth-century developments from a psychology that claimed to be experimental and was no doubt not entirely entitled to do so.

Nevertheless, this path has the drawback of pushing us in the direction of the classification of affects. Now, experience proves to us that in going too far in this direction, one merely winds up in obvious dead ends, even if one puts the emphasis firmly on that part of our experience that just now I distinguished as theory. This is borne out very nicely, for example, in an article by David Rapaport which you'll find in volume 34 of the *International Journal*, the third section from 1953. This text, which attempts a psychoanalytic theory of affect, is truly exemplary for the quite dismaying outcome it arrives at, without moreover the author's hand dreaming of concealing it. Announcing an article with the title *On a Psychoanalytic*

Theory of Affect could make us hope, after all, that something new, something original, might come out of it, concerning what the analyst may think about affect. The astonishing result is that the author limits himself to cataloguing the accepted uses of the term, staying strictly within analytic theory, only to realize at the end of it that these uses are irreducible to one another.

The first of these accepted uses is affect conceived of as constituting, substantially, drive discharge. The second professedly goes farther than the Freudian text, to turn affect into what connotes a tension across its different, ordinarily conflicting, phases – the variation of tension. In the third instance, affect is defined within the properly topographical reference of Freudian theory as a signal at the level of the ego of a danger coming from elsewhere. The important thing is that the author notices that among the most recent authors to contribute to the analytic discussion, divergent claims still remain concerning the primacy to be accorded each of these three meanings, such that nothing of it is resolved. That the author in question is unable to say any more about it is at any rate the sign that here the method known as cataloguing can ultimately only bear the mark of a profound aporia, in that it winds up in dead ends, even in a very particular lack of fecundity.

There is another method. I apologize for going on at such length today about the question of method, but it holds great interest as a preamble, with regard to the timeliness of what we're doing here, and I'm not introducing it just for the sake of it, as you shall see, in connection with anxiety. I'm going to call it, to form a consonance with the previous term, the method of the analogue.

This would lead us to distinguish some levels. One piece of work, which I won't cite otherwise today, presents an attempt at this kind of rounding-up, where in separate chapters one can see anxiety being conceived of biologically, then sociologically, then *culturally* as they say, the work being in the English language – as if all it takes, to do something other than isolate, not a classification this time, but a sort of type, is to reveal analogical positions at levels purported to be independent of one another.

We know what such a method ends up with. It ends up with what is known as an anthropology. Of all the paths we might go down, anthropology is in our eyes the one that entails the greatest number of the most hazardous presuppositions. Whatever eclecticism it may be characterized by, such a method always ends up, and necessarily so, with a central kernel that is Jungianism, or at least what we term thus in our habitual vocabulary, without making it the sign of someone who occupied such an eminent position. On the subject of anxiousness, this thematic lies very far from what is at issue in experience.

On the other hand, experience leads us to the third path, which I'll put under the heading of the function of the key. The key is a thing which unlocks and which, in unlocking, functions. The key is the form according to which the signifying function as such operates or not.

My announcing it, distinguishing it and daring to introduce it as what we may trust ourselves to, has nothing that should here be stamped with presumption.

What legitimizes it and that will, I think, be a sufficiently convincing reference, especially for those here who are teachers by profession, is that the dimension of the key is utterly connatural to any teaching, analytic or not.

Indeed, I will say that – regardless of the shock that may arise in some people as a result of me saying it, for my part, concerning what I teach – there is no teaching which does not refer to what I shall call an ideal of straightforwardness.

2

In taking the path of turning to the texts on affect, we saw earlier that neither head nor tail can be made of what we think, we analysts.

There is something deeply unsatisfying about this and it constitutes a weighty objection. Indeed it is to be expected, whatever capacity we're in, that we should satisfy a certain ideal of straightforward reduction.

What does this mean? Why so? Why, for all the time that we've been practising science – for this reflection bears on something very different from, as well as fields that are vaster than, the field of our experience – has the greatest possible straightforwardness been demanded? Why would the real be straightforward? What can lead us even for one minute to suppose that it is?

Well, nothing – nothing other than the subjective *initium* I emphasized during the whole of the first part of my teaching last year, namely, that there's no conceivable advent of a subject as such except on the basis of the prior introduction of a signifier, and the most straightforward of signifiers, known as the unary trait.

The unary trait precedes the subject. *In the beginning was the word* means *In the beginning stands the unary trait*. Everything that is teachable has to preserve the stigmata of this ultra-simple *initium*. It's the only thing that can justify in our eyes the ideal of straightforwardness.

Simplex, singularity of the trait, this is what we cause to enter the real, whether the real likes it or not. One thing is certain, it does enter and it has already entered before us. It's along this path that all those subjects who've been dialoguing for a few centuries now have already had to get by as best they can with the condition that, precisely, betwixt them and the real lies the field of the signifier, for it was already with the operation of the unary trait that they were con- stituted as subjects. Why should we be surprised to meet its stamp in our field, if our field is that of the subject?

In analysis, there is something that stands prior to everything we can elaborate or understand. I shall call this the presence of the Other, *l'Autre* with a capital A. There is no auto-analysis, even when one imagines there is. The Other is there. It's on this path and with the same intention that we meet the indication I've already given you concerning something that goes much farther still, namely, anxiety.

In this regard, I started to indicate a certain relationship for you, which so far I've merely embellished with an image. I recalled this image for you last time, with a second mention of the sketch of my rather modest and discomfited presence in the presence of the giant praying mantis. I've already said more about it, however, in specify- ing that this bore a relation to the desire of the Other.

First off, before knowing what my relation to its desire means when I'm in a state of anxiety, I put this Other here, capital A. To bring us closer to its desire, I'm going to take the paths I've already cleared.

As I told you, man's desire is the desire of the Other.

Excuse me for not being able to go back over what I spelt out on this subject during the recent Provincial Study Days, and this is why I'm so adamant that the transcript of that should reach me intact, so that it may be circulated. It concerned the grammatical analysis of what the desire of the Other means, including the objective meaning of this genitive. Those who have attended my Seminar up to now possess enough elements to situate it, however.

I alluded last time, at the start, to a short study that had been handed me that same morning. This article concerns the suspension of what may be called dialectical reason, on the structuralist level at which Lévi-Strauss is poised. In order to unravel this debate, to enter into its twists and turns, to sort out the tangles from the analytic point of view, its author makes reference, of course, to what I said about the fantasy as a support of desire. For my liking, however, he doesn't make enough of what I say when I speak about man's desire as desire of the Other. What proves it is that he thinks he can make do with reminding us that it's Hegel's formula.

Certainly, if there's someone who doesn't do any wrong to what the *Phänomenologie des Geistes* has brought us, that someone is me.

If, however, there's one point at which it's important to mark the progress, to employ this term – I'd much rather say the leap – that is ours with regard to Hegel, it's precisely concerning the function of desire.

In view of the field that I have to cover this year, I'm not in a position to go over Hegel's text with you step by step, as this article does, an article which I hope will be published because it displays a thoroughly sensitive familiarity with what Hegel says on this score. I won't even take up the passage, a quite original passage, that the author did well to recall on this occasion. But given the idea that the common run of my audience has already had the chance to get to grips with the Hegelian reference, I'll say right off, to make you feel what's at issue, that in Hegel, concerning the dependence of my desire with respect to the desirer who is the Other, I'm dealing in the most certain and articulated way with the Other as consciousness. The Other is the one who sees me.

You can already glimpse well enough in what way this concerns my desire, but I'll be coming back to it in a little while. For the moment, I'm setting out some broad oppositions.

In Hegel, the Other is the one who sees me and this is what, all by itself, kicks off the struggle, according to the foundations wherewith Hegel marks the start of the *Phänomenologie des Geistes*, on the plane of what he calls pure prestige, and it's on this plane that my desire is concerned. For Lacan, because Lacan is an analyst, the Other is there as an un-consciousness that is constituted as such. The Other concerns my desire to the extent of what he lacks and to the extent that he doesn't know. It's at the level of what he lacks, and at the level of him not knowing, that I'm concerned in the most prominent way, because there's no other path for me to find what I lack as object of my desire. This is why for me there is no, not simply access to my desire, but not even any possible means of sustaining my desire that would have any reference to any object whatsoever if not through coupling it, through tying it in, with this, the $, which designates the subject's necessary dependence on the Other as such.

This Other is of course the same one that I think over the years I've accustomed you to distinguishing at each step from the other, my *semblable*. It's the Other as locus of the signifier. It is my *semblable* amongst other things, but only in so far as it's also the locus at which the Other as such of the singular difference I was telling you about at the beginning is instituted.

Shall I now introduce the formulae I've written up? I'm not claiming, far from it, that the bag of tricks will spill right open. I ask you, today like last time, to jot them down. That's why this year I'm noting things up on the blackboard. You'll be seeing how they function afterwards.

First Formula
$$d(a) : d(A) < a$$

In the Hegelian sense, *desire for desire* is the desire for a desire to respond to the subject's appeal. It's the desire for a desirer. Why does the subject need this desirer who is the Other? It's plainly spelt out in Hegel that he needs the Other so that the Other may acknowledge him, so that he may receive the Other's acknowledgement. What does that mean? It means that the Other will institute something, designated by a, which is what is involved at the level of what desires. The whole impasse lies here. In demanding to be acknowledged, right where I get acknowledged, I only get acknowledged as an object. I get what I desire, I'm an object, and I can't stand myself as an object, since this object that I am is of its essence a consciousness, a *Selbstbewusstsein*. I can't stand myself acknowledged in the only type of acknowledgement I can obtain. Therefore it has to be settled at any cost between our two consciousnesses. There's no longer any mediation but that of violence. Such is desire's lot in Hegel.

Second Formula
$$d(a) < i(a) : d(\cancel{A})$$

In the Lacanian, or analytic, sense *desire for desire* is desire of the Other in a way that is, in its principle, far more open to a kind of mediation. At least, so it seems on first approach.

Notice that the formula I've put up on the blackboard goes a long way to wrong-foot what you might expect. I have in fact written the relation to the desire of the Other, $d(\cancel{A})$, with the image-support of this desire that I unhesitatingly write $i(a)$, precisely because of the ambiguity that this creates with the notation $i(m)$ with which I usually designate the specular image.

We don't yet know when, how or why this $i(a)$ can be the specular image, but it most certainly is an image. It's not the specular image, though it belongs to the realm of the image. Here, it's the fantasy which I don't hesitate on occasion to overlap with the notation of the specular image. I'm saying therefore that this desire is desire inasmuch as its image-support is equivalent to the desire of the Other. This is why the colon that was here is now here. This Other is connoted by a barred A because it's the Other at the point where it's characterized as lack.

There are two other formulae. Only two, since those that are bracketed together are just two ways of writing the same thing, in one direction, then in the palindromic direction. I don't know whether I'll have time today to get to their translation.

Third Formula
$$d(x) : d(A) < x$$

Fourth Formula
$$d(0) < 0 : d(\cancel{A})$$
$$d(a) : 0 > d(0)$$

I'd like you to know already, however, that the first is designed to highlight the fact that anxiety is what imparts truth to the Hegelian formula. The Hegelian formula is in fact partial and a little out, and even out of kilter. I've indicated for you on many occasions the perversion that results – and which is very far-reaching, as far as the political domain – from the whole of the beginning of *Phänomenologie des Geistes*, which is too tightly focused on the imaginary. It's very nice to say that the slave's servitude is brimming with the whole future right up to absolute knowledge, but politically this means that till the end of time the slave will remain a slave. One does have to tell it like it is once in a while.

Kierkegaard is the one who imparts the truth of the Hegelian formula. Next time, I think, I'll comment on what the third formula means.

The formula labelled fourth – hold on, while I think of it, that's not the letter *O* you should read there, but zero – is not Hegel's truth, but the truth of anxiety which, for its part, can only be grasped with reference to the second formula, which concerns desire at the psychoanalytic level.

3

Before I leave you today, I'd simply like to make a few remarks.

There is something that you can see appearing in like fashion in both Hegel's formula and mine. As paradoxical as it may seem, their first term is an object *a*. It's an object *a* that desires.

If the Hegelian concept of desire and the one I'm promoting to you here have something in common, it's this. At a moment which is precisely the unacceptable point of impasse in the process of the *Selbstbewusstsein* as Hegel would have it, the subject, being this object, is irremediably stamped with finitude. This object affected by desire which I'm putting forward here does indeed have something in common in this respect with Hegel's theory, except that our analytic level doesn't require the transparency of the *Selbstbewusstsein*. This is a difficulty, of course, but it's not of the sort that would lead us to retrace our steps, nor to commit ourselves to the struggle to the death with the Other.

Because of the existence of the unconscious, we can be this object affected by desire. Indeed, it is even in so far as we, subject of the unconscious, are stamped in this way by finitude that our own lack can be desire, finite desire. It looks to be indefinite, because lack, entailing as it does some emptiness, can be filled in several ways, though we know very well, because we're analysts, that we don't fill it in umpteen different ways. We're going to see why, and what these ways are.

From this perspective, the classic, moralistic, though not really theological, dimension of the infinity of desire has absolutely to be cut down to size. In fact, this pseudo-infinity is due to one thing alone, which a certain part of the theory of the signifier fortunately allows us to picture – and this is none other than the whole number. This false infinity is linked to the kind of metonymy that, concerning the definition of the whole number, is called recursion. It's the law we accentuated forcefully last year with regard to the recursive One. But what our experience demonstrates to us, and what I'll be articulating for you in the various fields offered to our experience, namely, and distinctly, the neurotic, the pervert, indeed the psychotic, is that this One, to which at the end of the day the succession of signifying elements, in so far as they are distinct, are reduced, does not exhaust the function of the Other.

This is what I've represented here in the form of these two columns, which are those under which the operation of division can be written. First off, you find A, the originative Other as locus of the signifier, and S, the subject as yet inexistent, who has to situate himself as determined by the signifier.

First table of division

With regard to the Other, the subject dependant upon this Other is inscribed as a quotient. He's stamped with the unary trait of the signifier in the field of the Other. It's not necessarily the case, if I may say so, that he slices the Other up. There is, in the sense of division, a remainder, a leftover. This remainder, this ultimate Other, this irrational entity, this proof and sole guarantee, when all is said and done, of the Other's otherness, is the *a*.

This is why the two terms, $ and *a*, the subject stamped with the bar of the signifier and the object *a*, the residue of the readying, if I can put it like that, of the Other, stand on the same side, the objective side, of the bar. Both of them stand on the side of the Other, because the fantasy, support of my desire, is in its totality on the side of the Other. What now stands on my side is what constitutes me as unconscious, namely Ⱥ, the Other in so far as I don't reach it.

Shall I take you further? No, time's too short. But I don't want to leave you on such a closed point as concerns the next part of the dialectic that's going to be inserted here.

What is the next step necessitated by this dialectic? You'll see that I'm going to have to explain to you what I'm bringing into this business, namely, into the subsistence of the fantasy. I'll give you a picture right now of the thrust of what I shall have to put forth, with a reminder that will be of some use to you regarding what, good gracious, concerns you most – I'm not the one who said so, it was Freud – to wit, the experience of love.

The point we're at in the theory of desire in its relationship to the Other actually delivers up the key to the following. Contrary to the hope that the Hegelian perspective might give you, the way by which the other party is conquered is not the way – too frequently adopted, alas, by one of the partners – of *I love you, even if you don't want me to*.

Don't believe that Hegel hadn't noticed this consequence of his doctrine. There's a very precious little note where he indicates that he could've made his whole dialectic pass through there. He also says that, if he didn't take this path, it's because it didn't seem serious enough. How right he was. Go ahead and try this formula out, you can let me know if you have any success.

There is, however, another formula, which doesn't demonstrate its efficacy any better, but perhaps this is so simply to the extent that it's not articulable. This doesn't mean, however, that it's not articulated. It is, *I desire you, even if I know it not*. Whenever it manages, as inarticulable as it is, to make itself heard, this one, I assure you, is irresistible.

And why so? I won't leave it as a conundrum.

Let's imagine it can be uttered. What would I be saying thereby?

I'm telling the other party that, desiring him or her, undoubtedly without knowing it, still without knowing it, I take him or her for the unknown object, unknown to me, of my desire. This means that, in our conception of desire, I identify you, thee to whom I'm speaking, with the object that you lack. In going via this circuit, which is obligatory if I am to attain the object of my desire, I accomplish for the other party precisely what he's seeking. If, innocently or not, I take this detour, the other as such, here object – observe – of my love, will necessarily fall into my toils.

I'll leave you with this recipe. Till next time.

21 November 1962

III

FROM THE COSMOS TO THE *UNHEIMLICHE*

The specular and the signifier
From the world to the world's stage
Hamlet and the stage on the stage
Lévi-Strauss's serenity
Anything whatsoever in the blank of the phallus

You'll have noted that I'm always pleased to latch onto some current affair in our dialogue.

All in all, there is only that which is current. That's precisely why it's so difficult to live in the world of, let's say, reflection. Because, truth be told, not much goes on there.

It can happen, just like that, that I take the trouble to see whether, somewhere, a little tip of a question mark might be rearing its head. I'm rarely rewarded. This is precisely why when it does so happen that someone poses me questions, and serious ones too, you won't hold it against me if I take advantage of this.

1

I'm continuing my dialogue with the person I've alluded to twice already, in my previous lessons.

With regard to the way that last time I punctuated the difference in conception that lies between the Hegelian articulation of desire and my own, I'm being urged.

I'm being urged to say more about what's being designated in so many words as a step further to be accomplished in my own disquisition. He would like a more precise articulation between the mirror stage – that is, as the Rome Report puts it, the specular image – and the signifier. It seems that a certain hiatus remains here, not without my interlocutor perceiving that the employment of words such as hiatus, cut, or scission, is perhaps none other than the response he's waiting for.

Nevertheless, in this form, the response could seem to be but an elusion, or an elision. This is why I'm going to try to reply to him today.

I shall do so all the more willingly given that here we find ourselves strictly on the path of what I have to describe this year. Indeed, anxiety is going to allow us to go back over the articulation that is hereby being required of me. I say *go back over*, because those who've been following me these last years and even those who, without necessarily having been assiduous in every respect, have read what I write, already possess more than a few elements to fill out this hiatus and make this cut function, as you shall see from the reminders with which I'm going to begin.

I don't believe there have ever been two phases to what I've taught, one phase that would supposedly be focused on the mirror stage and the imaginary, and then afterwards, at that moment of our history that is marked by the Rome Report, my supposedly sudden discovery of the signifier. I ask those interested in the question that's been put to me to consult a text that is no longer so easy to get hold of, but which can be found in all the good psychiatric libraries. This text, published in *L'Évolution psychiatrique* and entitled *Presentation on Psychical Causality*, is a disquisition that takes us back to 1946, if memory serves, just after the war. There they will see things that will prove to them that I've been intimately weaving the interplay between the two registers for a long while now.

If this text was followed, let's say, by a somewhat long silence on my part, you needn't be too astonished. A great deal of ground was covered thereafter, in order to open up a certain number of ears to this disquisition. Don't believe that at the time I gave this presentation on psychical causality ears were all that quick to hear it. Since the presentation was given in Bonneval and since a more recent meeting at the same location has signalled for some the ground covered, I can tell you that the reactions to those first remarks were somewhat astonishing.

At best, the term that would describe them is the discreet term of ambivalence, which we use in the analytic world, but this would be to say too little. As I'm sure to be queried on this subject and as I'm being taken back to that era which a certain number of you were already sufficiently trained to remember, the post-war period animated by whatever movement of regeneration could be hoped of it, I suddenly can't avoid recalling that those who certainly weren't, individually, the least inclined to hearing a disquisition that was very new at the time, people situated on the side that in politics is called the hard left, communists, to call a spade a spade, on that occasion made a quite special show of reactions whose style I must absolutely single out with a term that is of everyday use, though a moment's pause is necessary before endorsing its use, because it's a term that has become quite unjust for those it originally invoked, a term that has ended up taking on a depreciative meaning, but I'm using it in the courteous sense – the term *pharisaism*.

On that occasion, in the little teacup that our psychiatric milieu is, communist pharisaism really served to the full in the very thing to which we saw it apply itself, at least for our generation, in present-day France, that is, to wit, assuring the persistence of that sum of habits, good or bad, wherein a certain established order finds its comfort and security.

In short, I can't avoid testifying that it's to the utterly particular reservations of the communists that I owe the fact of having understood that my disquisition would take a long while to make itself heard. Hence the silence in question and the care I took to devote myself simply to making this disquisition enter the milieu whose experience rendered it the most apt to hear it, to wit, the analytic milieu. I'll spare you the subsequent adventures.

But if this can get you to reread the *Presentation on Psychical Causality*, you'll see, especially after what I'll have told you today, that the framework into which each of these two perspectives are inscribed, perspectives that my interlocutor quite rightly sets apart, already existed. These perspectives are here punctuated by these two coloured lines, the vertical one in blue, marked with the sign I for imaginary, the horizontal one in red, with S for symbolic.

In what I'm demonstrating for you, the connection between the subject and the little other and the connection between the subject and the big Other don't live separate lives. There'd be more than one way of reminding you of this, but I'm going to remind you of it by going over a certain number of moments that have already been punctuated as essential in my disquisition.

What you see jotted up there on the blackboard and onto which we'll be placing the elements involved is none other than a diagram already published in my *Remarks on Daniel Lagache's Presentation*. In this drawing, some terms have been linked up which have the strictest relationship with our subject, that is, the function of dependency. I'm taking them from the text of these *Remarks . . .*, but also from a previous disquisition which I delivered here back in the second year of my Seminar, concerning what at the time I called respectively the ideal ego and the Ego Ideal.

Let's recall, then, how the specular relation is found to take its place and how it is found to be dependent on the fact that the subject is constituted in the locus of the Other, constituted by its mark, in the relation to the signifier.

Already, just in the exemplary little image with which the demonstration of the mirror stage begins, the moment that is said to be *jubilatory* when the child, grasping himself in the inaugural experience of recognition in the mirror, comes to terms with himself as a totality functioning as such in his specular image, haven't I always insisted on the movement that the infant makes? This movement is so frequent, constant I'd say, that each and every one of you may have some recollection of it. Namely, he turns round, I noted, to the one supporting him who's there behind him. If we force ourselves to assume the content of the infant's experience and to reconstruct the sense of this movement, we shall say that, with this nutating movement of the head, which turns towards the adult as if to call upon his assent, and then back to the image, he seems to be asking the one supporting him, and who here represents the big Other, to ratify the value of this image.

This is nothing, of course, but an indication concerning the inaugural nexus between this relation to the big Other and the advent of the function of the specular image, noted by $i(a)$.

But need we stick at this level?

I asked my interlocutor for a written text concerning some doubts he had with regard to what Claude Lévi-Strauss has put forward in his book, *The Savage Mind*, which is in the spotlight at the moment and whose close relationship with what we have to say this year you're going to see.

If we do indeed have to broach here what's in question in this book, it's so as to mark out the type of progress the use of psychoanalytic reason constitutes, in so far as it comes precisely to respond to the gap in the face of which more than one of you have for the moment come to a standstill, the gap that Claude Lévi-Strauss indicates throughout his development in the opposition between what he calls analytic reason and dialectical reason.

It's in reference to this opposition that I'd like to put the following remark to you by way of an introduction on the path I'm treading today.

Recall if you will what I extracted from the inaugural step in Freud's thought that *The Interpretation of Dreams* constitutes, when I laid the emphasis on the fact that Freud initially introduces the unconscious as a locus that he calls *ein anderer Schauplatz*, an other scene. From the beginning, from the moment the function of the unconscious comes into the picture in reference to the dream, this term is introduced as essential. Well, I think that here we have a mode that is constitutive of what is, let's say, our reason.

We are searching for the path by which to discern the structures of this reason. I shall say that the first phase is as follows – there is *the world*. I'm saying it with no frills, to make you hear what I have to say to you, but we'll have to come back to this, for we don't know what it means yet.

This world as it stands is what analytic reason is concerned with, the same reason to which Claude Lévi-Strauss's disquisition tends to give primacy. With this primacy, the said reason also grants it an ultimately peculiar homogeneity, which is precisely what strikes and troubles the most lucid of you. And you cannot fail to discern the return this entails to what could be called primary materialism, in so far as, at the limit of this disquisition, the play of structure, the play of the combinatory that is so powerfully articulated in Claude Lévi-Strauss's disquisition, would merely join up with the structure of the brain itself, for example, indeed the structure of matter, and represent, in keeping with the form called *materialist* in the eighteenth-century sense, not even its *doublure*, its lining, but its doublet. I know very well that here we merely have a perspective that stands at the limit, but it is worthwhile grasping it since it is expressly articulated.

Now, the dimension of the stage, in its separation from the locus, worldly or otherwise, cosmic or otherwise, where the spectator is, exists precisely to picture in our eyes the radical distinction between the world and the locus where things, if only the things of the world, come to be voiced. All the things of the world come to be staged in keeping with the laws of the signifier, laws that we could never fancy in any way to be consistent with the laws of the world at the outset.

It is only too clear that the existence of the discourse in which we are implicated as subjects stands well prior to the advent of science. As admirably instructive as Claude Lévi-Strauss's effort is to homogenize the discourse he calls *magic* with the discourse of science, he cannot for one instant push this as far as the illusion of believing that there's no difference here, nor even a cut, and in a little while I'll be accentuating what we have to say about it. The effort in question is, in truth, marvellous in its hopelessness.

So, first phase, *the world*. Second phase, *the stage* that we make this world climb up onto. The stage is the dimension of history.

History has always had a character of staging. Claude Lévi-Strauss shows this well, notably in the chapter in which he replies to Jean-Paul Sartre and in which he critiques his latest development which was set down to perform the operation I last time called *putting history back between the shafts that pull its coach*. Lévi-Strauss recalls that the teasing-out of history has a limited span, that the time of history is distinct from cosmic time, and that dates themselves all of a sudden take on a different value within the dimension of history, whether they are called *le Deux-Décembre* or *le 18 Brumaire*. It's not the same calendar as the one you tear a page off each day. The proof of this is that these dates have a different meaning for you. They can be mentioned again on any other day of the calendar to signify that they impart it their stamp, their characteristic, their style of difference or recurrence.

Once the stage has come to the fore, what happens is that the whole world is put upon it, and with Descartes one can say, *Onto the world's stage go I,* as befits, *larvatus, masked.*

From this point on, the question may be posed as to what the world, what at the start we quite innocently called the world, owes to what has come back down to it from this stage. Everything that throughout the course of history we have called *the world* has left behind superimposed residues that accumulate without the faintest care for contradiction. What culture transports to us in the guise of the world is a stack, a shop crammed full of the flotsam and jetsam of worlds that have followed one after the other, and which, for all their incompatibility, don't get on any the worse with each other within every single one of us.

The particular field of our experience allows us to gauge the predominance of this structure. We know its depth, especially in the experience of the obsessional neurotic in whom Freud himself noticed a long time ago the extent to which these cosmic worlds could co-exist in a fashion which apparently doesn't raise the least objection, all the while displaying the most perfect heterogeneity from the very first examination onward. In short, as soon as we start making reference to the stage, nothing is more legitimate than to call into question what the world of cosmism is in the real. Isn't that which we believe ourselves to be dealing with as the world quite simply the accumulated remains of what came from the stage when, if I may say so, it was doing the rounds?

This reminder will lead us into a third phase, one which I already pointed out for you a long while ago without having enough time back then to accentuate it.

2

Since we're speaking about the stage, we know what function the theatre holds in the functioning of the myths that have given us, we analysts, such food for thought.

I'm going to take you back to *Hamlet* and to a crucial point that's already posed a question for a number of authors. Otto Rank in particular produced an article on this subject that is admirable in every respect, given the early period in which it was written, and particularly for the attention he draws to the function of the stage on the stage.

In *Hamlet*, what does Hamlet, the stage character, bring onto the stage with the players? Undoubtedly, it's the *Mouse-trap* with which, so he tells us, he'll *catch the conscience of the king*. But some very strange things come to pass besides, in particular the following, which at the time I spoke to you at such great length about *Hamlet* I didn't want to introduce, because it would have steered you towards a literature that is ultimately more Hamletic than psychoanalytic, and as you know, there's already plenty enough to paper the walls with.

When the scene is mimed by way of a prologue, before the players begin their speeches, it doesn't seem to stir the king all that much, even though the presumed gestures of his crime are being played out before him. On the other hand, if there is one thing that's really quite odd, then it's the veritable flood, the fit of agitation, that seizes Hamlet at the crucial moment when the character called Lucianus, or Luciano, arrives on stage and carries out his crime, as much against the character that represents the king – the play-acting king even though he affirms in his speech that he is the king within a certain dimension – as against the character representing his spouse.

All the authors who have paused on this scene have remarked that the garb in which the said Luciano is clad isn't that of the king whom it's a question of catching, but precisely that of Hamlet himself. Likewise, it's indicated that this character is not the brother of the play-acting king. He does not therefore stand in a relation to the play-acting king that would be equivalent to the usurper's relation to Hamlet's father in the tragedy, the usurper who, once the murder is carried out, is in possession of Queen Gertrude. Luciano is the nephew of the play-acting king, a position equivalent to Hamlet's own position with regard to the usurper.

What Hamlet has represented on the stage is, therefore, in the end, himself carrying out the crime in question. This character whose desire can't be roused to accomplish the will of the ghost, the ghost of his father – for reasons that I tried to spell out for you – attempts to give shape to something, which goes by way of the specular image, his image put into the situation, not of accomplishing his revenge, but of assuming first of all the crime that stands to be avenged.

Now, what do we see? We see that it's insufficient. Much as Hamlet is seized, after this kind of magic-lantern effect, by what may truly be qualified – in view of his remarks, their style, even the quite ordinary way in which the players bring this moment to life – as a veritable little fit of manic agitation when, just afterwards, he finds himself with his enemy within reach, he only manages to articulate what any listener can only feel to be evasion. He shirks away behind an excuse, namely, that he would be seizing his enemy at a moment that is too holy – the king is praying – for him to bring himself to send him straight to heaven by striking there and then.

I'm not going to spend time translating what all of this means, because I have to go further here. Alongside this failure, I showed you all the scope of one of Hamlet's identifications whose nature is altogether different. It's what I called the identification with Ophelia. In point of fact, in the second phase, Hamlet is seized by the furious soul we can legitimately infer to be that of the victim, the suicide victim, manifestly offered in sacrifice to the paternal manes, since it's right after the killing of her father that she falters and succumbs.

This refers back to long-held beliefs pertaining to the aftermath of certain types of demise, when the funeral ceremonies can't be fully carried out. Nothing is appeased of the vengeance Ophelia is calling out for.

At the moment of the revelation of what this neglected and misrecognized object was for him, we can see being played out in Shakespeare in all its nakedness the same identification with the object that Freud designated for us as the mainspring of the function of mourning. This is the implacable definition that Freud rightly gave to mourning, the sort of nether side he designated with the tears dedicated to the deceased, the background of reproach entailed by the fact that, of the reality of the one who's been lost, we only want to remember the regrets he's left behind.

What astonishing cruelty, and just what it takes to remind us of the legitimacy of those more primitive types of celebration that still live on today thanks to certain collective practices. Why shouldn't one rejoice at the fact that the deceased existed? The country folk we reckon to be drowning out some harmful insensitivity in their feasts are actually doing something quite different, they are celebrating the accession of *he that was* to the sort of simple glory that he deserves for having simply been a living being in our midst. Identification with the bereaved object was designated by Freud in its negative patterns, but let's not forget that it also has its positive phase.

It's the entry into Hamlet of what I've called *the fury of the female soul* that gives him the strength to become this sleepwalker who accepts everything, up to and including – I've marked this sufficiently – to become the one who in the combat fights for his enemy, the king himself, against his specular image, who is Laertes.

From that point on, things sort themselves out on their own and without him doing, all in all, anything other than exactly what he shouldn't, until he does what he has to. Namely, he will himself be mortally wounded by the time he kills the king.

Here we are able to measure all the distance that lies between two kinds of imaginary identification. There is the identification with *i(a)*, the specular image such as it is offered to us with the stage on the stage, and there is the more mysterious identification – whose enigma starts to be developed here – with the object of desire as such, *a*, designated as such in the Shakespearean articulation without any ambiguity whatsoever, since it's precisely as object of desire that Hamlet has been neglected up until a certain moment, and that he is reintegrated onto the stage via the path of identification.

It is to the extent that, as object, he comes to vanish, that the retroactive dimension imposes itself which is that of the imperfect tense in the ambiguous form in which it is employed in French, and which lends its force to the way in which I've been repeating before you *Il ne savait pas, He didn't know*. This means both *At the last instant, he didn't know* and *A little more, and he was going to know*. It's not for nothing that *désir* in French comes from *desiderium*. There is a retroactive recognition of *the object that used to be there*. It's down this path that Hamlet's return passes into the culmination of his destiny, of his Hamlet function, if I may put it like that, his Hamletic finish.

It's here that what I called the third phase, namely, the stage on the stage, shows us where our questioning ought to be directed.

This questioning – you've known this much for a long time because it's the same that I'm always repeating from multiple angles – concerns the status of the object as object of desire. Everything that Claude Lévi-Strauss says about the function of magic and the function of myth has its value, on the condition that we know that it's a matter of the relationship with this object that holds the status of the object of desire. This status, I admit, hasn't been established yet and this is very much what has to be pushed forward this year on the inroad to anxiety.

At any rate, this object of desire oughtn't to be confused with the object defined by epistemology. The advent of the object of our science is very specifically defined by a particular discovery of the efficacy of the signifying operation as such. This means that what is specific to our science, I'm saying to the science that has been in existence at our side for two centuries now, leaves open the question of what earlier I called the cosmism of the object. Whether or not there is a cosmos is uncertain, and our science advances precisely to the extent that it's given up maintaining any cosmic or cosmizing presuppositions.

This reference point remains nevertheless so essential that one can't fail to be astonished that in restoring in *The Savage Mind*, in a modern form, the permanence, the perpetuity, the eternity of the cosmism of the object's reality, Claude Lévi-Strauss doesn't bring everybody the security, the serenity, the Epicurean relief that ought to ensue. The question arises as to whether the psychoanalysts are the only ones who aren't happy, or whether it's everybody. Now, I claim, regardless of the fact that I don't yet have the proof, that it must be everybody. It's a matter of reasoning it out.

Why is it that people aren't happy about seeing totemism all of a sudden emptied of its content? A content I shall call, to make myself understood, emotive. Why is it that people aren't happy about the world being so in order, ever since the Neolithic period – because we can't go back any further – that everything should merely amount to insignificant wavelets on the surface of this order? In other words, why do we want so much to preserve the dimension of anxiety? There must be a reason for this.

Between returning to an assured cosmism and maintaining an historical pathos by which we don't set all that much store either, even though it does have its function, there is a way, a passageway. This passageway is precisely to be cleared by studying the function of anxiety.

3

Here then is the reason why I've been led to remind you precisely how the specular relation is tied into the relation to the big Other.

The apparatus I put together in the article to which I'm asking you to refer, because I'm not going to go through it all again here, is designed to remind us of this, which I accentuated at the end of my Seminar on desire, namely, that the function of specular investment is situated within the dialectic of narcissism such as Freud introduced it.

Investment in the specular image is a fundamental phase of the imaginary relation. It's fundamental inasmuch as there's a limit. Not all of the libidinal investment passes by way of the specular image. There's a remainder. I hope I succeeded in making you see why this remainder is the lynchpin of this whole dialectic. This is where I'll be taking up again next time, to show you, more than I've been able to as yet, how this function is privileged in the mode of the phallus.

This means that in everything that concerns taking one's bearings in the imaginary, the phallus will henceforth step in, in the form of

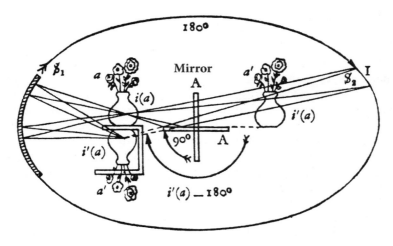

Complete diagram

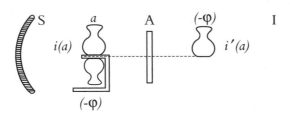

Simplified diagram

a lack. To the full extent that here, in $i(a)$, what I've called the *real image* comes to be realized – the body image functioning in the subject's material as specifically imaginary, that is to say, libidinalized – the phallus appears as a minus, as a blank. Despite the phallus undoubtedly being an operative reserve, not only is it not represented at the level of the imaginary, but it is circumscribed and, in a word, cut out of the specular image.

To add something to peg this dialectic together, I tried last year to articulate this for you with a figure borrowed from the ambiguous domain of topology, which planes the imaginary data right down and teases out a kind of trans-space, everything of which leads us to think in the end that it's fashioned from a pure signifying articulation, whilst still leaving a few intuitive elements within reach. For instance, those that support the quirky yet altogether expressive image of the cross-cap.

I manipulated this surface in front of you for over a month in order to bring you to form an idea of how the cut can establish two different pieces here, one which can have a specular image and the other which, quite literally, doesn't have one. It was a question of the relationship between minus-*phi* and the constitution of the little *a*. On one hand, there is the reserve that can't be grasped in the imaginary, even though it is linked to an organ, which, thank goodness, is still perfectly graspable, this instrument which will all the same have to go into action from time to time for the satisfaction of desire, the phallus. On the other hand, there is the *a*, which is this remainder, this residue, this object whose status escapes the status of the object derived from the specular image, that is, the laws of transcendental aesthetics. All the confusion has swept into analytic theory because its status is so hard to spell out.

This object *a* whose constituent characteristics we've merely touched on and which today we're putting on the agenda, is what is in question whenever Freud speaks about the object in connection with anxiety. The ambiguity is due to the fact that we can't do otherwise than to imagine it in the specular register. It's precisely a matter of establishing another type of imaginarization here, if I may express myself in this way, whereby this object may be defined. This is what we will manage to do if you will kindly follow me, that is to say, step by step.

In the article I've been speaking to you about, where do I place the starting point of the dialectic? At an S, the subject as possible, the subject because needs must speak about one if speaking there is, and whose model is given us by the classical conception of the subject, on the sole condition that we limit the subject to the fact that he speaks. As soon as he starts to speak, the unary trait comes into play. The fact of being able to say 1 and 1 and another 1 and another, constitutes the primary identification. You always have to start with 1. As the diagram from the article in question shows, it's on this basis that the very possibility of recognizing the unit called $i(a)$ is established.

This $i(a)$ is given in the specular experience, but, as I told you, it is authenticated by the Other. Without going back over all the elements of the amusing little physics experiment that served me in picturing it for you, I shall simply tell you that, at the level of $i'(a)$ which is the *virtual image* of a *real image*, nothing appears. I've written $(-\varphi)$ at the top, because we'll have to put it there next time. This minus-*phi* is no more visible, no more tangible, no more presentifiable up there than down here, under $i(a)$, because it hasn't entered the imaginary.

In its principle, the lot, the inaugural moment of desire, which you'll have to wait till next time for me to articulate, takes hold in the relation I've given you as that of the fantasy, ($ \$ \lozenge a$), which is read – barred S, diamond, with its meaning which we shall soon know how to read differently, little *a*.

If the subject could really, and not through the intermediary of the Other, be at the place labelled I, he would have a relation with what it's a question of plucking from the neck of the vase in the original specular image, *i(a)*, namely, the object of his desire, *a*. These two pillars, *i(a)* and *a*, are the support of the function of desire. If desire exists and sustains mankind in its existence as mankind, it's to the extent that the relation ($ ◊ *a*) is accessible via some detour, where artifices give us access to the imaginary relation constituted by the fantasy. But this isn't in the least bit possible in an effective way. What man has in front of him is only ever the *virtual image, i'(a)*, of what I was representing in my diagram with this vase. What the spherical mirror's illusion produces on the left in the real state, in the form of a *real image*, he has only the *virtual image* of, on the right, with nothing in the neck of the vase. The *a*, desire's support in the fantasy, isn't visible in what constitutes for man the image of his desire.

Elsewhere, on this side of this image, on the left, there is the presence of the *a*, which is too close to him to be seen, but which is the *initium* of desire. This is where the image *i'(a)* gets its prestige from. But the more man approaches, encircles and caresses what he believes to be the object of his desire, the more he is in fact diverted and distracted from it. Everything he does on this path to move closer to it gives ever more body to what, in the object of this desire, represents the specular image. The further he goes, the more he wants, in the object of his desire, to preserve, maintain and protect the face of this primordial vase that is intact – the specular image. The further he goes down this path that is often improperly called the way to the perfection of the object relation, the more he is taken in.

Here we are, then, in a position to reply now to the question – when does anxiety emerge? Anxiety emerges when a mechanism makes something appear in the place of what I'm going to call, to make myself understood, a natural place, namely, the place of (– φ), which corresponds, on the right-hand side, to the place that is occupied, on the left-hand side, by the *a* of the object of desire. I say *something* – you should understand *anything whatsoever*.

Before next time, I would ask you to take the trouble to reread – with this introduction I'm giving you here – Freud's article on the *Unheimliche*. It's an article that I've never heard anyone comment on and no one seems to have noticed that it's indispensable for broaching the question of anxiety. Just as I broached the unconscious with the *Witz*, this year I'm going to be broaching anxiety with the *Unheimliche*.

The *Unheimliche* is what appears at the place where the minus-*phi* should be. Indeed, everything starts with imaginary castration, because there is no image of lack, and with good reason. When something does appear there, it is, therefore, if I may put it this way, because lack happens to be lacking.

This is perhaps going to seem to you to be a touch, a *concetto*, not at all out of place in my style which has a certain *Gongorismo* about it, as everyone knows. Well, I don't give a damn. I'll simply point out to you that a good many things may arise in the sense of anomalies, but that's not what provokes anxiety in us. But should all the norms, that is, that which makes for anomaly just as much as that which makes for lack, happen all of a sudden not to be lacking, that's when the anxiety starts. Try applying that to a whole number of things.

I authorize you now to resume reading what Freud says in his last major article on anxiety, *Inhibitions, Symptoms and Anxiety*. The key I'm providing you with will enable you to see the true meaning to be given to the term he there sets down in writing – *object-loss*.

That's where I'll be taking up next time, when I hope I'll be able to impart to our research for this year its true meaning.

28 November 1962

IV

BEYOND CASTRATION
ANXIETY

The object as a spare part
The Hoffmannian object
The object *a* postiche
The object-demand
The object that is not missing

I've put up on the blackboard for you the diagram that I started to go into with you last time in the articulation of what constitutes our theme.

With anxiety, with its phenomenon, but also with the place that I'm going to teach you to designate as specific to it, it's a matter of going deeper into the function of the object in the analytic experience.

I want briefly to mention that the text I've taken the trouble to write up of a paper I gave, over two years ago now, on 21 September 1960, at a Hegelian meeting in Royaumont, will soon be coming out. I chose to treat the following topic – *The Subversion of the Subject and the Dialectic of Desire in the Freudian Unconscious*. I'm mentioning it to those who've already familiarized themselves with my teaching because there they will find, I think to their satisfaction, the phases of construction and the functioning of what together we have called *the graph*. This text will thus soon be seeing the light of day in a volume, which contains the other papers too, not all of which are psychoanalytic, published by a centre at 173, boulevard Saint-Germain, which is seeing to the publication of all the work from the Royaumont meeting.

This announcement isn't out of place today in so far as the subversion of the subject as dialectic of desire frames the functioning of the object that we're going to have to go into more deeply.

In those that have been coming here as novices, I don't think I've encountered the reaction, a most unpleasant reaction I must say, that greeted this piece of work at Royaumont, a work designed to put the function of the object very much into question, namely, the function of the object of desire. To my astonishment, this reaction was shown by philosophers whom I believed more inured to the unusual. Their impression, which I can't qualify any differently than they themselves did, was one of a kind of nightmare, a flight of fancy even, peppered with a certain diabolism. However, oughtn't everything in the experience that I shall call modern – with the profound modifications in the perception of the object that are brought to it by the era that I'm not the first to qualify as the technological era – to suggest the idea that a disquisition on the object inevitably has to go via complex relations that only afford us access to it through wide chicanes?

Take, for instance, this unit of the object that is called *the spare part* and which is so very characteristic of what is given to us in experience, the outermost experience, not analytic experience. Isn't this something that deserves to be paused on, something that introduces a new dimension to any noetic examination pertaining to our relation to the object? For in the end, what is a spare part? How does it subsist beyond its possible use in relation to a certain model? Today the model is functional, but tomorrow it could just as well become obsolete, it might just as easily not be updated, as they say – following which, what does the spare part become? What sense does it have?

Why shouldn't this profile of a certain enigmatic relation to the object serve us today by way of introduction so as to take up this diagram once again?

1

This diagram is not some pointless complication. There's nothing for us to be astonished at and no reason to stiffen up.

At this place, $i'(a)$, in the Other, in the locus of the Other, an image emerges that is merely the reflection of ourselves. It's authenticated by the Other, but it's already problematic, fallacious even.

This image is characterized by a lack, that is, by the fact that

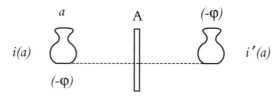

Simplified diagram

what is called upon there is unable to appear there. It orients and polarizes desire and it has a function of inveiglement for this desire. There, desire isn't simply veiled, but essentially brought into relation with an absence.

This absence is also the possibility of an appearance, which is controlled by a presence that lies elsewhere. This presence controls it very closely, but it does so from a site that is ungraspable for the subject. As I've indicated to you, the presence in question is that of the *a*, the object in the function that it fulfils in the fantasy.

At this place of lack where something can appear, last time I put, in brackets, the sign $(-\varphi)$. This indicates for you that there emerges here a relationship with the libidinal reserve, namely, with that something that doesn't get projected, doesn't get invested in, at the level of the specular image, which is irreducible, for the reason that it remains profoundly invested at the level of one's body, the level of primary narcissism, of what is called autoerotism, an autistic jouissance. All in all, it is a nutrient that stays there to animate if need be what will come into play as an instrument in the relation to the other, the other constituted on the basis of the image of my *semblable*, the other that will sketch its form and its norms – the image of the body in its seductive function – onto the one who is the sexual partner.

It is anxiety that, I told you last time, can come to be signalled at the place here designated by $(-\varphi)$, castration anxiety, in its relation to the Other. Here then is the question we shall be advancing into today. As you can see, I'm going straight to the nodal point.

By what path have we come to learn everything we know that is altogether new and original about the structure of the subject and the dialectic of desire that we analysts have to articulate? Well, by the path of the neurotic's experience. Now, what does Freud say on this score? He says that the final term he reached in developing this experience, its point of arrival, the point at which it runs aground, the term that for him is unsurpassable, is castration anxiety.

What does this mean? Is this term unsurpassable? What is meant by this halting of the analytic dialectic upon castration anxiety? Can't you see already, just from the way I've been making use of the diagrams, the path along which I mean to lead you being sketched out? It starts off from a better articulation of this fact of experience which Freud designated in the neurotic's running aground on castration anxiety. The opening I'm offering you, the dialectic I'm demonstrating for you here, permits of spelling out the fact that it really isn't castration anxiety that in and of itself constitutes the neurotic's ultimate impasse.

Indeed, the form of castration, that is, castration in its imaginary structure, is already produced here, at $(-\varphi)$, at the level of the fracture that occurs when the libidinalized image of the *semblable* is approached, at the phase of a certain imaginary drama. Hence the importance of the mishaps of the *scene* which for this reason is called *traumatic*. The imaginary fracture presents all sorts of variations and possible anomalies, which already indicates in and of itself that something in the material is useable for another function that gives its full meaning to the term *castration*.

What the neurotic shrinks back from is not castration, but from turning his castration into what the Other lacks. He shrinks back from turning his castration into something positive, namely, the guarantee of the function of the Other, this Other that steals away in the indeterminate echo of significations, this Other in which the subject no longer sees himself except as fate, but fate that has no end, fate that gets lost in the ocean of histories. Now, what are these histories, if not an immense fiction? What might ensure a relationship between the subject and this universe of significations, if not the fact that somewhere there is jouissance? This he can only ensure for himself by means of a signifier and this signifier is necessarily missing. The subject is summoned to this missing place to tender the exact change in the shape of a sign, the sign of his own castration.

Dedicating his castration to guaranteeing the Other is that before which the neurotic comes to a standstill. He comes to a standstill there for a reason that is in some sense internal to analysis and has to do with the fact that it's analysis that brings him to this appointment. At the end of the day, castration is none other than the moment of interpreting castration.

I might have been going faster with my disquisition this morning than I intended. Either way, you can see here an indication that there might be a possible way through, but we can only explore this possibility by retracing our steps, back to that place where imaginary castration functions to constitute what is properly speaking called, and quite rightly, the castration complex.

It's at the level of a reappraisal of castration that our concrete exploration of anxiety is going to allow us to study the possible way through – all the more possible for having already been got through on many an occasion. The study of the phenomenology of anxiety is going to enable us to say how and why.

2

Let's take anxiety in its *a minima* definition as a signal. Despite having been imparted by Freud at the end of the progress of his thought, this definition is not what people think it is.

It results neither from a relinquishment of his initial positions, which saw it as the result of a metabolism of energy, nor from a new conquest, because back when Freud saw anxiety as the transformation of libido he was already indicating that it could function as a signal. It would be easy for me to show you this in passing by referring to the text, but I've got too much to bring up with you this year to dwell too long at the level of textual explanations.

Anxiety, I've told you, is linked to anything that might appear at the place $(-\varphi)$. What assures us of this is a phenomenon for which the too scant attention that's been paid to it has meant that nobody has arrived at a formulation that would be satisfactory and unified for the functions of anxiety in their entirety in the field of our experience. This phenomenon is the *Unheimliche*.

I asked you last time to go to Freud's text yourselves, because I don't have time to spell it out to. Many of you, I know, did so right away, for which I thank you. Even from a superficial reading, the first thing that leaps to your attention is the importance Freud attaches to linguistic analysis. Were this not so striking wherever you care to look, this text would be enough on its own to justify the prevalence I give to the functions of the signifier in my commentary on Freud.

The second thing that will leap to your attention when you read the dictionary exploration with which Freud introduces his study, is that the *Unheimliche* is defined as *Heimliche*. The *Unheim* is poised in the *Heim*.

Freud doesn't trouble himself with explaining why. That's how it is. Since it's very clear from simply reading the dictionaries that that's how it is, he doesn't dwell on it any longer. He's like me today, he has to press on. Well, for the sake of staying within our conventions and for the sake of the clarity of our language for what is about to come next, we shall call the place designated last time as the minus-*phi* by its name – this is what is called the *Heim*.

Let's say that, if this word has a meaning in human experience, we have here man's home, his house. You may give this word all the overtones you like, including its astrological ones. Man finds his home at a point located in the Other that lies beyond the image from which we are fashioned.

This place represents the absence where we stand. Supposing that, which does indeed happen, it shows itself for what it is – namely, the presence that lies elsewhere, which means that this place is tantamount to an absence – then it becomes the queen of the game, it makes off with the image that underpins it, and the specular image becomes the image of the double, with all the radical uncanniness it brings. To employ terms that take on their signification in their opposition to the Hegelian terms, it makes us appear as an object, revealing the non-autonomy of the subject.

Hoffmann's texts, as everything that Freud has pinpointed within them by way of example shows, get to the heart of such an experience.

In the horrifying story of *The Sandman*, we can see how the subject goes from one inveiglement to the next, faced with this form of image that strictly speaking materializes the highly reduced diagram of it that I'm giving you here. The doll that the hero of the tale spies through the window of the sorcerer, who is conjuring up some magical operation or other, is strictly speaking this image, $i'(a)$, being finished off with what is absolutely singled out in the very form of the tale, to wit, the eye. The eye in question can only be that of the protagonist, the theme of someone wanting to rob him of this eye providing the thread that explains the whole tale.

It's indicative of goodness knows what awkwardness, no doubt linked to the fact that this was the first time the ploughshare was entering into the furrow of the discovery of subjective structure, that Freud throws in this reference for us as it comes to him. He says something along the lines of – *read* The Devil's Elixir, *I can't begin to tell you how complete it is, how it contains all the possible forms of the mechanism, how all the occasions when the reaction of the* unheimlich *may occur are clarified here*. It's plain to see that he doesn't go into it, as if overwhelmed by the luxuriance that this short novel does indeed present.

It's not easy to get hold of a copy, but through the kindness of one person present here, I find myself furnished with one, which is here on the lectern and for which I thank him. It's very useful to have more than one copy at one's disposal.

At this point *Heim,* what shows itself isn't simply what you've always known, that desire reveals itself as desire of the Other, here desire *in* the Other, but also that my desire, I shall say, enters the lair where it has been awaited for all eternity in the shape of *the object that I am* in so far as it exiles me from my subjectivity, by deciding on its own all the signifiers to which this subjectivity is attached.

Of course, this doesn't happen every day, and perhaps indeed it only ever happens in Hoffmann's tales. In *The Devil's Elixir*, it's utterly clear. At every turn in this long and so torturous truth, the accuracy of the footnote given by Freud to the effect that one gets a little lost in it is borne out. Indeed, *getting lost in it* itself goes to make up part of the function of the labyrinth, which has to be brought to life. In following each of these twists and turns, however, it's clear that the subject only gets to his desire by always substituting himself for one of his doubles.

Freud doesn't insist just for the sake of it on the quintessential dimension that the field of fiction imparts to our experience of the *Unheimliche*. In reality, this experience is too fleeting. Fiction demonstrates it far better and even produces it as an effect in a more stable way because it's better articulated. It's a kind of ideal point, but how precious it is for us, since this effect allows us to see the function of the fantasy.

This major effect of fiction, spelt out over and over in a work like *The Devil's Elixir*, but evident in so many others too, is that which, in the actual flux of existence, remains in the fantasy state. If we take it up like this, what is the fantasy if not something that we rather suspected, *ein Wunsch*, a wish, and even, like all wishes, a somewhat naïve one? To put it light-heartedly, I'd say that the formula of the fantasy, $ \$ $ desire of *a*, can be translated into the following perspective – that the Other faints, swoons, faced with this object that I am, a deduction I reach on account of being able to behold myself.

So as to put you in the picture, and to put it in an apodictic way, before I show you how it functions, I'll tell you right away that the two phases whose relations of $ \$ $ to *a* I've written up here, situating this last term differently in relation to the reflexive function of the A as a mirror, correspond exactly to the distribution of the terms of the fantasy for the pervert and the neurotic.

$$ a \ \Big|\ \overset{\text{A}}{\$} \qquad\qquad S\ \Big|\ \overset{\text{A}}{a\,\$} $$

The pervert's fantasy   The neurotic's fantasy

For the pervert, things are, if I may say so, in their right place. The *a* is right where the subject can't see it and the capital S is in its place. This is why one can say that the perverse subject, whilst remaining oblivious to the way this functions, offers himself loyally to the Other's jouissance.

Only, we'd never have known anything about it had it not been for the neurotics, for whom the fantasy doesn't possess at all the same functioning. The neurotic is the one who reveals the fantasy in its structure because of what he makes of it, but also, at the same time, through what he makes of it, he cons you, like he cons everyone.

Indeed, as I'm about to explain, the neurotic makes use of his fantasy for particular ends. What one reckoned one could make out, beneath the neurosis, to be perversion, and which I've spoken to you about on other occasions, is simply this, which I'm in the process of explaining to you, namely, that the neurotic's fantasy

is entirely situated in the locus of the Other. The support the neurotic finds in the fantasy is what, when it's met, presents itself as
perversion.

Neurotics have perverse fantasies and analysts have been racking
their brains for a good while wondering what this means. At any
rate, one can very well see that it's not the same thing as perversion, that it doesn't function in the same way, and a whole mix-up is
produced, and questions mount up, and people wonder for example
whether a perversion is really a perversion, in other words whether
perchance it might not be functioning as does the fantasy for the
neurotic. This question merely duplicates the first one – of what use
is the perverse fantasy to the neurotic?

Based on what I've just laid out for you concerning the function
of the fantasy, we need to begin by saying that there is indeed something of the order of *a* that appears at the place above the image
i'(a) that I'm designating for you on the blackboard, the place of
the *Heim* which is the locus of the appearance of anxiety. It's striking that the fantasy the neurotic makes use of, which he organizes
at the very moment he uses it, is precisely what serves him best in
defending himself against anxiety, in keeping a lid on it.

Naturally, this can only be conceived of starting off from presuppositions that I had to put forward initially in their extreme form.
As with any new discourse, you'll have to judge it as it takes shape,
by appreciating whether it tallies with the functioning of experience.
I don't think you'll have any doubt about it.

This object *a* that the neurotic makes himself into in his fantasy
becomes him much like gaiters do a rabbit. That's why the neurotic
never makes much of his fantasy. It succeeds in defending him
against anxiety precisely to the extent that it's a postiche *a*. I illustrated this function for you a long while ago with the dream dreamt
by the butcher's beautiful wife.

The butcher's beautiful wife is fond of caviar, of course, only she
doesn't want any, because it may well give too much pleasure to her
big brute of a husband who's capable of gobbling it up along with
the rest. Even that won't bring him to a stop. Now, what interests
the butcher's beautiful wife is not in the slightest, of course, feeding
her husband caviar, because, as I told you, he'll add on a whole
menu. He's got a big appetite, this butcher. The only thing that
interests the butcher's beautiful wife is her husband fancying the
little negligible amount, the *nothing*, that she keeps in reserve.

This formula, which is utterly clear as far as hysterics are concerned, trust me on this one, is applicable to all neurotics. The
object *a* functioning in their fantasy, which serves them as a defence
against their anxiety, is also, contrary to all appearances, the bait

with which they hold onto the Other. And, praise be, this is what we owe psychoanalysis to.

There was a certain Anna O. who knew a thing or two about the manoeuvre of the hysteric's game. She presented all of her little story, all her fantasies, to Herren Breuer and Freud, who leapt on them like little fish into water. Freud, on page 271 of *Studien über Hysterie*, marvels at the fact that, really, she didn't betray the faintest defence. She handed over the whole thing, just like that. No need to do any delving to get the whole caboodle. Clearly, Freud found himself before a generous form of hysterical functioning and this is why, as you know, Breuer jolly well took it full on, since, along with the wonderful bait, he swallowed the little *nothing* too, and it took him a certain while to regurgitate it. He didn't go there again.

Fortunately, Freud was neurotic and since he was both intelligent and courageous, he knew how to make use of his anxiety faced with his desire, which lay at the heart of the principle of his ridiculous attachment to that impossible woman who moreover buried him and who went by the name of Frau Freud. He knew how to make use of it so as to project the case onto the radiographic screen of his fidelity to this fantasmatic object and he was able to recognize there, without for one second batting an eyelid, what all that was for, to the point of well and truly admitting that Anna O. had him quite perfectly, Freud himself, in her sights. But he was clearly a bit harder to take in than the other fellow, Breuer. It's very much to this that we owe the fact of having gained access via the fantasy to the mechanism of analysis and a rational use of transference.

It's also perhaps what will enable us to take the next step and recognize what constitutes the limit point between the neurotic and the others.

3

There's another jump to be made now, which I ask you to note, since, as with the others, we're going to have to justify it afterwards.

What is actually functioning in the neurotic at the level, a level that is displaced in him, of the object a? What reality lies behind the fallacious use of the object in the neurotic's fantasy? This is sufficiently explained by the fact that he's been able to transport the function of the a into the Other. This reality has a very simple name – *demand*.

The true object sought out by the neurotic is a demand that he wants to be asked of him. He wants to be begged. The only thing he doesn't want is to pay the price.

This is a basic experience, from which analysts – no doubt not sufficiently enlightened by Freud's explanations of this not to have thought themselves duty-bound to get back onto the slippery slope of morality – have deduced a fantasy that lingers on in the oldest moralistic religious preaching, that of oblativity. As he doesn't want to give anything – this clearly bearing a certain relation to the fact that his difficulty belongs to the realm of receiving – then, if only he should care to give something, everything would be all right.

Only, what they don't perceive, these smooth talkers who tell us that genital maturity is the locus of the gift, is that what you've got to teach the neurotic to give is this thing he doesn't imagine, it's nothing – it's precisely his anxiety.

This is what brings us back to our point of departure today, designating the point at which one runs aground on castration anxiety.

The neurotic won't give up his anxiety. You're going to see that we're going to find out a bit more about this. We're going to find out why. It's so true, it's so very much this that's involved, that the whole process, the whole chain of analysis, consists in him at least giving over its equivalent, because he begins by giving over his symptom a little. This is why an analysis, as Freud said, begins with a shaping of symptoms. We endeavour to snare him, my goodness, in his own trap. We can never do otherwise with anyone. He makes you an offer, a fallacious offer when all is said and done – and, well, we accept it. By virtue of this, we enter a game by way of which he makes an appeal to demand. He wants you to ask something of him. As you don't ask anything, he starts modulating his own, his own demands, which come to the place *Heim*. That's what the first entry into analysis consists of.

I'll tell you in passing, further to what is articulated almost of its own accord in the diagram, that I don't really see how people have up until now been able to justify the frustration/aggression/regression dialectic, unless it's with a false and crude comprehensibility. What happens when you leave demand without a reply? The aggression you're being told about, where have you ever seen it arise if not outside analysis, in practices known as group psychotherapy, which we've been hearing about? No aggression arises in analysis. On the other hand, the dimension of aggressiveness comes into play to call into question what it aims at by its very nature, namely, the relation to the specular image. As the subject exhausts his rages against this image, the succession of demands is produced that leads back to an ever more original demand, historically speaking, and regression as such comes to be modulated.

We're now coming to another point that until now has never been satisfactorily explained. How come it is by the regressive path that the subject is led back to a time that we're very much forced to situate historically as progressive?

There are some who, faced with this paradox of knowing that it's in going back to the oral phase that the phallic relation is uncovered, have tried to have us believe that after regression it's necessary to go back up the path in the opposite direction, which is absolutely contrary to experience. No one's ever heard of an analysis, however successful it's reckoned to have been in the process of regression, going back through the opposite stages, as would be necessary were it a question of genetic reconstruction. On the contrary, it's to the extent that every form of demand is exhausted to its full term, to the bottom of the barrel, up to and including the D_0 of demand, that in the end we see the castration relation appear.

Castration is found inscribed as a relation at the far limit of demand's regressive cycle. It appears there as soon as, and in so far as, the register of demand is exhausted.

This has to be understood topologically. But not being able to push things much farther today, I'll finish with a remark that, converging as it does with the remark on which I finished my last talk, will focus your reflection on a direction that may facilitate the next step, such as I've just signposted it. Once again, I won't go round the houses, I'm going to take things up right in the middle of the pool.

In *Inhibitions, Symptoms and Anxiety*, Freud tells us, or sounds like he's telling us, that anxiety is the reaction-signal to the loss of an object. He lists – loss of the intrauterine environment that occurs in one fell swoop at birth – eventual loss of the mother, considered as an object – loss of the penis – loss of love from the object – and loss of the superego's love. Now, what was it I told you last time so as to put you on a certain track that it's so essential to grasp? I told you that anxiety isn't the signal of a lack, but of something that has to be conceived of at a duplicated level, as the failing of the support that lack provides. Well, with this indication, go back to Freud's list, which I snatched in full flight, as it were.

Don't you know that it's not longing for the maternal breast that provokes anxiety, but its imminence? What provokes anxiety is everything that announces to us, that lets us glimpse, that we're going to be taken back onto the lap. It is not, contrary to what is said, the rhythm of the mother's alternating presence and absence. The proof of this is that the infant revels in repeating this game of presence and absence. The security of presence is the possibility of absence. The most anguishing thing for the infant is precisely the moment when the relationship upon which he's established himself, of the lack that turns him into desire, is disrupted, and this relationship is most disrupted when there's no possibility of any lack, when the mother is on his back all the while, and especially when she's wiping his backside. This is one model of demand, of the demand that will never let up.

At a higher level, in the next temporal phase, that of the so-called loss of the penis, what's at stake? What can we see at the start of Little Hans's phobia? The stress gets laid, not very squarely, on anxiety being linked, so they say, to the mother forbidding masturbatory practices, which is perceived by the child as the presence of the mother's desire being exerted upon him. But what does experience teach us here about anxiety in its relation to the object of desire, if not simply that prohibition is temptation? Anxiety isn't about the loss of the object, but its presence. The objects aren't missing.

Let's move up to the next level, that of the superego's love, with everything that this is deemed to entail on what is said to be the path to failure. What does that mean, if not that what is feared is success? Once more, *there's no lack*.

I'll leave you today on this point, which is designed to clear away a mix-up and turn it round, a mix-up that is entirely due to the difficulty of identifying the object of desire. Just because it's difficult to identify, this doesn't mean it's not there. It *is* there, and its function is decisive.

As regards anxiety, consider that what I've told you about it today is merely a preliminary way in. The precise way of locating it, which we shall be entering as of next time, is to be situated amid the three themes that you've seen being sketched out in my disquisition today.

One is the Other's jouissance. The second is the Other's demand. The third, which only the sharpest ears would have picked out, is that sort of desire that is evinced in interpretation, and of which the analyst's incidence in the treatment is the most exemplary and the most enigmatic form.

It's the one that's been leading me for a long while now to pose for you the question – in the economy of desire, what is represented by this privileged sort of desire that I call the analyst's desire?

5 December 1962

V

THAT WHICH DECEIVES

Pavlov, Goldstein and the Other's demand
Jones and the Other's jouissance
The traces of the subject
The cuts of the drive
Pascal and the vacuum experiment

It's been seen, it's been read, it will be seen, and it will be read again that one segment of psychoanalysis, the one that's being pursued here, has a more philosophical character than any of the others, that it supposedly tries to match up with an experience that is more concrete, more scientific, more experimental, it doesn't much matter which word you use.

It's not my fault, as one says, that psychoanalysis puts into question, on the theoretical plane, *le désir de connaître*, the desire to take cognizance, and that, in its discourse, it places itself of its own accord further upstream, at a spot that precedes the moment of cognizance. This would justify in and of itself the questioning that lends a certain philosophical hue to our discourse.

Besides, I was preceded in this by the inventor of analysis, who stood very much, as far as I know, at the level of a direct experience, that of the mentally ill, especially those who are called, with greater rigour following Freud, neurotics.

This wouldn't be a reason to stay any longer than necessary at the level of an epistemological reappraisal, if the place of desire, the way in which desire hollows itself out, were not presentified for us at each moment in our therapeutic position by a problem, the most concrete problem of all, that of not allowing ourselves to be taken down a false track, of not responding to it falsely or beside the point, at least as regards a certain goal we are pursuing and which is not all that clear.

I remember causing the indignation of one of those kinds of

colleagues who know how to shield themselves on occasion behind a swell of good intentions designed to reassure someone or other, when I said that, in analysis, cure is an additional bonus. This was seen as some kind of disdain for the person we have charge of, and who is suffering, when in fact I was speaking from a methodological point of view. It's quite certain that our justification, like our duty, is to improve the subject's position. But I claim that nothing is shakier, in the field we're in, than the concept of cure.

Is an analysis that finishes with the patient, male or female, joining the Third Order a cure, even if the subject finds himself better off as far as his symptoms are concerned now that, fortified by a certain faith, by a certain order that he's recovered, he voices the most express reservations about the paths, which now he sees as perverse, along which we made him pass in order to have him enter heaven's kingdom? This can happen.

This is why I don't think for one second that I'm moving away from our experience when my disquisition calls to mind how, in this experience, every question may be asked, and we have to conserve the possibility of a certain thread that can guarantee at the very least that we don't cheat with the very thing that constitutes our instrument, that is, the plane of truth.

This necessitates an exploration that has to be not only serious, but even to a certain degree, not exhaustive – who could be? – but encyclopaedic. On a subject like anxiety, it certainly isn't easy to gather together, in a disquisition like mine, everything that has to be functional for analysts. What shouldn't be forgotten for a single instant is that the place which we've designated on this little diagram as the place of anxiety, and which is currently being occupied by the $(-\varphi)$, constitutes a certain void. Everything that may show itself in this place throws us off route, as it were, as regards the structuring function of this void.

This topology will only have value if you can find the clues it gives you confirmed by whatever approach might have been taken to the phenomenon of anxiety, by any serious study, whatever its presuppositions may be. Even if these presuppositions seem to us to be too narrow for our purposes and have to be situated afresh within the radical experience that is ours, something has still been grasped at a certain level. Even if the phenomenon of anxiety appears thereby limited, contorted, and insufficient with regard to our experience, one ought at least to know why this is so. And it isn't always so.

We have to take our pickings, at whatever level this may be, right where the examination on the topic of anxiety has up to now been formulated.

My purpose today is to give an indication of it, for want of being

able to go over the sum total of what's been put forward on this
score, which would necessitate a whole year's Seminar.

1

There's a certain type of examination that's called, rightly or
wrongly, the objective or experimental approach to the problem of
anxiety.

We wouldn't know anything but how to get lost in it had I not
given you at the start the lines of sight, the points of support, which
we simply cannot let go of and which enable us to guarantee and
narrow down our object, and to see what conditions it in the most
radical fashion. Last time my talk ended by circumscribing them, as
it were, with three reference points that I did no more than introduce, three points in which the dimension of the Other remains
dominant.

These are, to wit, the Other's demand, the Other's jouissance, and
in a modalized form, which moreover stayed at the level of a question mark, the desire of the Other, inasmuch as this is the desire that
corresponds to the analyst in so far as he intervenes as a term in the
experience.

We shan't do what we reproach all the others with doing, namely,
to elide the analyst from the text of the experience we're examining. The anxiety unto which we have to bring a formula here is
an anxiety that corresponds to us, an anxiety that we provoke, an
anxiety with which we have on occasion a decisive relationship.

In this dimension of the Other we find our place, our efficient
place, inasmuch as we know how not to shrink it down. This
grounds the question I'm posing, namely, to what extent our desire
oughtn't to make this dimension of the Other shrink. I should like
to make you feel this. This dimension is by no means absent from
any of the ways in which people have tried, up to this day, to circumscribe the phenomenon of anxiety.

At the level of mental exercise to which I've trained you, accustomed you, perhaps indeed you now find the emphasis but futile,
the success but vain, the triumph but groundless, which some take
from the fact that, for instance, supposedly to the contrary of how
analytic thought would have it – and how exactly would it be the
contrary? – neuroses are produced in animals, in the lab, on the
laboratory table.

What do these neuroses, which Pavlov and those who followed
him have on occasion accentuated, show us? We are told in what
way an animal reflex is conditioned. A reaction said to be natural is

associated with a stimulus that belongs to a register that is presumed
to be completely different from the one involved in the reaction.
Then, these conditioned reactions are made to converge in a certain
fashion by obtaining effects of contrariety. What we've obtained,
conditioned, broken in, in the organism's responses, allows us to
put the organism in a position where it may respond in two contrary ways at the same time, thereby generating, as it were, a sort of
organic perplexity.

To go further, we shall even say that we have the idea that
in certain cases we obtain an exhaustion of the possibilities of
response, a more fundamental disarray generated by diverting them,
which concerns in a more radical fashion the ordinary field of the
reactions involved, an objective translation of what may be interpreted in a more general perspective as defined by certain patterns
of reaction that will be called instinctive. More recently, in other cultural spheres, they've theorized something they've qualified with the
term *stress*. We've got to the point where the demand made upon
the function leads to a deficit that overwhelms the function itself,
going so far as to involve the system in a way that modifies it beyond
the register of the functional response, verging in the end, in the
lasting traces it engenders, on a lesional deficit.

In this overview of experimental examination, it would no doubt
be important to point out where something shows itself that is
reminiscent of what is called the anxious form that we sometimes
come across in neurotic reactions. There's something, however, that
always seems to be sidelined in this way of posing the problem of
experiments. It's doubtless impossible to criticize he who reports
one of these experiments for this, since this sidelining is constitutive
of the experiment itself, but whoever might care to compare this
experience with ours – our experience which occurs with a speaking
subject – really shouldn't fail to mention the following. However
primitive the animal organism under examination may be in comparison with a speaking subject – and in Pavlov's experiments this
organism is very far from being primitive, since they are performed
on dogs – the dimension of the Other is present in the experiment.

This isn't the first time I've noted this. When speaking at one
of our scientific meetings on some phenomena that were being
reported to us concerning the creation of experimental neurosis, I
remarked to the one who was relating this research that his own
presence, as a human figure, handling a certain number of things
around the animal, had to be counted at any one moment as part
of the experiment. When you know how a dog behaves vis-à-vis the
one who calls himself, or doesn't, his master, you know that in every
case the dimension of the Other counts for a dog. But even were it

not a dog, were it a grasshopper or a leech, the very fact that there is an array of apparatuses means that the dimension of the Other is present.

You'll tell me that a grasshopper or a leech, the object organism of the experiment, doesn't know anything about this dimension of the Other. I agree entirely. This is precisely why my whole effort was for a certain while to demonstrate to you the scale of a comparable level in us, the subject. In this subject that we are, the subject that we learn to handle and determine, there is also a whole field in which we know nothing of what constitutes us.

The *Selbstbewusstsein*, which I've taught you to name *subject supposed to know*, is a deceptive supposition. The *Selbstbewusstsein*, considered to be constitutive of the cognizing subject, is an illusion, a source of error, because the dimension of the subject deemed to be transparent in his act of taking cognizance of some entity only begins with the coming into play of a specified object, which is the one that the mirror stage attempts to circumscribe, namely, the image of one's body, in so far as, faced with this image, the subject has the feeling of jubilation on account of being indeed faced with an object that renders him transparent to himself. The extension of this illusion of consciousness to all types of cognizance is prompted by the object of cognizance being constructed and modelled in the image of the relation to the specular image. It's precisely in this respect that this object of cognizance is insufficient.

Were there no psychoanalysis, we would still know this from the fact that there are moments when the object appears that cast us into a completely different dimension, which is given in experience, and deserves to be set apart as primary in experience. This is the dimension of the uncanny.

This dimension may in no way be grasped as leaving the subject who is faced with it transparent to his cognizance. In contending with this new entity, the subject quite literally falters, and everything of the so-called primordial relation of the subject to any effect of cognizance is brought into question.

This sudden appearance, within the field of the object, of an unknown entity that is experienced as such, of an irreducible structuration, doesn't only pose a question for analysts, for this is already given in experience. All the same, one ought to try to explain why children are afraid of the dark. At the same time, it can be seen that they aren't always afraid of the dark. So, people do a little psychology. The so-called experimenters embark on theories of the inherited, ancestral, primordial reaction of a thinking – since thinking there is, it seems that the term ought still to be kept up – that would be structured differently from logical, rational thinking. And they construct, they invent. That's where a little philosophy gets done. Here we stand in wait for those with whom we have to pursue this dialogue when the opportunity arises, on the very ground upon which this dialogue must be judged. Let's see if we can account for the experience in a less hypothetical way.

Here's one conceivable reply, I offer it up to you. It is articulated based on the constitution of the object that is correlative to a first pattern of approach, that of the recognition of our own form. It says that this recognition is in itself limited, for it allows something to escape of that primordial investment in our Being that is given by the fact of existing as a body. Isn't this a reply that's not only reasonable but verifiable, to say that it's this remainder, this un-imaged residue of the body, that comes along, by a certain detour that we know how to designate, to make itself felt in the place laid out for lack, and in a way that, not being specular, cannot thereafter be marked out? This failing of certain markings is indeed one dimension of anxiety.

We won't be in disagreement here with the way that a certain Kurt Goldstein broaches this phenomenon. When he speaks to us of anxiety, he does so with great pertinence. How's this whole phenomenology of lesional phenomena, in which he's hot on the trail of this experience that interests us, articulated? It is articulated on the basis of the precondition that the organism functions as a totality in all its relational effects. There's not a single muscle that's not involved in just one tilt of the head. Any reaction to any given situation implies the totality of the organismal response. If we follow him, we can see two terms appear that are tightly woven together, *catastrophic reaction*, and, within its phenomenal field, the marking-out of *anxiety phenomena* as such.

I ask you to look up Goldstein's texts, very accessible texts since they've been translated into French, to see both how close these formulations are to our own, and how much they'd gain in clarity by referring to ours more expressly. This you shall see if you follow the text with the key I'm handing you.

Take, for example, the difference that lies between the reaction of disorder and the reaction of anxiety.

Through the reaction of disorder, the subject responds to his inoperativeness, to the fact of being faced with a situation that's insurmountable, undoubtedly because of his deficit. This is a way of reacting that's not at all foreign to a non-deficient subject contending with a situation of *Hilflosigkeit*, of insurmountable danger.

For the reaction of anxiety to occur, two conditions, which are present in the concrete cases mentioned, always have to be met. The first is for the deficiencies to be fairly limited so that the subject can make them out in the test he's undergoing, and so that, owing to this limit, the lacuna can appear as such in the objective field. This sudden emergence of lack in a positive form is the source of anxiety – only, second condition, here again it mustn't be omitted that the subject has Goldstein in front of him, or some such person from his laboratory, who's subjecting him to an organized test. Thus, the field of *lack* is produced under the effect of a *question*.

When you know where and when to look for these terms, you find them without fail, if need be.

To skip to an altogether different realm, I'll just mention the experience that is the heaviest, which is never reconstituted, an ancestral experience, flung back into a darkness of ancient times from which we're supposed to have escaped, but which bears out a necessity that unites us to these times, an experience that's still current, and which, most curiously, we don't speak about any more except very rarely – the experience of the nightmare.

One wonders why analysts, for some time now, have taken so little interest in it. I'm introducing it here because all the same we really must spend some time on it this year. I'll tell you why, and where to find the material, for a literature has already been put together on the subject, and it's one of the most remarkable, and to which you ought to refer. I'm thinking, as forgotten as it is, of Jones's work *On the Nightmare*, a book of incomparable richness.

I'll remind you of its fundamental phenomenology. I wouldn't dream for an instant of eluding its principal dimension – the nightmare's anxiety is felt, properly speaking, as that of the Other's jouissance.

The correlative of the nightmare is the incubus or the succubus, the creature that bears down on your chest with all its opaque weight of foreign jouissance, which crushes you beneath its jouissance. The first thing that appears in the myth, but also in the nightmare such as it is experienced, is that this creature that weighs down with its jouissance is also a questioning being, and even reveals itself in the developed dimension of the question known as the riddle. The Sphinx, don't forget, who in the myth arrives on the scene prior to all of Oedipus' drama, is both a nightmarish figure and a questioning figure.

This question furnishes the most primordial form of what I called the dimension of demand, whereas what we usually call demand, in the sense of a requirement that's claimed to be instinctual, is only a reduced form of it.

So, here we're led once more to examine the relationship between an experience that may be called pre-subjective, in the usual sense of the term *subject*, and the question in its most closed form, in the form of a signifier that is put forward as opaque, which is the stance of the riddle.

This allows you to call my bluff, by citing the definitions I've already offered you, so that I have to put them to the test of using them.

2

The signifier, so I told you at one turn in the path, is a trace, but an effaced trace. The signifier, so I told you at another such turn, is distinguished from the sign by the fact that the sign is what represents something for someone, whereas the signifier is what represents a subject for another signifier.

We're going to put this to the test in connection with what's at stake.

What's at stake is our anxious relation to some lost object, but which certainly isn't lost for everyone. I'm going to show you where it can be found, since it's not enough to forget something for it not to go on being there, only we no longer know how to recognize it. To find it again, we must go back over the subject of the trace.

To liven up the interest of this research for you, I'll give you right away two newsflashes on our most common experience.

The correlation is clear between what I'm trying to sketch out for you and the phenomenology of the hysteric symptom, in the widest sense, for don't forget that there aren't just the little hysterias, there are the big ones too, there are anaesthesias, paralyses, scotomata, there are restrictions of the visual field. Anxiety doesn't appear in hysteria to the exact extent that these lacks are misrecognized.

There's something that's not often noticed, that you hardly ever let into the picture, which nevertheless explains a whole part of the obsessional's behaviour. In his very particular way of treating the signifier, namely, of casting doubt on it, of giving it a good rub, of effacing it, of pummelling it, of smashing it to smithereens, of behaving towards it like Lady Macbeth and the damned spot of blood, the obsessional, by a dead-end path, but whose aim is not to be doubted, operates precisely in the direction of finding the sign beneath the signifier. *Ungeschehenmachen, making unhappened* the inscription of history.[1] It came to pass like that, but it's not sure. It's not sure, because they're just signifiers, it's just history, and so it's a doodad. The obsessional is right, he's grasped something, he wants to get to the origin, to the previous level, to the level of the sign.

Now I'll try to lead you along the path in the opposite direction. I didn't begin today with our laboratory animals just for the sake of it. After all, we could try unlocking the doors for them to see what they do with the trace.

Effacing traces, operating with traces, isn't just one of mankind's properties. We see animals effacing their traces. We even see complex behaviour that consists in burying a certain number of traces, dejecta for example – this is well known in cats.

One part of animal behaviour consists in structuring a certain field of its *Umwelt*, its surroundings, by way of traces that punctuate this field and define its limits for the animal. This is what is called the constitution of territory. Hippopotami do that with their dejecta and also with a product from certain glands that are, if memory serves, peri-anal. The stag will rub his antlers against the bark of certain trees, and will also do so where the traces can be made out. I don't want to go into the infinite variety of what a developed zoology can teach you on this score. What's important to me is what I have to say to you concerning the effacement of traces.

Animals, I tell you, efface their traces and lay false traces. Do they for all that make signifiers? There's one thing that animals don't do – they don't lay false traces to make us believe that they are false, that is, traces that will be taken for false. Laying falsely false traces is a behaviour that is, I won't say quintessentially human, but quintessentially signifying. That's where the limit is. That's where a subject presentifies himself. When a trace has been made to be taken for a false trace, though in fact they are the traces of my true passage, we know that there's a speaking subject, we know that there's a subject as cause.

The very notion of cause has no other support but this. Afterwards we try to extend it to the universe, but the original cause is the cause of a trace that presents itself as empty, that wants to be taken for a false trace. What does this mean? It means, indissolubly, that the subject, when he arises, addresses what I shall for the time being call the most radical form of the Other's rationality. Indeed, this behaviour has nothing else within its range but to take up ranks in the locus of the Other in a chain of signifiers, signifiers that do or don't have the same origin, but which constitute the only possible term of reference for the trace that has become a signifying trace.

This happens in such a way that you can grasp here that what feeds the emergence of the signifier at the origin is the aim that the Other, the real Other, should not know. The *he didn't know* takes root in a *he mustn't know*. The signifier does undoubtedly reveal the subject, but by effacing his trace.

Thus, first of all there is an *a*, the object of the hunt, and an A, in whose interval the subject S appears with the birth of the signifier, but as barred, as unknown. All the subsequent mapping-out

$$a \quad A$$
$$\$$$

Schema of the effaced trace

of the subject leans on the necessity of a reconquest of this original unknown dimension. You can see here appearing already, in connection with the Being that stands to be won back, the subject's Being, the truly radical relationship that there is between the *a* and the first apparition of the subject as unknown, which means, unconscious, *unbewusst*. The word is justified by the philosophical tradition, which makes the *Bewusste* of consciousness coincide with absolute knowledge. This won't do for us, in so far as we know that this knowledge and consciousness don't coincide.

Freud leaves open the question as to where the existence of the field defined as that of consciousness might stem from. I can claim that the mirror stage, articulated as it is, provides the beginning of a solution to this, much as I know in what dissatisfaction it can leave such minds as have been trained in Cartesian meditation. I think we can take a step further this year, which should lead you to grasp where the real origin, the original object, of the system called consciousness is, for we shall only be satisfied that the perspectives of consciousness really have been refuted when we finally realize that it attaches itself to an isolable object that is specified in the structure.

Earlier I indicated the neurotic's position in this dialectic. If you've managed to grasp the sinews of what's involved concerning the emergence of the signifier, you'll soon understand what slippery slope we're presented with concerning what happens in neurosis. All the traps into which analytic dialectic has fallen are due to the intrinsic part of falsity that lies in the neurotic's demand having been misrecognized.

The existence of anxiety is linked to the fact that any demand, even the most archaic, always has something illusory about it with respect to what preserves the place of desire. This is also what explains the anguishing side of anything that gives a response to this false demand in such a way as to fill it in.

I saw this arise, not so long ago, in what one of my patients said, a patient whose mother had never left him so much as an inch, up to a certain age – could it be put any better? She only ever gave a false response to his demand, a response that really fell wide of the mark, because, if demand is actually structured by the signifier, then it's not to be taken literally. What the child asks of his mother is designed to structure the presence/absence relation for him, as is demonstrated by the originative *Fort-Da* game which is a first exercise of mastery. A certain void is always to be preserved, which has nothing to do with the content, neither positive nor negative, of demand. The disruption wherein anxiety is evinced arises when this void is totally filled in.

Our algebra furnishes us with a ready-made instrument with which we may clearly see the consequences of this. Demand comes unduly to the place of what is spirited away, *a*, the object.

3

What is an algebraic equation? It's something very straightforward that's designed to make something very complicated manageable, to make it pass into a mechanical state, without you having to understand it. It's a lot better like that. As has been seen in mathematics from the start, the equation just has to be correctly put together.

I've taught you to write the drive ($ ◊ D), to be read – barred S, cut of capital D, demand. We're going to come back to this cut – all the same, you started to get a little idea of it just now, what has to be cut off is the hunter's momentum – but already the way I've taught you to write the drive explains to you why it was that the drives were described in neurotics – it's to the extent that the fantasy ($ ◊ a) is presented in a privileged way in the neurotic as ($ ◊ D).

In other words, it was an illusion of the neurotic's fantasmatic structure that allowed this first step called the drive to be taken. Freud designated it, always and perfectly, without the slightest wavering, as *Trieb*. This word has a history in German philosophical thought, and it's absolutely impossible to mix it up with the word *instinct*. In view of which, even in the *Standard Edition*, I recently came across, and, if memory serves, in the text *Inhibitions, Symptoms and Anxiety*, translated as *instinctual need*, something which in the German text is called *Bedürfnis*. Simply replacing *Bedürfnis* with *need*, if one so wished, would be a good translation from German to English. Why add this *instinctual* which is absolutely not in the text, and which is enough to falsify the entire meaning of the sentence? A drive has nothing to do with an instinct.

I've no objection to the definition of what may be called instinct, nor even to the customary use of the word, as for example calling the needs that living beings have to feed themselves *instincts*. But the oral drive is something else. It pertains to the mouth's erotogeneity, which brings us straight to the problem of why only the mouth is involved? Why doesn't it also involve gastric secretion, since we were speaking earlier about Pavlov's dogs? And even, if we look closely, why more particularly does it only involve the lips and, from a certain age onwards, what Homer called the *fence of teeth*?

In fact, from the very first analytic approach to instinct, we come across this fault line which is crucial to the dialectic established by the reference to the other in the mirror.

I thought I'd brought along for you today, though I haven't found it in my papers, Hegel's phrase from the *Phänomenologie des Geistes*, which I'll give you next time, where it's categorically said that language is work, and that it's through this that the subject makes his inside pass outside. The sentence is such that it's very clear that what's involved is an *inside out*, as is said in English. It really is the metaphor of the glove turned inside out. But to this reference I've added the idea of a loss, in so far as something doesn't undergo this inversion. At each stage, a residue remains which can't be turned inside out and isn't signifiable in the articulated register.

We shan't be surprised that these forms of the object appear in the form that's called partial. This fact struck us strongly enough to name them thus, in their divided-off form. For example, when we're led to bring in the object that is correlative to the oral drive, we speak of the maternal nipple. All the same, we oughtn't to omit its initial phenomenology, that of a dummy, I mean something that presents itself with an artificial character. This is precisely what allows it to be replaced by any old feeding bottle, which functions in exactly the same way in the economy of the oral drive.

Biological references, references to need, are of course essential, they're not to be sniffed at, but only as a way of seeing the utterly primitive structural difference that introduces here, de facto, both ruptures and cuts, along with, without further ado, the signifying dialectic. Is there something here that might be impenetrable for a conception that I shall call *all that's most natural*?

The dimension of the signifier is nothing, if you will, but the very thing an animal finds itself caught up in while pursuing its object, in such a way that the pursuit of this object leads it into another field of traces, where the pursuit itself thenceforth assumes a merely intro-ductive value. The fantasy, the $\$$ in relation to *a*, here takes on the signifying value of the subject's entry into this dimension that will lead him to that indefinite chain of significations called destiny. Its ultimate mainspring may elude him indefinitely, but precisely what has to be found is the point of departure – how did the subject get into this business of the signifier?

So it's quite clear that it's worthwhile recognizing the structure I gave you for the drive in the first objects that were singled out by analysis. Already we have the one that earlier I called the cut-off breast. Later, demand addressed *to* the mother swings round into demand *from* the mother, and we have the object called the scybalum. One can't really see what this object's privilege could be if one can't see that it too has a relation to a zone that's called erogenous. It should be seen that, once again, the zone in question is separated by a limit from the entire functional system that it affects, and which is a good deal larger. Among the different excretory functions, why single out the anus, if not for its decisive sphincter function which contributes to cutting an object? This cut is what gives its value, its accent, to the anal object, with everything that it can come to represent, not simply, as they say, on the side of the gift, but on the side of identity.

The function that may be given to it in analytic theory in what goes by the name of *object relations* – I'm not talking about a theory that's brand new, but it's pretty recent all the same – finds itself justified by what I've just been saying, with nevertheless one slight difference, which is that everything about it gets falsified when one sees in it a model of the patient's world, wherein a process of maturation would allow for the progressive restoration of a reaction that is presumed to be total and authentic. No, it's just a question of a piece of waste that designates the only thing that's important, namely, the place of a void.

I'm going to show you that other, so much more interesting, objects will take up position here. Moreover, you're already familiar with them, but you don't know how to place them. For today, consider the place of this void to have been reserved.

Since, likewise, something in our project shall not fail to evoke the existential theory of anxiety, and even the *existentialist* theory of anxiety, you can tell yourselves that it's not by chance that the one who may be considered to be one of the fathers, at least in the modern era, of the existential perspective didn't fail to take an interest in the void.

I'm talking about Pascal, who is fascinating for us, though we don't really know why, when going by the theoreticians of the sciences he screwed up on everything. At least, he screwed up on infinitesimal calculus, which he was apparently a whisker away from discovering. I think that he rather didn't give a hoot, because he had something that interested him more, and that's why he touches us still, even those of us who are complete unbelievers. Being the good Jansenist he was, Pascal was interested in desire, and that's why, I'm telling you in confidence, he carried out the Puy de Dôme experiments on the vacuum.

The vacuum doesn't interest us at all from the theoretical point of view. It's almost meaningless for us now. We know that in a vacuum there can be hollows, plenums, masses of waves and anything else you like. But for Pascal, whether or not nature abhors a vacuum was essential, because this signified the abhorrence that all the learned men of his day had for desire. Until then, if not nature, at least all thought had abhorred the possibility that somewhere there might be a void.

So there we have what's being offered to our attention. It remains to be seen whether from time to time we too don't succumb to this abhorrence.

12 December 1962

VI

THAT WHICH DECEIVES NOT

One of Ferenczi's precious points
Anxiety is framed
Anxiety is not without object
From anxiety to action
On the demands of the God of the Jews

So, what I've been conjuring up for you here isn't metaphysics. It's more of a brainwashing.

I let myself use this term a few years back, before it started cropping up here, there and everywhere in the news. What I mean to do is to teach you to recognize, in the right place, by means of a method, what presents itself in your experience. Of course, the efficacy of what I'm claiming to do can only be tested out in experience.

The presence at my teaching of certain people who are in analysis with me has sometimes been objected to. All in all, the legitimacy of the co-existence of these two relationships with me – one where they hear me and one where they get heard by me – can only be judged from within. Can what I teach you here effectively make – for one and all, and thus equally for those who work with me – the way in to recognizing one's own pathway any easier? At this locus, there is of course a limit where any external monitoring stops, but seeing that those who partake of these two positions at least learn to read better isn't a bad sign.

Brainwashing, I said. Showing you I know how to recognize in the comments of those I analyse something other than what's written in the books is tantamount to offering myself up to this monitoring. Conversely, for them, they show that they know how to recognize in the books what is effectively in the books.

This is why I can only applaud myself for a little sign like the one, a recent one, imparted to me from the mouth of someone I have in analysis.

Indeed, the scope of a point that may be clutched in passing in one of Ferenczi's books didn't escape his notice, a book that recently appeared in translation, but how late.

1

The original title of the work is *Versuch einer Genitaltheorie*, that is, quite precisely, *Research on a Theory of Genitality*, and not *Origins of Sexual Life* as it has been lost in the translation.

This book is disturbing in some respects. For those who know how to hear, I pointed out a long time ago what therein can, on occasion, partake of delusion. But since it brings with it great experience, it does all the same, in its twists and turns, allow more than one point that will be precious for us to be set down.

I'm sure that the author himself doesn't give the point all the accentuation it deserves, given that his intention in his research is to arrive at an altogether too harmonizing, too totalizing notion of his object, namely, genital realization.

Here are the terms in which he expresses himself in passing. *The development of genital sexuality, whose broad outlines we have just sketched out for man* – he's talking about males – *undergoes in woman* what is translated as *a rather unexpected interruption,* a quite improper translation since in German it's, *eine ziemlich unvermittelte Unterbrechung,* which means *an interruption that in most cases is pretty much unmediated.* This means that it isn't part of what Ferenczi qualifies as amphimixis, and which when all is said and done is merely one of the naturalized forms of what we call thesis/antithesis/synthesis, that is, dialectical progression, if I may say, a term which despite doubtless not being valorized in Ferenczi's mind doesn't animate his whole construction any the less effectively. If the interruption is said to be *unvermittelte,* it's because it runs parallel to this process, and let's not forget that here it's a question of finding the synthesis of genital harmony. It needs to be understood, therefore, that this interruption lies rather in a cul-de-sac, that is to say, beyond the progress of mediation.

This interruption, says Ferenczi, *is characterized by the displacement from the erogeneity of the clitoris, the female penis, to the vaginal cavity.* Here, he's merely accentuating what Freud tells us. *Analytic experience inclines us to suppose, however, that for the woman, not only the vagina, but also other parts of the body can be genitalized, as is likewise borne out by hysteria, in particular the nipple and its surrounding area.*

As you know, in hysteria, a good many other zones are concerned besides that one. Moreover, the translation, in failing to follow effectively what's precious in what's being brought to us here by way of material, again shows itself to be vague, and slightly blurry. In German, there's no *likewise borne out*, but simply *nach Art der Hysterie*, that is, *in the manner of* or *in keeping with the pattern of*.

What does that mean, for someone who's learnt, be it here or elsewhere, how to hear, if not that the vagina comes to function in the genital relation through a mechanism that is strictly equivalent to all the other hysterical mechanisms?

And why should we be surprised? Our diagram for the place of the empty locus in the function of desire allows you at least to locate the paradox at stake, and which is defined as follows.

The locus, the house of jouissance, is ordinarily found, since it's naturally found, placed in an organ that is, as experience and anatomo-physiological investigation teach you in the most certain fashion, non-sensitive, in the sense that it can't even be stimulated when it's being irritated. The ultimate locus of genital jouissance is a place – this is no mystery – where you can pour torrents of boiling water, brought to a temperature that no other mucous membrane could withstand, without provoking any immediate sensory reactions.

There is every reason to pinpoint correlations such as these before entering the diachronic myth of a so-called maturation, which would turn the port of arrival, namely, the accomplishment of the sexual function in the genital function, into something other than a process of maturation, something other than a locus of convergence, of synthesis, of everything that up to that point had presented itself in terms of partial aims. Recognizing the necessity of the empty place in a functional point of desire, and noticing that this is right where nature itself, right where physiology, has found its most favourable functional point, frees us of the weight of paradoxes that would lead us to devise so many mythical constructions around so-called vaginal jouissance, and also thereby puts us in a clearer position, though not of course without something being able to be indicated beyond this.

Those of you who attended our Amsterdam Congress on female sexuality may remember that many things, praiseworthy things, were said there without being effectively linked up and mapped out, for want of that structural register I'd indicated in my opening to the proceedings, and whose articulations I'm trying to give you here. And yet, how precious it is for us to know what's here on the blackboard, when one is acquainted with all the paradoxes one is beset with concerning the place to be ascribed to hysteria on what could be called the scale of neuroses.

Due to the obvious analogies with the hysteric mechanism, whose centrepiece I've pointed out to you, people consider hysteria to be the most advanced neurosis because it stands nearest to genital achievement. According to this diachronic conception, we have to put it at the end point of infantile maturation, but also at its beginning, since the clinic shows us that we really have to consider it to be the most primary neurosis on the neurotic scale, because it's upon hysteria that the constructions of obsessional neurosis are built. Moreover, hysteria's relationships to psychosis, to schizophrenia, are obvious and have been highlighted.

The only thing that might allow us to avoid constantly flitting back and forth as the needs of the case to be presented dictate, to avoid placing hysteria sometimes at the end, sometimes at the beginning, of what are deemed to be progressive phases, is first and foremost to bring it back to what is prevalent, namely, structure, the structure that's both synchronic and constitutive of desire as such, wherein what I'm designating as the place of the blank, the place of the void, always plays an essential function. The fact that this function comes to the fore in the final structure of the genital relation is both the confirmation of our method's validity and the point at which a more clear-cut, more orderly view of the phenomena specific to the genital dimension gets under way.

Doubtless there's some obstacle that stops us seeing it directly, since to reach it we have to pass via a somewhat winding path, the path of anxiety. That's why we're here.

2

This moment at which a first phase of our disquisition is coming to a close, along with the year itself, is the right moment for me to underscore the fact that there is a structure of anxiety.

I broached this for you with the aid of the tachygraphic form that's been up on the blackboard since the start of my disquisition, and with the keenly traced lines and edges it brings, which is to be taken on in all its specified character. There's one point, however, that I've not yet sufficiently stressed.

This feature is the mirror that is seen from one edge. Now, a mirror doesn't stretch out to infinity. It has limits. If you refer to the article from which this diagram has been extracted, you'll see that I make a point of mentioning the limits of the mirror. This mirror allows the subject to see something from a point located somewhere within the space of the mirror, a point that isn't directly perceivable for him. In other words, I don't necessarily see my eye in the mirror, even if the mirror is helping me to perceive something that I wouldn't see otherwise. What I mean by this is that the first thing to be put forward concerning the structure of anxiety – and which you always neglect in the observations because you're fascinated by the content of the mirror and you forget its limits – is that anxiety is framed.

Those who heard the presentation I gave at the Provincial Study Days dedicated to the fantasy – the transcript of which I'm still waiting to receive two months and one week on – may recall the metaphor I used of a painting that comes to be placed in the frame of a window. No doubt an absurd technique were it a matter of better seeing what's in the painting, but that's not what it's about. Regardless of the charm of what's painted on the canvas, it's about not seeing what stands to be beheld outside the window.

It so happens that in dreams people see appearing, and in an unambiguous way, a pure, schematic form of the fantasy. This is the case in the dream from the study on *The Wolf Man*. This recurring dream takes on all its importance, and Freud chooses it as central, because it is the pure fantasy unveiled in its structure. This observation has an unexhausted and inexhaustible character because it essentially concerns, from beginning to end, the fantasy's relation to the real. Now, what can we see in this dream? The sudden opening – these two terms are indicated – of a window. The fantasy is beheld on the other side of a windowpane, and through a window that opens. The fantasy is framed.

As for what you can behold on the other side, you'll recognize there the same structure as you can see in the mirror in my diagram. There are always two rods, one of a more or less developed support and one of something that is supported. In this dream, they are the wolves on the branches of the tree. I only have to open up any old collection of drawings by schizophrenics to scoop this up by the basketful, as it were. You'll also find a tree on occasion, with something on the end of it.

I'm taking my first example from the presentation Jean Bobon gave at the recent Antwerp Congress on the phenomenon of expression.

Look at this drawing by a schizophrenic woman. What is there on the tip of the branches? For the subject in question, the role that the wolves play for the Wolf Man is fulfilled by signifiers. Beyond the tree's branches she's written out the formula of her secret, *Io sono sempre vista*. It's what she'd never been able to say until then. *I'm always in view*. I still have to pause to make you see that in Italian, as in French, *vista* is ambiguous. It's not only a past participle, it's also *view*, with its two meanings, subjective and objective, the function

Io sono sempre vista – drawing by Isabella
(observation by Jean Bobon, Liège)

of viewing, of sight, and the fact of being a view, as one says *a coun-tryside view*, the view that's taken as an object on a postcard.

What I simply want to accentuate today is that *the dreadful, the shady, the disturbing*, everything by which we translate, as best we can in French, the magisterial German *Unheimliche*, presents itself through little windows. The field of anxiety is situated as something framed. Thus, you're coming back to what I introduced the discussion with, namely, the relationship between the stage and the world.

Suddenly, all at once, you'll always find this term the moment the phenomenon of the *Unheimliche* enters. You'll always find the stage that presents itself in its own specific dimension and which allows for the emergence in the world of that which *may not* be said.

What do we always expect at curtain up, if not this brief moment of anxiety, which quickly passes, but which is never lacking in the dimension where, in going to the theatre, we do more than just come along to settle our behinds into a seat that has cost us perhaps dear, perhaps less – the moment when the three knocks are sounded and the curtain rises? Without this introductive moment of anxiety, which quickly dies away, nothing would be able to take on its value of what will be determined thereafter as tragic or comic.

I said – *that which may not*. Once again, not every language furnishes you with the same resources. It's not about *können* – of course, a good many things *can* be said, materially speaking – but *dürfen*, a *may* that is poorly translated as *allowed* or *not allowed* when in fact the word refers to a more original dimension. It's even because *man darf nicht*, it may not, that *man kann*, one can all the same. Here, the forcing takes effect, the dimension of unwinding, which constitutes the dramatic action properly speaking.

No matter how much time we spend on the nuances of this framing of anxiety, it will never be too long. Will you say that I'm seeking out this anxiety in the sense of reducing it to expectation, to preparation, to a state of alertness, to a response that is already a defensive response faced with what's about to happen? This, indeed, is the *Erwartung*, the constitution of the hostile as such, the first line of recourse beyond *Hilflosigkeit*. Although expectation can indeed serve, amongst other means, to frame anxiety, it isn't indispensable. There's no need for any expectation, the framing is still there. But anxiety is something else.

Anxiety is the appearance, within this framing, of what was already there, at much closer quarters, at home, *Heim*. It's the occupant, you'll say. In a certain sense, yes indeed, of course, this unknown occupant that appears in an unexpected way is absolutely related to what's encountered in the *Unheimliche*, but it's too little to designate it like that because, as the term indicates very well for you in French, this *hôte*, in its ordinary meaning, is already someone well wrought through with expectation.

This *hôte* is what had already slipped into the *hostile* with which I began this talk on expectation. This occupant, in the ordinary sense, isn't the *Heimliche*, it's not the inhabitant of the house, it's the sof-tened up, appeased and admitted hostile. That which is *Heim*, that which belongs to the realm of *Geheimnis*, has never passed through the twists and turns, the networks, the sieve of recognition. It has stayed *unheimlich*, not so much inhabituable as in-habiting, not so much in-habitual as in-habituated.

The phenomenon of anxiety is the sudden appearance of the *Heimliche* within the frame, and this is why it's wrong to say that anxiety is without object.

Anxiety has a different sort of object from the object whose perception is prepared and structured. By what? By the model of the cut, of the furrow, of the unary trait, of the *there it is*, which in operating always remain tight-lipped – the tight lip or lips of the cut – which become a closed book on the subject, unopened letters sending him off again under closed seal to further traces.

Signifiers turn the world into a network of traces in which the transition from one cycle to another is thenceforth possible. This means that the signifier begets a world, the world of the subject who speaks, whose essential characteristic is that therein it's possible to deceive.

Anxiety is this cut – this clean cut without which the presence of the signifier, its functioning, its furrow in the real, is unthinkable – it's the cut that opens up, affording a view of what now you can hear better, the unexpected, the visit, the piece of news, that which is so well expressed in the term *pressentiment*, which isn't simply to be heard as the premonition of something, but also as the pre-feeling, the *pré-sentiment*, that which stands prior to the first appearance of a feeling.

Things can branch off in every possible direction starting off from anxiety. What we were waiting for, when all's said and done, and which is the true substance of anxiety, is *that which deceives not*, that which is entirely free of doubt.

Don't let yourselves be taken in by appearances. Just because anxiety's link to doubt, to hesitation, to the obsessional's so-called ambivalent game, may strike you as clinically tangible, this doesn't mean that they are the same thing. Anxiety is not doubt, anxiety is the cause of doubt.

This isn't the first time, and it won't be the last, that I shall have to point out here how the function of causality has been kept up after two centuries of critical misgivings precisely because it lies somewhere other than where they've been gainsaying it. If there is one dimension wherein we have to search for the true function, the true weight, the sense behind keeping up the function of cause, then it lies in the direction of the opening that anxiety affords.

The effort that doubt expends is exerted merely to combat anxiety, and precisely through lures, to the extent that what it strives to avoid is what holds firm in anxiety with dreadful certainty.

3

I think that you'll stop me here to remind me that more than once have I stated, aphoristically, that all human activity opens out onto certainty, or else it generates certainty, or, more generally, that certainty's reference point is essentially action.

Well, yes, of course. And it's precisely what allows me now to introduce how it may well be from anxiety that action borrows its certainty.

To act is to snatch from anxiety its certainty. To act is to bring about a transfer of anxiety.

And since we're now at the end of the term, I'll let myself put forward the following, a little rapidly, in order to fill in, or almost fill in, the blank spaces I'd left in the chart from my first lesson of this year's Seminar, the chart organized on the basis of the Freudian terms, *inhibition*, *symptom* and *anxiety*, completed with *impediment*, *embarrassment*, *emotion* and *turmoil*. What's in the empty spaces? There are the *passage à l'acte* and *acting-out*.

Inhibition	Impediment	Embarrassment
Emotion	**Symptom**	*Passage à l'acte*
Turmoil	Acting-Out	**Anxiety**

The anxiety chart

I don't have time today to tell you why. This is why I said that I would merely be *almost* completing the chart. All the same, I'm going to help you to move forward a little on this path by stating for you, in the closest possible relationship to our theme from this morning, the opposition that was already implied, and even expressed, in my first introduction of these terms, between what there's too much of in embarrassment, and what there's too little of in turmoil, *esmayer*. Turmoil is essentially, so I told you, the evocation of the power that fails you, the experience of what you lack in need.

Linking up these two terms is essential for our topic because it highlights its ambiguity. If what we're dealing with is too much, then you're not lacking it. If it so happens that we're lacking it, why then say that elsewhere it's embarrassing us?

Let's be careful not to give in to the most gratifying of illusions here.

In tackling anxiety ourselves, let's acknowledge what all those who've spoken about it from a scientific point of view say. Heavens! This is where what I had to put forward at the start as necessary to the constitution of a world, the signifier as the possibility of deception, shows itself not to have been in vain. This can be seen better precisely when anxiety is what's at issue. And what exactly can be seen? Well, you see that approaching it scientifically always boils down to showing it to be one great big deception.

People don't realize that everything over which the conquest of our discourse extends always boils down to showing it to be a great big deception. Mastering the phenomenon by thought always amounts to showing how it can be redone in a deceitful way, it amounts to being able to reproduce it, that is, to being able to turn it into a signifier. A signifier of what? The subject, in reproducing it, can tamper with the books, which shouldn't surprise us, if it's true that, as I've taught you, the signifier is the subject's trace in the course of the world. Only, if we believe we can keep up this game for anxiety, well, we're sure to fail, for anxiety precisely escapes this game.

Therefore, this is what we have to be on guard against at the moment of grasping what is meant by embarrassment's relation to too much of the signifier and lack's relation to too little of the signifier. I'll give an illustration of this. I'd like you to know that, were it not for analysis, I wouldn't be able to speak about it. But analysis encountered it at the first bend, the phallus for instance.

Little Hans, who is as much of a logician as Aristotle, postulates the equation *All animate beings have a phallus*. I assume I'm addressing people who followed my commentary on the analysis of Little Hans, and who also remember what I took care to accentuate last year concerning the proposition known as the universal affirmative, namely, that the universal affirmative is only meaningful in defining the real on the basis of the impossible. It's impossible for an animate being not to have a phallus. As you can see, logic is now poised in this essentially precarious function of condemning the real to stumble over endlessly into the impossible. We don't have any other means of apprehending it but to go stumbling on and on.

An example. There are living beings, Mum, for instance, who don't have a phallus. So, this means that there are no living beings – anxiety.

The next step is to be taken. The most convenient thing is to say that even those who don't have one have one. That's why by and large we stick to this solution. The living beings who don't have any phallus shall have one, in spite of everything. Since they shall have a phallus – which we others, psychologists, will call unreal, and which will simply be the phallus signifier – they shall be living. Thus, going from stumble to stumble, there's a progression, I daren't say in knowledge, but certainly in understanding.

By the by, I can't resist the pleasure of sharing a discovery with you, a find, that chance, good chance, what is called chance but which is hardly that at all, brought within my reach for you no later than this last weekend, in a dictionary of English slang.

My God, it might've taken me a while to get to it, but what a beautiful language the English language is! Who here knows then that, already since the fifteenth century, slang has found this marvel of replacing on occasion *I understand you perfectly* by *I understumble you perfectly*? I'm writing it up, since my pronunciation has perhaps made you miss the nuance. This *understumble*, untranslatable in French, incorporates *stumble* into *understand*. Understanding always amounts to struggling forward into misunderstanding.

Classical psychology teaches that the stuff of experience is composed of the real and the unreal, and that men are tormented by the unreal in the real. Were this the case, hoping to rid themselves of it would be utterly futile, for the good reason that the Freudian conquest teaches us that the disturbing thing is that, in the unreal, it's the real that torments them.

One's *care*, *Sorge*, the philosopher Heidegger tells us. Of course, but we've come a long way now. If, before getting a move on, before speaking, before getting down to work, care has been presupposed, does that make the term *care* an ultimate term? What does it mean? Can't we see that here we're already at the level of an art of care? Man is clearly a major producer of something that, with regard to him, is called care. But then, I prefer learning this from a holy book, which is at the same time the most sacrilegious book there is, and which is called Ecclesiastes.

This title is the Greek translation, by the Septuagint, of the term *Qoheleth*, which is a hapax, a unique term employed on this sole occasion, and comes from *Qahâl*, assembly. *Qoheleth* is both an abstract and feminine form of it, and is strictly speaking the assembling virtue, the one that gathers together, the ἐκκλησία, as it were, rather than the ἐκκλησιαστής.

What does this book, which I've called a sacred book and the most profane, teach us? The philosopher doesn't fail to stumble here, reading as he does some Epicurean echo or other. That's what I read. The Epicurean with regard to Ecclesiastes, well, let's see about that! I know very well that Epicurus stopped calming us down a long time ago, as was, you know, his intention, but to say that Ecclesiastes had so much as a moment's chance of producing the same effect on us is really to have never even taken a peep at it.

God asks me to jouir, *to enjoy* – it's in the text. The Bible is, after all, the word of God. And even if it's not the word of God for you, I think you've already noticed the absolute difference that lies between the God of the Jews and Plato's God. Even though Christian history believed, a propos the God of the Jews, that it had to find its little psychotic evasion with Plato's God, it's nevertheless high time to recall the difference that lies between Aristotle's universal mover God, the God of sovereign good, Plato's delusional conception, and the God of the Jews, who's a God one speaks to, a God who asks something of you, and who, in Ecclesiastes, gives you the order *Jouis* – which really crowns it all.

To *jouir* on order is all the same something about which each of us can sense that, if there's a wellspring, an origin, of anxiety, then it must be found somewhere there. To the imperative *Jouis*, I can only reply one thing, and that is *J'ouïs, I hear*, but naturally I don't *jouir* so easily for all that. This is the order of presence within which the God who speaks is activated for us, the one who tells us expressly that He is what He is.

So that I may move forward, while it's within reach, into the field of His demands, I shall introduce, because it's very close to our subject, because it's the moment – you know very well that my remarking on this is nothing new – when, amongst God's demands to His chosen people, His privileged people, there are some that are very precise, and it seems that, in order to specify their terms, this God didn't require the prescience of my Seminar – and notably, there's one that's called circumcision. He orders us to *jouir*, and what's more, He goes into the instructions. He specifies the request, He isolates the object.

It's in this respect, I think, that the extraordinary muddle, the bungling, that there is in referring circumcision to castration surely appeared to you just as it did to me a long time ago.

Of course it's got an analogical relationship, because it's related to the object of anxiety. But saying that castration is either the cause or the representative, the analogue, of what we call castration and its complex amounts to a basic error. It amounts to not going beyond the symptom, namely, what in any circumcised subject can establish some confusion between its mark and what may be at stake in his neurosis relative to the castration complex.

Nothing is less castrating than circumcision. When it's done well, we can't deny that the result is rather elegant, especially when compared with all those male organs from Magna Graecia which the antique dealers, under the pretext that I'm an analyst, bring to my door by the caseload, and which my secretary hands back to them, and I see them go off again into the courtyard laden with a suitcase of these organs, whose phimosis is always accentuated in a fashion that is, I must say, particularly distasteful. There is all the same something salubrious in the practice of circumcision from the aesthetic point of view.

Moreover, most of those who go on repeating the confusion on this matter that can be found knocking around in analytic texts nevertheless grasped a long time ago that it was also a question of significantly reducing the ambiguity of what is known as the bisexual type. *I am the cut and the knife*, Baudelaire says somewhere. Well, why consider it normal to be both the spear and the scabbard? The ritual practice of circumcision can clearly generate something of a salubrious repartition as regards the division of roles.

These remarks, as you can sense very well, are not digressional. Already, circumcision can no longer strike you as being some ritualistic whim, because it conforms to what I've been teaching you to consider in demand, namely, the circumscription of the object and with it the function of the cut. What God demands as an offering in this delimited zone isolates the object once it's been circumscribed. Whether afterwards those who recognize each other by this traditional sign see their relation to anxiety being scaled down, far from it perhaps, is where the question begins.

One of those being alluded to here, and it really isn't anyone in my audience, one day called me, in a private message, *the last of the Christian cabalists*. Rest assured, whilst it can happen that some of my investigations play, strictly speaking, on the calculus of signifiers, my gematria isn't about to get lost in its computus. I daresay it shall never take my bladder for the lantern of knowledge.[1] Much rather, should this lantern turn out to be a dark lantern, it will lead me instead, if need be, to recognize it as my bladder.

But, more directly than did Freud because I'm coming after him, I ask his God – *Che vuoi?* What wouldst thou with me? In other words, what is desire's relation to law? A question always elided by philosophic tradition, but to which Freud gives a reply, and you depend on it, even if, like everyone else, you haven't yet realized. The reply – it's the same thing.

What I teach you, what you're led to by what I teach you, and which is already in the text, masked beneath the myth of Oedipus, is that the terms that seem to stand in a relation of antithesis – desire and law – are but one and the same barrier to bar our access to the Thing. *Nolens, volens*, desiring, I go down the path of the law. This is why Freud refers the origin of the law back to the ungraspable desire of the father. But what his discovery leads you back to, as does the entire analytic enquiry, is not to lose sight of what is true behind this lure.

Whether or not one normalizes my objects, so long as I desire, I know nothing of what I desire. And then, from time to time, an object appears amongst the others, and I really don't know why it's there.

On one hand, there's the one from which I've learnt that it covers over my anxiety, the object of my phobia, though I don't deny that it had to be explained to me because until then I knew only what I had in my head, and all I could say was that I had it, and I was afraid of it. On the other hand, there's the one for which I really can't find any justification as to why this is the one I desire – and why, not being one who detests girls, I'm even fonder of a little shoe.

On one side there's the wolf, on the other the shepherdess.

This is where I'm going to leave you at the end of these first talks on anxiety.

There's more to be heard besides God's anxiety-provoking order, there's Diana's hunt, which, at the time I chose, that of Freud's centenary, I said was the way of the Freudian quest. For the coming term, I'm making you an appointment with the slaying of the wolf.

19 December 1962

REVISION OF THE
STATUS OF THE OBJECT

VII

NOT WITHOUT HAVING IT

Physics
Linguistics
Sociology
Physiology
Topology

In the thirty-second of his introductory lessons on psychoanalysis which you'll find in the series called *Nouvelles Conférences sur la psychanalyse*, this being how the title has been retranslated in French, Freud specifies that what is involved is to introduce something that has in no way whatsoever, so he says, the character of sheer speculation.

It's been translated for us in a French whose unintelligibility you'll be able to judge. *Mais il ne peut vraiment être question que de conceptions. But it can truly only be a question of conceptions.* Full stop. *En effet, il s'agit de trouver les idées abstraites, justes, qui, appliquées à la matière brute de l'observation, y apporteront ordre et clarté. Indeed, what is involved is to find the right abstract ideas which, when applied to the raw material of observation, will bring order and clarity to it.* Clearly, it's always unfortunate to entrust such a precious thing as the translation of Freud to Women of the Bedchamber.

There's no full stop in the German text where I pointed that one out to you and there's no riddle in the sentence. *Sondern es handelt sich wirklich um Auffassungen*, it's a matter *wirklich*, really, effectively – and not *truly* – of conceptions, that is, by that I mean that the accurate abstract representations, *Vorstellung*, it's a matter of *einzuführen*, of bringing them to light, and of applying them to the *Rohstoff der Beobachtung*, the raw stuff of observation, which will allow one to get *Ordnung und Durchsichtigkeit* out of it, order and transparency.

This effort, this programme, is indeed the same to which we've been applying ourselves here for some years now.

1

On our path to anxiety, we find ourselves having to specify the status of what I designated at the outset with the letter a.

You can see it reigning over the outline of the vase that symbolizes for us libido's narcissistic container. This can be brought into relation with the image of one's body, $i'(a)$, through the intermediary of the mirror of the Other, A. Betwixt the two of them, a communicating oscillation is played out which Freud designates as the reversibility of the libido of one's own body into object libido. In relation to the economic oscillation of this libido that pours from $i(a)$ into $i'(a)$, there's something that doesn't so much escape from it as step in as an incidence whose pattern of disruption is precisely what we're studying this year. The most striking manifestation of this object a, the signal that it is intervening, is anxiety.

That doesn't mean that this object is merely the nether side of anxiety, but it only steps in, it only functions, in correlation with anxiety.

Anxiety, Freud taught us, plays the role of a signal function in relation to something. I say that it's a signal in relation to what occurs in connection with the subject's relation to the object a in all its generality. The subject is only ever able to enter this relation within the vacillation of a certain fading, the same that the notation barred S designates. Anxiety is the signal of certain moments of this relation. This is what I'll be endeavouring to show you more fully today, by specifying what I mean by this object a.

We designate this object with a letter. This algebraic notation has its function. It's like a thread designed to enable us to recognize the identity of the object behind the various incidences in which it appears to us. The algebraic notation has precisely the purpose of giving us a pure identity marker, we having stated already that marking something out with a word is only ever metaphorical, that is to say, it can only leave the function of the signifier itself outside of any signification that is induced by introducing it. The word *good*, if it gives rise to the signification of good, isn't good in and of itself, far from it, because by the same token it gives rise to the bad.

Likewise, designating this little a with the term *object* is merely a metaphorical use of this word, since it's borrowed from the subject–object relation, from which the term *object* is constituted. It's no doubt suitable for designating the general function of objectivity, but the object we have to speak about under the term a is precisely an object that is external to any possible definition of objectivity.

I'm not going to speak here about what happens by way of objectivity in the field of science, I'm speaking about our science in

general. You know that since Kant some misfortunes have befallen
this object, which are all due to the overly large share that people
wanted to give to certain evident elements and especially to those
that come from the field of transcendental aesthetics. In holding
that the separation of the dimensions of space from the dimension
of time was evident, the development of the scientific object found
itself running into what is very improperly translated as a crisis
of scientific reason. A big effort had to be made to realize that, at
a certain level of physics, the two registers, spatial and temporal,
couldn't go on being held to be independent variables, which,
and this is a surprising fact, seems to have posed some insoluble
problems to a few minds. They don't, however, seem worthy of
our attention when we notice that it's precisely to the status of the
object that one ought to turn to give the symbolic the exact place
that falls to it in the constitution and translation of experience,
without making any risky extrapolation from the imaginary into the
symbolic.

In truth, the time that's involved, at the level at which it is irreal-
ized in a fourth dimension, has got nothing to do with the time that,
in intuition, seems very much to present itself as a kind of insurmountable clash with the real. Worrying about the fact that what
appears to all of us by way of time, and which is held to be something self-evident, can only be translated into the symbolic by an
independent variable is simply to commit an error of categorization
at the start. The same difficulty arises, you know this, at a certain
limit of physics, with the body.

We're on our home turf here. On what has to be done at the
start to give experience its rightful status, we have our word to say.
Indeed, our experience posits and establishes that no intuition, no
transparency, no *Durchsichtigkeit*, as Freud's term has it, that is
founded purely and simply upon the intuition of consciousness can
be held to be originative, or valid, and thus it cannot constitute the
starting point of any transcendental aesthetics. This is for the simple
reason that the subject cannot be situated in any exhaustive way in
consciousness since he is first of all, primordially, unconscious, due
to the following – we have to maintain the incidence of the signifier
as standing prior to his constitution.

The problem is one of the signifier's entry into the real and of
seeing how the subject is born from this. Does this mean that we
find ourselves before some kind of descent of the spirit, a kind
of apparition of winged signifiers, that they would start making
their holes in the real all by themselves and that, out of the midst
of them, one hole would appear which would be the subject? I
think that, when I introduce the division between the real, the

imaginary, and the symbolic, no one attributes such a design to me. Today the point is to know precisely what allows this signifier to be incarnated.

What allows it to be incarnated is first and foremost what we've got here by which to presentify ourselves to one another, our body. Except that this body isn't to be taken up in the pure and simple categories of transcendental aesthetics either. This body can't be constituted in the same way that Descartes establishes it in the field of extension. Nor is it given to us in a pure and simple way in the mirror.

Even in the experience of the mirror, a moment can come about when the image we believe we abide by undergoes modification. If this specular image we have facing us, which is our stature, our face, our two eyes, allows the dimension of our gaze to emerge, the value of the image starts to change – above all if there's a moment when this gaze that appears in the mirror starts not to look at us any more. There's an *initium*, an aura, a dawning sense of uncanniness which leaves the door open to anxiety.

This passage from the specular image to the double that escapes me is the point at which something occurs whose generality, whose presence within the entire phenomenal field, can be shown through the articulation we have been giving to the function of the *a*. This function goes far beyond what appears in this odd moment, which I simply wanted to mark out for its character of being at once the most commonly known and the most discreet in its intensity.

How does this transformation of the object come about, one which from an object that can be located, pinpointed, and exchanged, forms this kind of private, incommunicable and yet dominant object that is our correlative in the fantasy? Where exactly is the moment of this metamorphosis, this transformation, this revelation, to be placed? Certain paths, certain approaches I prepared for you over the course of the previous years, enable us to designate this place and, better still, to explain what's going on. The little diagram I've put up on the blackboard for you gives you something of these *richtigen Vorstellungen*, these accurate representations, that enable us to turn the appeal to intuition and experience, an appeal that's always more or less opaque and obscure, into something *durchsichtig*, transparent – in other words, to reconstitute for ourselves the transcendental aesthetics that fits our experience.

It's generally accepted that anxiety is without an object. This, which is not extracted from Freud's disquisition but a part of his disquisition, is specifically what I've been rectifying through my disquisition. You can therefore take it as read that, since I've gone to the lengths of writing it up on the blackboard for you in the style of a little memento – why not this one amongst others? – *it is not without an object.*

This is the exact formula in which anxiety's relation to an object must be suspended.

This object is not properly speaking the object of anxiety. I've already made use of this *not without* in the formula I gave you concerning the subject's relation to the phallus, *he is not without having it.*

This relation of being *not without having* doesn't mean that one knows which object is involved. When I say, *He's not without resources, He's not without cunning*, it means, at least for me, that his resources are obscure, his cunning isn't run of the mill.

Likewise, at the linguistic level, the term *sans*, in Latin *sine*, is deeply correlative to the apposition *haud*. One says *non haud sine, non pas sans*. It's a certain type of conditional liaison, which links *being* to *having* in a kind of alternation. There, he is not without having it, but elsewhere, right where he is, it's not to be seen.

Isn't this what the sociological function of the phallus demonstrates to us, on the condition that we take it at the upper-case level, Φ, where it incarnates the most alienating function of the subject in exchange? Even in social exchange, the male subject roams around reduced to being the bearer of the phallus. That's what makes castration necessary for a socialized sexuality, where doubtless there are prohibitions, but also and above all preferences, as Claude Lévi-Strauss has remarked. The true secret, the truth of everything that Freud makes revolve around the exchange of women in the structure, is that, underneath the exchange of women, the phalli will fill them out. The phallus mustn't be seen to be involved. If it gets seen, then there's anxiety.

I could branch off on more than one line here. It's clear that, with this reference, we've got to the castration complex straightaway. Well then, my goodness, why not go down this route?

2

As I've repeated in front of you on numerous occasions, the castration of the complex is not a castration. Everyone knows this, everyone suspects as much, and, strangely enough, no one pauses on it. It does, however, hold great interest.

Where are we to situate this image, this fantasy? In the imaginary or in the symbolic? What's going on here? Is it the emasculation that we know well from the savage practices of war? It's certainly closer to that than to making eunuchs. Of course, there's the maiming of the penis evoked by the fantasmatic threats issued by mother or father, depending on the psychoanalytic era you're in. *Do that and we'll snip it off.* This accent of cutting needs to bear its full import for the practice of circumcision to be considered as castration, the circumcision to which you saw me make some, if I may say, prophylactic references last time.

The mental impact of circumcision is far from ambiguous. I'm not the only one to have noticed that. One of the most recent works dedicated to this subject, Nunberg's quite remarkable book on *Problems of Bisexuality as Reflected in Circumcision*, is there to remind us what numerous authors had introduced before him, namely, that circumcision has just as much the aim of reinforcing the term of masculinity in men by isolating it as to provoke the said effects of the castration complex, at least in their anxiety-provoking impact. It's precisely this common denominator of the cut that allows us to bring into the field of castration the circumcisory operation, the *Beschneidung* of the foreskin, the *'ârêl* in Hebrew.

Is there not, in this term *cut*, something that enables a further step to be taken in the function of castration anxiety? *I'll snip it off*, says the mum who gets qualified as a castrating mother. Yes, and afterwards, where will it be? Where will the *Wiwimacher*, as Little Hans calls it, be? Well, if we imagine that this threat which has always been presentified in our experience were actually to be followed through, it would be in the operational field of the common, exchangeable object, it would be there in the hands of the mother who has cut it off, and this is precisely what would be uncanny about the situation.

It often happens that our subjects dream they've got the object in hand, either some gangrene has detached it, or some partner in the dream has taken it upon himself to perform the slicing operation, or else there's been some mishap or other. These dreams, which are variously nuanced with uncanniness and anxiety, possess a character that is especially unsettling. The way that the object suddenly passes over into what could be called its *Zuhandenheit*, as Heidegger would say, its handiness in the sense of commonplace objects and utensils, comes to be designated in the observation on Little Hans by a dream, the dream of the tap fitter who will unscrew it, screw it back on again, and make the *eingewurzelt*, which either was or wasn't well-rooted in the body, pass over into the register of the detachable. This phenomenological turnaround allows us to designate something that contrasts two types of object.

When I began to set out the fundamental function of the mirror stage in the general institution of the field of the object, I moved through several phases. First of all, there is the plane of the first identification with the specular image, the original misrecognition of the subject in his totality. Next, there is the transitivist reference that is established in his relation with the imaginary other, his *semblable*. This means that his identity is always poorly disentangled from the other party's identity. Hence the introduction of mediation by means of a common object, an object of competition, whose status will be derived from the notion of belonging – it's yours or its mine.

There are two kinds of object in the field of belongings – those that can be shared and those that can't. I can still see those objects that can't be shared circulating in the domain of sharing, alongside the other objects, whose status leans squarely on competition, an ambiguous function that is at once rivalry and agreement. A price can be set on these objects, they are objects of exchange. But there are others.

I've been foregrounding the phallus because it's the most illustrious one, due to the fact of castration, but there also exist the equivalents of this phallus, among which you are familiar with those that precede it, the scybalum and the nipple. There are perhaps some that you are less familiar with, though they are perfectly legible in the analytic literature, and we are going to try to designate them. When these objects freely enter this field which they have nothing to do with, the field of sharing, when they show up there and become recognizable, anxiety signals to us the particularity of their status. Indeed, they are objects from before the constitution of the status of the common, communicable, socialized object. This is what is involved in the *a*.

We shall name these objects and we shall draw up a catalogue that perhaps will be exhaustive, let's hope so. I've already named three of them. There are only two missing. As a whole, they correspond to the five forms of loss, of *Verlust*, that Freud designated in *Inhibitions, Symptoms and Anxiety* as the major moments when the signal appears.

Before getting any deeper into this, I'd like to switch back to another track that you saw me in the process of choosing earlier on, in order to make a remark whose sidelines will carry some illuminating aspects for you.

I already designated one shortcoming in analytic research by saying that we hadn't led anyone to take a step forward into the physiological question of women's sexuality. We can accuse ourselves of the same failing with regard to male impotence.

After all, in the process of the male part of copulation, which can be clearly ascertained in its normative phases, we are still referring to what can be found in any old physiology textbook concerning first the process of erection, then of orgasm. We content ourselves with a reference to the stimulus–response circuit, as though the homology between orgasmic discharge and the motor part of this circuit were acceptable in any process of action. Of course, we're not at that level, far from it, even in Freud. He raised the problem as to why in sexual pleasure the circuit is not, as it is elsewhere, the shortest one by which to return to the level of minimum excitation, but instead entails a *Vorlust*, a *preliminary pleasure* as it is translated, that consists precisely in raising this minimal level to the highest possible pitch. And why does orgasm intervene the moment that – when? – the rising level that is normally linked to foreplay is broken off?

Have we not even come close to providing an outline of what intervenes? If one wants to give a physiological representation of it, have we distinguished, singled out, and designated the mechanism of the circuit of innervation – Freud would say *Abfuhrinnervationen* – that brings discharge into play as its underpinning? It really needs to be considered as distinct from what was functioning beforehand, because what was functioning beforehand was precisely a process that was not leading up to discharge. It was an execution of the function of pleasure that tended to be confined to its own limit, that is, it tends to stop before arriving at a certain level in the mounting stimulus, before pain arises.

So, where does the feedback come from? Nobody has so much as dreamt of telling us. Well, be that as it may, it is certain that, either way, the function of the Other must be intervening here.

I'm not the one who should be saying so, but rather those for whom that which constitutes a normal genital function is linked to oblativity. By the by, I'm still waiting for them to intimate how the function of the gift steps in as such, *hic et nunc*, when we're fucking.

You know that a large part of analytic experience lies in the disruptions of love life and that a large part of our speculation concerns what is termed the choice of love object. In this field, the reference to the primordial object, the mother, is held to be crucial and its impact wide-ranging. For some the result is that they can only function for orgasm with prostitutes, whilst for others it will be with partners chosen in a different register. As we know from our analyses, the relationship with the prostitute is almost directly engrained in the reference to the mother, whilst in other cases the degradations of *Liebesleben* are linked to a choice made in opposition to the maternal term, which bears on woman in so far as she becomes a support, in so far as she is the equivalent, of the phallic object.

Well, how does all that come about? The diagram that I reproduced once on the board allows us to provide a reply.

The attraction that decks out the object of glamour, of desirable

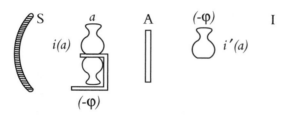

The choice of object

brilliance, of preferential colour – that's how sexuality is designated in Chinese – means that the object becomes stimulating at the level of excitation. This preferential colour is situated on the side of *i'(a)* at the same signalling level that can also be that of anxiety. How so? This happens by connecting onto the original erogenous investment that is here in *a*, both present and concealed.

Or else what functions as a sorting element in the choice of love object is produced here, in the ego, on the other side of the mirror, at the level of the framing of the object by an *Einschränkung*, a narrowing that Freud refers directly to a mechanism of the ego, a limitation of the field of libidinal interest which excludes a certain type of object precisely due to the relation it bears to the mother.

These two mechanisms stand at either end of the chain that starts at inhibition and finishes with anxiety, whose diagonal line I marked out in the chart I gave you at the start of the year. Between inhibition and anxiety, one ought to distinguish between the two mechanisms and conceive of how both one and the other can enter the fray right across sexual manifestation from top to bottom.

When I say *from top to bottom*, I include what in our experience is called transference.

Recently I heard an allusion to the fact that we in our Society are people who know a thing or two about transference. Now, since one work on transference, which moreover was written before our Society was founded, I only know of one other devoted to it and that is the work I did here with you two years ago. I said a good many things here, in a form that was certainly most appropriate to it, that is, a partially veiled form. It is quite certain that the other piece of work brought you a great distinction that contrasts *need of repetition* with *repetition of need*, proof that having recourse to wordplay to designate things, which moreover is not without interest, is not my privilege alone.

I believe that the reference to transference, when limited solely to effects of reproduction and repetition, is too narrow and would deserve to be expanded. In insisting on the historical element, or on the repetition of lived experience, one runs the risk of sweeping aside a whole dimension that is no less important, the synchronic dimension, the dimension of what is precisely included, latent, in the position of the analyst and where lies, in the space that determines this position, the function of the partial object.

If you remember, this is what, in speaking to you about transfer-ence, I designated by way of a metaphor, which seems fairly clear to me, of a hand reaching over to a log. Just as the hand is about to reach the log, the log catches light, and in the flame another hand appears, reaching back to the first. This is what I also designated, when studying Plato's *Symposium*, using the function that is termed ἄγαλμα in the speech by Alcibiades. I think that the insufficiency of the reference made to the synchronic dimension of the function of the partial object in the analytic relation of transference explains the neglect of a domain that I am not surprised to see being left in the dark, namely, the field of what might be called the post-analytic result, across which a certain number of examples of hitches in the sexual function are distributed.

The function of analysis as a space or field of the partial object is precisely what Freud made us pause in front of in his article on *Analysis Terminable and Interminable*. If one sets off from the idea that Freud's limit, which we meet throughout his observations, is due to his not having grasped what stood to be analysed in the synchronic relationship between the analysed party and the analyst concerning the function of the partial object, one can see that this is the very mainspring of the failure of his intervention with Dora and with the young woman from the case of female homosexuality. And this is why Freud designates for us what he calls the limit of analysis in castration anxiety. He remained for his patient the locus of this partial object.

Freud tells us that analysis leaves both man and woman wanting, one of them in the field of the castration complex, the other in *Penisneid*. But this is not an absolute limit. It is the limit at which finite analysis ends with Freud, in so far as it continues to follow the indefinitely approached parallelism that characterizes the asymp-tote. There you have the principle of analysis that Freud calls *unendliche*, indefinite, boundless, and not *infinie* as it has been trans-lated in French. This limit is instituted to the extent that something has been, not unanalysed, but revealed in a way that is only partial and I may at least pose the question as to how it is analysable.

Don't think I'm contributing something that should be considered as standing completely beyond the bounds of the pared-down forms already sketched out by our experience. To make reference to more recent work, familiar in the French field, one analyst, over many years, those that comprised the time during which his life's work

came together, made his analyses of obsessional neurosis in particular revolve around penis envy. How many times did I comment
on them with what we had to hand back then, to criticize them and
show where they trip up, which I shall formulate now more precisely.

On reading his observations in detail, we can see the author covering the field that I designate as the field of the interpretation to be
given of the phallic function at the level of the big Other, with the
fantasy of fellatio, concerning the analyst's penis in particular. This
is a very clear indication. The problem had indeed been spotted and
let me tell you that it was not by chance, I mean in connection with
what I'm developing for you here. Only, this is just one angle on
it and one that is insufficient. Centring an analysis on this fantasy
could never exhaust what is really involved, because in reality it only
links up with a symptomatic fantasy of obsessionals.

To designate what I mean, I shall go to an exemplary reference
in the literature, namely, the Rat Man's famous nocturnal conduct
when, having obtained by himself an erection in the looking-glass,
he goes to open the hallway door to the imagined phantom of his
dead father, in order to present, to the eyes of this spectre, the
state of his member. Were one only to advise analysing what is
involved at the level of the analyst fellatio fantasy – which is so
strongly linked by the author to what is involved in what he called
the technique of *getting closer*, where distance is considered to be a
fundamental factor of obsessional structure, notably in its relations
with psychosis – what would happen? I believe one would merely
allow the subject, even encourage him, to take up in this fantasmatic
relation the role of the Other in the type of presence that is here constituted by death, this Other, I would say by pushing things a little,
who watches the fellatio fantasmatically.

This last point is only addressed to those whose practice allows
these remarks to be put in their right place.

3

I'm going to end with these two images which I've put up on the
board.

The first represents a vase and its neck. I've made it so that you're
looking down the hole of the vase as a way of stressing that what
matters to me is the rim. The second is the transformation that can
be brought about in connection with this rim.

Starting off from this, it will appear to you just how opportune
last year's long insistence on these topological considerations was,
concerning the function of identification at the level of desire,

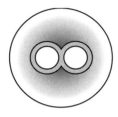

The doubling of the rim

namely, the third type designated by Freud in his article on identification, the one which finds its major example in hysteria.

Here then is the impact and the scope of these topological
considerations.

I told you that I spent such a long time with you on the cross-cap
so as to afford you the possibility of intuitively forming a conception
of the distinction between the object *a* and the object constructed on
the basis of the specular relation, the common object.

To go quickly, what is it that makes a specular image distinct
from what it represents? It's that right becomes left and vice versa.
Let's put our confidence in the idea that we normally find our
reward in trusting in what Freud says, even in his more aphoris-
matic moments. The ego is not only a surface but, so he says, the
projection of a surface. Thus the problem has to be posed in the
topological terms of pure surface. In relation to what it duplicates,
the specular image is exactly a right glove becoming a left glove,
which one can obtain on a single surface by turning the rim inside
out.

Don't forget that I've been speaking to you about the glove and
the hood for a while now. The dream in one of Ella Sharpe's cases
that I commented on for you not so long ago revolves for the most
part around this model.

Let's see for ourselves now with what I've taught you to find
in the Möbius strip. In taking this band – having opened it – and
joining it back to itself by giving it a half twist on the way, you get
with the greatest of ease a Möbius strip.

An ant walking along one of the apparent faces will pass over to the
other face without needing to go over the edge. In other words, the
Möbius strip is a surface that has just one face and a surface with just
one face cannot be turned inside out. If you turn it over, it will still be
identical to itself. This is what I call *not having a specular image*.

Furthermore, I told you that, in the cross-cap, when you single
out one part of it through a section, a slice, which has no other condition than that of joining up with itself after having included the
point on the surface where the hole lies, it is still a Möbius strip.

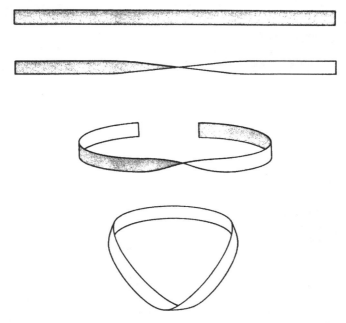

The band/The Möbius strip

This is the residual part, here. I've constructed it for you and I'll pass it around. It does hold a little interest because, let me tell you, this is the *a*. I give it to you much as one might administer the Host, because you'll make use of it afterwards. The *a* is put together like that.

It's put together like that when the slice has been made, whatever it may be, the slice of the umbilical cord, the slice of circumcision, and a few others besides that we are going to have to designate. After the slice, there remains something comparable to the Möbius strip, which has no specular image.

Now see what I mean to tell you by returning to the vase.

Phase one. The vase has its specular image, which is the ideal ego, constitutive of the entire world of the common object.

Add *a* in the form of a cross-cap. Then separate off, in this cross-cap, the small *a* object I've put in your hands. It remains, attached to *i(a)*, a surface that joins up as does a Möbius strip. From then on, the whole vase becomes a Möbius strip because an ant walking on the outside comes onto the inside without any difficulty at all.

The specular image becomes the uncanny and invasive image of the double. This is what happens little by little at the end of Maupassant's life, when he starts failing to see himself in the mirror,

Figure i
This closed surface bearing a line of
auto-intersection is considered to be
topologically equivalent to the projective
plane.

Figure ii
The surface obtained by removing the
lower portion of the previous surface
is a cross-cap.

Figure iii
If one slices into the cross-cap along its
line of auto-intersection, the resulting
surface can be given the shape of a
circular disc with a circular hole at its
centre whose diametrically opposing
points are identified in pairs.

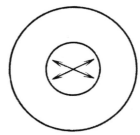

Figure iv
This residual surface can be materialized
in the shape that is known as an inner
eight.

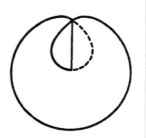

The cross-cap and its transformations

or when he glimpses something in a room, a phantom that turns its back on him, whereupon he knows it to be something that bears a certain relation to himself, and when the phantom turns round, he sees that it is he.

There you have what is involved when *a* enters the world of the real, to which in fact it is simply returning.

It might seem odd to you as a hypothesis that something should resemble this. Observe, however, the following. Let's step outside of the visual field. Close your eyes for a moment, and feel along the rim of this transformed vessel. *But it's a vase just like the other one,* you'll say, *there's only one hole because there's only one rim.* Looking at it, however, it does look like it's got two, as the drawing from earlier shows you, the drawing of the transformed rim.

Those of you who have read a bit know that this ambiguity between one and two is a common ambiguity with regard to the appearance of the phallus in the field of the oneiric apparition, and not only oneiric, of the sexual member. Right where apparently there is no real phallus, its ordinary pattern of apparition is to appear in the form of two phalli.

That's enough for today.

9 January 1963

VIII

THE CAUSE OF DESIRE

The object behind desire
The sadist's identification with the fetish object
The masochist's identification with the common object
The presence of real love in transference
The young homosexual woman, dropped

I should like to manage today to tell you a certain number of things about what I've taught you to designate as the object a, to which the aphorism I put forward last time concerning anxiety steers you, namely, that *it is not without object*.

This year, the object a is taking centre stage in our topic. It has been set into the framework of a Seminar that I've titled *Anxiety* because it is essentially from this angle that it's possible to speak about it, which means moreover that anxiety is the sole subjective translation of this object.

The a that arises here was, however, introduced a long while ago. It was announced in the formula of the fantasy as support of desire, ($\$ \lozenge a$), $\$$ desire of a.

1

My first point will be to add a further detail which those who have been listening to me should be able to master for themselves, though underlining it today does not strike me as needless.

What stands to be specified concerns the mirage that stems from a perspective that may be termed subjectivist inasmuch as, in the constitution of our experience, it lays the entire accent on the structure of the subject.

This line of elaboration, which the modern philosophical tradition carried to its most extreme point in the circles around Husserl by bringing out the function of intentionality, holds us prisoner to a misunderstanding concerning what is commonly called the object of desire. Indeed, we are taught that there is no noesis, no thought, that is not turned towards something. This would seem to be the only point that would enable idealism to find its way back towards the real. But can the object of desire be conceived of in this way? Is this how things stand for desire?

With respect to the level of our listening ear which exists in each of us and which calls for intuition, I will ask – does the object of desire lie out in front of it? This is the mirage at stake here. It sterilized everything that, in analysis, meant to move in the direction known as object relations and I've already taken a good number of different routes to rectify that. What I'm about to put forward now is a new way of accentuating this rectification.

No doubt I won't be making it as developed as it should be, setting aside this formulation for another piece of work of mine that will come to you via another path. I think that for most of you it will be enough to hear the broad formulas with which I think I can accentuate for you today the point I've just introduced.

You know to what extent, in the progress of epistemology, isolating the notion of cause has produced problems. This notion of cause has not been maintained in the development of our physics without a stream of reductions that ultimately lead it back to one of the most tenuous and equivocal functions.

Furthermore, it is clear that, whatever reduction is forced upon it, the mental function, as it were, of this notion cannot be eliminated or cut down to a kind of metaphysical shadow. It may well be made to subsist by resorting to intuition, but this says too little. I claim that it is on the basis of the reassessment we can make of the function of cause in starting off from the analytic experience that any critique of pure reason brought up to date with our science may be carried out.

To set our target, I shall say that the object a – which is not to be situated in anything analogous to the intentionality of a noesis, which is not the intentionality of desire – is to be conceived of as the cause of desire. To take up my earlier metaphor, the object lies *behind* desire.

From this object a emerges the dimension whose elusion in the theory of the subject has produced the insufficiency of the whole coordination whose centre comes to the fore as a theory of cognizance, a gnoseology. Likewise, the structural, topological novelty that is required by this function of the object is perfectly tangible in Freud's formulations, especially those regarding the drive.

If you want to check this up against a text, I would send you to the

thirty-second lesson of the New Series of *Vorlesungen* on the introduction to psychoanalysis that I cited last time. The distinction you
can find there between *Ziel*, the goal of the drive, and its *Objekt* is
very different from what initially presents itself to thought, namely,
that this goal and this object would be in the same place. Freud
employs very striking terms, the first of which is *eingeschoben* – the
object slides in, passes through somewhere. It's the same word that
serves *Verschiebung*, displacement. The object as something that, in
its essential function, steals away at the level of our grasp is being
pointed out there as such.

On the other hand, there is at this level an express contrast
between two terms – *äußeres*, external, outside, and *inneres*, internal. It is specified that the object is to be situated *äußeres*, on the
outside, and, on the other hand, that the satisfaction of the aim is
only brought about in so far as it meets up with something that is to
be considered as standing *inneres*, inside the body, where it finds its
Befriedigung, its satisfaction.

The ego and the non-ego

The topological function that I have presented you with allows
for a plain formulation of what needs to be introduced to clear up
this enigma, namely, it is the notion of an outside that stands prior
to a certain internalization, which is located in *a*, before the subject,
in the locus of the Other, grasps himself in specular form, in *x*, which
will introduce for him the distinction between ego and non-ego.

The notion of cause belongs to this outside, the locus of the
object, prior to any internalization. I shall illustrate this straightaway in the most direct way of getting it through your ears, because
I'm also going to refrain from doing any metaphysics today. To give
an image of it, it isn't by chance that I am going to use the fetish as
such, because this is where the veil is drawn back on the dimension
of the object as cause of desire.

What is desired? It's not the little item of footwear, nor the breast,
nor anything else with which you can embody the fetish. The fetish
causes desire. Desire goes off to hook on wherever it can. It is not
absolutely necessary for her to be wearing the little shoe, it just has
to be in the vicinity. It's not even necessary for her to be the one that

bears the breast, the breast can be in one's head. But all and sundry know that for the fetishist the fetish has to be there. The fetish is the condition by which his desire sustains itself.

I shall indicate in passing the following term, which I believe to be seldom used in German – the vague translations that we have in French let it slip through entirely – it is the relation that Freud indicates, when anxiety is involved, using the word *Libidohaushalt*. Here we are dealing with a word that lies between *Aushaltung*, which would indicate something along the lines of interruption or lifting, and *Inhalt*, which would be the content. It's neither one nor the other. It is the sustaining of libido. To spell it out, this relation to the object that I've been discussing with you today allows for a synthesis between anxiety's signal function and its relation with something that we may call an interruption in the sustaining of libido.

Assuming that, with the reference to the fetish, I've made myself understood well enough on the enormous difference that lies between the two possible perspectives on the object as object of desire and on the reasons that lead me to place the *a* in an essential precession, I would like to make you understand where our research is going to lead us.

2

In the very locus where your mental wont tells you to seek out the subject, right where, despite yourself, the subject emerges when, for example, Freud indicates the source of the aim, right where, in discourse, there stands that which you articulate as being you – in a word, right where you say *I* – that is where, at the level of the unconscious, the *a* properly speaking is located.

At this level, you are *a*, the object, and everyone knows that this is what is intolerable and not only to discourse itself, which, after all, betrays this. I'm going to illustrate this right away with a remark that is designed to shift, even to shake up, the ruts in which you are accustomed to leaving the functions known as sadism and masochism, as if what were involved were merely a register of a kind of immanent aggression and its reversibility. As we go into their subjective structure, the features that set them apart will appear to you. I'm going to designate the crux of this difference right now.

Here is a figure in which you meet the distinctions that organize the graph into an abridged four-point formula. On the right we have the side of the Other, on the left the side of the S, which is the side of the still-to-be-constituted *I*, the subject which stands to be reviewed in our experience and which we know cannot coincide with

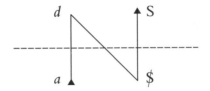

The sadist's desire

the traditional formula for the subject, namely, its exhaustive aspect in any relationship with the object.

The sadist's desire, with everything it entails by way of enigma, can only be formulated on the basis of the split, the dissociation, that he aims to introduce in the subject, the other party, by imposing upon him, up to a certain limit, what he is unable to tolerate – up to the precise limit at which a division appears in this subject, a gap, between his existence as a subject and what he is undergoing, what he may be suffering from, in his body.

It is not so much the other party's suffering that is being sought in the sadistic intention as his anxiety. I noted this with the little sign, $ 0. In the formulae from my second lesson of this year I taught you to read it as a zero, and not the letter O.

The anxiety of the other party, his essential existence as a subject in relation to this anxiety, is precisely the string that sadistic desire means to pluck and this is why I didn't hesitate in one of my previous Seminars to relate its structure to what is specifically homologous in what Kant spelt out as the condition for practising a pure practical reason, a moral will properly speaking, where he locates the sole point at which a relation with a pure moral good can emerge. I apologize for the brevity of this reminder. Those who attended the Seminar will remember this. The rest of you will be seeing in the not too distant future what I took from this in a preface I have written to *La Philosophie dans le boudoir*, the text around which I organized this comparison.

The new feature I mean to put forward today is the following, which is characteristic of the sadist's desire. In carrying through his act, his rite – because it has specifically to do with this kind of human action in which we find all the structures of rite – what the agent of sadistic desire doesn't know is what he is seeking, and what he is seeking is to make himself appear – to whom? because in any case this revelation can only ever be obtuse to himself – as a pure object, as a black fetish. At its final term, the manifestation of sadistic desire boils down to this, in so far as he who is its agent moves towards a realization.

Likewise, if you recall the figure of Sade, you will see that it's not by chance that what remains of him after a kind of transubstantiation accomplished down through the ages, after the imaginary elaboration of his figure across generations, is precisely the form with which Man Ray found it apt to furnish him the day he set about making his *Imaginary Portrait*, to wit, a petrified form.

This could not be more different from the masochist's position, for whom this embodiment of himself as object is the declared goal – whether he becomes a dog under the table or a piece of merchandise, an item dealt with by contract, sold amongst other objects put on the market. In sum, what he seeks is his identification with the common object, the object of exchange. It remains impossible for him to grasp himself for what he is, inasmuch as, like all of us, he is an *a*.

As to finding out why this interests him so much, this acknowledgement that nevertheless remains impossible, this is what his analysis can reveal. Before he can even comprehend its particular conditions, however, there are certain structural conjunctions that need to be established here.

Mark my words, I didn't say, without further comment, that the masochist attains his object identification. As with the sadist, this identification only appears on a stage. Except that, even on this stage, the sadist cannot behold himself, he can only behold the remainder. There is also something that the masochist cannot behold and we shall see what later.

This allows me to introduce some formulas, the first of which is that to recognize oneself as the object of one's desire, in the sense I have been spelling it out, is always masochistic.

This formula carries the interest of making you sensitive to how difficult this is. It's very convenient to make use of our little Punch puppet and say, for example, that if masochism is involved then it's because the superego is a real meanie. Of course, we are aware of all the necessary distinctions to be drawn within masochism – erogenous masochism, women's masochism and moral masochism. But simply setting out this classification is a little bit like saying – there's this glass, there's Christian faith and then there's Wall Street turning bearish. It leaves us wanting rather. If the term *masochism* is to have a meaning, a formula needs to be found for it that is valid across the board. If we were to say that the superego is the cause of masochism, we wouldn't get far beyond this satisfying intuition, except that we still need to take into account what I have taught you today about the cause. Let's say that the superego is part of the functioning of this object as its cause, such as I have introduced it today. I could even bring it into the series of objects that I will be calling upon for you.

They can be listed, but I'm avoiding setting out this catalogue at the outset so that you won't get dizzy, so that you won't think that the things to be found here are the same as those you've always found yourself with in connection with analysis, because it's not true. Though you might believe you know the function of the maternal breast or that of the scybalum, you know very well what obscurity still lingers in your minds regarding the phallus. And when it comes to the object that follows in the series – I'll give it to you nevertheless, as a way of giving your curiosity something to feed on, it's the eye, as such – well, there, you really don't know any more. This is why this should only be approached with care and for good reason, because if this is the object without which there would be no anxiety, then it's a dangerous object indeed. Let's be careful then, because it bites.

For the time being, this care will provide me with the opportunity to show what I meant, two lessons back, in saying the following, which caught the ear of one of my listeners, that desire and law are one and the same thing.

Desire and law are the same thing in the sense that their object is common to both of them. It is not enough to comfort oneself with the notion that they stand in the same relation as do the two sides of a wall, or the topside and the lining of a garment. This passes the difficulty off lightly. The central myth that enabled psychoanalysis to get under way has no other worth than to make you sense this.

The Oedipus myth means nothing but the following – at the origin, desire, as the father's desire, and the law are one and the same thing. The relationship between the law and desire is so tight that only the function of the law traces out the path of desire. Desire, as desire for the mother, is identical to the function of the law. It is inasmuch as she is forbidden by the law that the law imposes this desire for the mother, because, after all, in and of herself the mother is not the most desirable object there is. If everything is organized around the desire for the mother, if one must prefer woman to be other than the mother, what can this mean but that a commandment is introduced into the very structure of desire? To spell it right out, one desires with a commandment. The Oedipus myth means that the father's desire is what laid down the law.

From this perspective, what is the value of masochism? This is its only value for the masochist. When desire and the law find themselves together again, what the masochist means to show – and I'll add, on his little stage, because this dimension should never be lost sight of – is that the desire of the Other lays down the law.

We can see one of its effects straightaway. The masochist himself appears in the function that I would call the function of the ejectum.

It's our object *a*, but in the appearance of a cast-off, thrown to the dog, in the rubbish, in the bin, on the scrapheap of common objects, for want of being able to put it anywhere else.

This is one of the aspects that the *a* can take on such as it is illustrated in perversion. Mapped out thus at the level of masochism, this in no way exhausts what we can only discern by moving around it, namely, the function of the *a*.

The central effect of this identity that conjugates the father's desire with the law is the castration complex. The law is born from the mysterious metamorphosis or mutation of the father's desire once he has been killed, and the consequence of this in the history of analytic thought, as well as in everything that we have been able to conceive of as the most certain nexus, is the castration complex. This is why you have already seen the notation $(- \varphi)$ appearing in my diagrams at the very place where *a* is missing.

Therefore, point one, I spoke to you about the object as cause of desire. Point two, I told you that to recognize oneself as the object of one's desire is always masochistic. In this connection I indicated what emerges under a certain influence of the superego and I underlined a particularity of what happens in the place of this object *a* in the form of $(- \varphi)$.

And so we come to our third point, which concerns the structural possibilities of the manifestation of the object *a* as a lack. The mirror diagram has been presentified for you for a while now to provide a conception of this.

What is the object *a* at the level of what subsists as a body and which hides from us, so to speak, its will? This object *a* is the rock that Freud speaks of, the final irreducible reserve of libido, whose contours we can see being literally punctuated with such pathos in his texts each time he meets it, and I won't end today's lesson without telling you where you ought to go to refresh this conviction.

In what place does the *a* stand? At what level could it be recognized, if indeed this were possible? I told you earlier that to recognize oneself as the object of one's desire is always masochistic, but the masochist only does so on the stage and you're going to see what operates when he can't stay on the stage any longer. We aren't always on the stage, even though the stage stretches out far and wide, right up to the domain of our dreams. When we aren't on the stage, when we stay just shy of it, and when we strive to read in the Other what it revolves around, we only find there, at *x*, lack.

Indeed, the object is bound to its necessary lack right where the subject is constituted in the locus of the Other, that is, as far away as possible, even beyond what can appear in the return of the repressed. The *Urverdrängung*, the irreducible *incognito*, we cannot say *unknowable* because we speak about it, this is where, in our analysis of transference, what I put forward with the term ἄγαλμα is structured and located.

To the extent that this empty place is targeted as such, the dimension of transference, which always gets neglected and for good reason, is established. This place, inasmuch as it is circumscribed by something that is materialized in the image, a rim, an opening, a gap, where the constitution of the specular image shows its limit, is the elective locus of anxiety.

You can find this rim phenomenon, for example, on privileged occasions in the opening window that marks the limit, the illusory aspect of the world of recognition, the one I have been calling *the stage*. This edge, this frame, this gap, is illustrated at least twice over in this diagram – in the mirror's edge and also in the little sign, ◊. This is the locus of anxiety and this is what you must always bear in mind as the signal of what is standing there to be sought out in the midst of it.

Freud's text on Dora, to which I ask you to refer, is ever more astounding to read for the double face it presents. On one hand there are the weaknesses and inadequacies that strike novices as the first items to be pointed up, but on the other hand there is the depth reached by everything Freud comes up against, revealing to what extent he was right there, turning around the very field we are trying to map out.

To those who heard my disquisition on *The Symposium*, the Dora text – of course, you have to be familiar with it first – may recall the dimension that is always eluded when transference is at issue, namely, that transference isn't simply that which reproduces and repeats a situation, an action, an attitude or an old trauma. There is always another coordinate, which I stressed in connection with Socrates' analytic intervention, to wit, in the case I'm mentioning here, *a love present in the real*. We cannot understand anything about transference if we do not know that it is also the consequence of this love, this present love, and analysts must keep this in mind in the course of analysis. This love is present in different ways, but they should at least remember this when it is visibly there. Contingent on this, let's say, real love, the central question of transference is established, the question the subject asks himself concerning the ἄγαλμα, namely, what he lacks, because he loves with this lack.

It is not for nothing that I'm always drumming it into you that to love is to give what one hasn't got. This is even the principle behind the castration complex. To have the phallus, to be able to make use of it, needs must not *be* it.

When one goes back to the conditions in which one does turn out to *be* it – because one *is* it both for a man, there's no doubt about it, and for a woman, we shall say again by what incidence she is led to *be* it – well, it's always very dangerous.

3

Before I take leave of you, suffice it to ask that you reread attentively the text Freud devotes entirely to his dealings with his patient known as the young homosexual woman.

I remind you that the analysis shows that it was essentially at the time of an enigmatic disappointment concerning the birth of a little brother in her family that she steered towards homosexuality in the form of a demonstrative love for a woman of doubtful reputation, in relation to whom she conducts herself, says Freud, in an essentially virile fashion.

We are so used to speaking about it without knowing, that we don't realize that here he means to stress what I tried to presentify for you in the function of courtly love. He does it with a touch, a science of analogy, that is utterly admirable. She behaves like the knight who suffers everything for his Lady, who contents himself with the most lifeless and least substantial favours, who even prefers to have these and nothing more. The more the object of his love moves in the opposite direction to what might be termed reward, the more he overestimates this object of eminent dignity.

When open hearsay cannot fail to impress upon her the fact that her beloved's conduct is indeed highly suspect, the loving exaltation finds itself reinforced by the supplementary aim of saving her. All of this is admirably underlined by Freud.

You know how the young woman in question was brought to his consultation. This affair was carried out for the whole town to see, with a style of defiance which Freud spotted right away as constituting a provocation aimed at someone in her family, and very quickly it turned out that this someone was her father. The affair ends with an encounter. The young woman, in the company of her beloved, runs into her father on his way to his office. He casts her an irritated glance. The scene unfolds very rapidly. The loved one, for whom this adventure is doubtless but a somewhat lowly entertainment, who clearly starts to get a bit fed up with all this and doesn't want to expose herself to any great difficulties, says to the young woman that this has gone on long enough, that they are going to leave it at that, and for her to stop lavishly sending her flowers every day and following her around on her heels. With that, the young woman flings herself straight off a bridge.

Once upon a time I pored over the maps of Vienna in great detail to give the case of Little Hans its full meaning, but today I won't be going so far as to tell you the exact place. It's very probably something comparable to what you can still see up on boulevard Pereire, namely, a little cutting with a railway track at the bottom for a small line that is now disused. That's where the woman flings herself, *niederkommt*, lets herself drop.

Simply recalling the analogy with giving birth is not sufficient to exhaust the meaning of this word. The *niederkommen* is essential to any sudden moment at which the subject is brought into relation with what he is as *a*. It is not for nothing that the melancholic subject has such a propensity to fling himself out of the window, which he always does at such disconcerting speed, in a shot. Indeed, inasmuch as it calls to mind the limit between the stage and the world, the window indicates for us what is meant by this act – in some way, the subject comes back to the state of fundamental exclusion he feels himself to be in. The leap is taken at the very moment that, in the absolute of a subject that only we analysts can form an idea of, the conjunction of desire and the law is brought about. This is specifically what happens at the moment when the couple formed by the knightly lass of Lesbos and her Anna Karenina object, if I may say so, meet the father.

To understand how the *passage à l'acte* occurred, it is not enough to say that the father cast an irritated glance. There is something here that touches on the very foundation of the relationship, its structure as such. What is at issue? Let's be brief and to the point, I think you've been sufficiently primed to hear this.

The young woman, whose disappointment with her father because of the birth of her younger brother was the turning point in her life, had therefore set about making of her womanly castration what the knight does with his Lady, namely, to offer her precisely the sacrifice of his virile prerogatives, which, through the inversion of this sacrifice, made her the support of what lacks in the field of the Other, namely, the supreme guarantee of the following, that the law is truly and verily the father's desire, that one can be sure of this, that there is a glory of the father, an absolute phallus, Φ.

Without doubt, resentment and revenge are decisive in the young woman's relationship with her father. Her resentment and her revenge are this law, this supreme phallus. This is where I place the capital Φ. *Because I have been disappointed in my attachment to you, Father, and I can be neither your submissive woman nor your object, She will be my Lady, and I shall be the one who sustains, who creates, the idealized relationship with that part of me that has been spurned, with that part of my womanly Being that is inadequate.* Indeed, let's not forget that she gave up cultivating her narcissism, she lost interest in her appearance and her coquetry, her beauty, to become the Lady's devoted knight.

All of this, this entire scene, is what meets the father's eye in the simple encounter on the bridge. And this scene, which had gained the subject's full approval, nevertheless loses all its value with the disapproval felt in this look. It is to this extent that there next occurs what we might call, in referring to the first chart I gave you of anxiety's coordinates, supreme *embarrassment*.

Then comes *emotion*. Go back to the chart. You will see its precise coordinates. Emotion comes to her through the sudden impossibility of facing up to the scene her beloved is making.

Here, I'm addressing someone who asked me to anticipate a little what I might have to say on the distinction between acting-out and *passage à l'acte*. We shall have to come back to this, but we can already reveal that the two essential conditions of what is known, properly speaking, as *passage à l'acte* are realized here.

What occurs then is the subject's absolute identification with the *a* to which she is reduced. Here, it is a matter of the confrontation between the father's desire, upon which her entire conduct is built, and the law that is presentified in the father's gaze. This is what leads her to feel definitively identified with *a* and, by the same token, rejected, evacuated, from the stage. And only the *being dropped*, the *letting oneself drop*, can realize this.

I don't have enough time today to indicate to you in what direction this is heading. Let's say, however, that Freud's famous note on mourning, about the identification with the object as that upon which bears what he expressed as a vengeance on the part of the griever, is not sufficient. We mourn and we feel its effects of devaluation inasmuch as the object we are mourning was, without us knowing, the one that had become, the one that we had made, the support of our castration. When this comes back at us, we see ourselves for what we are, in so far as we have essentially gone back to this position of castration.

You can see time is getting on and I can only give you an indication here. Two things designate very well to what extent this is what is involved.

First of all the way Freud senses that, regardless of the spectacular advance the subject might be making in her analysis, it passes over her, so to speak, like water off a duck's back. He perfectly designates, through all the possible coordinates, the place specific to *a* in the mirror of the Other. Of course he hasn't got the elements of my topology at his disposal, but you can't put it more clearly than that. I'm coming to a standstill, I'm coming up against something, so he says, akin to what happens in hypnosis. Now, what happens in hypnosis? The subject, in the mirror of the Other, is capable of reading everything that stands at the level of the little vase traced out in a dotted line, that is, he goes straight for everything that can be made specular. It's not for nothing that the mirror, the carafe stopper, even the hypnotizer's gaze, are the instruments of hypnosis. The only thing one doesn't see in hypnosis is precisely the stopper itself, or the hypnotizer's gaze, namely, the cause behind the hypnosis. The cause of hypnosis does not deliver itself up in the consequences of hypnosis.

The other reference is the obsessional's doubt. And what does this radical doubt bear on, this being also what makes the analyses of obsessionals go on for ages and ages, and very nicely so? The obsessional's treatment is always a veritable honeymoon between analyst and patient, in so far as it is centred right where Freud designates very well what kind of discourse the obsessional holds, namely – *he's really very fine this man, he tells me the most beautiful things in the world, the trouble is, I don't altogether believe in it.* If it's central, it's because it's right here, in *x*.

In the case of the young homosexual woman, what's at stake is a certain promotion of the phallus, as such, in the place of *a*. This is precisely what should enlighten us as to the outcome of the treatment.

I hesitate to broach it here because it's such a marvellously illuminating text that I don't need to give you its other properties. I beg you at least not to take the closing remarks of this text for one of those ritornellos to which we have since become accustomed. Here he gives us what he was in the course of uncovering, namely, the distinction between inborn constitutional elements and acquired historical elements, small matter which, in the determination of homosexuality. By setting apart the *Objektwahl* as such, the choice of object, by showing that it entails originative mechanisms, he singles out the object as such, as the field specific to analysis. Effectively, everything turns around the subject's relation to *a*.

The paradox of this analysis borders on what I indicated for you last time as the point at which Freud bequeaths us the question of how to operate at the level of the castration complex. This paradox is designated by something that is part and parcel of the observation and I'm surprised that this is not the most common object of surprise among analysts, namely, that this analysis comes to an end with Freud dropping her.

We are now better able to articulate what happened with Dora, and I'll be coming back to this. All of that was very far from being just some mere tactlessness and we can say that, though Dora was not analysed right up to the end, Freud saw clearly right up to the end. But with the young homosexual woman – which is a case where the function of the *a* is in a way so prevalent that it even went to the point of passing over into the real, a *passage à l'acte*, whose symbolic relation he nonetheless comprehends so well – Freud gives in. *I won't manage anything*, he tells himself, and he passes her on to a female colleague. He is the one who takes the initiative of *dropping* her.

I'll leave you with this term as an offering to your reflection.

You can sense that my concern is to target an essential reference in the analytic handling of transference.

16 January 1963

IX

PASSAGE À L'ACTE AND ACTING-OUT

Letting oneself drop and *getting up on the stage*

Egoization
The natal cut
The jouissance of the symptom
The lies of the unconscious
Freud's passion

Today we are going to continue to speak about what I have been designating for you as the *a*.

I'll begin by calling to mind the relation it bears to the subject, so as to maintain our axis and not to let you drift off course through my explanation. What we have to accentuate today, however, is the relation it bears to the big Other.

The *a* is isolated by the Other and it is constituted as a remainder in the subject's relation to the Other. This is why I have reproduced this table, which is homologous with the apparatus of division.

$$
\begin{array}{c|c}
A & S \\
\$ & \cancel{A} \\
a & 0
\end{array}
$$

Second table of division

At the top right stands the subject, inasmuch as, through our dialectic, it finds its point of departure in the function of the signifier. This is the hypothetical subject at the origin of this dialectic. The barred subject, the only subject to which our experience has access, is constituted in the locus of the Other as marked by the signifier. Conversely, the Other's entire existence hangs upon a guarantee that is missing, hence the barred Other.

But there is a remainder after this operation and this is the *a*.

1

Last time, starting off from the case of homosexuality in a woman, which was not a unique example because the Dora case was looming behind it, I brought out for you a structural characteristic of the subject's relation to *a*.

This essential possibility, this relation which may be called universal because you always find it across all the levels pertaining to the *a* – and this is its most characteristic connotation precisely because it is linked to the function of the remainder – I called, using a term borrowed from Freud's vocabulary regarding the *passage à l'acte* that brings his case of female homosexuality to him, *being dropped, niederkommen lassen*.

Now, no doubt you remember that I ended with the remark that, strangely enough, a same *being dropped* marked the response from Freud himself to an exemplary difficulty in this case. In everything of which Freud has given us an account with regard to his action, his conduct, and his experience, this *being dropped* is unique and at the same time is so evident in his text, almost provocative, that for some it becomes practically invisible when reading it.

This *being dropped* is the essential correlate of the *passage à l'acte*. But which side this *being dropped* is seen from still needs to be specified. If you would care to refer to the formula of the fantasy, the *passage à l'acte* is on the side of the subject inasmuch as he appears effaced by the bar to the greatest extent. The moment of the *passage à l'acte* is the moment of the subject's greatest *embarrassment*, with the behavioural addition of *emotion* as a disorder of movement. It is then that, from where he is – namely, the locus of the stage where alone, as a fundamentally historicized subject, he is able to maintain himself in his status of subject – he rushes and topples off the stage, out of the scene.

This is the very structure of the *passage à l'acte*.

The woman in the observation on female homosexuality leaps over a little barrier that separates her from the channel where the partially underground tram passes by. Dora's *passage à l'acte* happens at the moment of embarrassment she is put in by the trapline, Herr K.'s tactless trap, *My wife means nothing to me*. The slap she gives him can only express the following perfect ambiguity – does she love Herr K. or Frau K.? The slap certainly won't tell us which. But such a slap is one of those signs, one of those crucial, fateful moments, that we can see rebounding from generation to generation, with its value as a junction where one's destiny switches from one track to another.

The subject moves in the direction of an escape from the scene.

This is what allows us to recognize the *passage à l'acte* in its specific value and to distinguish it from something quite different, as you shall see, to wit, acting-out.

Shall I tell you about another example, of the most glaring variety? Who would dream of contesting the application of this label to what is known as a fugue? What is it that we call a fugue in subjects who have always more or less been put into the infantile position, who cast themselves into it, if not this stage exit, roving off into the pure world where the subject sets off in search of something that's been rejected and refused everywhere? *Il se fait mousse*, as one says, he goes off to become a ship's lad and, of course, he comes back, which can be his opportunity to *se faire mousser*, to sing his own praises. The departure is precisely the passage from the stage to the world.

This is precisely why it was so useful to set out in the first phases of this disquisition on anxiety the essential distinction between these two registers – on one hand, the *world*, the place where the real bears down, and, on the other hand, the *stage* of the Other where man as subject has to be constituted, to take up his place as he who bears speech, but only ever in a structure that, as truthful as it sets itself out to be, has the structure of fiction.

Before I delve any further into the function of anxiety, let me inform you that later on I'll be speaking to you about acting-out, even though initially it looks more like something along the lines of an avoidance of anxiety. Furthermore, dwelling on this subject right now doubtless strikes you as yet another detour – and one more detour would surely be one detour too many. Observe if you will, however, that here you're simply meeting up with a line of questioning that my disquisition had already punctuated at the outset as something essential. It is the question as to whether anxiety, between the subject and the Other, is not such an absolute mode of communication that one may wonder whether it is not, properly speaking, common to both of them.

In this regard, I note that we have to take into account the fact of anxiety in certain animals. This is one of the features which gives us great difficulty, but which we have to preserve and which no disquisition on anxiety ought to misrecognize. I am placing here, in order to find it again later, a little marker, a little white pebble. How can we be so sure about a feeling in an animal? Now, anxiety is indeed the only feeling we can have no doubt about when we meet it in an animal. We find there, in an outer form, the character that I have already noted as included in anxiety – *that which does not deceive*.

2

So, having drawn up the diagram for what I hope to cover today, I'll begin with a few reminders.

Freud's ultimate thinking points out that anxiety is a signal in the ego.

If this signal is in the ego, it must be somewhere in the locus of the ideal ego. I think I've gone far enough into this for you to know that it must be at x on the diagram.

This signal is a rim phenomenon in the imaginary field of the ego. The term *rim* derives its legitimacy from the affirmation by Freud himself that the ego is a surface and even, he adds, a surface projection, as I reminded you in its time. Let's say, therefore, that it's a colour, a term whose metaphorical use I'll be justifying on a later occasion. This colour is produced on the rim of the specular surface, $i'(a)$, itself a mirroring, being specular, of the real surface $i(a)$.

The ideal ego is the function whereby the ego is constituted through the series of its identifications with certain objects, with respect to which Freud underlines, in *Das Ich und das Es*, a problem that leaves him baffled, the ambiguity between identification and love. We won't be surprised, therefore, that we can only approach it ourselves with the help of the formulas that test out the very status of our specific subjectivity in discourse – to be understood as learned discourse, the disquisition of the teacher. The ambiguity at issue here designates the relationship I've been stressing for a long time now, the relationship between *being* and *having*.

To emphasize this with a reference point taken from the salient points of Freud's oeuvre itself, it is the identification that lies essentially at the root of mourning, for example. How is it that a, the object of identification, is also a, the object of love? Well, it is to the extent that it metaphorically wrenches the *lover*, to use the medieval and traditional term, from the status in which he presents himself, the status of the loveable one, ἐρώμενος, to make him ἐρῶν, a subject of lack, whereby he constitutes himself properly in love. This is what gives him, so to speak, the instrument of love inasmuch as – we fall back into this – one loves, when one is a lover, with what one hasn't got.

The a is called a in our discourse not merely for the algebraic function of the letter that we were promoting the other day, but, if I may say so, light-heartedly, because it's what *on n'a plus*, what we $a$in't got no more. This is why this a that in love we $a$in't got no more can be found again along the regressive path in identification in the form of the identification with *being* it. This is why Freud qualifies the passage from love to identification using precisely the term *regression*, but, in this regression, *a* remains what it is, an instrument. It is *with* what one is that one can have or have not, as it were.

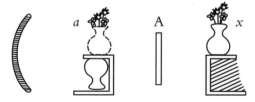

The real image encloses the objects *a*

It is *with* the real image, constituted, when it emerges, as *i(a)*, that one clasps or not the multiplicity of objects *a*, here represented by the real flowers, in the neck of the vase, and this is thanks to the concave mirror at the far end, a symbol of something that must stand to be found in the structure of the cortex, the foundation of a certain relationship that man has with the image of his body, and with the different objects that can be constituted from this body, with the fragments of the original body grasped or not at the moment when *i(a)* has the opportunity of being constituted.

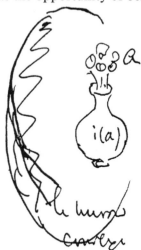

Prior to the mirror stage, that which will be *i(a)* lies in the disorder of the objects *a* in the plural and it is not yet a question of having them or not. This is the true meaning, the deepest meaning, to be given to the term *autoeroticism* – one lacks any self, as it were, completely and utterly. It is not the outside world that one lacks, as it is quite wrongly expressed, it is oneself.

This is where the possibility of the fragmented-body fantasy that some of you have met in schizophrenics lies. This does not enable us, however, to decide upon the determinism of this fantasy and this is why I pointed out the worth of a recent piece of research concerning the coordinates of this determinism. This research did not claim to exhaust it in the least, but it connoted one of its features by observing strictly, and without further ado, what the schizophrenic's mother voices regarding what her child had been for her when he was in her belly – nothing more than a body that was conversely convenient or cumbersome, namely, the subjectification of a as sheer real.

Let's stay for a while with this state that stands prior to the emergence of the image $i(a)$ – prior to the distinction between all the objects a and the real image in relation to which they will be the remainder that one has or has not – in order to make the following remark.

Freud tells us that anxiety is a rim phenomenon, a signal that is produced at the ego's limit when it is threatened by something that must not appear. This is the a, the remainder, which is abhorred by the Other. How is it that the movement of reflection, like the guide rails of experience, led the analysts, first Rank and then Freud, to the following point in this connection – to find the origin of anxiety at the pre-specular and pre-autoerotic level of birth, where no one in the analytic circle has ever dreamt of speaking about the constitution of an ego? This really is the proof that, though it is indeed possible to define anxiety as a signal, a rim phenomenon, within the ego when the ego has been constituted, this is surely not exhaustive.

We find this quite clearly in some of the most well-known phenomena that accompany anxiety, those that are designated as phenomena of depersonalization. These are precisely the most contrary phenomena to the structure of the ego as such. This raises a question that we cannot avoid, that of locating depersonalization authentically, all the more so given that under this heading, when we see the points of divergence among the different authors, the phenomena are grouped together in a way that is certainly ambiguous from the analytic point of view.

We know about the place depersonalization has taken in the specific way it has been marked out by one or several authors from the French school whom I've already had occasion to reference. You will easily recognize the relationships between this way of marking things out and what I've been developing here, and it is even to be presumed that the outlines I gave previously are not foreign to it. The notion of distance is indeed almost palpable in this diagram, where I have always marked the distance that had to be kept from the mirror in order to afford the subject this distancing from himself that the specular dimension is designed to offer him. We cannot conclude from this, however, that any *getting closer* could provide us with the solution to any of the difficulties that are generated by the necessity of this distance.

In other words, what should be said is not that the objects are invasive in psychosis. What is it that constitutes their danger as far as the ego is concerned? Well, the very structure of these objects makes them unsuitable for egoization.

This is what I tried to get you to grasp with the help of what you might call, if you like, topological metaphors – but I think it takes things further – in so far as they introduce the possibility of a non-specularizable form in the structure of certain of these objects.

Phenomenologically speaking, it seems to go without saying that depersonalization begins with the non-recognition of the specular image. We all know just how tangible this fact is in the clinic and with what frequency the subject starts to be gripped by a depersonalizing vacillation whenever he cannot find himself in the mirror, or anything else analogous to one in a situation of this kind. But this formula, which does set out the fact, is no less inadequate. If what is seen in the mirror is anguishing, it is in so far as it cannot be proposed to the Other's acknowledgement.

It's enough just to refer to the moment I marked out as characteristic of the experience of the mirror and paradigmatic of the constitution of the ideal ego in the space of the Other – the moment the child turns his head, with that familiar movement I've described for you, towards this Other, this witness, this adult who stands behind him, to communicate to him by way of a smile the manifestations of his jubilation, let's say, the manifestations of something that makes him communicate it through the specular image. Should the relationship that is struck up with the specular image be such that the subject is too captive to the image for this movement to be possible, it's because the purely dyadic relationship dispossesses him of his relation to the big Other.

Moreover, this sense of dispossession has been well observed by clinicians in psychosis. There, specularization is strange, *odd* as the English say, unpaired, devoid of symmetry. It is Maupassant's *Horla*, the *hors-l'espace*, outside space, inasmuch as space is the dimension of the superposable.

At the point we've reached, let's pause on what is meant by the separation linked to birth anxiety. Some imprecision lingers here, which gives rise to all kinds of confusion. I won't have time to do any more than indicate it and I will be coming back to it, but you should know, however, that some major reservations ought to be voiced pertaining to the structuring of the phenomenon of anxiety at the place of birth.

You just have to go and look at Freud's text. He says that at the level of birth anxiety a whole constellation of movements are constituted, principally vasomotor and respiratory ones, a real constellation that will be carried over to anxiety in its function of signal in the same way as the hysterical access point is constituted, which is itself a reproduction of inherited movements for the expression of certain emotional moments. This is assuredly altogether inconceivable. It is impossible to locate such a complex relationship between anxiety and the ego right back at the start. Although, thereafter, it will be able to serve as the ego's signal, this is only through the intermediary of the relationship between $i(a)$ and a, and precisely the intermediary of what we have to seek out here in terms of a structural operator, namely, the cut.

But then, the initial typical separation, the one that enables us to approach and form an idea of this relationship, is not the separation from the mother. The cut in question is not the one that cleaves child from mother.

The way the child dwells within the mother at the origin poses the whole problem of the character of the egg's relation to the mother's body in mammals. You know that there's a whole side on which it is, in relation to the mother's body, a foreign body, a parasitic body, a body lodged by the arteriovenous stems of its chorion in the specific organ that houses it, the uterus, along with the mucous membrane with which it interrelates in a certain fashion. The cut that interests us, the cut that leaves its stamp on a certain number of clinically recognizable phenomena and for which we cannot elude it, is a cut that, thank goodness, for our idea of it, is much more satisfying than the cut of the child who is born when he falls into the world.

A cut from what? From the embryonic envelopes.

I need only send you off to any old textbook on embryology from the last hundred years for you to grasp that, to have a complete notion of this pre-specular bundle that the a is, you have to consider the envelopes as an element of the child's body. The envelopes are differentiated starting off from the egg and you will see in what forms they are, most curiously, distinguished – I trust you quite far now after last year's work on the cross-cap. In the diagrams illustrating the envelopes you can see all the varieties of the inside/outside relationship appearing, the outer coelom in which the foetus floats, enveloped in its amnion, the amniotic cavity itself being enveloped by an ectodermal lamina, presenting on the outside a face that is in continuity with the endoblast.

In sum, you will see just how tangible is the analogy between what is detached from these envelopes with the cut of the embryo and the separation, on the cross-cap, of a certain enigmatic *a* that I insisted on. Should we come across this analogy again later on, I think I've indicated it enough for you today to facilitate it for us.

Therefore, what's left to be done today is what I announced concerning what acting-out indicates about the essential relationship between the small *a* and the big A.

3

Everything that amounts to acting-out stands in contrast to the *passage à l'acte*. It presents itself with certain characteristics that are going to allow us to single it out.

The profound and necessary relationship between acting-out and the *a* is what I wish to lead you into, by the hand in some sense, without letting you slip over.

Observe if you will to what extent, in what you have ascertained in the clinic, taking someone by the hand so that they won't slip over is utterly essential to a certain type of relation that the subject can have. When you meet it you can be quite certain that it's an *a* for the subject. This makes for a kind of union that is very widespread, but which is not for all that any more convenient to manage because the *a* that is involved for the subject may well be the most inconvenient superego.

There exists a type of mother that we call a phallic woman, a term which is not unsuitable but which we use without entirely knowing what we mean. I advise prudence before you apply this label, but if you are dealing with someone who tells you that, as very precious as an object is for her, inexplicably, she will be dreadfully tempted not to hold onto it in a fall, expecting goodness knows what miraculous outcome to such a catastrophe, and that the most beloved child is precisely the one that one day she inexplicably dropped, well then, there you can identify her as what may conveniently be called on this occasion a phallic mother. There are without doubt other modalities. We shall say that this one here strikes us as the least deceptive. In Greek tragedy, and this did not escape Giraudoux's perspicacity, Electra's deepest grievance against Clytemnestra is that one day she let her slip from her arms.

Let's move now into acting-out.

In the *Case of Homosexuality in a Woman*, whilst the suicide attempt is a *passage à l'acte*, the whole affair with the lady of doubtful reputation who is elevated to the function of a supreme object amounts to acting-out. Whilst Dora's slap is a *passage à l'acte*, all her paradoxical behaviour in the K. household, which Freud uncovers right away with such perspicacity, amounts to acting-out.

Acting-out is essentially something in the subject's conduct that is on show. The demonstrative aspect of any acting-out, its orientation towards the Other, must be noted.

In the case of the young homosexual woman, Freud insists on this. Her conduct is on display to the eyes of all and sundry. The more scandalous this display becomes, the more her conduct is accentuated. And what is on show is essentially on show as something other than what it is. What it is, nobody knows, but nobody doubts that it is something else.

What it is, Freud says so himself, is that she would have liked a child from her father. But should you content yourselves with that, then you're really not hard to please because this child has nothing to do with a maternal need. This is why I insisted at least on indicating that, contrary to the whole direction that analytic thinking has slid off in, the child's relation to the mother ought to be placed in a position that is in some sense lateral in relation to the main current of the elucidation of unconscious desire.

In what we can at least grasp of this from its economic impact, there is in the mother's ordinary relation to her child something fullish, roundish, closed off, something just as complete as during the pregnancy phase, to the extent that it takes some very special care to make it enter our conception and to see how its impact is applied to the cut relationship between $i(a)$ and a. After all, our experience of the transference is enough to see at what moment in the analysis our female patients fall pregnant and how it serves them – it's always the bulwark of a return to the deepest narcissism. But let's leave that aside.

She did indeed want that child as something else and this something else doesn't escape Freud's notice either, thank goodness. She wanted the child as a phallus, that is, as it is spelt out in doctrine in the most developed fashion in Freud, as a substitute, as ersatz, as something that here falls squarely into our dialectic of cut and lack, of the a as an offcut, as something missing.

This is what allows her, having failed in the realization of her desire, to realize it both differently and in the same way, as ἐρῶν. She turns herself into a *lover*. In other words, she poises herself in what she hasn't got, the phallus, and to make a good show of having it, she gives it. It is indeed an utterly demonstrative way. Freud tells us that she behaves towards the Lady as a devoted knight, as a man, as one who can sacrifice for her what he has, his phallus.

So, let's combine these two terms, showing, or displaying, and desire, so as to single out a desire whose essence is to show oneself as other, and yet, in showing oneself as other, thereby to designate oneself. In acting-out, we shall say therefore that desire, to assert itself as truth, sets out on a path that doubtless it only manages to take in a way we would call peculiar if we didn't already know, from our work here, that truth is not in desire's nature. If we call to mind the formula that desire cannot be articulable even though it is articulated, we will be less astonished by the phenomenon with which we are faced. I even gave you a further link in the chain – it is articulated objectively, articulated to the object that last time I called cause of desire.

Acting-out is essentially *monstration*, showing, which is doubtless veiled, but not veiled in and of itself. It is only veiled for us, as the subject of acting-out, inasmuch as it speaks, inasmuch as it could be truthful. Otherwise, on the contrary, it is as visible as can be and this is precisely why it is invisible in another register, showing its cause. The crux of what is on show is this remainder, this offcut, which falls away in the affair.

Betwixt the subject $, here Othered, so to speak, in his structure of fiction, and the Other, A, which cannot be authenticated, never fully authenticated, what emerges is the remainder, *a*, the pound of flesh. This means that you can borrow as much as you like to fill the holes of desire, like those of melancholia, and there you have the Jew who knows a thing or two about balancing the books and who in the end asks for the pound of flesh – I think you know whom I'm quoting. This is the trait you always meet up with in what amounts to acting-out.

Remember what I had occasion to write in my report on *The Direction of the Treatment* about Ernst Kris's observation with respect to the case of plagiarism. Being on a certain path that perhaps we shall have to name, Kris seeks to silence his patient by means of the truth. He shows him in the most irrefutable way that he is not a plagiarist, he has read his book and it is well and truly original. On the contrary, the others are the ones who've been copying him. The subject cannot dispute this. Only, he doesn't give a damn. And when he leaves, what does he go and do? As you know – I think there are nonetheless a few people, a majority of you, who read what I write now and then – he goes and gobbles down a plate of fresh brains.

I'm not in the process of calling to mind the mechanism of the case. I'm teaching you to recognize acting-out and what it means, namely, what I'm designating for you as the *a* or the pound of flesh.

With the fresh brains, the patient simply gives a sign to Ernst Kris. *Everything you say is true, only it leaves the question unscathed.*

There are still the fresh brains. To make a point of it, I'm going to eat some right afterwards so that I can tell you about it in the next session.
I insist, on matters such as these it's impossible to move too slowly. You will ask me – well, I'm doing the asking and the answering, you might tell me if I haven't stressed this enough – *What is original about this acting-out and this demonstration of an unknown desire? The symptom is the same. Acting-out is a symptom. The symptom shows itself as something else too. The proof is that it has to be interpreted.* – Well, let's dot the *i*'s then. You know that the symptom is not to be interpreted directly, that it takes transference, that is, the introduction of the Other.

Perhaps you're still not quite grasping this and you'll be telling me – *Well, yes, that's what you're telling us about acting-out.* – No, it's not. It is not in the essential nature of the symptom to have to be interpreted. It doesn't call upon interpretation in the way that acting-out does, contrary to what you might think.

Besides, it does need to be said, acting-out does call upon interpretation, but the question is one of knowing whether the interpretation is possible. I am going to show you that, yes, it is, but it's hanging in the balance, in analytic practice and analytic theory alike.

Regarding the symptom, interpretation is clearly possible, but only given a certain additional condition, namely, that transference should have been established. In its nature, the symptom is not like acting-out, which calls upon interpretation, because, and this is too often forgotten, what analysis uncovers in the symptom is that the symptom is not an appeal to the Other, it is not what shows itself to the Other. The symptom, in its nature, is jouissance, don't forget this, a jouissance under wraps no doubt, *unterbliebene Befriedigung*, it has no need of you, unlike acting-out, it is sufficient unto itself. It belongs to the realm of what I taught you to distinguish from desire as jouissance, that is, it steers towards the Thing, having crossed the barrier of the good – this is a reference to my Seminar on ethics – that is, the barrier of the pleasure principle, and this is why this jouissance can be translated as an *Unlust* – for those who haven't heard it yet, this German term signifies *displeasure*.

I'm not the one who invented all that and I'm not even the one to voice it, I've put it in Freud's own specific terms.

Let's come back to acting-out.

Unlike the symptom, acting-out is an inroad into transference. It's wild transference. There doesn't have to be analysis for there to be transference, and you suspected as much, but transference without analysis is acting-out. Acting-out without analysis is transference. The result of this is that one of the questions that arises concerning the organization of transference, by this I mean its *Handlung*, is that of knowing how wild transference may be domesticated, how the wild elephant is to be got into the enclosure, how the horse is to be made to walk the lunge ring, to trot round the pen.

This is one of the ways of setting out the problem of transference. It would be very useful to set it out from this angle because this is the only way of knowing how to take action with regard to acting-out.

To those of you who are soon going to be looking at acting-out, I'll tell you that there exists, in the *Psychoanalytic Quarterly*, the article by Phyllis Greenacre, *General Problems of Acting Out*. It's in the fourth issue of volume XIX, 1950, so it's not impossible to find. It's a very interesting article in many respects, but for me it also conjures up a memory.

It was at a time, already some ten years ago, when a few investigators were paying us a visit. Phyllis Greenacre, who was among them, gave me occasion to observe a fine acting-out, namely, the frantic masturbation, which she gave herself over to before my very eyes, of a little female clam digger, a Japanese netsuke that was in my possession, and still bears the traces of this, the object I mean. I must also say that her visit was the occasion of a very agreeable conversation, much better than the one I had with Mrs Lampl De Groot, which was punctuated by various *passages à l'acte*, including leaps and bounds that nearly took her up to the ceiling, low as it admittedly is, of my consulting room.

So, in the article *General Problems of Acting Out*, one finds some very pertinent remarks, albeit that – as you'll see, those of you who read it – they stand to gain from being clarified by the original outlines I'm sketching out for you here. The question is one of knowing how to take action with regard to acting-out. There are three ways, she says. To interpret it, to prohibit it, or to strengthen the ego.

When it comes to interpreting it, she doesn't labour under any illusion. Phyllis Greenacre is a very fine woman. Interpreting it, given what I've just been saying, is not destined to have much effect, if only for the fact that acting-out is made for that. When you look closely, more often than not you notice that the subject knows very well what he's doing in acting-out. It is to offer himself to your interpretation. Only there you have it, it is not the meaning of what you interpret that counts, whatever it may be, it's the remainder. So, this path, at least without adding anything, is a dead end.

It's very interesting to take the time to punctuate these hypotheses.

Prohibiting it, naturally, raises a smile, even from the author herself, who says – *well, one can do all kinds of things, but telling the subject that there'll be no acting-out is rather hard to do*. Anyway, no one dreams of doing that. All the same, one can observe in this regard the interlocutory prohibitions that are always to be found in analysis. Indeed, much more forbidding goes on than is thought. A good many things are done, clearly, to avoid any acting-out in the session. And then, patients are also told not to take any essential life decisions during analysis. It is a fact that, wherever one is applying one's grip, there is a certain relationship to what may be called danger, either for the subject or for the analyst.

Why does one do all that?

Essentially – I shall say, to illustrate my point – both because we are doctors and because we are good people. As it was put by I no longer recall whom, we don't want the patient who comes to confide in us to get hurt. And the most astonishing thing is that we manage this. The fact that we notice acting-out is all the same the sign that we prevent a great deal of it. Is that what Mrs Greenacre is speaking about when she says that a true transference has to be allowed to establish itself more solidly?

I should like to point out here one aspect of analysis that people don't see. Its accident insurance aspect, its health insurance aspect. It's very funny, though – at least once an analyst has got what is known as experience under his belt, that is, everything that, in his own specific attitude, he is most often unaware of – just how rare short-term illnesses are during analyses, just how much, in an analysis which goes on a bit, colds, bouts of flu and suchlike, vanish, and even where long-term illnesses are concerned, if there were more analyses in society, we'd all be faring much better. I think national insurance and life insurance too should take into account the proportion of analyses in the population to alter their rates.

Conversely, when accidents do occur, I'm not only speaking about acting-out, it is very frequently ascribed, by the patient and those around him, to the analysis. It is in a way ascribed to the analysis by its very nature. They are right, it's acting-out, so it's addressed to the Other, and if one is in analysis, then it's addressed to the analyst. If he has taken up this place, then too bad for him. He still has the responsibility that comes with this place that he has agreed to occupy.

These questions are perhaps designed to clarify for you what I mean when I speak about the analyst's desire and when I pose the question of this desire.

I won't be stopping, however, to examine what shifted the question of the way in which we domesticate the transference in the direction of strengthening the ego – the third of the hypotheses – because as you've heard me say, it's not straightforward. Nor will I be stopping to affirm what I've always stood in opposition to, because, as is admitted by those who have been walking this path for well over a decade, and more precisely for so many decades that people are starting to speak about it much less now, this is a matter of leading the subject to identification. An entire literature admits as much.

It is not about identifying with an image as the reflection of the ideal ego in the Other, but with the analyst's ego, resulting in what Balint speaks of, the veritable manic fit that he describes as standing at the end of an analysis thus characterized.

What exactly does this fit represent? It represents the insurrection of the *a* that remains entirely untouched.

4

Let's come back to Freud and to the observation on the case of homosexuality in a woman, in which we find all kinds of altogether admirable remarks.

Even though he tells us that there is nothing to indicate that anything called transference is occurring here, he says at the same time that it would be out of the question to give any time to the hypothesis that there is no transference. A kind of blind spot in his position is being indicated here, because this misrecognizes entirely what the transference relation is about and we even find it expressly worded in the disquisition of Freud himself on this case.

This patient – this is spelt out as such – was lying to him in her dreams. For Freud this is the characteristic feature of the case. The precious ἄγαλμα of this disquisition on homosexuality in a woman lies in the fact that Freud comes to a halt, gobsmacked, faced with the following – he too does the asking and the answering – *What! The unconscious can lie!*

Indeed, this patient's dreams mark, day by day, great strides towards the sex to which she is destined, but Freud doesn't believe in it for one minute, and quite rightly, because the same sufferer who reports these dreams to him also says to him – *But yes, of course, that will allow me to marry and, at the same time, the best part, to occupy myself with women.*

Therefore, she tells him herself that she is lying. And besides, Freud doesn't doubt it. This is precisely what gives the appearance of an absence of any relationship of transference. He comes to a halt on the following – *But then, this unconscious that we are accustomed to considering as the most profound, the true truth, can therefore deceive us.* And his whole debate revolves around the *Zutrauen,* the confidence to be put in the unconscious – *Can we keep up this confidence in the unconscious?* he asks.

He affirms this in a sentence that is very characteristic because it is so elliptical and concentrated that it almost has the character of tripping up in one's speech that I speak about in my Rome Report. I will read you the sentence, I haven't brought it with me today, I'll bring it next time, it is very fine, it concerns a snag with regard to the unconscious. The unconscious always merits our confidence, he says, and the discourse of the dream is something other than the unconscious, it is forged from a desire stemming from the unconscious – but he admits at the same time, without going so far as to formulate it, that therefore she does indeed desire something and, stemming from the unconscious, this desire is what is being expressed through these lies.

She tells him as much herself, her dreams lie. Freud comes to a halt faced with the problem of any symptomatic lie – look what lies are for children – it's the problem of what the subject means when lying. And the odd thing is that Freud lets everything drop when all the parts seize up. He's not interested in what's jamming them, namely, the waste object, the little remainder, which brings everything to a stop and which nevertheless is what is in question here.

Without seeing what he is being encumbered by here, he is moved, as he most certainly shows, faced with this threat to the fidelity of the unconscious. And then, he follows through on his impulse, he commits a *passage à l'acte*.

This is the point at which Freud refuses to see, in truth – which is his passion – the structure of fiction that stands at its origin.

This is the point at which he has not sufficiently pondered over something on which, in speaking of the fantasy, I laid the accent for you in a recent talk, namely, the Epimenides paradox. The *I am lying* is perfectly admissible in so far as what is lying is desire, at the moment when, affirming itself as desire, it delivers the subject to this logical cancelling-out on which the philosopher comes to a standstill when he sees the contradiction of the *I am lying*.

But after all, what Freud lacks here is, as we know, what lacks in his disquisition. It is something that always remained for him in the state of a question – *what does a woman want?* This is where Freud's thinking trips up over something that we may call, provisionally, femininity.

Don't make out that I'm saying that woman per se is mendacious when I say that femininity is evasive and that there's something of an angle here, to employ the terms of the *I Ching*, of *pliant gentleness*,[1] something over which Freud nearly choked to death when he found out, shortly after the fact, about the night-time stroll his fiancée had taken, on the very day they exchanged their final vows, with some cousin or other without telling him. I'm saying some cousin or other, I don't remember very well whom, I haven't checked in the biography, never mind whom, one of those swains with an assured future, as some say, which means that they don't really have any future at all.

That's where the blind spot is. Freud wants the woman to tell him everything. Well, so she did – with the talking cure and the chimney sweeping. Ah, they gave her chimney a fine old sweeping!

For a while, they do all right for themselves in all that, the important thing was to be together, up the same chimney. Only, when they climb back out again, a question arises – you're familiar with this, I recalled it at the end of one of my articles, it's borrowed from the *Talmud* – when they come out of a chimney together, which of the two is going to dust himself off?

Yes, I advise you to reread that article and not only that one but also the one I wrote on *The Freudian Thing*. You can see the Freudian Thing designated there, I daresay with some accentuation.

Diana is the one I designate as showing where we are to give chase in this ongoing hunt.

The Freudian Thing is what Freud dropped – but it goes on after his death, and it is still what leads the stalk, in the shape of the hunting party we form.

We shall continue this pursuit next time.

23 January 1963

X

ON A LACK THAT IS IRREDUCIBLE TO THE SIGNIFIER

Differential topology of holes
A lack for which the symbol cannot compensate
The object in transference
Margaret Little and her capital R
Cut-interpretation

We've always been taught that anxiety is a fear without an object.

Claptrap! we may already say here, where another discourse has been voiced. Claptrap that, as scientific as it is, resembles the song with which a child reassures himself. For the truth I'm setting out for you I formulate as follows – *anxiety is not without an object.*

This doesn't mean that this object is accessible by the same path as all the rest. I've already emphasized that to say that a discourse that is homologous or similar to any other part of scientific discourse can symbolize this object, can put us alongside it in this relationship of symbol to which we shall be coming back later, would be yet another way of getting rid of anxiety. Although anxiety sustains this relationship of not being without an object, it is on the condition that we are not committed to saying, as one would of another object, which object is involved – nor even to being able to say which.

In other words, anxiety introduces us, with the accent of utmost communicability, to a function that is, for our field, radical – the function of lack.

1

The relation to lack is so intrinsic to the constitution of any logic that it may be said that the history of logic is the story of its successes in masking this, in which it resembles an enormous bungled action, if we give this term its positive meaning.

This is indeed why you can always see me wending my way back to these paradoxes of logic that are designed to suggest the paths, the gates of entry through which is impressed upon us, by which is fixed, that certain style that allows us to bring off this bungled action, that is, not to bungle lack.

This is also why I thought I would once more introduce my talk today by means of an apologue.

It is but that and you cannot base yourselves on any analogy to find anything in it that might lend support to a situating of this lack. But this apologue is, however, useful when it comes to reopening the dimension – whose rut any discourse, any discourse from the analytic literature itself, necessarily leads you back into, in the intervals, I would say, between my talks for your catching up week in week out – the dimension of something which can be sealed off in our experience, and which any gap whereby it would designate this lack would still be something that any such discourse could fill.

So, a little apologue, the first that came to me, there could be others, I simply want to go quickly.

I once said to you that, in sum, there is no lack in the real, that lack is only graspable through the intermediary of the symbolic. At the level of the library, one can say – *Volume* x *is missing from its place*. This place is a place that is designated by the prior introduction of the symbolic in the real. By virtue of this, the lack I'm speaking about is easily filled by the symbol. It designates place, it designates absence, and it presentifies what is not there.

But now take a look at the volume I acquired this week and which inspired this little apologue.

On the first page it carries the note – *The four prints from page* y *to page* z *are missing*.

Would this mean, though, that the function of double negation comes into play? Would this mean that, if the volume happens to be missing from its place, the lack of the four prints would be undone and they would be back in the volume?

It's blindingly obvious that it wouldn't.

This apologue might strike you as somewhat foolish. This is, however, the whole question of logic when one transposes into intuitive terms what the Eulerian diagram imparts to the inclusion of lack. What position does the family have in the genus? The individual in the species? Within a circle inscribed on a plane, what is the hole?

If I made you do so much topology last year, it was precisely to suggest that the function of the hole is not univocal.

Something always introduces itself onto the path of thought, something to which we give various different forms, metaphorical forms – the *plan*-ning, the im-*ply*-cation of the *plane* pure and simple – but which does indeed always refer to something, namely, a plane as necessarily constituting the natural, intuitive support of the surface. Now, the relation to the surface is infinitely more complex, as I showed you simply by introducing you to the ring or the torus. This surface has the appearance of being one of the most readily imaginable, but if one develops it in order to be able to refer to it, and on the condition that you consider it to be precisely what it is, a surface, you will have noticed that one can see the function of the hole varying rather oddly.

I'll point out to you once more how this has to be understood.

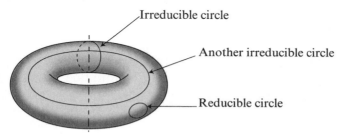

The two types of hole on the torus

It's a matter of knowing how a hole can be filled, how it can close up. It can be represented as a shrinking circle. Even though any old circle drawn on the plane can shrink down to nothing more than a point, a vanishing limit point, and then disappear altogether, this is not the case on the surface of the torus. There are circles on the surface of the torus on which we can operate in this way, but we only have to draw our circle in a different way to see that it cannot shrink down to zero. Structures exist that do not entail the hole being filled in.

I'm drawing so as not to express myself otherwise.

The essence of the cross-cap, such as I showed it to you last year, is that it doesn't furnish us with the diversity of the two kinds of circle. Whatever cut you trace onto the surface, you will never get a circle that can be reduced to a point.

Whether we draw it in a way that is homologous with the cut that on the torus partakes of the two kinds of circle, or whether we go via the privileged point γ to which I drew your attention last year, at the level of the cross-cap you will always get something that, in its appearance, can be reduced to the minimal surface, but not without there remaining at the end, regardless of how the cut may vary, something that is symbolized, not as a concentric reduction, but in an irreducible form – that one there or this one here, which is the

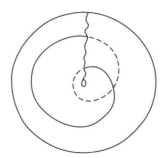

The minimal surface of the cross-cap

same, the one known as the inner eight – which one must distinguish from the concentric ponctification.

This is how the cross-cap came to be another way for us to approach the possibility of an irreducible type of lack.

Lack is radical, radical in the very constitution of subjectivity such as it appears to us on the path of analytic experience. I should like to set it out in the following formula – as soon as it becomes known, as soon as something comes to knowledge, something is lost and the surest way of approaching this lost something is to conceive of it as a bodily fragment.

There you have, in a broad and opaque form, and in its irreducible character, the truth which the analytic experience affords us and which it introduces into any possible subsequent reflection on any conceivable form of our condition.

It really needs to be said that this point entails an aspect that is sufficiently unbearable for us to strive endlessly to circumvent it. The fact doubtless has two faces, namely that, in the very effort of circumventing it, we only trace out its contour all the more, and that, even as we approach it, we are always tempted to forget it, in conformity with the structure that this lack represents. From which there results another truth, namely, that every twist and turn in our experience is down to the fact that the relation to the Other, wherein any possibility of symbolization and of the locus of discourse are situated, meets up again with a structural fault.

The step further that is to be taken is that of noticing that here we're touching on the very thing that makes the relation to the Other possible, that is, on that whence emerges the fact that there is such a thing as a signifier.

This site whence emerges the fact that there is such a thing as the signifier is, in one sense, the site that cannot be signified. It is what I call the site of the lack-of-signifier.

2

I recently heard someone, someone who understands me quite well, ask me whether this doesn't amount to making reference simply to what is in some sense the imaginary material of any signifier, the shape of the word or the form of the Chinese character, if you like, that is, the irreducible aspect that lies in the fact that the signifier needs to have an intuitive support, like the others, like all the rest. Well, no, it doesn't.

Of course, this is what is on offer, this is the temptation, but it's not what's involved where lack is concerned. To give you a sense of this, I'm going to refer to definitions I've already given you and which ought to serve us well.

I told you that nothing lacks that is not part of the symbolic order. But as for privation, that is something real.

What we are speaking about here, for example, is something real. That which my disquisition turns around when I try to re-presentify for you this decisive site that nevertheless we always forget, not only in our theory but in our practice of the analytic experience as well, is a privation, which shows itself as much in theory as in practice. This privation is real and as such it cannot be scaled down. To flush it out, is it enough to designate it? If indeed we are to manage to circumscribe it scientifically, which is perfectly conceivable, we only need to work at the analytic literature. I'll be giving you a sample of this in a little while.

To begin with, I took the first issue of the *International Journal* that came to hand and at just about any point therein we meet the problems involved, whether one is speaking about anxiousness, acting-out or *R* – I'm not the only one who uses letters – *The Analyst's Total Response* in the analytic situation. The author of the article that bears this title is someone we're meeting again, because I've already spoken about Margaret Little. It was back in the second year of my Seminar.[1] We meet up again with the problem, which is very tightly focused in her article, of knowing where privation is to be located, because clearly it slides away the more the author means to close in on the problem that a certain type of patient poses her.

It is not, however, the reduction of privation, its symbolization, and its articulation, that will for all that remove the lack. This is what we have to get into our heads first of all, if only so as to understand what is signified by this mode through which lack appears in the analytic experience, a mode that is called castration. Privation is something real whereas lack is symbolic. It is clear that a woman hasn't got a penis, but, if you don't symbolize the penis as the essential element that one either has or has not, she shall know nothing of this privation.

Castration, I've told you, is symbolic. This means that it refers to a certain phenomenon of lack. Castration appears in an analysis inasmuch as the relation to the Other, which moreover didn't have to wait for the analysis before being constituted, is fundamental here. At the level of this symbolization – that is, in the relation to the Other in so far as the subject has to constitute himself in analytic discourse – one of the possible forms in which lack appears is the (– φ), the imaginary support of castration. But this is just one of the possible translations of the original lack, of the structural fault inscribed into the specific being-in-the-world of the subject we are dealing with. In these conditions, isn't it normal to ask oneself why the analytic experience could be brought to this point but not beyond? The term that Freud gives us as the final term, the castration complex in men and *Penisneid* in women, may be called into question. It is not necessary for this to be the final term.

This is precisely why conceiving of the function of lack in its originative structure is an essential inroad into our experience and this has to be gone over several times so as not to miss it. So, another tale.

If the insect that wanders along the surface of the Möbius strip forms a representation of the fact that it is a surface, he can believe from one moment to the next that there is another face that he hasn't explored, the face that is always on the back of the face along which he is walking. He can believe in this other side, even though there isn't one, as you know. Without knowing it, he is exploring the only face there is, and yet, from one moment to the next, it does indeed have a back.

What he is lacking in order to realize that he has gone over to the other side is the little piece that I made concrete for you at the start of the year by constructing it and putting it in your hands, the one that sketches out for you this way of slicing through the cross-cap. This little missing portion is a kind of short-circuiting that brings him back by the shortest possible route to the other side of the point he was at just before.

Is the matter settled because we are describing this little missing piece, the *a* on this occasion, with this paradigmatic shape? Absolutely not, because the very fact that it is missing is what forms the reality of the world the insect is walking about in. The little interior eight is well and truly irreducible. In other words, it is a lack for which the symbol cannot compensate. This is not an absence that the symbol can counter.

This isn't a cancelling-out either, nor is it a denegation. Cancelling-out and denegation are forms constituted by the relation that the symbol allows to be introduced into the real, namely absence. To cancel out and to negate is to attempt to undo that which in the signifier draws us away from the origin and the original structural fault, that is, to attempt to meet up in the signifier with its function of sign, this being what the obsessional forces himself to do and wears himself out doing. Cancelling-out and denegation target, therefore, this point of lack, but they don't for all that get there because as Freud explains they merely duplicate the function of the signifier by applying this function to itself. Now, the more I say that it's not there, the more it is there.

The bloodstain, whether it's the one that Lady Macbeth tires herself out with or the one that Lautréamont designates with the term *intellectual*, is impossible to remove because the nature of the signifier is precisely to strive to wipe away a trace. And the more one seeks to wipe out the signifier, to find the trace again, the more the trace insists as a signifier. From which it results that, concerning the relationship with that whereby the *a* manifests itself as the cause of desire, we're always dealing with an ambiguous problematic.

Indeed, when this is written into our diagram, which is always to be renewed, there are two ways in which the *a* can appear in the relation to the Other. If we can make them join up, then it is precisely through the function of anxiety inasmuch as anxiety, wherever it is produced, is the signal thereof – at least to the extent that there is no other way to interpret what we are told about it in the analytic literature.

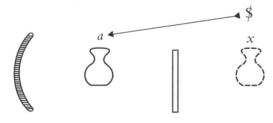

Simplified diagram

The analytic discourse is divided over anxiety and presents two faces. Observe if you will how strange it is to compare them.

On one hand, anxiety is referred to the real and we are told that it is the major and most radical defence, the response to the most primary danger, to the insurmountable *Hilflosigkeit*, to the absolute distress at entering the world. On the other hand, one maintains that it is thereafter taken up by the ego as a signal of infinitely slighter dangers, with respect to which the analytic discourse is often carried to grandiloquence, bringing up what it calls the threats of the *Id*, the *Es*. On this point, Jones shows a tactfulness and a moderation that our colleagues lack, speaking simply in one text of a *buried desire* in order to ask – *after all, is the return of a buried desire really as dangerous as all that?* Does it merit the deployment of a signal as major as anxiety purportedly is, if to explain it we are forced to resort to the most absolute vital danger?

This paradox can be found again a bit further down, because there is no analytic discourse that, having made anxiety the ultimate entity of each and every defence, does not speak to us about defence against anxiety. Thus, the instrument that is so useful in warning us of danger is the very thing against which we are supposed to be defending ourselves. And this is how, by means of this defence against anxiety, all kinds of reactions, constructions and formations in the psychopathological field get explained. Is there not something of a paradox here, one that would require us to formulate things differently? Namely, that the defence is not against anxiety but against that of which anxiety is a signal.

In reality, what is involved is not defence against anxiety, but against this certain lack, with the proviso that we know that there are different structures of this lack, which are definable as such. The lack of a single rim, the lack of relation with the narcissistic image, is not the same as the lack of the duplicated rim, which relates to the slice that is pushed further on the cross-cap and concerns the *a* as such in so far as it is what we must be dealing with at a certain level of the handling of the transference.

Here it will appear, so it seems to me, better than elsewhere, that the lack of handling is not the handling of lack.

Each time a disquisition is pushed fairly far with regard to the relationship that we, as Other, have with the one who is in analysis with us, the question arises as to what our relationship to this *a* ought to be. It needs to be made out, and you will always find it. Once again, there is a glaring gap between the two sides of the analytic discourse.

On one hand, the analytic experience is spoken of as a deep and permanent calling into question that always sends the subject back to something else with respect to what he shows us, whatever its nature may be. As one of my patients said to me not so long ago – *If I were sure that it was just transference*. The function of the *ne que* in *ce n'est que du transfert* is the other side of its function in *il n'a qu'à faire ainsi, there's nothing to be done but to . . .* This form of the verb can be conjugated, but not as you think, as *il n'a qu'avait* – a form you can sometimes hear spring up when people talk spontaneously.

On the other side, they explain to us that it is incumbent upon the analyst-hero, it is his responsibility, to have to internalize this *a*, to take it inside himself, as an object good or bad, but in any case as an internal object, and it is from here that all the creativity emerges by which he must restore to the subject his access to the world.

Both are true, although they cannot be made to join up. But in not joining them up, people mix them up, and in mixing them up, nothing gets said with any clarity on the topic of the handling of the transferential relationship, the relationship that revolves around the *a*.

But this is explained well enough in the remark I made on what distinguishes, in the clinic, the subject's position in relation to *a* from the very constitution of his desire.

To put it crudely, if it has to do with a pervert or a psychotic, the fantasy relation ($\$ \lozenge a$) is established in such a way that *a* is in its place on the side of $i'(a)$. In this case, to handle the transferential relation, we do indeed have to take within us the *a* at issue, like a foreign body, like an incorporation of which we are the patient, because the object in so far as it is the cause of his lack is utterly foreign to the subject who is speaking to us.

In the case of neurosis, the position is different, inasmuch as something of his fantasy appears on the side of the image $i'(a)$. In *x*, something appears which is an *a* and which only seems to be – because the *a* cannot be made specular and can only appear in person, as it were. This one is only a substitute. Only here can the deep questioning of any authenticity in the classical analysis of transference be applied.

But this is not to say that the cause of transference lies here. We are still dealing with the little *a*, which is not up on the stage, but which is constantly asking to get up there to introduce its discourse into the one who still holds his place on the stage, even if it means to wreak havoc, to cause mayhem, by saying *That's enough tragedy!* or equally *That's enough comedy!*, though it's a bit better like that.

Why does Ajax get so worked up, as they say, when at the end of the day, all he's done is kill some sheep, and that's much better, much less serious than if he really had killed all those Greeks. Since he hasn't killed the Greeks, he is all the less dishonoured, and though he gave himself over to that ridiculous display, everyone knows that it was because Minerva had cast a spell on him. In short, it's no big deal.

Comedy isn't so easy to exorcize. As everyone knows, it's more light-hearted, and even if one does exorcize it, what's happening on stage can very well carry on. It starts over, like in a goat-hoof song, the same old story that was there right from the start, at the origin of desire. This is precisely why the very name τραγῳδία refers to the billy-goat and the satyr, who moreover always had a place set aside for them at the end of a trilogy.

The goat that leaps onto the stage is the acting-out. The acting-out I'm speaking about is the movement that goes in the opposite direction to what modern theatre aspires to, where the actors step down into the stalls. Here the spectators get up on stage and say what they have to say.

This is why I'm summoning, as it were, Margaret Little, selected from amongst others, as I told you, just as one might slip on a blindfold and push the point of a knife blade between the pages of a book for divinatory purposes.

3

In her article on *'R' – The Analyst's Total Response to his Patient's Needs*, May–August 1957, parts III to IV of Volume XXXVIII, Margaret Little pursues the disquisition I paused on for a while in my Seminar, before this article was published.

Those of you who were there will remember the remarks I made regarding a certain anxiety-ridden discourse of hers and her attempts to master this anxiety by speaking about countertransference. I didn't dwell on the first appearance of the problem, namely, the effects of an imprecise interpretation.

One day, an analyst sees one of his patients who has just made a radio broadcast on a subject that interests the analyst himself – we can see something of the kind of milieu in which this occurred. He tells him – *You spoke very well yesterday, but I see you thoroughly depressed today. It's surely because you're afraid of having wounded me by encroaching on my territory.*

It takes two more years for the subject to realize, in connection with an anniversary that has come around, that what had produced his sadness was due to the fact that the broadcast had brought back the sense of bereavement he had felt with the recent passing away of his mother. A mother who, so he says, had not been able to see the success that being promoted to a momentary position in the limelight represented for her son.

Margaret Little, who took over the patient from this previous analyst, is struck by the fact that the analyst, in his interpretation, had merely interpreted what was going on in his own unconscious, the analyst's unconscious, namely, that he had effectively been very upset by his patient's success.

What is at issue, however, lies elsewhere. To wit, it is not enough to speak about bereavement, nor even the repetition of the bereavement the subject was in, back then, for the man he made his analyst two years hence. Rather, one has to see what is at issue in the function of bereavement itself and, therefore, by the same token, to push a little further what Freud said about mourning as an identification with the lost object. This is not an adequate definition of mourning.

We mourn but for he of whom we can say *I was his lack.* We mourn people that we have treated either well or badly, but with respect to whom we don't know that we fulfilled the function of being in the place of their lack. What we give in love is essentially what we haven't got and when this *not having* comes back at us there is most certainly regression and at the same time a revelation of the way in which we left him wanting, so as to represent this lack. But here, given the irreducible character of the misrecognition of this lack, this misrecognition simply switches round, namely, we believe we can translate our function of being his lack into us having left him wanting – even though it was in this respect that we were precious and indispensable for him.

This is what I ask you to ascertain, if you would care to go to it, in Margaret Little's new article which constitutes a later phase in her reflection, which has been considerably deepened, though not enhanced, because, indeed, enhanced it is not.

The author doesn't venture to provide any definition of countertransference, which is always such a problematic question, and up to a certain point we may be grateful because though she did indeed venture into it, it was, mathematically, in error. She only wants to consider the analyst's total response, which means everything, as much the fact that the analyst is there as analyst and that things from his own unconscious may escape his notice as the fact that, like any living being, he experiences feelings during the analysis and that, in the end – she doesn't put it like this, but this is what's involved – being Other, she is in a position of complete responsibility. Therefore, it is with this immense *Total* of her position as analyst that she means to set out frankly her conception of the analyst's response.

The result is that she will go so far as to take up positions that couldn't be further from the classical positions, which does not mean that they are false positions. Far from staying outside the field of play, the analyst has to suppose herself, in principle, engaged right to the hilt, to consider herself effectively responsible and, for example, not to discount bearing witness should she be called before a court of law to answer for what has been occurring in the analysis.

I'm not saying that this isn't a tenable attitude. I'm saying that placing the function of the analyst at the heart of this perspective betrays an originality that exposes itself to a snag. The analyst may, on any occasion, be required to justify any one of his feelings not only at the analyst's own tribunal, which anyone will admit, but even to the subject. The weight of all the feelings that the analyst can experience with regard to any given subject engaged with him in the analytic enterprise may have to be not only mentioned, but set forth in something that will not be an interpretation but an admission. With this, a path opens up whose first introduction into analysis by Ferenczi was the object of the most extreme reservation on the part of the classical analysts.

Our author shares out the patients she sees into three groups. As she seems to agree to take on the widest caseload, we have, in the first group, psychosis. There, she has to agree to delegate a part of her responsibilities to other supports, if only, every now and then, for necessary hospitalizations. In the group of neuroses, she tells us that the larger share of responsibilities we delegate are put on the patients' shoulders, which evinces remarkable lucidity on her part. Between these two groups, she defines a third class, that of neurotic character disorders or *personnalités réactionnelles*, what Alexander designates as neurotic characters. In short, a good many problematic attempts at classification are developed around this, when in reality it's not about a sort of subject but a relational zone in which what I have been defining here as acting-out is prevalent.

Indeed, this is very much what is involved in the case she develops for us. It is the case of a female subject who came into analysis because she commits acts that may be classed in the frame of kleptomania. For a whole year she doesn't make the slightest allusion to these thefts. For a long period of the analysis, she finds herself under the unremitting fire of repeated interpretations on the current state of the transference in the sense it is currently considered. On the path that has been taken, they consider that the transference must, from a certain point on, be slaked and absorbed, without let-up, throughout the course of the analysis. Not one of these interpretations, as subtle and varied as the analyst makes them, so much as grazes her subject's defence.

If one of you would be kind enough to do me the favour, on a date we shall set, of going into the case in detail, which I cannot do for you here because I have other things to tell you, you will see the pertinence of the remarks I've been making show through.

The analysis only gets moving, she tells us, when one day the patient arrives with her face swollen from the tears she has shed over the death – in a country she left long ago with her parents, namely, the Germany of back then, Nazi Germany – of a person who only differed from any of the others who had watched over her during her childhood for having been, not simply a friend of her parents, but a woman with whom she had very different relations than she had with her parents. It is a fact that she has never grieved so sorely over anyone else.

Faced with this surprising, stirred reaction, what is the reaction from our analyst? Her reaction is to interpret, as she always does. Once again, she varies her interpretations, just to see which one might work. They are classical interpretations, to the effect that this mourning is a need to retaliate against the object, that this mourning might be addressed to the analyst, a way of bringing back to her, the analyst, all the reproaches that she has to level at her through the screen of the person she is mourning. None of this works. A little something starts to kick in when the analyst admits to the subject that she can make neither head nor tail of it and that seeing her in this state saddens her. And straightaway our analyst deduces from this that it was the positive, real, living aspect of a feeling that gave the analysis its movement back. The author chooses both the style and the order of her development so that we can say that what gets through to the subject and allows her to transfer, properly speaking, into the relationship with the analyst the reaction that was involved in the mourning, is owing to the appearance of the fact that there was someone for whom she could be a lack.

The intervention showed the patient that the analyst was har-bouring what is known as anxiety. Here we are standing at the limit of something that designates the place of lack in the analysis. This insertion, this graft, this marcotting, opens up a dimension that allows this female subject to grasp herself as a lack, when she was absolutely unable to do so in her relationship with her parents.

The interpretation did not hit home as a positive feeling, if we can qualify what is described for us in the observation as an interpreta-tion. The fact remains that the subject does open her arms and let slip that this interpretation has indeed hit home. This is because what is in question has been introduced, unwittingly, as it must always come into question in analysis at some point, even at its end, namely, the function of the cut.

What will enable you to spot this are the changes of direction that ensue and which were to be decisive for the analysis. There are two moments.

The first moment is when the analyst, summoning up her courage, in the name of ideology, in the name of life, in the name of the real, in the name of whatever you like, all the same intercedes in a way that is most peculiar in relation to a perspective that I shall call sen-timental. One fine day, as the subject is turning over all her money issues with her mother, the analyst says, word for word – *Listen, that's enough of that, I won't hear another word, you're sending me to sleep*. I'm not giving you this as a model for technique, I'm asking you to read an observation and to follow the problems that can arise for an analyst like this who has considerable experience and burns with authenticity.

The second moment concerns the slight modifications the analyst has made to what she calls the decor of her consulting room – going by what we usually see in our colleagues' offices, this must be a nice one. Margaret Little has already been badgered by a whole day's worth of remarks from her patients – *That's great, that's horrible, that brown is disgusting, that green is really very fine* – and then along comes our patient at the end of the day and puts it in slightly more aggressive terms than all the others. The analyst tells her in so many words – *Listen, I really don't care what you think about it*. Just like the first time, the patient is shocked, gobsmacked, whereupon she comes out of her silence with gasps of enthusiasm – *What you've done there is really wonderful*, and so on.

I'll spare you the further progress of this analysis. What I should simply like to designate here in connection with a case chosen from a portion of the field that is particularly open to this problematic, is that the decisive factor in the progress of the treatment is down to having introduced the function of the cut. The first interpretation consisted in saying to her – *You're having the same effect on me as a hypnotist's crystal stopper, you're sending me to sleep*. The second time she literally puts her back in her place – *Think what you like about the decor of my office, I couldn't care less*. And this is when something is decisively mobilized in the transferential relationship at issue here.

This allows her to point out that one of her problems was that this subject had never been able to feel the slightest hint of a sense of bereavement for her father, whom she admired. But the stories that are reported show us above all else that she was unable to represent in any shape or form anything that her father might have lacked. There is one very significant scene – during a short stroll with him, she is holding a little wooden stick, very symbolic of the penis, and the patient herself stresses this. Quite innocently, so it seems to her, the father tosses the little switch into the water without the slightest comment. We're a long way from *Sundays and Cybele*.

As for her mother, whose influence lies at much closer quarters in the determinism behind the thefts, she was never able to turn her child into anything other than an extension of herself, a piece of furniture, or even an instrument, occasionally an instrument of threat and blackmail, but never, ever, something that might have stood in a causal relation to the desire of this subject. This is precisely to designate the following, namely, that her desire – she doesn't know which, of course – could indeed be taken into consideration. Each time her mother moves closer and enters into the field of induction in which she can have some effect, the subject very regularly gives herself over to a theft, which, like all kleptomaniacs' thefts, has no signification of any particular interest, it simply means – *I'm showing you an object I've stolen, by hook or by crook, because somewhere else there is another object, mine, the a, which deserves to be considered, to be allowed to emerge for a moment.* This function of isolating, of being-alone, is in some way the pole that is correlative to the function of anxiety. *Life,* says someone somewhere, who is not an analyst, Étienne Gilson, *existence is an unbroken power of active separations.*

I think that after today's talk you won't confuse this remark with the one that is usually made with regard to frustrations.[2] This is something quite different. This is about the limit point at which the place of lack is established.

An ongoing and varied reflection on the diverse metonymic forms that the focal points of this lack assume in the clinic will make up the next part of our disquisition. But we cannot avoid a reappraisal of the goals of analysis as well. The positions taken up in this regard are so instructive, so rich in lessons, that I would like, at the point we've reached, for the article by a certain Szasz to be taken up, *On the Theory of Psychoanalytic Treatment*, in which he puts forward that the goals of analysis are given in its rule and that, by the same token, the final end of any analysis, didactic or otherwise, can only be defined as the patient's initiation into a scientific point of view on his movements.

This is an extreme position, most certainly a very peculiar and specialized one. I'm not asking – *Is this a definition we can accept?* I'm asking – *What can this definition teach us?* You have heard, right here, enough to know that if there's one thing I've put in question time and time again, then it's the scientific point of view, inasmuch as its aim is always to consider lack as something that can be filled, in stark contrast to the problematic of an experience that includes within it the taking into account of lack as such.

The fact remains no less that it is useful to mark out a view-point such as this, above all if one brings it to bear on an older article by another woman analyst, Barbara Low, on what she calls *Entschädigungen*, the compensations of the analyst's position. There you will see a reference to the analyst's position that is diametrically opposed, a reference not to the scientist but to the position of the artist. What is involved in analysis, she tells us, is something entirely comparable – this is not an analyst who is any the less remarkable for the firmness of her conceptions – to the sublimation that governs artistic creation. The article is in German in the twentieth year of the *Internationale Zeitschrift*. In spite of its rarity, I'll make sure it's available to whoever might care to go into it.

On 20 February, the day I come back, because I'm going away for a while, could the two people present here whom I asked earlier take charge of the three articles I've just been speaking about by sharing out the roles as they see fit and adding on a third person for the third article, and might they not also see to it that this rostrum doesn't stay unoccupied for too long and occupy it in my stead if I'm not there, or with me in the audience if I do come back?

I believe I have their consent – I'm referring respectively to Granoff and Perrier. So, the next appointment, to hear them, will be on 20 February, that is, exactly three weeks from now. *(In the event, Lacan returned on 27 February.)*

30 January 1963

XI

PUNCTUATIONS ON DESIRE

From countertransference to the analyst's desire
Desire as a will to jouissance
Desire, from conflict to love

Well, here I am back from my winter holidays.

As usual, the bulk of my reflections were turned towards your service, though not exclusively so.

Aside from having done me good this year, which isn't always the case, the winter-sports resort struck me as somehow harbouring something that in the end appeared to me and led me back to a problem of which these resorts seem to be a glaring incarnation, a very vivid materialization – the contemporary problem of the function of the concentration camp.

Winter-sports resorts are a kind of concentration camp for the elderly well-to-do, which as everyone knows is going to pose an ever greater problem as our civilization advances, given the increase of the average age over time.

This reminded me that the problem of the concentration camp and its function at this time in our history has thus far truly been entirely missed. It was completely masked over by the immediate post-war era of cretinous moralization and the absurd idea that we would be able to do away with all that just as quickly – I'm still talking about the concentration camps. I won't go on any longer about the various travelling salesmen who've become specialists in hushing up the affair, including in the front line one who walked off with the Nobel Prize. We saw to what extent he measured up to his heroism of the absurd when it was a matter of seriously taking sides on one particular burning question.

In parallel with these reflections, I reread, still in your service, my Seminar on ethics from a few years back, with an eye to refreshing the validity of the most essential part of what I believe I articulated there following our master, Freud, and which I believe I accentuated in a way that is worthy of the truth involved, namely, that any morality is to be sought out, in its principle and in its origin, on the side of the real. We still need to know what is meant by that.

The fact that morality is to be sought out on the side of the real and more specifically in politics is not, however, an incitement to seek it out on the side of the Common Market.

Now I'm going to hand over not only the floor but also the chairmanship to the one who held it last time, Granoff. Since he made a general introduction to the three parts, he can at least give a quick word of reply to Mme Aulagnier, who today is going to bring to a close what she started last time on the Margaret Little article.

[*Mme Aulagnier's paper and Granoff's commentary*]

The Barbara Low article is certainly by far the most extraordinary and the most remarkable of the three. I caught sight of a slight sign of avoidance in the fact that Granoff referred us to a more modern form of intervention, in the shape of the article by Lucia Tower. On the other hand, I am quite grateful to him because now that this article has been introduced, which I wouldn't have done this year, we can no longer avoid it. I'm also very grateful to Perrier for having sent me yesterday a short summary of what he contributed. I'm going to give myself some time, and perhaps await some harder information, and turn now to some points of detail that I will have to bring up.

Therefore, the authors of these papers won't lose anything in waiting a bit.

1

I think that, for the most part, you know enough about what I mean to bring up in referring to these articles, which are each centred on countertransference, a subject I don't claim to be able to specify right now in the way it deserves. I only mentioned it within the perspective of what I've got to say to you about anxiety, more precisely the function that the reference to anxiety has to fulfil in the overall continuation of my teaching.

The topic of anxiety can no longer be kept at a distance from a more precise approach to what has been coming up in my disquisition for a while now in an ever more insistent way, namely, the problem of the analyst's desire.

At the end of the day, even the stoniest ears cannot fail to hear that, in the difficulty these authors have in approaching countertransference, the problem of the analyst's desire is what creates the obstacle. Taken as a whole, without the support of any elaboration comparable to the one we've undertaken here, any intervention of this order, as surprising as this may seem after sixty years of analytic elaboration, seems to smack of a fundamental impudence.

None of the authors involved – whether Szasz, whether Barbara Low herself, or even Margaret Little, and in a little while I'll be telling you in what way the thing has been pushed forward in what Lucia Tower, the most recent author to date, prodigiously confides in the very profound avowal of her experience that she gives – can avoid placing things on the plane of desire.

The term *countertransference* broadly aims at the analyst's participation. But what is more essential than the analyst's engagement – regarding which you can see the most extreme wavering occurring in these texts, going from *one hundred percent* responsibility to entirely taking a back seat – the most recent article, the one by Lucia Tower, points out, not for the first time, though it's the first time in an articulate way, what is most evocative in this realm, namely, what she calls a *minor change* that can arise on the side of the analyst. She tells us that countertransference is everything the psychoanalyst represses of what he receives in the analysis as a signifier.

This is not about giving a strict definition of countertransference, which could be given quite straightforwardly. This comment completely relieves what is at issue of its impact. Besides, the question of countertransference is not really the question because it derives its signification from the state of confusion in which it is brought to us. The only signification from which none of the authors can escape is precisely the analyst's desire.

If the question of this desire stands not only unresolved, but hasn't even begun to be resolved, it's simply for the following reason, that until now in analytic theory there has never been, apart from this Seminar, any exact positioning of what desire is.

Doubtless this is because doing so is no small matter. Likewise, you may notice that I've never claimed to do so in just one step. I started by teaching you to locate desire in how it is distinct from demand. Then, namely at the start of this year, I introduced something new, initially suggesting to you – to see your response, your reactions as they say, which indeed were forthcoming – the identity between desire and law.

It is somewhat curious that something as obvious as this, which is written into the first steps of analytic doctrine, has only been able to be introduced, or reintroduced, with such precautions. This is why I'm coming back to this plane today to show you some of its different aspects and even its implications.

2

So, desire is law.

This isn't true only in analytic doctrine, where it's the central body of structure. It's clear that what makes for the substance of the law is desire for the mother and that conversely what makes desire itself normative, what situates it as desire, is the law known as the prohibition of incest.

Let's take things from the angle defined by a word that carries meaning, a meaning that is being presentifed in our times, eroticism.

As we know, its Oedipal manifestation, even its Sadean one, is the most exemplary. Desire presents itself as a will to jouissance, whichever angle it appears from, whether from the Sadean angle, I didn't say sadistic, or from the side of what is known as masochism.

Even in perversion, where desire is given as what lays down the law, that is, as a subversion of the law, it is in fact truly and verily the support of a law. If we know something now about the pervert, it is that what appears from the outside to be an unbounded satisfaction is actually a defence and an implementation of a law inasmuch as it curbs, suspends, and halts the subject on the path to jouissance. For the perverts, the will to jouissance is, as for anyone else, a will that fails, that encounters its own limit, its own reining-in, in the very exercise of desire. As has been very well underlined by one of the people who took the floor earlier at my behest, the pervert doesn't know what jouissance he is serving in exercising his activity. It is not, in any case, in the service of his own jouissance.

This is what allows us to situate what is involved at the level of the neurotic. The neurotic has been the exemplary path for leading us to the discovery, which is a decisive step in morality, of the true nature of desire. This decisive step was only taken when attention was directed, right here, to what I am in the process of expressly articulating for you. The neurotic shows us that he does indeed need to go via the institution of the law itself in order to sustain his desire. More than any other subject, the neurotic highlights the exemplary fact that he can only desire in accordance with the law. He can only give his desire its status as unsatisfied or as impossible.

The fact remains that I'm sitting pretty by only speaking to you about the hysteric and the obsessional, because that leaves outside the field what is still confusing us, namely anxiety neurosis, on which I hope to bring you to take the necessary step with what I'm getting under way here this year. Let's not forget that this was where Freud set off from and that if his death deprived us of something, then it's that it didn't leave him the time to come back to this.

As paradoxical as this may seem, the subject of anxiety thus brings us back to the critical plane that I shall call the myth of moral law, namely, that any sound position of the moral law is purportedly to be sought out in the direction of an autonomy of the subject.

The ever greater accentuation, over the course of the history of ethical theories, of the notion of autonomy shows well enough what is involved, namely, a defence. What has to be swallowed is this first truth, this obvious truth, that moral law is heteronomous.

This is why I'm insisting on the following – that it stems from what I call the real inasmuch as it intervenes, when it intervenes, just as Freud tells us it does, namely, by eliding the subject therefrom and by determining, through its very intervention, repression. What is known as repression only takes on its full meaning on the basis of the function of the synchronic function I spelt out for you in speaking about what, in a first approximation, is called quite simply *effacing the traces*.

Clearly, this is just a first approximation because everyone knows that the traces cannot be effaced and that this is what makes for the aporia of the affair. This aporia is not one for you, because the notion of the signifier has been developed here in front of you precisely so as to resolve it. It is not a matter of effacing the traces, but of the signifier's return to the state of a trace. The abolishing of the passage from trace to signifier is what I tried to give you an inkling of by putting the trace in parentheses, an underlining, a barricading, a mark of the trace. The signifier is what is missed out when the real intervenes. The real sends the subject back to the trace and, by the same token, abolishes the subject too, because there is only a subject by virtue of the signifier, by virtue of the passage to the signifier. A signifier is what represents the subject for another signifier.

The mainspring of what's involved here is not to be grasped from the perspective of history and memory, which is always overly facile. Forgetting seems to be something too material, too natural, for us not to think that it goes without saying, when in fact it's the most mysterious thing in the world as soon as memory is posited as existing. This is why I'm trying to introduce you to a transverse dimension, the synchronic one.

Let's take the masochist, the *maso* as people are apparently saying now in French.

He is the most enigmatic one that can be singled out in the field of perversion. You'll tell me that he knows very well that the Other is the one who enjoys. This would therefore be the pervert stepping into the light of his truth. He would be the exception to everything I said earlier, that is, that the pervert doesn't know who's enjoying. Of course, it's always the Other and the *maso* ostensibly knows this. Well, what escapes the notice of the masochist and puts him in the same position as the rest of the perverts is that he believes, of course, that what he is seeking is the Other's jouissance, but precisely because he believes this, this is not what he is seeking. What escapes his notice, even though this is a tangible truth, lying around all over the place in everybody's reach, though never seen at its true functional level, is the fact that he is seeking the Other's anxiety.

This doesn't mean that he seeks to bother him. For want of any understanding of what it means to seek out the Other's anxiety, this is the crude level, even the daft level, that things are brought down to by a kind of common sense. For want of being able to see the truth that lies behind it, people abandon this shell which houses something deeper, which is formulated in the way I've just told you.

This is why it is necessary for us to come back to the theory of anxiety.

3

What is new in the dimension introduced in Lacan's teaching on anxiety?

Freud, at the end of his elaboration, speaks of an anxiety-signal occurring in the ego and concerning an internal danger. It is a sign, representing something for someone, to wit, the internal danger for the ego.

The essential transition that permits of using this structure, thereby giving it its full sense, is to suppress this notion of internal danger. As I told you – paradoxically for distracted ears – when I went back over the topology of the *Entwurf* when giving my Seminar on ethics, there is no internal danger for the reason that this envelope that the neurological apparatus is has no interior, because it's a single surface, and because the Ψ system, as *Aufbau*, as structure, as that which is interposed between perception and consciousness, is located in another dimension, as Other qua locus of the signifier. Since last year, I have been introducing anxiety as the specific manifestation of the desire of the Other.

What does the desire of the Other represent when it arises from this angle? This is where the signal assumes its value. If it occurs in a place that topologically speaking one may call the ego, then it concerns someone else. If the ego is the locus of the signal, then the signal isn't given for the ego. This is quite clear. If it lights up at the level of the ego, then it's so that the subject may be warned of something, namely a desire, that is, a demand that doesn't pertain to any need, which pertains to nothing other than my very Being, that is, which puts it in question. Let's say that it cancels it out. In principle, it doesn't address me as someone here in the present, it addresses me, if you like, as expected and far more still as lost. It solicits my loss, so that the Other can find itself there again. That's what anxiety is.

The desire of the Other doesn't acknowledge me as Hegel believes it does, and which makes the question altogether easy, because if the Other acknowledges me, as it will never acknowledge me sufficiently, I just need to use violence. In truth, the Other neither acknowledges me nor misrecognizes me. It would be too easy, I could always come out of it through conflict and violence. The Other puts me in question, it interrogates me at the very root of my desire as *a*, as cause of this desire and not as object. And because this is what the Other targets, in a temporal relation of antecedence, I can do nothing to break this hold, except to engage with it.

This temporal dimension is anxiety and this temporal dimension is the dimension of analysis. I am taken up in the efficacy of the analysis because the analyst's desire creates in me the dimension of expectation. I really would like him to see me like this or like that, for him to turn me into an object. The Hegelian relationship with the other is very convenient in this respect, because then I do indeed possess all manner of resistances against it, whereas a good part of the resistance slips off when deployed against the other dimension. Only, needs must find out what desire is. Its function doesn't only lie on the plane of the conflict, but right where Hegel, and for good reason, didn't want to go looking for it – on the plane of love.

The more I think about it and the more I speak about it the more indispensable I find it to illustrate the things I'm speaking about. If you read the article by Lucia Tower you will see two blokes and their love stories – to speak in a way one used to speak after the war when in certain social classes they would refer to women as *bonnes femmes*. In one case, the subject has put her on the plane of love. In the other case, he hasn't managed to, and she says why. I'm indicating this so as to lead us to a few reflections on the fact that, if there are a few people who've said something sensible about so-called countertransference, they are all women.

You'll tell me – Michael Balint. Only he wrote his article with Alice. Ella Sharpe, Margaret Little, Barbara Low, Lucia Tower. Why are the vast majority of those who have dared to speak about this, and who have said interesting things, women? The question will be thoroughly clarified if we take it from the angle I'm speaking about, namely, the function of desire in love. You're ready to hear this, which moreover is a truth that's always been well known, but which has never been given it's rightful place – inasmuch as desire enters the fray of love and is one of its major stakes, desire doesn't pertain to the loved object.

So long as you rank this first truth, which only a valid dialectic of love can orbit, as a mishap, an *Erniedrigung* of love life, an Oedipus that trips over its feet, well, you won't understand anything about the way the problem ought to be posed concerning what the analyst's desire might be. You have to start off from the experience of love, as I did in the year of my Seminar on transference, to situate the topology into which this transference can be inscribed.

As I'm going to end now, my disquisition will no doubt assume a broken-off aspect. What I've put forward in the utmost term as a formula might only be taken for a pause, a chapter heading, or a conclusion, as you will. After all, you have the liberty to take it as a rock of offence or, if you prefer, as a banality.

This is where I mean us to take up the next part of this disquisition, next time, to situate exactly the function that is indicative of anxiety and the way in which it will thereafter allow us to gain access to it.

27 February 1963

ANXIETY BETWEEN JOUISSANCE AND DESIRE

XII

ANXIETY, SIGNAL OF THE REAL

Chekhov's panic fears
Agatha and Lucy
Perversion and the Other's anxiety
The mamma and the deciduous object
From detumescence to castration

So, we're going to be making some more inroads into anxiety, the anxiety I've been getting you to understand as itself being something of an inroad.

You've already been sufficiently forewarned by what I've come up with here to know that anxiety is not what some unthinkingly maintain.

Nevertheless, reading back through the main texts on the question of anxiety afterwards, you will be able to see that what I will have taught you is far from being absent from them, only it is simultaneously unveiled and masked over by formulas that are perhaps overly cautious, under the cover of their carapace, so to speak.

The best authors allow what I've accentuated to show through, namely, that anxiety is not *objektlos*, it is not without object.

1

In *Hemmung, Symptom und Angst*, addendum B, *Ergänzung zur Angst*, the *Supplementary Remarks on Anxiety*, you can read the sentence in which, following tradition here, Freud brings up the indeterminacy, the *Objektlosigkeit*, of anxiety. I will only need to remind you of the main body of the article to say that this characteristic of being without an object cannot be upheld. But look at the preceding sentence. Freud himself says that anxiety is essentially *Angst vor etwas*, anxiety faced with something.

Can we content ourselves with this formula? Of course we can't. We have to go further and say more about this structure. This structure stands in contrast to the structure I introduced by placing the cause of desire behind desire. How has it moved in front? This is perhaps one of the mainsprings of the problem.

Be that as it may, let's be sure to emphasize that here we find ourselves faced with an almost literary theme, a commonplace – fear and anxiety. All the authors who refer to the semantic formation of the words pit them against each other, at least at the start, even if some bring them closer together thereafter, or reduce them to each other, which is not the case among the best of these authors. They tend to accentuate the contrast between fear and anxiety by drawing a distinction between their positions with regard to the object, and it is significant of the error that is thereby committed that they are led to accentuate that fear, for one, has an object.

There is objective danger, *Gefahr, dangéité*, fraught with danger, *Gefährdung*, a danger-situation, an endangering of the subject. This deserves to be paused over. What is a danger? It will be said that fear, of its nature, is adequate to, corresponds to, *entsprechend*, the object from which the danger stems.

The Goldstein article on the problem of anxiety, on which we will be making a stop later on, is very significant in this regard of a pen that lets itself get carried away in an author who otherwise knew how to broach the most precious characteristics of our subject. He insists on the oriented character of fear, as if it were completely formed with the marking-out of the object, with an organization of the response, with the opposition, the *Entgegenstehen*, between what is *Umwelt* and everything that has to face up to it within the subject.

I think I've already underlined for you what is to be found in this connection in what amounts to not even a short story, but a note, an impression, by Chekhov, which has been translated under the title *Panic Fears*. I've tried to have the Russian title explained to me, but in vain because, inexplicably, though perfectly marked out with its year of publication in the French translation, none of my listeners who speak Russian have been able to find the text in the editions of Chekhov, despite them being set out chronologically. This is quite baffling and I can't say I'm not disappointed.

It's about the panic fears that he, Chekhov, experienced. One day, with a young boy who is driving his trolley, his *droschka*, he rides onto a plain and, at sundown, as the sun has already set on the horizon, he spies a belfry in the distance, which nonetheless appears near enough for him to make out the details. He sees flickering through a tiny window, high up in the top turret which, because he's familiar with the place, he knows to be quite inaccessible, a mysterious, inexplicable flame, which nothing allows him to attribute to any reflection. He makes a brief reckoning of what might have been behind this phenomenon and, having ruled out any known cause, is suddenly overcome by something which, when you read the text, can in no way be called anxiety and which has been translated by the term *terror*. What is involved here is not anxiety, but fear. What he is afraid of is not anything that threatens him, but something that has the character of being referred to the unknown aspect of what is making itself felt.

Second example. One day he sees a kind of goods truck come into his field of vision, giving him the impression of a phantom wagon, nothing being able to explain its movement. It darts past at great speed, following the curve of the rails just in front of him. Where does it come from? Where is it going? This apparition, apparently torn free from any determinant he can make out, once again casts him, for an instant, into the disarray of a real panic, which well and truly belongs to the realm of fear. Nor is there any threat here either. The characteristic of anxiety is missing in the sense that the subject is neither seized, nor concerned, nor implicated in his inmost depths.

The third example is the pedigree dog he comes across in a forest, whose presence at that hour and that place he cannot explain. He starts to foment the mystery of Faust's poodle. Here, fear takes shape truly and verily on the side of the unknown. He doesn't know in which form the devil is approaching him. It is not an object that makes him afraid, it's not the dog, it's something else, something that lies behind the dog.

People insist that the effects of fear have in principle a character of appropriateness, namely, they trigger flight. This thesis is sufficiently contradicted by the fact that, in a good many cases, fear paralyses, it is evinced in inhibiting actions, even fully disorganizing ones, or it casts the subject into a turmoil that is least adapted to the response. Therefore, the reference by which anxiety is distinguished needs to be sought out elsewhere.

You do realize that it's not simply out of some desire to play around with a switcheroo, a paradox, that I affirm here before you that anxiety is not without object. Of course, the term *object*, which I've been preparing for a long while, here carries an accent that is distinct from the one it carries in the authors who speak about the object of fear. This formula sketches out a subjectified relationship. It marks a stage from which I want to venture further today.

It is easy to give Freud's *vor etwas* its support straightaway, because he articulates it in all manner of ways in his article. It is what he calls danger, *Gefahr* or *Gefährdung*, internal danger, danger that comes from within. As I told you, however, we cannot make do with this notion of danger. I already pointed out for you earlier its problematic character when it's a matter of external danger. What warns the subject that it is a danger if not fear itself, if not anxiety? The meaning that the term *internal danger* can carry is linked to the function of a structure to be conserved. It belongs to the realm of what we call defence. In the very term *defence*, the function of danger is itself implied, but it is not for all that clarified.

Let's try, therefore, to follow the structure in a more step-by-step manner and designate precisely where we mean to mark out the signal feature on which Freud came to a halt as the feature that is most apt to indicate to us, we analysts, the use we can make of the function of anxiety.

Only the notion of the real, in the opaque function which is the function I set off from in order to contrast it with the function of the signifier, enables us to orient ourselves. We can already say that this *etwas*, faced with which anxiety operates as a signal, belongs to the realm of the real's irreducibility. It is in this sense that I dared to formulate for you that anxiety, of all signals, is the one that does not deceive.

Therefore, the real, an irreducible pattern by which this real presents itself in experience, is what anxiety signals. This is the guiding thread I ask you to hold onto in order to see where it leads us.

2

The place of this real can be inscribed, with the support of the sign of the bar, in the operation that we term, arithmetically, division.

$$
\begin{array}{c|c}
A & S \\
\hline
a & \cancel{A} \\
\$ & \\
\end{array}
$$

Third table of division

I've already taught you to locate the process of subjectification, inasmuch as the subject has to be constituted in the locus of the Other, and primarily so in the shape of the signifier. The subject is constituted in the locus of the Other upon what is given by the treasure of the signifier, which is already constituted in the Other and which is just as essential to any advent of human life as everything we can conceive of with respect to the natural *Umwelt*. The treasure of the signifier in which he has to situate himself already awaits the subject who, at this mythical level, doesn't yet exist. He will only exist on the basis of the signifier that precedes him and which bears a constituent relation to him.

Let's say that the subject performs a first interrogative operation in A – how many times? The operation being a supposed one, there then appears a difference between the response-A, marked by inter-rogation, and the given A, something which is the remainder, the irreducible aspect of the subject. This is the a. The a is what remains of the irreducible in the complete operation of the subject's advent in the locus of the Other and it is from this that it will derive its function.

The a's relation to the S, the a inasmuch as it is precisely what represents the S in its irreducible real, this a over S is what brings the operation of division to a close, because, indeed, A has no common denominator, it lies outside the common denominator between the a and the S. If we want to bring the operation to a close nevertheless, in a conventional way, what do we do? We put the remainder in the place of the numerator and the divisor in the place of the denomina-tor. The $\$$ is equivalent to a over S.

$$\$ = \frac{a}{S}$$

Inasmuch as it is the cast-off, as it were, of the subjective opera-tion, we recognize in this remainder, through a computational analogy, the lost object. This is what we are dealing with, on one hand in desire, on the other in anxiety. In anxiety, we are dealing with it at a moment that logically precedes the moment at which we deal with it in desire.

A	S	x
a	$\mathring{A}$	anxiety
$\$$		desire

Anxiety between x and desire

To connote the three stages of the operation of division, we shall say that here at the start there is an x that we can only name retroactively, which is properly speaking the inroad to the Other, the essential target at which the subject has to place himself. Here we have the level of anxiety, constitutive of the appearance of the a function. And it is with the third term that the $\$$ appears as subject of desire.

To bring to life the doubtless extreme abstraction I've just out-lined, I'm going to take you back to the fact of the image, which is all the more reasonable given that the image is what's involved, given that this irreducible aspect of the *a* belongs to the realm of the image.

The one who possessed the object of desire and of law, the one who found jouissance with his mother, Oedipus, to give him his name, takes one step further, he sees what he has done. You know what happens then. How can one express what belongs to the realm of the inexpressible and whose image I want nevertheless to make emerge? He sees what he has done, which brings with it the consequence that he *sees* – this is the word I'm coming up against – a moment after, his own eyes, their vitreous humour swollen, lying on the ground in a sorry heap of waste. Having torn them from their sockets, he has clearly lost his sight, and yet, he is *not without seeing* them, seeing them as such, finally unveiled as object-cause of the last, the ultimate, not guilty but uncurbed, concupiscence, that of having wanted to know.

Tradition has it that it was from then on that he became truly a seer. At Colonus, he sees as far as one can see, as far ahead as the future destiny of Athens.

What is the moment of anxiety? Is it the *possibility* of that action whereby Oedipus tears out his eyes, sacrifices them, offers them at the price of the blinding that fulfils his destiny? Is that what anxiety is? Is it man's possibility of maiming himself? No, it isn't. It is what I'm trying to designate through this image, it is the impossible sight that threatens you, of your own eyes lying on the ground.

This is the surest key to what you can always find in the phenomenon of anxiety, by whichever line of approach it presents itself to you.

As expressive, as provocative, so to speak, as the narrowness of this place is that I'm designating for you as what is delimited by anxiety, you must see that it's not through some preciosity in my selection that this image finds itself there as though it stood beyond the limits. This is not an eccentric selection. It is commonly met.

Go to the first exhibition you come across, for example, the one that is showing now at the Museum of Decorative Arts, where you can see two Zurbaráns, one from Montpellier, the other from elsewhere, which present you one with Lucy, the other with Agatha, one with her eyes, the other her pair of breasts, on a platter. Both are martyrs, which means witnesses.

It's not the *possible*, that is, the fact that these eyes have been enucleated, that those breasts have been torn off, that makes for anxiety. It should be remarked that these Christian images are not especially hard to bear, even though some people, for what are not always the best reasons, like to pull a face. Speaking of the Santo

Stefano Rotondo in Rome, Stendhal finds the images on the walls distasteful, and certainly they are sufficiently artless as to introduce us a little more vividly to their signification, but the beguiling characters that Zurbarán brings us, presenting us these objects on a platter, present us nothing other that what can on occasion, and we don't deprive ourselves of this, constitute the objects of our desire. These images do not in any way introduce us, for what is common to us all, to the realm of anxiety.

For that to occur, the subject would have to be concerned more personally, he would have to be a sadist or a masochist, for example. I'm not speaking about someone who can have fantasies that we might mark out as sadistic or masochistic, but a bona fide masochist, a bona fide sadist, whose essential condition, whose fundamental situation, we can map out, coordinate, and construct through successive eliminations, by the necessity of teasing out the map of his position further than what is given to us by others as *Erlebnis* – a term more homogeneous to the neurotic – but which is merely the image of something beyond, which forms the specificity of the perverse position, which the neurotic takes reference from and leans on for all kinds of ends that we shall be coming back to. Let's try, therefore, to say what we can presume the sadistic or the masochistic position to be. The key to what Zurbarán's images of Lucy and Agatha might truly concern is indeed anxiety. But it has to be hunted out.

As I said last time, what is the masochist's position? What is masked over for him by his fantasy of being the object of a jouissance of the Other – which is his own will to jouissance, because after all, the masochist does not necessarily meet his partner, as a light-hearted apologue once quoted here bears out? What does this position of object mask over, if it is not the fact of meeting up with himself again, of positing himself in the function of a human wreck, the poor bodily scrap that is laid out for us on these canvases? This is why I'm saying that targeting the Other's jouissance is a fantasmatic target. What is sought out is the response in the Other to the subject's essential downfall into his final misery, and this response is anxiety.

Where is the Other at issue here? This is precisely why the third term in this range has been given, which is always present in perverse jouissance. We are meeting again the profound ambiguity in which an apparently dyadic relation is located. Indeed, we might say – and the thing is borne out well enough by all kinds of features in history – that this anxiety, which is the masochist's blind aim because his fantasy masks it from him, is scarcely less, in real terms, what we might call God's anxiety.

Need I call upon the most fundamental Christian myth to flesh out what I'm advancing? The entire Christian venture is set afoot by a fundamental attempt incarnated by a man whose every word still needs to be heard afresh, on account of him being the one who pushed things right up to the utmost term of an anxiety that truly comes full circle only at the level of He for whom the sacrifice has been established, that is, the Father.

God is soulless. That is quite evident, not a single theologian has ever dreamt of attributing Him with a soul. The radical change of perspective in the relation to God began, however, with a drama, a passion, in which someone made himself God's soul. The place of the soul is to be situated at the level of the residue, a, the fallen object. There is no vivid conception of the soul, with the whole dramatic procession through which this notion appears and functions in our cultural sphere, unless it is accompanied in the most essential fashion by the image of the fall. Everything that Kierkegaard articulates is but a reference to these major structural markers.

Observe if you will that I started with the masochist. It was the most difficult one, but also the one that avoided any confusion, because starting from there one can better understand what the sadist is, and the trap that lies there of merely making him the inverse, the nether side, the back-to-front position of the masochist, which is what one habitually does, unless one proceeds in this opposite direction.

In the sadist, anxiety is less concealed. It is even so barely concealed as to come right to the fore in the fantasy, which makes the victim's anxiety a required condition. Only, this is the very thing that ought to make us wary.

What does the sadist seek out in the Other? It is very clear that, for him, the Other exists, and just because he takes him for an object, this doesn't mean we should say that we have some kind of immature or even pre-genital relation here. The Other is absolutely essential and this is precisely what I wanted to spell out when I gave my Seminar on ethics by bringing Sade and Kant together and showing you that Sade's essential act of putting the Other to the question goes so far as to simulate, and this is not by chance, the exigencies of moral law, which are there to show us that the reference to the Other as such is part and parcel of his aim.

What does he seek? This is where the texts, those that leave some leeway for a sufficient critique, have their value, signalled by the oddity of those moments, those detours that stand out, that are out of place with respect to the thread that is being followed. I leave it to you to look up in *Juliette*, even in *The 120 Days*. . ., the few passages in which the protagonists, entirely absorbed as they are in satisfying their avidity for torments on their chosen victims, enter the strange, peculiar and curious trance that is expressed in these odd words, which I really do have to voice here – *I triumph* – exclaims the tormentor – *cunt-skin!*

This is not a feature that slips of its own accord into the furrow of the imaginable. Its privileged character, the moment of enthusiasm that connotes it, its status as a supreme trophy brandished at the height of the chapter, is sufficiently indicative of the following, that it is in some respect the subject's nether side that is being sought out, which takes on its signification from the characteristic of the glove turned inside out underlined by the victim's womanly essence. That which is most concealed passes over to the outside. Observe too that the text itself indicates in some way that this moment is totally unfathomed by the subject and leaves the characteristic of his own anxiety masked to him.

To say it all, if there is something that is evoked as much by the scant light shed on the authentically sadistic relation as by the form of the explanatory texts in which its fantasy is deployed, if there is something that they suggest, then it is the instrumental character to which the function of agent is reduced. What robs him, except in a fleeting moment, of the aim of his action is the belaboured character of his operation.

He too has a relation with God. This is splashed out here, there and everywhere in Sade's text. Sade cannot take a single step forward in Supremely-Evil-Being without it turning out – and it's just as plain for him as for the one who speaks – that God is the one involved. He gives himself a dickens of a time, a considerable and exhausting devil of a time to the point of missing his goal, trying to realize – which, thank the Lord and make no mistake about it, Sade spares us having to reconstruct because he spells it out as such, namely – to realize God's jouissance.

I think I've shown you here the play of occultation by which, in the sadist and in the masochist, anxiety and object are brought to the fore, one term at the expense of the other.

In these structures, anxiety's radical link to the object is exposed as failing. Its essential function is to be the subject's leftover, the subject as real.

Certainly, this incites us to lay greater accent on the real status of these objects.

3

Moving on to the next chapter, I cannot fail to remark the extent to which the real status of the objects, which has already been mapped out for us, has been left to one side or poorly defined by people who nevertheless like to think they possess biological markers.

This is the opportunity to take note of a certain number of outstanding features that I'd like to introduce you to as best I can, putting my cart before my horse, because in the end, we've got them right here, for example, on Saint Agatha's platter. Isn't this an opportunity to reflect on what people have been saying for a long while, namely, that anxiety appears in separation? Indeed, we can see very well that these are separable objects. They are not separable by chance, like the leg of a grasshopper, they are separable because they already have a certain anatomical character of having been stuck on, of having been fastened on.

This very particular character that certain anatomical parts possess specifies one sector of the animal scale, the one that is called mammalian. It is rather curious that the signifying character, properly speaking, of this feature has not been noticed before. It seems that there are more structural things besides the mamma to designate this animal group, which presents a good many other features of homogeneity by which it may be designated. No doubt they weren't wrong to choose this feature, but this is very much one of those cases in which one can see that the spirit of objectification is not free of influence from the psychological salience of certain significations in which we are engaged to the utmost.

The division between the viviparous and the oviparous is really a befuddling one. All animals are viviparous because they generate eggs in which there is a living being and all of them are oviparous because there are no viviparous beings that have not vivipared inside an egg.

But why not give its full importance to the following fact, which is truly analogous with what I said about the breast, namely that, for those eggs that have a certain period of intrauterine life, there is an element that is irreducible to the division of the egg and this is known as the placenta. There too, this is somewhat stuck on. To spell it right out, what milks the mother is not so much the child as the breast itself and so too it is the placenta that gives the child's position inside the mother's body its character of parasitic nidation, which is sometimes evident on the plane of pathology. You can see that I mean to lay the accent on the privilege of elements that we may qualify as amboceptors.

On what side does the breast stand? On the side of what sucks or on the side of what is sucked? There is an ambiguity here which analytic theory has sometimes been led to speak about in connection with the breast and the mother, by emphasizing of course that they aren't the same thing. Does qualifying the breast as a partial object say it all? When I say *amboceptor*, I'm emphasizing that it is just as necessary to spell out the maternal subject's relation to the breast as the nursling's relation to the breast. The cut does not pass through the same spot for one as it does for the other.

There are two cuts, which are so far apart that they leave different off-cuts. For the child, the cutting of the cord leaves the envelopes apart. These envelopes are consistent with him, continuous with his ectoderm and his endoderm. For the mother, the cut lies at the level of the placenta as it falls away. This is even why it is called the decidua. The deciduous character of the object *a*, which shapes its function, lies there. The falling-away, the *niederfallen*, is typical when approaching an *a* that is nonetheless more essential to the subject than any other part of himself.

This hurried brush-up of the lines of separation along which this falling-away occurs is not meant to lead you right away into any imprudent revisions, but to enable you to navigate straight onto the level to which this examination carries over, that of castration.

There too, we are dealing with an organ. Might we not search out, by analogy with the image I've put forward for you today, whether we don't already possess the indication that anxiety is to be placed elsewhere than in the threat of what I called the *possible* action of castration?

People always revel in biology with an incredible shallowness in the way they approach the phenomenon. A penis is not limited to the field of mammals. There are loads of insects, repugnant in different ways, from the black-beetle to the cockroach, which have darts. That goes a long way in animals, the dart. I wouldn't want to give you a lesson in comparative anatomy today, I beg you to refer to the authors, if necessary I'll tell you whom, but in many cases the dart is an instrument that is used as a hook.

We know nothing of the amorous jouissance of the cockroach or the black-beetle. Nothing indicates, however, that they are deprived of any. Don't jouissance and sexual conjunction always bear the closest relation? It's fairly likely, but never mind. We can presume that our experience, we men, is that of the mammals who most resemble us, conjoining the locus of jouissance with the instrument, the dart. Moreover, we take it as read, everything indicates this, that when the copulatory instrument is a dart, a claw, a hooking object, in any case an object that is neither tumescent nor detumescent, jouissance is tied to the function of the object.

The fact that for us, to stay at our level, the jouissance of orgasm coincides with the instrument's sidelining, *hors de combat*, out of the game, on account of detumescence, warrants not being taken for a feature that belongs to the *Wesenheit*, the essentiality of the organism, this being Goldstein's term. When you think about it, this coincidence has nothing rigorous about it and it is not, if I may say so, in the *nature* of men's stuff.

In fact, Freud's first intuition leads him to locate a particular source of anxiety in *coitus interruptus* where, through the very nature of the operations under way, the instrument is brought to light in its function, which is suddenly stripped away, of being an accompaniment to orgasm in so far as orgasm is supposed to signify a common satisfaction. There are questions here that I'm going to leave on hold and I'll simply say that anxiety is promoted by Freud in its quintessential function right where the accompaniment to orgasmic build-up is precisely uncoupled from the engagement of the instrument. The subject may well be reaching ejaculation, but it's an ejaculation on the outside and anxiety is provoked by the sidelining of the instrument in jouissance. Subjectivity is focalized in the falling-away of the phallus.

This falling-away does exist in normally accomplished orgasm as well. Detumescence in copulation deserves to hold our attention as a way of highlighting one of the dimensions of castration. The fact that the phallus is more significant in human experience through its possibility of being a fallen object than through its presence is what distinguishes the possibility of the place of castration in the history of desire. It is crucial to foreground this, because so long as desire has not been structurally distinguished from the dimension of jouissance and so long as the question hasn't been posed as to whether for each partner there is a relation, and which, between desire, namely the desire of the Other, and jouissance, the whole affair is doomed to obscurity.

Thanks to Freud, we have this cleaving point in our grasp. This in itself is miraculous. Thanks to Freud's very early perception of its essential character, we have in our grasp the function of castration. It is closely linked to the characteristics of the deciduous object. Its deciduous character is essential. It is only on the basis of this deciduous object that we can see what it means to have spoken about the partial object. In point of fact, I'll tell you right away, the partial object is an invention of the neurotic. It's a fantasy. The neurotic is the one who turns it into a partial object.

As for orgasm, it bears an essential relation to the function we define as the falling-away of what is most real in the subject. Those of you who have an analyst's experience, surely you have had at

Francisco de Zurbarán, *Saint Lucy of Syracuse*, oil on canvas (1636),
Musée des Beaux-Arts, Chartres; © Photo RMN/Lagiewski

Francisco de Zurbarán, *Saint Agatha of Catania*, oil on canvas (1630–3),
Musée Fabre, Montpellier; © Photo Lauros/Giraudon/Bridgeman

least once a testimony to this. How many times have you been told that a subject had, I'm not saying his first, but one of his first orgasms, when he had to hand in hurriedly an end-of-term exam paper or some drawing he had to rush off quickly? And then, what gets scooped up? His work, the thing that was essentially expected of him. Something is wrenched from him. It's time to gather up the papers, and right then and there, he ejaculates. He ejaculates at the height of his anxiety.

We are told of the famous eroticization of anxiety. Isn't it necessary first of all to find out what relations anxiety has with Eros?

We'll try to make some headway next time on the study of the respective faces of anxiety, on the side of jouissance and on the side of desire.

6 March 1963

XIII

APHORISMS ON LOVE

Negation in Russian
Desire and the professor
The subject of jouissance
The *a* is not a signifier
Man and woman

страхи.
ч страха глаза велики.
я боюсь чтоб он не пришёл.
небось боюсь, что он не придёт.

Several people were kind enough to respond to my complaint from last time, about not having been able to acquaint myself with the Russian term that corresponds to the Chekhov morsel Pierre Kaufmann brought to my attention. Even though he doesn't speak Russian, he was the one who brought me the precise term, which I then asked Smirnoff, who is a Russian speaker, to give a brief commentary on.

I hardly dare utter these words for which I do not possess the phonology. The word in the title is страхи, which is the plural of страх. This word, like all words that have to do with fear, fright, anxiety, terror and torment, poses us some very difficult problems of translation. I was just thinking that it's rather like colours whose overtones vary from one language to another. Be that as it may, I believe I'm right in understanding, from the debates amongst the Russian speakers present here, that what I put forward last time was correct, namely, that Chekhov didn't mean to speak of anxiety.

With that, I'm coming back to what I wanted to convey to Pierre Kaufmann. I used this example last time to shed a little side light on the reversal I wanted to bring about, namely, to assert, as moreover

I did once before, that anxiety is not without an object. Introducing this object by saying that it would be just as legitimate to maintain that fear has no object held a certain interest for me. But it's clear that this does not exhaust the question of the nature of the frights, panic fears, or terrors designated in the examples from Chekhov. This is the right moment to point out for you in this regard that in an upcoming piece of work Kaufmann takes the trouble to give a precise articulation focused on these Chekhovian dreads.

Before I begin, I'm going to let you profit from another little discovery, once again due to Kaufmann.

He found the most frequent term used to say *I fear* and that is боюсь. With that, he amused himself hunting out in Russian the function of negation known as the expletive, on which I have laid such a strong emphasis. You can find it in French in the sentence, *je crains qu'il ne vienne*, when you're saying that what you fear is him coming. It is not enough to qualify the *ne* as *discordantiel*, because it marks the discordance that lies between my fear, because I fear he may come, and my hope, since I hope he won't. For my part, I see it as nothing less than the signifying trace of what I call the subject of the enunciation, distinct from the subject of the statement.

Well, going by the Russian, it seems that we see how it has to be accorded even greater specificity and this goes altogether in the direction of the value I ascribe to the expletive *ne*, namely, that it really does represent the subject of the enunciation as such and not simply his sentiment. If I understood Smirnoff rightly, in Russian the discordance is indicated by a special nuance. The чтоб is already in itself a *ne que*, but one that is also marked by a further nuance, inasmuch as the *que* that distinguishes this чтоб from the simple что that is in the second sentence,[1] nuances the verb with a sort of conditional aspect, in such a way that the discordance is already marked at the level of the letter б. The negation is therefore even more expletive in Russian from the simple standpoint of the signified.

This doesn't prevent it from working in exactly the same way in Russian as it does in French, thus leaving the question of its interpretation open. I've just said how I parse it.

So, now, how am I going to proceed?

1

This morning, remarkably enough, as I was thinking about what I'd be coming out with here, I suddenly conjured up the time when one of my most intelligent patients – this species does still exist – asked me pointedly *What on earth is it that drives you to such lengths to tell them that?* This was back in the barren years when linguistics and even probability calculus had some place here.

I said to myself that reminding you that there is such a thing as a teacher's desire wasn't such a bad angle from which to introduce the analyst's desire.

I won't give you the word right now, and for good reason, but when I feel the stirrings of guilt at the level of what might be called human tenderness, when it so happens that I think of the calm I'm upsetting, it is quite striking how I willingly put forward the excuse that, for example, I wouldn't be teaching were it not for the 1953 scission. It's not true. Well, clearly I would have liked to devote myself to more limited works, even more intermittent work, but deep down that doesn't change anything.

That one may pose someone the question of the teacher's desire is, to state the obvious, the sign that the question exists. It is also the sign that there is a teaching. And, at the end of the day, this introduces us to the curious observation that, right where the question doesn't get asked, there stands the professor. The professor comes into existence each time the response to this question is, as it were, already written out, written into his manner or his behaviour, into the kind of conditioning that may be situated at the level of what we call the pre-conscious, that is to say, at the level of something that, wherever it comes from, from institutions or even from what one calls one's penchants, one is able to come out with.

It is useful to take a look at how the professor is defined as he who teaches on teachings. In other words, he snips into teachings, he does something analogous to collage. Were this truth better known, it would allow professors to go about it with more consummate art, whose path is shown precisely by collage such as it has taken on its own meaning through artworks. Were they to make their collage in a way that was less concerned with the join, less tempered, they would stand a chance of achieving the same result that collage aims at, namely, to evoke the lack that makes for the entire worth of the figurative work itself, when it is an accomplished one, of course. And along this path, they would thereby manage to meet up with the effect that is specific to what, precisely, teaching is.

So, that's been said as a way of situating, even of lauding, those who are good enough to take the trouble to see, through their presence, what gets taught here, and of thanking them too.

With that, since I can also see listeners who only come along intermittently, I am going to become for a moment the professor of my own teaching and remind you of the major point in what I brought along last time.

Starting off from the distinction between anxiety and fear, I strove, at least as a first step, to overturn the opposition that is currently accepted by everyone at the point at which the final elaboration of this distinction has come to a standstill.

The movement certainly doesn't lie in the direction of a transition from one to the other. Though traces of this remain in Freud, to attribute him with the idea of reducing one to the other would only be an error. Despite the term *objektlos* cropping up in one sentence, he says quite clearly that anxiety is *Angst vor etwas*, anxiety faced with something. He certainly doesn't do this just to reduce it to another form of fear because he underlines the essential distinction between the points of origin of what provokes the one and the other. What I said in passing about fear has to be borne in mind on the side of the refusal of any accentuation that might isolate the fear of *entgegenstehen*, what is placed to the fore, from fear as a response, *entgegen*.

In anxiety, on the other hand, the subject is seized, concerned and implicated in his inmost depths. We already find a first hint of this on the phenomenological plane. In this respect, I called to mind the tight relationship between anxiety and the apparatus of what we call defence, and then, along this same path, I pointed out again how it is on the side of the real, in a first approximation, that we have to seek out what in anxiety does not deceive.

This does not mean that the real exhausts the notion of what anxiety targets. What anxiety targets in the real, in relation to which it presents itself as a signal, is what I've tried to show you by means of the table of the subject's signifying division, as it were. It includes the x of a primordial subject moving towards his advent as subject, in accordance with the figure of a division of the subject S in relation to the A of the Other, since the subject has to realize himself on the path to the Other.

$$\frac{A}{S}$$

I left this subject, in its first position, indeterminate with regard to its denomination, but the end of my talk allowed you to recognize how it could be denoted at this mythical level, prior to the operation being played out in its entirety. It is the subject of jouissance, in so far as this term has a meaning, but precisely, for reasons we shall be going back over later, it can in no way be isolated as a subject, unless mythically.

Last time, I wrote up the three levels that correspond to the three phases of this operation. They are, respectively, jouissance, anxiety and desire. I'm going to move through this layering today to show

A   S   Jouissance

a   Ⱥ   Anxiety

\$ Desire

Anxiety between jouissance and desire

you, not the *mediating* function of anxiety between jouissance and desire, but its *median* function.

How else might we comment on this important phase of our account, except to say the following, whose various terms I ask you to take up by providing them with their fullest meaning – jouissance shall know nothing of the Other except by this remainder, *a*.

What arrives on the bottom level, what comes about at the end of the operation, is the barred subject, namely, the subject as it is implied in the fantasy where it is one of the two terms that constitute desire's support. The fantasy is \$ standing in a certain relation of opposition to *a*, a relation whose polyvalence is sufficiently defined by the composite character of the rhomb, which represents disjunction, ∨, just as much as conjunction, ∧, which is as much *greater than* > as *lesser than* <. \$ is the term of this operation in the form of division, since *a* is irreducible, it is a remainder, and there is no way of operating with it. With this way of embellishing it with an image through mathematical forms, this can only stand as a reminder that, were the division to come about, what would be concerned in \$ is the relation of *a* to S.

What does this mean? To sketch out the translation of what I am designating, I might suggest that *a* comes to assume the function of the metaphor of the subject of jouissance. This would only be right if *a* were deemed equivalent to a signifier. Now, the *a* is precisely what resists any assimilation to the function of a signifier and this indeed is why it symbolizes that which, in the sphere of the signifier, always presents itself as lost, as what gets lost in signifierization. Now, it is precisely this waste product, this scrap, which resists signifierization, that comes to find itself constituting the foundation of the desiring subject as such – not the subject of jouissance now, but the subject on the path of his search, which is not a search for his jouissance. In wanting to bring this jouissance into the locus of the Other as locus of the signifier, however, the subject precipitates himself, anticipating himself as a desiring subject. If there is precipitation and anticipation here, it is not in the sense that this step might skip over or move more quickly than its own stages, it is in the sense that it broaches, just shy of its realization, the gap between desire and jouissance. This is where anxiety is situated.

This is so definite that the anxiety phase will not be absent from the constitution of desire, even if this phase is elided and cannot be concretely ascertained. Those to whom I need to suggest an authority for them to trust in my not being mistaken will remember in this respect Freud's first analysis of the fantasy in the analysis of *Ein Kind wird geschlagen*, which is not only a structural analysis but a dynamic one too. Freud too speaks precisely of a second phase which is always elided in the constitution of the fantasy and to such an extent that even analysis can only reconstruct it. This doesn't mean that this anxiety phase is always this inaccessible. On a good many levels, it can be ascertained phenomenologically.

Anxiety is thus an intermediary term between jouissance and desire in so far as desire is constituted and founded upon the anxiety phase, once anxiety has been got through.

2

The next part of my talk was designed to illustrate something we first caught sight of a long while ago, but which we don't know how to turn fully to our advantage when it comes to understanding what the castration complex corresponds to, which takes on a quite different value in the discourse of the analysts we are.

I tell you that at the heart of the experience of desire lies what remains when desire has been, let's say, satisfied, what remains at the end of desire, an end that is always a false end, an end that is always the result of having got it wrong. I spelt out well enough last time, with regard to detumescence, the value that the phallus assumes in its worn-out state. This synchronic element, as simple as a cabbage[2] and even alike to a cabbage stem as Petronius had it, stands to remind us that essentially the object falls away from the subject in his relation to desire.

The fact that the object lies in this falling-away is a dimension that deserves to be accentuated in order to take a small step further to the place I should like to bring you today and which, given a little attention, might already have emerged for you in what I said last time when I tried to show you the form in which the object *a* of the fantasy, the support of desire, is embodied.

When I used Zurbarán to tell you about breasts and eyes, using his Lucy and Agatha, were you not struck by the fact that these objects *a* present themselves in a positive form? Those breasts and those eyes that I showed you on the platter that these two dignified saints use to bear them, even on the bitter earth that carries the footsteps of Oedipus, appear with a sign that is different from what I next showed you with respect to the phallus, which is specified by the fact that at a certain level of an animal realm jouissance coincides with detumescence, without there being any necessity to it nor anything that would be linked to the organism's *Wesenheit* in Goldstein's sense. Since the phallus functions in human copulation not only as an instrument of desire but also as its negative, it presents itself in the *a* function with a minus sign.

It is essential to distinguish between castration anxiety and what is maintained in the subject at the end of an analysis, and which Freud designates as the threat of castration. This point is surmountable. It is not altogether necessary for the subject to remain suspended, when he is male, from the threat of castration, nor, when she is of the other sex, from *Penisneid*. To know how we might cross this limit point we need to know why analysis, when it is led in a certain direction, winds up in this dead end whereby the negative that stamps the physiological function of copulation in the human being finds itself promoted to the level of the subject in the form of an irreducible lack. This will be met up with further down the line as a question and I think it is important to have marked it out already.

Next I showed the articulation between two points pertaining to sadism and masochism, and I shall summarize for you now its essential part, the part that it is crucial to uphold inasmuch as it allows you to give full meaning to the most developed elements of what has been said on this score from where we currently stand. To my surprise and also to my delight, on reading one author recently I saw that he has taken things very far concerning masochism, as close as can be to the point to which I am going to try to lead you this year from our angle of approach. The fact remains that even this article, whose title I'm going to give you, is still, like all the others, strictly incomprehensible for the reason that the proof of what I am about to set out has been elided from it.

We have come to free ourselves of laying the accent on what at first approach clashes most strongly with our finalism, namely, the fact that the function of pain comes into the picture in masochism. We have come to understand that this is not the essential point. In the analytic experience, we have come to perceive, thank goodness, that the Other is being targeted, that the masochistic manoeuvres in the transference are situated at a level that bears a relation to the Other. Many authors stop there, sinking into an *insight* whose superficiality is blindingly obvious, even though certain cases have turned out to be manageable by getting to this level and no further. One cannot say that the function of narcissism, for example, which has been accentuated by one author who betrays some talent for exposition, Ludwig Eidelberg, will suffice us.

Without leading you into the structure of masochistic functioning, I wanted last time to accentuate for you, because this will shed an entirely different light on the details in the table, what is not seen in the masochist's aim. It is said that the masochist aims at the Other's jouissance. I showed you that what is concealed by this idea is that he aims in fact, as the ultimate term, at the Other's anxiety. This is what allows the manoeuvre to be outmanoeuvred. And now an analogous remark on the side of sadism – analogous in the sense that the first term is likewise elided. It is patent that the sadist seeks the Other's anxiety. What is thereby masked is the Other's jouissance.

Therefore we find ourselves, betwixt sadism and masochism, in the presence of what presents itself as an alternation. That which, at the second level, is veiled and concealed in each of these two subjects appears in the other party at the level of what is targeted. There is an occultation of anxiety in the first case, of the object a in the other. This is not, however, a process in reverse, a switch-around. Sadism is not masochism back to front. This is not a reversible couple. The structure is more complex. Though I'm only singling out two terms today, you may presume, in reference to several of my main schemas, that it has to do with a fourfold function, a foursquare function. One passes from one to the other by rotating it 90 degrees, and not through any symmetry or inversion.

Last time I indicated that what lies concealed behind the search for the Other's anxiety in sadism is the search for the object a. I qualified it using an expressive term taken from the text of Sadean fantasies, which I won't remind you of now.

I'm going to end with a brief reminder that will go back over what I said about the a, this object, by stressing one of the evident characteristics it possesses, which we are very familiar with, even though we don't notice its importance. I mean to speak about anatomy, of which Freud was wrong to say without further qualification that it is destiny.

The limitation to which the destiny of desire is submitted in man has the conjunction with a certain anatomy as its mainspring, the same conjunction that I tried to qualify last time between the existence of what I called decidua, deciduous appendages that only exist at the mammalian level of organisms, and what is effectively destiny, namely ἀνάγκη, through which jouissance has to contend with the signifier. Desire is destined to meet the object in a certain function that is localized and precipitated at the level of deciduous adnexa or anything that may serve as a deciduous appendage. This term will enable us better to explore the cut-off points where anxiety may be expected, to confirm that this is precisely where it emerges, and to draw up an exhaustive catalogue of these frontiers.

I ended with one of the better-known clinical examples illustrating the tight connection, which is much less fortuitous than is thought, between orgasm and anxiety in so far as both may be defined through an exemplary situation, that of the Other's expectation. The exam paper, blank or otherwise, that the examinee has to hand in is a gripping example of what, for a short instant, the *a* can be for a subject.

3

After all these reminders, we're going to try to move on a bit. I shall do so on a path that might not, as I said, be quite the one I'd have settled on myself. You'll see what I mean by that.

With regard to countertransference, I mentioned how women seemed to navigate it with greater ease. If they navigate it with greater ease in their theoretical writings, it is, I presume, because they navigate it fairly well in their practice too, even if they don't see – or rather don't articulate, because why shouldn't they be credited with a little mental restriction? – its mainspring in a way that's entirely clear.

Here it's a matter of tackling something of desire's relation to jouissance. When we refer to pieces of work like this, it seems that women have a very fine understanding of what the analyst's desire is. How is that so?

To grasp this, we have to take things up where I left them in this table, by telling you that anxiety forms the middle register between desire and jouissance. I'm going to bring in a few formulas, which I'll leave each of you to find your own way in, through your experience, because they're aphoristic, and it's easy to understand why.

On a subject as delicate as the relations between man and woman, spelling out everything that makes the persistence of a necessary misunderstanding both licit and justified can only have the reductive effect of letting each of my listeners drown out his own personal difficulties, which fall far short of what I'm aiming at, in the certainty that this misunderstanding is structural. If you know how to hear me, however, speaking about misunderstanding is in no way equivalent to speaking about necessary failure. If the real is always implied, then I don't see why the most efficient jouissance shouldn't be reached along the paths of misunderstanding themselves.

The only thing that sets aphorism apart from doctrinal development is that it foregoes any preconceived order. I'm going to put forward a few different forms of these aphorisms. To begin with, I'll choose the following, which might touch you in a way that's less likely to have you falling about laughing – *Only love allows jouissance to condescend to desire.*

We shall be putting forward a few more of them, which can be deduced from our little table on which it is shown that the *a*, as such, and nothing else, is the port of access, not to jouissance, but to the Other. It is all that's left of it when the subject wants to make his entrance into this Other.

At the end of the day, this is suitable for clearing away the ghost of oblativity which has been exerting its poisonous influence since 1927, invented by the grammarian Pichon. Goodness knows I acknowledge his worth in grammar, but it can only be regretted that an analysis that was, as it were, absent, should have delivered him up entirely, in his exposé of psychoanalytic theory, to the mercy of ideas he held prior to that time and which were none other than Maurrassian ideas.

When S re-emerges from this access to the Other, it is the unconscious, that is, the barred Other. As I told you earlier, all he has left to do is to turn A into something for which it is less the metaphorical function that matters than the relation of falling-away he will find himself in with regard to this *a*. Therefore, to desire the Other, big A, is only ever to desire *a*.

To deal with love, just as one deals with sublimation, one has to recall what the pre-Freudian moralists – I mean those from the fine tradition, notably those from the French tradition, which passes over into the man of pleasure whose scansion I have already called to your minds – spelt out in full, and whose acquired knowledge we ought not to take for old-hat, namely, that love is the sublimation of desire.

The result is that we really cannot use love as either the first or the last term, however primordial it looks to be in our theorization. Love is a cultural fact. It is not only *How many are they who might never have loved but for hearing talk of love*, as La Rochefoucauld put it so well, it is that love would be out of the question were it not for culture. This should prompt us to set down elsewhere the arcs of what we have to say on the conjunction between man and woman, namely, at the very point that Freud himself indicates, underlining that this detour could have been otherwise produced.

I'll continue down my aphoristic path. *To put myself forward as the one who desires, ἐρῶν, is to put myself forward as the want of* a, *and it is by this path that I open the door to the jouissance of my Being.*

The aporic character of this position cannot fail to emerge for you, but there are still a few more steps to be taken. I think you have already grasped, because I've been telling you for a long while now, that if I am standing at the level of the ἐρῶν, opening the door to the jouissance of my Being, it is clear that the nearest slope that offers itself to this enterprise is for me to be appreciated as ἐρώμενος, loveable. This is what does not fail to come about, and without any conceit, but where already the fact that something has gone amiss in the affair can be read.

This is not an aphorism, but already a commentary. I believed it necessary for two reasons, firstly because I made a kind of double negative slip, which ought to warn me of something, and secondly because I believed I could see the miracle of incomprehension shining across a few faces.

I continue. *Any requirement of a on the path of this enterprise to encounter woman* – since I've taken the androcentric perspective – *can only trigger the Other's anxiety, precisely because I don't make any more of the Other than a, because my desire* ays *the Other, as it were.* This is precisely why sublimation-love allows jouissance to condescend to desire. Here, my little circuit of aphorisms chases its tail.

What noble words are these. You see, I don't fear ridicule. All this might sound a bit preachy and each time one advances on this ground one always runs this risk. But still, you seem to be taking your time before laughing at it. I can only thank you and be off again.

I shall only start off again for a short while today, but allow me to take a few more small steps forward. This same path that I've just trodden in a tone that strikes you as somewhat heroic can be taken in the opposite direction and there we shall see something emerge that may sound less triumphant, which once again will confirm the non-reversibility of these routes.

On the path that condescends to my desire, what the Other wants, what he wants even if he doesn't know in the slightest what he wants, is nevertheless, necessarily, my anxiety. It is not enough to say that woman overcomes hers through love. That remains to be seen.

Moving along the path I've chosen today, I'm leaving to one side, for another time, how the partners are defined at the outset. The way things stand, such as we are moving through them, always entails picking things up en route and even sometimes at the port of arrival, because we can't pick them up at the start.

Be that as it may, it is in so far as she wants my jouissance, that is, to enjoy me, that woman generates anxiety in me. This is for the very simple reason, which for a long time now has been part of our theory, that no desire can be fulfilled without entailing castration.

To the extent that jouissance is involved, that is, that she has my Being in her sights, woman can only reach it by castrating me.

May this not lead the male portion of my audience into any resignation with regard to the ever palpable effects of this basic truth in what is called, using a classificatory term, conjugal life. Defining a basic ἀνάγκη has absolutely nothing to do with its incidental points of impact. Nonetheless, a good many things are clarified when it is properly spelt out.

Now, spelling it out properly as I have just done, even though it overlaps with the most palpable experience, risks the danger of you seeing here what is commonly called inevitability, which means that it's already written out. Just because I'm saying it, this doesn't mean you should think it is already written. Moreover, were I to write it, I would add more shape to it. This shape consists precisely in going into the details, that is, in going into the whys and wherefores.

With reference to what makes for the key to the function of the object of desire, what is blindingly obvious is that woman lacks nothing. We would be quite wrong to consider *Penisneid* to be an ultimate term. I've already announced that herein lies the originality of what I'm trying to pursue for you this year.

The fact is that on this point she has nothing wanting. Perhaps I'll try to spell out why anatomically. The clitoris/penis analogy is far from being a well-founded one. A clitoris is not simply a smaller penis, it is a part of the penis that corresponds to the corpus cavernosa. To the best of my knowledge, except in hypospadias, a penis is not limited to the corpus cavernosa. This is an aside.

The fact of having nothing wanting on the road to jouissance does not resolve the question of desire for her in the slightest, precisely in so far as the function of the *a* plays its full role for her as for us. But all the same, this simplifies the question of desire a great deal for her – though not for us in the presence of her desire. But in the end, taking an interest in the object as an object of our desire entails far fewer complications for women.

Time is getting on. I'll leave things at the point to which I've steered them today. This point is tempting enough for many of my listeners to want to know what comes next.

To give you a few first fruits, I'll tell you that, if a title can be given to what I'm going to be speaking about next time, it would be something along the lines of – *On the Relationships of Woman, as Psychoanalyst, to the Position of Don Juan.*

13 March 1963

XIV

WOMAN, TRUER AND MORE REAL

Tiresias struck blind
The hole, the void, and the pot
Woman lacks nothing
Don Juan, a woman's dream
Lucia Tower and her desire

To situate anxiety for you, I announced that I would have to come back to the central field already sketched out in the Seminar on ethics as the field of jouissance.

Today we'll be moving forward by trying to spell out why this is so.

1

A certain number of inroads, notably those I made in the year of the said Seminar, have already taught you that, as mythical as the point at which we must locate it is, we have to conceive of jouissance as being profoundly independent of the articulation of desire.

Indeed, desire is constituted upstream of the zone which separates out jouissance and desire, and which is the fault-line where anxiety is produced. This does not mean that desire doesn't concern the Other involved in jouissance, which is the real Other. I will say that it is normative for desire, for the law that constitutes desire as desire, not to manage to concern this Other in its centre. It only concerns it elliptically and off to one side – small *a*, substitute for big A. This means that all the *Erniedrigungen*, the debasements in the sphere of love that come pointed out and punctuated by Freud, are the effects of this fundamental structure, which is irreducible. Here lies the gap that we do not mean to mask over, if, more-over, we think that the castration complex and *Penisneid*, which thrive here, are not themselves the final terms that designate this structure.

Woman turns out to be superior in the domain of jouissance, on account of her bond with the knot of desire being much looser. Lack, the *minus* sign that stamps the phallic function for man and means that his nexus with the object has to pass via the negativizing of the phallus and the castration complex, the status of the (– φ) at the centre of man's desire, all of that does not form a necessary knot for woman.

This does not mean that she is without any relation to the desire of the Other. On the contrary, the desire of the Other as such is precisely what she has to contend with, and all the more so given that, in this confrontation, the phallic object only comes in second place for her, and in so far as it plays a role in the desire of the Other. This is a considerable simplification.

This simplified relationship with the desire of the Other is what allows women, when they apply themselves to our noble profession, to be with respect to this desire in a relationship that we can feel to be much freer, notwithstanding each particularity that they may represent in a relationship that is, if I may say, *essential*. This is shown each time they broach the field confusingly labelled the field of countertransference. She possesses this greater freedom because she doesn't clasp onto this relation to the Other as *essentially*, in such a *wesentlich* manner, as men do, in particular in anything to do with jouissance.

With that, having incarnated for you the other day the *a* in the falling eyes of Oedipus, I cannot fail to call to your minds Tiresias struck blind.

Tiresias, the one who ought to be the patron saint of psychoanalysts, Tiresias the seer, the soothsayer, was blinded by the supreme goddess Juno, the jealous one, who thereby took vengeance for his offence to her in circumstances that Ovid explains to us very well in the third book of the *Metamorphoses*, line 316 to line 338. I ask you to refer to this text whose *great anthropological interest* is underlined by T. S. Eliot in an endnote to *The Waste Land*.

One day, engaging this one time in somewhat mellow intercourse with his wife, Jupiter teases her over the fact that *most certainly the voluptuousness you women experience* – that's him speaking – *is much greater than the pleasure men feel*. With that, off they go to consult Tiresias, just like that, for a lark – the gods don't always measure the consequences of their acts. *But, by the by,* he says, *how did it slip my mind? Tiresias was seven years a woman.*

The baker's wife / every seven years switched her skin, chanted Guillaume Apollinaire, and Tiresias changed sex, not from straightforward periodicity, but by mishap. Having been careless enough to disturb two coupling snakes, those of our caduceus, he became a woman. Then, repeating the deed, he came back to his initial position. Whatever the meaning might be behind these snakes that one can only disentangle at great peril, he is called to bear witness before Jupiter and Juno on the question of jouissance for having spent the full seven-year interval as a woman. And so, what does he say? Out with the truth, regardless of the consequences. *I corroborate*, he says, *what Jupiter has told. Women's jouissance is greater than men's.*

By a quarter or a tenth? There are also more precise versions, but the ratio matters little. It depends only, in sum, on the limitation that man's relation to desire imposes on him, which inscribes the object into the negative column. This is what I designate as $(-\varphi)$. Whereas the prophet of absolute knowledge teaches this man that he makes his hole in the real, which in Hegel is called negativity, I say something else, namely, that the hole begins at the base of his abdomen, at the very least if we want to go right back to the source of what forms the status of desire in him.

On this score, Sartre, being post-Hegelian, doesn't fail to slip in an image you know well, with his wonderful talent for sidetracking – the image of the infant, which naturally he makes a born-bourgeois, just to spice things up a bit, who sticking his finger into the sand mimes, in his eyes, and to our attention, the act that is supposed to be the fundamental act.

Some thoroughly warranted scorn could be poured on what here amounts to a new form of the little-man-within-the-man that we are incarnating in the character of this child without realizing that it warrants all the philosophical objections that have been levelled at the said little-man. But in the end, scorn is not enough. The figure Sartre presents us with hits home, it makes something resonate in the unconscious. What exactly? Well, my goodness, none other than the desired engulfing of one's entire body into the bosom of Mother Earth, whose meaning Freud exposes, as it deserves to be, when he says, in so many words, at the end of one of the chapters of *Hemmung, Symptom und Angst*, that the return to the mother's womb is a fantasy of impotent men. This is precisely why the ward that Sartre applies himself to incubating in this man, and whom he invites throughout his oeuvre to share the only glue of existence, will let himself be the phallus. The accent here is on *being*.

You may see the phallus that is involved by portraying it with an image that is within easy reach of your research, the one to be found harboured in the valves of those little animals called razor shells. They will on occasion stick their tongues out at you, from the tureen in which you have gathered your pickings. You pry them up in much the same way as you crop asparagus, with a long-bladed pocketknife and a simple piece of wire that you hook down into the sand. I don't know if you've ever seen these tongues poking out of the razor shell in a state of opisthotonus, but if you haven't, it's a unique experience you really have to treat yourselves to and one which strikes me as bearing a clear relation to the fantasy Sartre insists on in *Nausea*, that of seeing tongues suddenly darting out from a wall or some other surface, which fits into the thematic of the image of the world being rejected into an unfathomable artificiality.

So what? you may wonder. Since, when all is said and done, he's exorcizing the cosmos, after having undermined the fundamental terms of theology, cosmology here being deemed to partake of the same nature, I will say that this curious use of tongues doesn't seem to be on the right track. But much rather than believing it, just as earlier I doubled up *essentially* and *wesentlich* – and I would have liked to have been able to voice the word in many other languages besides – I find myself here faced with a certain Babelism, which you will wind up making, if you nettle me, one of the key points of what I have to forbid.

Be that as it may, this reference indicates why my own experience is not the same, my experience of what one can see, when one is young, on the beach, that is, where one cannot make a hole without water welling up in it. Well, to come out with it, this is an annoyance which also wells up in me faced with the crab's sideways walk, ever ready to hide its intention to pinch your fingers. They're very dexterous things, crabs. You can give one a pack to shuffle, which is nowhere near as hard as opening a mussel, something it does every day – well, even were there no more than two cards, it would still try to scramble them.

So it goes that one says, for example, that the real is always full. That produces an effect, it's got a ring to it that lends credence to the thing, a little ring of tasteful Lacanianism. Who else but me can speak of the real like that? The rub is, I never said that. The real is teeming with hollows and you can even create a vacuum in it. What I say is altogether different. It is that the real doesn't lack anything.

I added that, if you make a few pots, even if they are all alike, it's a sure thing that these pots are different. All the same, it's incredible that, in the name of the Principle of Individuation, this should give classical thought so much cotton to spin with. Look where we're at, even now. We're at the Bertrand Russell level, mobilizing all time and space just to uphold the distinction between individuals. You have to admit it's a laugh.

My pot story continues. The next phase is that their identity, that is, what can be substituted between the pots, is the void around which the pot is formed. And the third phase is that human action has begun when this void is barred, in order to be filled with what will constitute the void of the pot beside it, when, for a pot, being half-full is the same thing as being half-empty. This presupposes that a pot is something that doesn't leak all over the place.

In all cultures you can be sure that a civilization is already complete and in place when you can find its first ceramics. Sometimes I contemplate a really very fine collection of vases I have in my country house. Evidently, for those people, in their time, as many other cultures show, it was their main asset. Even if we are unable to read what is wonderfully and lavishly painted on their sides, even if we are unable to translate them into an articulated language of rites and myths, one thing we do know – in this vase, there is everything. The vase is enough, man's relation to the object and to desire is there in its entirety, tangible and enduring.

This is indeed what legitimizes the famous mustard pot that once set my colleagues' teeth on edge for a year or so, to the point that, kind as I am, I ended up putting it back up on the shelf with the pots of glue. I did still make use of it, though. It served as an example of how striking it is that on the dinner table the mustard pot is always empty, as you know from experience.

The only time there is any mustard is when it gets up your nose, as we say in French. You start to see red.

Contrary to what people think, I am not in the least bit fussy about how pots are used. I'm saying this because a problem of this order was recently set out for us. Piera Aulagnier, who is a steadfast spirit as women can be, and this is even what will do her a disservice, knows very well that it is permissible to put the *Redcurrant Jam* label on the pot that contains the rhubarb. You just have to know whom you want to purge by this means and then wait, so as to gather up what you wanted from the subject.

All the same, when I bring along a full array of carefully finished pots, don't imagine that there wasn't a whole load of them that got chucked on the scrapheap. I too, in my time, gave entire talks in which the action, the thought and the words spun on their wheel in such a way that things went all wonky. Well, that went in the bin.

When I put *impediment* at the top of the column that includes *acting-out* and *embarrassment* at the top of the one next to it, which includes *passage à l'acte*, if, Piera, you want to single out the case of acting-out that you observed, and very finely so, if you want to distinguish it as what you call *acted-out transference* – which, of course, is a distinct idea, which is your idea and which is worthwhile discussing – it is still the case that you are referring to my chart because in your text you invoke the *embarrassment* your subject found himself in. Not really being used anywhere else but here, this is where you took note of the term.

It was evident in your observation that the patient had been impeded by the obstetrician from seeing his offspring come out of the maternal gates and that his turmoil at being powerless to overcome a fresh impediment of this sort drove him to throw the peacekeepers into a state of anxiety with the written assertion of his father's right to what I will call hylophagia, to specify the notion represented by the image of the devouring Saturn. Indeed, this fellow presents himself at the police station to say that nothing in the law prevents him from eating his baby, who has just died. On the contrary, it's evidently the embarrassment into which he is plunged by the calmness of the superintendent on this occasion, who didn't come down in the last shower, and the shock of the turmoil he wanted to provoke that leads to his *passage à l'acte*, that makes him carry out the kind of acts that get him put inside.

So, not to acknowledge, when clearly you're right on it, that I couldn't find a finer observation to explain what you know, that you're really right on it, that you've put your finger on it, is to betray yourself a bit.

This, which of course couldn't be reproached of anyone when it's a matter of handling things like this, fresh out the mould, authorizes me all the same to recall that my work, mine, is only of any interest if one uses it in the right way, that is to say, not as people have generally got into the habit of doing, the bad habit of doing, in the teaching – this is not directed at you, Piera – of notions that are grouped together in a sort of rounding up, just for the sake of padding things out.

Having given this reminder to indicate to you what gives you some right to be watchful of what I bring you and have chosen for you with such care, I'll resume my topic.

2

What I intend to say now on woman's relation to jouissance and to desire, I shall try, I too, to give you some inkling of through one of my observations.

One day a woman tells me that her husband, whose insistences are, if I may, part and parcel of the foundation of the marriage, leaves her alone a little too long for her not to notice. Given the way that she always feels what she gets from him to be more or less clumsy, she finds this something of a relief. This is when she comes out with a sentence that I'm nevertheless going to extract from her monologue, counting on you not to jump straightaway at the chance of savouring an irony that it would be quite unwarranted to attribute to me. She expresses herself as follows – *Small matter whether he desires me, provided he doesn't desire others.*

I won't go so far as to say that this is a commonplace or regular position. It can only assume its value from the ensuing part of the constellation such as it was to unfold in the associations that make up her monologue.

So here she is now, speaking about her state. She speaks about it, for a change, with peculiar precision, which brings out the fact that tumescence is not a man's privilege. This woman, whose sexuality is quite normal, bears witness to what occurs for her if, when she is driving, for example, an alert flashes up for a moving entity that makes her say to herself something along the lines of *God, a car!* Well, inexplicably, she notices the existence of a vaginal swelling. This is what strikes her that day and she notes that, during some periods, the phenomenon will occur when just any old object comes into her visual field, to all appearances utterly foreign to anything of a sexual nature. This state, which she says is not disagreeable, which is rather of an awkward nature, stops of its own accord.

With that, and *it bothers me to follow on with what I'm about to tell you,* she says, *this bears no relation,* of course, she tells me that each of her initiatives are dedicated to me, her analyst. *I can't say devoted,* she adds, *that would mean it was done with a certain aim, but no, any old object forces me to evoke you as a witness, not even to have your approval of what I see, no, simply your gaze, and in saying that, I'm going slightly too far, let's say that this gaze helps me to make each thing assume meaning.*

With that, she wryly mentions coming across, at an early date in her life, the well-known title of Steve Passeur's play, *Je vivrai un grand amour.* Has she come across this reference at other moments in her life? This question takes her back to the start of her married life, then further back, to speak about what was indeed her first love, the love one never forgets. He was a student from whom she soon parted, but with whom she remained in correspondence, in the full sense of the term. And everything she wrote to him, she says, was truly, I quote her, *a web of lies. Stitch by stitch, I created a character, what I wanted to be in his eyes, which I in no way was. I'm afraid it was a purely fictional enterprise, which I pursued most doggedly, enveloping myself,* she says, *in a kind of cocoon.* She adds, very gently – *You know, he had a tough time getting over it.*

With that, she comes back to what she does with me. *What I strive to be here with you is quite the opposite. I strive always to be truthful with you. I'm not writing a novel when I'm with you. I write it when I'm not with you.* She comes back to the threading, still stitch by stitch, of this dedicating of each gesture, which is not necessarily a gesture supposed to please me, nor one that would necessarily be in conformity with my thinking. You can't say she was forcing her talent. After all, what she wanted was not so much for me to look at her as for my gaze to replace hers. *I appeal to the assistance of your person. The gaze, my gaze, is insufficient when it comes to capturing everything that stands to be absorbed from the outside. It's not about watching me do something, it's about doing it for me.*

I'll bring this reading to an end, though I've still got a full page left. I just want to extract the only word of poor taste that comes out – *I am*, she says, *remote-controlled*. This does not express any metaphor and there is no *sentiment d'influence*, believe me, no feeling of being influenced. I'm only isolating this formula because you may have read it in the papers in connection with that left-wing politician who, after getting embroiled in a staged shooting, thought he ought to give us the immortal example of how, in politics, the left is always effectively remote-controlled by the right. Moreover, that's precisely how a tight relation of equal representation can be set up between the two sides.

So, where's all this leading us? To the vessel. Is the female vessel empty or full? It matters not, because it is sufficient unto itself, even if it is *to be consummated stupidly*, as my patient puts it. Nothing is lacking. The presence of the object is, so to say, an extra. Why? Because this presence is not linked to the lack of the object cause of desire, to the $(-\varphi)$ to which it is bound in men.

Men's anxiety is linked to the possibility of *not being able*. Hence the myth, a very male one, that makes the woman the equivalent of one of his ribs. One of his ribs was removed, we don't know which, and besides, he's not missing any, but it's clear that in this myth of the rib the lost object is what's involved. For man, woman is an object fashioned therefrom.

Anxiety exists in women too. Kierkegaard, who must have had something of the Tiresias about him, probably more than I because I prize my peepers, even says that women are more susceptible to anxiety than men. Should we believe it? In truth, what matters to us is to grasp the woman's bond to the infinite possibilities or rather indeterminate possibilities of desire in the field that stretches out around her.

She tempts herself by tempting the Other, in which myth will serve us here too. As the complement to the earlier myth shows, that of the famous story of the apple, you can tempt him with just about any old object, even one that is dispensable for her, because, after all, what was she going to do with that apple? Nothing more than a fish would.[1] But it so happens that this apple was already good enough, little fish that it was, to hook the angler. The desire of the Other is what interests her.

To accentuate this slightly better, I would say that desire is a mercantile thing, that there is a pricing of desire that one pushes up and down culturally and that the pattern and the level of love depend from one minute to the next on the price one sets on desire in the marketplace. Love, in so far as it is itself a *value*, as the philosophers say very well, is made from the idealization of desire. I say idealization, because our patient from earlier on didn't speak about her husband's desire as a sick desire. Her prizing it, that's what love is. She's not really so keen on him evincing it, that's not essential, but that's the way it is.

With respect to woman's jouissance, which fully warrants all kinds of care from the partner being focused upon her, and she knows very well how to obtain this, experience teaches us that the partner's impotence can be very well accepted, along with his technical offences, because the thing also rears its head on the occasion of the fiasco, as Stendhal remarked. In cases where this impotence is lasting, although one occasionally sees her enlisting after a certain while some aid that is reputed to be more efficient, it seems that this is more out of a kind of delicacy, so that it won't be said that anyone is being refused, for any reason that may be evoked.

If you call to mind my formulas on masochism from last time, which are designed, you will see, to restore to masochism, be it the pervert's masochism, moral masochism, or women's masochism, its otherwise ungraspable unity, if you call to mind what I emphasized about the occultation, by the Other's jouissance, or by the jouissance that looks to be alleged of the Other, of an anxiety that it's incontestably a matter of awakening, you will see that women's masochism takes on a completely different meaning, a fairly ironic meaning, and a completely different scope.

It can only be caught hold of when one has really grasped that one has to assert, in principle, that women's masochism is a male fantasy.

Second point. In this fantasy, it is by proxy and in relation to the masochistic structure that is imagined in woman that man sustains his jouissance through something that is his own anxiety. This is what the object covers over. In men, the object is the condition of desire. Jouissance depends on this question. Now, desire is merely covering over anxiety. You can see the margin he still has to cover to be in range of jouissance.

For women, the desire of the Other is the means by which her jouissance will have an object that is, as it were, suitable. Her anxiety is only anxiety faced with the desire of the Other and, at the end of the day, she doesn't really know what it covers over. To go further into my formulas, I will say that in man's realm there is always the presence of some imposture. In the woman's, if something corresponds to this, then it's the masquerade, as we already said in its time in reference to Joan Riviere's article, but that's something altogether different.

By and large, woman is much more real and much truer than man, in that she knows the worth of the yardstick of what she is dealing with in desire, in that she takes this route with the greatest peace of mind and in that she has, if I may, a certain disdain for its being mis-deigned, which is a satisfaction man cannot give himself. He cannot disdain the mis-deigning of desire, because it is his very nature to deign.

Letting his desire for a woman be seen can clearly be anguishing on occasion. Why so? In passing, I would ask you to note the distinction between the dimension of *letting something be seen* and the voyeurism/exhibitionism couple. There isn't only showing and seeing, there is also *letting something be seen*. For women, whose danger at the very most comes from the masquerade, the something that is there to be let seen is *what there is*. Of course, if there's not very much, it's anxiety provoking, but it's still *what there is*, whereas for men, letting their desire be seen essentially amounts to letting *what there is not* be seen.

So, you see, don't believe that this situation, whose demonstration might strike you as fairly complex, is for all that to be taken as something especially desperate. Though it most certainly doesn't represent it as something easy, can you fail to spot the access to jouissance that it opens for the man?

The fact no less remains that all of this is very easy to handle if all you expect from it is happiness.

This remark is a conclusive one, so now we shall move into the example I find myself, all told, poised to make you benefit from, on account of the favour that we all owe to Granoff for having introduced it here.

3

To understand what Lucia Tower tells us in her article on the two men she had in her charge, I don't think I can find a better preamble, as I told you, than the image of Don Juan.

I've gone back over the question a great deal lately. I can't make you go back through the maze. Read the dreadful book by Rank called *Die Don-Juan-Gestalt*. A cat couldn't find her kittens, it's such a mess. But if you have the thread I'm about to give you, it will seem much clearer. Don Juan is a woman's dream.

Sometimes it takes a man who would still be his same old self, as woman can in a certain way pride herself on being in relation to man. Don Juan is a man who would lack nothing. This is perfectly tangible in the term I'm going to have to come back to in connection with the general structure of masochism. This almost sounds like some jape, but Don Juan's relation to the image of the father qua un-castrated is a pure feminine image. This relation is perfectly legible in what you can uncover in Rank's labyrinthine twists and turns. If we manage to link him back to a certain state of myth and rite, Don Juan would represent, so he tells us, and there his intuition guides him, he who in times now passed was capable of putting a bit of soul into things without losing his soul. The notorious practice of the *Jus primae noctis*, just like the practice, a mythical one as you know, of the deflowering priest on the *Prima noctes*, are purportedly founded on this. But *Don Juan* is a fine story, which functions and produces its effect for those who are not acquainted with all these acts of kindness. Certainly they are not absent from Mozart's song, to be found more on the side of *Le nozze di Figaro* than *Don Giovanni*.

The palpable trace of what I'm putting forward concerning Don Juan is that for him man's complex relation to his object is effaced, but at the price of accepting his radical imposture. Don Juan's prestige is linked to his acceptance of this imposture. He is always in the stead of someone else. He is, if I may, the absolute object.

Notice that it's not said that he inspires desire in the least. Though he slips into women's beds, no one knows how he got there. One might even say that he doesn't have any desire either. He stands in relation to something with respect to which he fulfils a certain function. You may call this something the *odor di femmina* and that takes us a long way. But desire plays such a paltry role in the affair that, when the *odor di femmina* does pass by, he is quite capable of failing to notice that it's Donna Elvira – to wit, the one he's had it up to here with – who's just crossed the stage.

It really needs to be said that he is not an anxiety-provoking character for women. When it happens that a woman really feels she is the object at the centre of a desire, well, believe me, that's when she really takes flight.

We're going to move now, if we can, into Lucia Tower's story.

She has two men, in analysis I mean. As she says, she always has very satisfying relations with them on the human level. Don't make out that I'm saying that this is a straightforward business, nor that they don't go on for quite a while. They are both cases of anxiety neurosis. At least that is the diagnosis she settles on, having examined every angle. Both men have had, as is fitting, a few difficulties with their mothers and their *female siblings*, that is, sisters, but put on the same level as brothers. They are both hitched up with women that they've chosen, so we are told, so as to be able to give vent to a certain number of aggressive tendencies, and others besides, and thereby protect themselves by means of an inclination, which, my goodness, is analytically incontestable, towards the other sex. *With both men, she tells us, I was quite aware of the contributions which they themselves made to the difficulties with their wives, namely,* she says, *that both were too submissive, too hostile, in a sense too devoted, and both wives,* she tells us, because she fixes her spy-glass on the situation with the greatest of ease to make her assessment, *both wives were frustrated for lack of sufficient uninhibited masculine assertiveness from their husbands.* In other words, these chaps don't affect enough semblance. There we enter the thick of things. She has her own idea about the affair.

As for her, of course, without knowing what might ensnare her in all that, she goes through *phases of protectiveness,* she is a bit *too protective,* albeit differently in each case. In the case of the first man, she protects his wife a bit too much. In the case of the second, the man himself, a bit too much. What reassures her is that she is much more favourably inclined towards the second man, because the first *presented some not too attractive psychosexual problems.* We really need to read things in their innocence and freshness. But the first man presents himself in a way that is not really so distinct from the other.

Both of them irritate her with their *mumbling, halting speech, circumstantiality* – which means they say it all and then some – *repetitiveness, minutiae.* Well, all the same, she's an analyst and what she notices in the first man is his tendency to destroy her *power as an analyst.* For the second, rather than destroy her as a frustrating object, it's a matter of acquiring an object from her. In this regard, she remarks that it might be because the second is more narcissistic. In truth, as those of you who are a little cultivated may notice, this doesn't really sit well with the other references we might have on narcissism. On the other hand, it's not really narcissism that is at stake here in his regard, but what is known as the anaclitic side, as she is about to see in what comes next.

As long and fastidious as the path trodden with one and the other is, without anything evincing any efficacy in analysing the transference, it is still nonetheless the case that something endures in her that is not fundamentally unpleasant and the countertransference responses she perceives in herself are, she says, *of a reasonably normal character*, they are a long way from crossing the limit to what could be stirred up *in any female analyst who might*, with fellows such as these, *be somewhat off guard.* She is *consistently and reasonably well on guard.*

Especially so where her first patient is concerned. She is attentive to what is going on with his wife. A bit more precisely, perhaps, she watches over her. When she learns that his wife has had a little psychosomatic mishap, she tells herself that it might not be so bad, she had feared that the woman was drifting off a bit towards psychosis, but now her anxiety is well bound.

And then, she thinks no more of it and the same situation goes on. Analyse as she might everything that occurs in the transference, right up to the use that the patient, this first one, makes in the analysis of his conflicts with his wife so as to obtain from his analyst even more attention and compensations that he never got from his mother, things still won't move on.

What is it that was to trigger the movement and make things advance? A dream, she tells us, that she, the analyst, has. Through this dream she realizes that it's perhaps not so sure that things are really going so badly with his wife.

In the dream, this woman welcomes her into her home most hospitably and shows her in every which way that she has no intention of sabotaging her husband's analysis, which until then had been one of the presuppositions of the affair, and that she is therefore quite ready to stand alongside the analyst in a position that we shall call, to translate the atmosphere of the dream, cooperative. This sets the wheels in motion for our analyst. She understands that something needs to be completely revised in her conception of her patient, that this fellow really is seeking in his couple to do what has to be done to put his wife at ease, in other words, that this bloke's desire is not nearly as adrift as all that, that the chap nevertheless takes himself seriously, that there is a way of attending to him. In other terms, he's capable of going along with it, of being a man, the dignity of which had until then been denied him.

Once she's made this discovery, once she's realigned the axis of her relation to her patient's desire, once she's realized that she had misrecognized how things stood, she can really undertake with him a review of everything that up until then had been played out illusively, the transference claims turn out to have been an imposture, and from that moment on, she tells us, everything changes.

But how does it change, and in what direction?

You have to read her to understand that from that moment on the analysis becomes particularly hard for her to bear. Everything happens, she says, in the midst of a storm of *profound depressive feelings and naked rage*, as if he were putting her to the test *cell by cell*. If a moment's inattention, she tells us, should lead her to make *even one slightest false move*, should any gesture or word ring hollow, she feels *he would fall apart*. Though she can't see everything, she nevertheless knows how to name what's involved. It is, she says, *phallic sadism couched in oral language*.

What holds our attention here? Two things.

Firstly, the very terms that are employed here confirm what I designated for you as being in the nature of sadism, namely, that the sadistic quest aims at the object and, within the object, the little piece that's missing. Once the truth of his desire has been recognized, what's really involved in the way the patient behaves, whose anomalies described as *not too attractive* are certainly of a sadistic order, is a search for the object.

Secondly, putting oneself on the line through which the sadistic object-search passes in no way amounts to being a masochist. Our Lucia Tower accuses herself of nothing of the sort and we have no need to impute it to her. Simply, she kicks up a storm and it comes down on her from a character to whom she only really started to relate in the transference once her desire was implicated, as she emphasizes with particular courage, and in the function where she herself is in the posture of a third-party rival to characters from her own history. Therefore, she bears the consequences of this desire, to the point that she feels what analysts include under the label *carry over*, which designates the phenomenon in which the effects of countertransference are most evident. It's when you carry on thinking about one patient when you're with another one.

And yet, she tells us, though she was *feeling at a very low ebb*, all this *was dispelled suddenly and amusingly*. Setting off on vacation during one of her annual breaks, she realizes that she's not carrying anything of this business with her. It doesn't concern her one bit. She is truly in the mythical position of the superlatively free and ethereal Don Juan as he exits the bedchamber where he was up to his usual tricks.

Once this scission, this un-sticking, has been accomplished, she finds once more her efficacy, her adaptation to the case, and, if I may say so, the implacable nakedness of her gaze. She had to take stock of her relation to her desire and realize that, as complex as one can suppose it to be – because she indicates that she's got her own problems as well – it is only ever something that at the end of the day she can keep a distance from.

That's where I'm going to pick up from next time.

20 March 1963

XV

MEN'S BUSINESS

Lucia Tower and the Oedipal comedy
What lacks, men's business
What is ridiculously termed perversion
A vessel with neither inside nor outside
Circumcision, an institution

So, we're getting straight back to the point.

I'm going to ask you a collective question. Would those who think they won't be able to make our appointment next Wednesday due to the school holidays please raise their hands?

OK. Well, there won't be any Seminar next Wednesday, nor the following one, in the week known as Palm Week, nor the one after that, in the week known as Easter Week. So we'll resume on the Wednesday of the week known as Quasimodo Week, that is, 24 April.

1

I'm taking up the items set down by Lucia Tower, whom I find myself having taken as an example, from a certain angle of what I shall call the easiness of women's position with respect to the relation to desire.

The term *easiness* has an ambiguous scope here. Let's say that a lesser implication in the difficulties of desire allowed her to reason within the psychoanalytic position if not more soundly then at least more freely, in her article, the said article on countertransference.

Through the effect of what there she calls, quite soundly, her countertransference, and which I will call her inner auto-critic, she realized she'd neglected something of what might be called the fitting appreciation or axiation of her patient's desire. She doesn't give us specifically what she said at that moment, she only tells us that she reviewed the patient's transferential requirements, this time setting things straight for him.

Now, while doing this, she was only able to give him the impression that she was sensitive to what she herself had just discovered – namely, that he takes much greater care with his wife, he arranges much more of what goes on in the marital situation, than she'd suspected. And the patient was only able to translate this rectification, so it seems, in the following terms – his desire is much less lacking in sway over his analyst than he thought, and it is not ruled out that this woman, who is his analyst, might be made, up to a certain point, *to bend* to his desire – *to stoop* in English, to bend. *She Stoops to Conquer*, the title of a comedy by Sheridan.[1] This at least is what Lucia Tower brings us in these terms. We can but trust her.

She also underlines for us that it's out of the question for such a thing to occur. In this respect she's *well on guard*, she's *aware* of it. She's no baby, and anyway, when is a woman a baby? But that's not where the question lies. Through this rectification, which appears to him as a concession, an opening that is made for him, the patient's desire is truly put back in its place. Now, the whole question is that he was never able to find this place. That's what his anxiety neurosis is.

What she encounters at that moment, as we said last time, is an outburst from her patient. It might not be a bad idea for me to go back over this a bit.

This outburst puts pressure on her. She is subjected to scrutiny, *scrutinized* as one says in English, which makes her feel like she can't make the *slightest false move*. She says that she's being put to the test, *cell by cell*, and, *if I were to fail to meet this test, he would fall apart*.

What does that mean? Precisely that, having sought out the man's desire, what she encounters from him by way of response is not a search for her desire but the search for *a*, for the object, the true object, for what's at stake in desire, which isn't the Other, but this leftover, the *a*. She sustains this search. This is what she refers to as developing a greater *amount of masochism* than she thought she had.

I'm telling you this because that's what she wrote. But hear this – she's mistaken. She's not at all cut out for going into the masochistic dialogue. Her relationship with the Other, the patient-Other, the male Other – whom she misses so entirely, as you'll see – demonstrates this quite well enough.

She copes extremely well, in spite of how exhausting it is. As the holidays approach, she's *feeling at a very low ebb*. Fortunately, vacation time arrives and *suddenly and amusingly* she realizes that, after all, none of that is going on any longer now that the sessions have come to a stop. She shakes herself off and thinks about other things.

Why? Because she knows quite well that search as he might, he will never find anything. That's precisely the point, for him to realize that there's nothing to be found, because that which for the man, for male desire, forms the object of his search concerns no one, as it were, but him.

This is the object of today's lesson. What he's looking for is $(-\varphi)$, what she lacks – but that's men's business.

Let me tell you this, and don't get all worked up – she knows very well that she doesn't lack anything. Or rather, that the mode by which lack plays a role in feminine development is not to be situated at the level at which the man's desire is seeking it out, when what's really involved is the sadistic search I stressed at the start of the year, which consists in making emerge what must be in the partner at the supposed place of lack.

That is what he has to grieve for. In the text she states very clearly that what they're doing together is a work of mourning. He has to mourn ever being able to find in his partner – in so far as she has positioned herself as a female partner, without really knowing what she was doing – his own lack, $(-\varphi)$, primary castration, man's fundamental castration as I designated it for you at the level of its biological root, of the particularities of the instrument of copulation at this level of the animal scale.

Once he'd mourned it, everything went well, Lucia Tower tells us. What does that mean? Precisely that with this fellow, who's never got to this level before, we'll be able to move into what you'll permit me to call for this occasion the Oedipal comedy. We'll be able to start having a laugh – *Dad's the one who did all that.*

That's the point. We've known it for a long while, don't forget Jones and the *moralisches Entgegenkommen*, the readiness to oblige moral prohibition. If he's castrated, it's because of the law. The comedy of the law is going to be played out. We are very much at ease here, this is well known and it's been set down. In a word, here we have this chap's desire taking the paths traced out by law, demonstrating once again that the norm of desire and the law are one and the same thing.

Have I made that sufficiently audible to take the next step?

Ah, not quite, because I haven't told you the difference between what was there beforehand and what's been surmounted thanks to this mourning.

Well now, what was there before was, properly speaking, his fault. He was buckling under the weight of his burden, under the weight of his (– φ). He was *exceedingly sinful* – remember the use I made of that passage from Saint Paul back when.

So I'm taking the next step.

2

Women have no trouble and up to a certain point run no risk in seeking out what's at stake in men's desire.

I can do no less on this occasion than remind you of the famous passage I cited a long time ago from the text attributed to Solomon. I'll give you it in Latin, which brings out its full flavour – *Tria sunt difficilia mihi*, says the wise king, *et quartum penitus ignoro*, there are four things I can say nothing of, because no trace is left behind, *viam aquilae in caelo*, the trace of the way of an eagle in the air, the way of a serpent upon a rock, the way of a ship in the midst of the sea, *et viam viri in adulescentula*, and the trace of a man on a maid. No trace.

It is desire that is involved here and not what comes about when the object as such comes to the fore. That leaves to one side the effects on the *adulescentula* of a good many things, starting with exhibitionism and, behind that, the primal scene. Something else is involved.

So, how are things to be tackled if we want to get an idea of what's going on in the woman regarding this thing we have an inkling of, namely, her having a port of entry towards lack?

People keep harping on about this business of *Penisneid*. This is where I think it necessary to stress the difference.

Of course there is a constitution of the object *a* of desire for her as well. It so happens that women speak. Some might regret it, but it's a fact. Therefore she too wants the object, and even one object in so far as she doesn't have it. That indeed is what Freud explains to us, her demand for the penis will remain to the end bound to the relationship with her mother, that is, with demand. It is in the dependence on demand that the object *a* is constituted for a woman. She knows very well that, in the Oedipus complex, it's not about being stronger and more desirable than her mother – because she notices quite quickly that time's on her side – but having the object. The fundamental dissatisfaction that's involved in the structure of desire is, if I may say so, pre-castrative. If it comes about that she takes an interest in castration as such, (– φ), it's to the extent that she will venture into men's problems. It's secondary. It's deutero-phallic, as Jones quite rightly put it.

This then is what the whole obscurity of the debate revolves around, a debate that ultimately has never been unravelled, on the famous phallicism of women, a debate in which every author is just as right as the next, for want of ever having found out where the genuine articulation lies. I won't make out that you're going to keep it present and right away marked out in your minds, but I mean to lead you right around it, along enough paths for you to end up knowing where it is and where a skip is made when people theorize.

For the woman, it is what initially she doesn't *have* that consti-tutes the object of her desire at the start, whereas, for the man, it is what he *is* not, and that's where he falters.

This is why I made you move along the path of the Don Juan fantasy. The Don Juan fantasy is a woman's fantasy because it corresponds to a woman's wish for an image that would fulfil its function, a fantasmatic function, that there be one of them, one of these men, who has it – which, from experience, is clearly a mis-recognition of reality – better still, that he always has it, that he can't lose it. Precisely what is implied by the position of Don Juan in the fantasy is that no woman may take it from him, and that's the crux of it. That's what he has in common with women, whom one cannot take it from, of course, because they don't have it.

What women see in the homage of men's desire is that this object – let's be careful with our terminology – becomes her belonging. This means nothing more than what I just put forward, that it can't be lost. The lost member of Osiris, that is the object of a woman's search and attention. The fundamental myth of the sexual dialectic between man and woman has been sufficiently accentuated by a whole tradition. And likewise women's psychological experience, in the sense this word carries in Paul Bourget's writings, tells us that a woman doesn't always think that a man goes astray with another woman. Don Juan assures her that there is one man who never gets lost.

Clearly, there are other privileged and typical ways of solving the difficult problem of woman's relationship with *a*. There is, if you will, another fantasy, but it's not the first that springs to mind, she's not the one who came up with it, she finds it ready-made. To take an interest in it, she's got to have the stomach for it.

I have in mind, in a normal register, the kind of tough fucker of which Saint Teresa of Ávila gives us the noblest example. A point of access is also given to us by the example of the lover of priests, though for her it is a more imaginary one. Move up a notch and you've got an erotomaniac. The difference depends on the level at which the man's desire collaborates with what he represents, more or less imaginarily, as wholly merging with the *a*.

I've alluded to Saint Teresa of Ávila. I could've spoken of the blessed Marguerite Marie Alacoque, who has the advantage of letting us see the very shape of the *a* in the Sacred Heart. For the lover of priests we aren't able to say starkly, and crudely, that institutionalized castration is enough to establish it, but at any rate this is the sense in which we're going to state that the *a* as such, having been singled out perfectly, is brought to the fore and offered her as the object elect of her desire. For the erotomaniac, there's no need for the work to be prepared for her, she does it herself.

So we find ourselves brought back to the previous problem, namely, the problem of what we can articulate of the relationship between the man and these various *a* objects such as they are proposed, or imposed, and which one has more or less at one's disposal, as furnishing the object of desire with its ultimate status in its relation to castration.

I ask you to think back for a moment to my mirror stage.

A while ago now, a film was shown that had been shot in a special school in England, in an effort to make what could be provided through the observation of children tie in to psychoanalytic genetics. The worth of the document was all that much greater for having been filmed without the faintest preconceived idea. The whole field of what can be observed in the infant's confrontation with the mirror was covered, which moreover fully confirmed the initial and final dates I set down.

I remember that this film was one of the last things presented in the Société psychanalytique de Paris before we went our separate ways. The separation was quite close at hand and maybe the film was only watched somewhat distractedly. But for my part I had my wits about me and I still recall the gripping image of the little girl before the mirror. If there is something that concretizes this reference to the non-specularizable dimension that I pointed up last year, then it's this little girl's gesture, her hand quickly passing over the gamma of the junction where her belly meets her thighs, like a moment of giddiness faced with what she sees.

As for the little boy, the poor mug, he looks down at the problematic little tap. He vaguely suspects that something's odd down there. Then, he has to learn, and to his cost, that what he's got there doesn't exist, I mean, up against what dad's got, what the big brothers have got, and so on. You're familiar with the whole initial dialectic of comparison. Next, he will learn that not only does it not exist, but that it doesn't want to know anything, or more precisely that it does as it pleases. To spell it out, he will have to learn step by step, through his individual experience, to strike it off the map of his narcissism, precisely so that it can start to be useful.

I'm not saying that it's as easy as all that and it would be nonsense to attribute me with such a thing because, naturally, there's also the fact that the more you push it down, the more it bobs back up to the surface. At the end of the day this game is the principle of homosexual attachment, namely – *I play loser takes all.*

I'm just giving you an indication here, but one that will meet up with what you've been indicated regarding the fundamental structure of what is ridiculously called perversion. At each moment of homosexual attachment, castration is what's at issue. This castration is what assures the homosexual that the (– φ) is the object of the game, and it is inasmuch as he loses that he wins.

I'm coming round to illustrating what posed a problem last time, much to my surprise, in my reminder about the mustard pot.

One of my listeners, a particularly attentive one, told me – *That was going well, that mustard pot, at least there were a number of us who didn't find it too off-putting, but now you're reintroducing the question of its content, you're filling it halfway, and with what?*

Let's go then.

The (– φ) is the emptiness of the vessel, the same vase that defines *Homo faber*. If women, so we are told, are primordially weavers, men are surely potters. This is even the sole angle that, in the human species, provides a footing for the tedious refrain that runs, *the thread is to the needle as girl is to boy*. A reference that makes itself out to be natural. It's not as natural as all that. Of course, women do present themselves with the appearance of the vase, the vessel, and that's clearly what tricks her partner, the *Homo faber* in question, the potter. He imagines that this vessel might contain the object of his desire.

Only, look where this leads us. It's inscribed in our experience, it's been spelt out step by step, which removes any appearance of deduction or reconstruction from what I'm telling you. It was spotted without starting off from the right place in the premises, but spotted it was, long before any understanding of what it meant. The fantasmatic presence of the phallus at the bottom of the vessel, I mean the phallus of another man, is an everyday object of our analytic experience. I don't need to go back to Solomon again to tell you that this presence is entirely fantasmatic.

Of course, there are things that can be found in this vessel and they're very interesting as far as desire is concerned, the egg, for instance. But in the end, that comes from the inside and proves for us that, if vessel there is, it complicates this scheme ever so slightly. The egg can benefit from the encounters that are in the offing for it thanks to this fundamental misunderstanding, I mean that it doesn't encounter the spermatozoon in vain, but, after all, parthenogenesis is not ruled out in the future. In the meantime, insemination can take on quite different forms. Moreover, it's back shop that the really interesting vessel is to be found, the uterus. It's objectively interesting and it's psychically interesting too, as interesting as can be – I mean that, as soon as there is maternity, it's largely enough to invest the woman's interest as a whole. At the time of pregnancy, as everyone knows, all that fuss about men's desire becomes slightly superfluous.

So, let's get to our pot from the other day, our decent little pot among the very first ceramics, and match it to $(-\varphi)$. It's the pot of castration.

Just for a moment, for the sake of demonstration, allow me to put into a neighbouring pot what for men can form the a, the object of desire.

These two pots are here for an apologue that is designed to stress that a, the object of desire, only has any meaning for men when it has been poured back into the emptiness of primordial castration.

The first tying-in between male desire and castration can only be produced on the basis of secondary narcissism, that is, when a becomes detached, when it falls away from $i(a)$, from the narcissistic image. There is a phenomenon here which is the constitutive phenomenon of what may be termed the *rim*. As I told you last year with regard to my topological analysis, nothing has a greater structuring function than the shape of the vessel, than the shape of its rim, than the cut whereby it is singled out as a vessel.

A long while back, the possibility of a genuine logic forged in accordance with the psychoanalytic field was just starting to take shape. This is still to be done, though I've given you more than just a taste – of Greater and Lesser Logic – I'm saying logic and not dialectics. One Imre Hermann started to devote himself to it, admittedly in a very confused way for want of any dialectical articulation, but in the end he sketched out the phenomenon he qualified as *Randbevorzugung*, the predeliction, the preference in the analytic phenomenal field for rim phenomena.

The rim of the pot of castration is a good round rim, a perfectly decent rim that has none of those sophisticated complications I introduced you to with the Möbius strip. It's very easy, however, to introduce them. All we have to do is make two opposite points on the rim of the vessel join up by turning the surfaces inside out as we go along, so that they join up as they do on the Möbius band, and we're looking at a vessel that allows us to pass with the greatest of ease from the inner face to the outer face without ever having to go over the rim.

This is what happens at the level of the other little pots, the a pots, and this is where anxiety starts.

A metaphor like this would never be enough, of course, to repro-

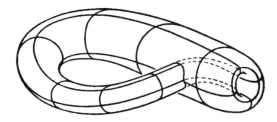

Structure of the *a* pots (the Klein bottle)

duce what has to be explained, namely, that the little originative pot has the closest relationship to what's at stake in sexual potency, with the intermittent surging of its force. A whole series of images – Chinese, Japanese and others – which it's quite easy to get a look at, of an eroto-propaedeutics, or even an erotics properly speaking, make this quite accessible. It wouldn't be hard to find a stack of images of this kind in our culture either.

This is not what provokes anxiety. The decanting allows us to grasp how the *a* takes on its value by coming over into the minus-*phi* pot and there being minus-*a*. The vessel is henceforth half-empty at the same time as it is half-full. But, as I told you last time, the phenomenon of decanting is not what's essential. What's essential is the phenomenon of the transfiguration of the vessel. If then this vessel becomes more anguishing, it's inasmuch as the *a* comes to half fill the already constituted hollow of originative castration.

We still need to add that this *a* comes from elsewhere and that it's only constituted by the intermediary of the desire of the Other. This is where we meet up with anxiety again and the ambiguous shape of the edge of the other vessel which, built in this way, allows neither inside nor outside to be distinguished.

Anxiety thus comes to be constituted and to take up its place in a relationship that is instituted beyond the emptiness of a first phase, if I may say so, of castration. This is why the subject has but one desire when it comes to this first castration and that is to get back to it.

After the coming break, I'm going to be speaking to you at length about masochism. Looking at it today is out of the question. If you want to get ready to hear what I have to say about it, I'll give you right now – it's a slip on my part not to have done it sooner – a reference to a precious article that draws on the most substantial experience and whose author is someone I'm really very sad circumstances have forbidden me from collaborating with. The article in question is by Grunberger, *Esquisse d'une théorie psycho-dynamique du masochisme*, in the April–June 1954 issue of the *Revue française de psychanalyse*, number two of volume XVIII.[2] I know not whether this work has been given the attention it deserves, even though it was published in London, thanks to the wealth of the Foundation of the Institute of Psychoanalysis. To what is this oversight due? I'm not about to settle the matter.

In this article, you will find noted – I'm only mentioning it here briefly to show you the value of the material that can be got from it – how recourse to the imaginary dimension of castration, to an *I'd like them to be snipped off*, can be a soothing, welcome way out of the masochist's anxiety.

I find here merely an indication of the first phase of castration inasmuch as the subject comes back to it, in so far as it becomes a point that he targets. This is certainly not a phenomenon that provides in the slightest the last word on this complex structure and, moreover, I've already got things under way in such a fashion that you now know that when it comes to the links between anxiety and masochism, I'm aiming at a point that is quite different from the subject's momentary turmoil.

This brings us back to what I stressed once before, at the end of one of my recent lessons, with regard to circumcision.

3

Stein, I don't know where you've got to in your ongoing commentary on *Totem and Taboo*, but this might also lead you to approach *Moses and Monotheism*.

I think you cannot do otherwise than go to it and then you will be struck by the complete evasion of the problem – which is nevertheless a structuring problem if ever there was – of knowing whether something at the level of the Mosaic institution reflects the inaugural cultural complex and what the function of the institution of circumcision might have been in this regard.

In any case, you cannot fail to compare the excision of the foreskin with the odd little twisting object I put in your hands at the start of the year, materialized, so that you could see how it is structured when fashioned in the form of a little piece of card. It had to do with what results from the central cut of the cross-cap, in so far as it isolates something that is defined as embodying what is non-specularizable. This can be linked in with the constitution of the autonomy of the small *a* of the object of desire.

Circumcision embodies, in the proper sense of the word, the fact that something akin to an order may be brought into this hole, into this constitutive failing of primordial castration. All the coordinates of circumcision, the ritualistic, even mythical configuration of the primordial access points of initiation where it is operative, show that it has the clearest possible relation to the normativation of the object of desire.

The circumcised man is consecrated – consecrated less to a law than to a certain relation to the Other, and this is why it has to do with the *a*. The fact remains that we've now reached the point to which I mean to bring the fire of sunlight, namely, the level at which we can find in the configuration of history something that is supported by an A, which here is pretty much the God of Judeo-Christian tradition. What circumcision signifies remains to be seen.

It is absolutely astonishing that, in a setting as Judaic as psychoanalysis is, there has been no further examination of the texts that were gone over a hundred thousand times from the Church Fathers to the fathers of the Reformation, as it were, and on up to the eighteenth century, I mean the fertile period of the Reformation.

What we are told in Chapter XVII of Genesis concerns the fundamental character of the law of circumcision inasmuch as it is part of the Covenant imparted by Yahweh out of the midst of the bush. This chapter dates the institution of circumcision back to Abraham. Without doubt, in the eyes of exegetic criticism this passage seems to be a sacerdotal addition, very appreciably later than the Jehovist and Elohist traditions, that is, the two primordial texts that make up the books of the Law.

In Chapter XXXIV, however, we have the famous episode, which is not lacking in humour, concerning the abduction of Dinah, sister of Simeon and Levi, daughter of Jacob. For Shechem, the man who has taken her, it is a matter of obtaining her from her brothers. Simeon and Levi demand that he be circumcised – *We cannot give our sister to one that is uncircumcised, we would be dishonoured.* There has clearly been a superposition of the two texts here. Indeed, we don't know if it's just one man who is to be circumcised, or all the Shechemites as one. Of course, this alliance could not be struck in the name of two families alone, but in the name of the two races. All the Shechemites get circumcised, which leaves them sore for three days and which the others take advantage of to slay them.

This is one of the beguiling episodes that was a bit beyond Monsieur Voltaire's *comprenoire*, leading him to speak so unfavourably of this book, a book which is quite admirable when it comes to the revelation of what is called the signifier as such.

All the same, this is designed to make us think that the law of circumcision doesn't date back only to Moses. I'm merely highlighting here the problems that have already been raised on this score.

Since this has to do with Moses and since Moses has ostensibly

been acknowledged in our sphere as having been Egyptian, it would
not be entirely misplaced to ask ourselves about the relationships
between Judaic circumcision and the circumcision of the Egyptians.
This will excuse me for drawing out what I have to say to you today
for another five minutes or thereabouts, so that what I've written up
on the blackboard doesn't get lost.

A certain number of writers from antiquity speak of the Egyptians'
circumcision. Notably, the aged Herodotus, who certainly witters
on in some parts but who is often very precious, doesn't leave any
room for doubt that in his time, when Egypt was well into the Late
Period, all Egyptians practised circumcision. So widespread is it in
his report that he states that all the Semites of Syria and Palestine
owe this custom to the Egyptians. Some have passed censure on
this, and at length, and, after all, no one's forcing us to believe him.
Oddly enough, he says the same for the Colchians, claiming them to
be an Egyptian colony, but let's leave that be.

Being Greek and being of his time, no doubt he can't understand
this to be anything other than a cleanliness measure. He underlines
for us how the Egyptians always prefer being clean, καθαροί, over
looking good. By which Herodotus, in being Greek, doesn't hide
the fact that in his eyes to be circumcised is always to be somewhat
disfigured.

Fortunately, we have more direct accounts of the circumcision of
the Egyptians. We have two accounts that I shall call iconographic
– and you will tell me that's not much.

One is from the Old Kingdom. It is in Saqqara, in the tomb
of the physician Ankhmahor. They say that he was a physician
because the tomb walls are covered with scenes of operations. One
of these walls shows us two scenes of circumcision, the left-hand
one I've reproduced here. I don't know if I've managed to make my
drawing legible, it just accentuates the lines that are visible. Here is
the boy who is being circumcised. Here is his organ. Another boy
behind him is holding onto his hands, because that's what it takes.
A character who is a priest, this being a qualification I won't dwell
on today, is here. He is holding the organ in his left hand and in the
other this oblong object which is a cutter made of stone.

We meet this cutter again in another text that until now has
remained completely enigmatic, a biblical text. It tells how, after
the episode of the burning bush, Moses is informed that all those
in Egypt who remembered his murder of an Egyptian have now
passed away and so he may return. He does return, but when he
stops on the road back – it is translated in the old way as an inn,
but let's leave that – Yahweh attacks him, seeking to kill him. That
is all we are told. Zipporah, his wife, then circumcises her son, who

is an infant, and, touching Moses with the foreskin, through this operation, this contact, mysteriously protects Moses, who is not circumcised, from Yahweh's attack. Yahweh then backs off.

It is written that Zipporah circumcises her son with a sharp stone. We find this cutter forty-odd years later because there is also the episode of the ordeals imposed on the Egyptians, the Ten Plagues, when, as he is about to enter the land of Canaan, Joshua receives the order – *Take thee flint knives and circumcise all who are here, all who will enter the land of Canaan.* This refers to all those who were born during the desert years, when they could not be circumcised. Yahweh adds – *This day I have rolled away from off you* – which is translated as lifted, suspended – *the reproach of Egypt.*

I'm reminding you of these texts not because I intend to make use of all of them, but because at least they may stimulate your desire or need to go and look them up.

For the time being, I shall stick with the flint cutter. At the very least, it indicates that the ceremony of circumcision has a very ancient origin. This is confirmed by the discovery – by Elliot Smith, near Luxor if memory serves, probably at Naga ed-Deir – of two corpses bearing the trace of circumcision. They are from the prehistoric period, in other words they were not mummified in accordance with the forms that would allow them to be dated in history. The simple fact of the flint cutter assigns to this ceremony an origin that stretches back at least to the Neolithic Age.

As for the rest, to lay any doubt to rest, three Egyptian letters, these three here, which are respectively an S, a B and a T, *SeBeTh*, expressly indicate that circumcision is involved. The sign marked out here is an hapax. It has only been found here. It would seem that this is a *forme fruste* of the determinative for the phallus that we can find much more sharply chiselled in other inscriptions.

Another way of designating circumcision features on this line and reads *FaHeT*. F is the horned viper. The aspirated H, which is also this sign here, is the placenta. The T, here, is the same sign you can see here. Here, a determinative which is the determinative for linen – I ask you to take note of this today because I'll be coming back to it – is unvoiced.

Here, there is another F, which designates *He.* And here there is *TaM*, which means foreskin. With the *iM*, which is the preposition *from*, *FaHeT iM TaM* means *to be separated from one's foreskin.* This also carries its full importance because circumcision is not to be taken solely as a totalitarian operation, as it were, as a sign. The *to be separated from something* is being articulated, properly speaking, right there in an Egyptian inscription.

Given the value, the weight, that is given in these inscriptions, so to speak, to the slightest word, maintaining the foreskin as the object of the operation just as much as he who is undergoing it, is something whose accentuation I ask you to heed. We are going to meet it again in the text of Jeremiah, which is just as enigmatic and to this day just as bereft of interpretation as the one I've just been alluding to, namely, the one of Zipporah's circumcision of her son.

I think I've gone far enough into the functioning of circumcision – not only into its coordinates of festivity, of initiation, and of introduction to a special consecration, but into its structure as a reference to castration as far as its relationships with the structuring of the object of desire are concerned – to be able to go further with you on the day I've set you for our next meeting.

27 March 1963

THE FIVE FORMS OF
THE OBJECT *a*

XVI

BUDDHA'S EYELIDS

The cause, a syncope of the object
The certainty of anxiety
The Jews and the function of the remnant
Christian masochism
Man or woman?

I left you with a comment that called into question the function of circumcision in the economy of desire, in the economy of the object in the sense that analysis grounds it as an object of desire.

The lesson ended on a passage from Jeremiah, verses 24 and 25 of Chapter IX, which has posed a few problems for translators down through the ages because the Hebrew text would give – *I will smite all them which are circumcised in their prepuce.* A paradoxical term that the translators have tried to get around, even one of the most recent and one of the best, Édouard Dhorme, with the wording – *Je sévirai contre tout circoncis à la façon de l'incirconcis, I will mete out punishment to all them which are circumcised in the way of the uncircumcised.*

I'm only calling this point to mind to indicate that what's really involved here is some permanent relation to a lost object as such. This object *a* as something cut off presentifies a quintessential relation to separation as such. The passage I've quoted is not unique in the Bible, but through its extreme paradox it sheds light on what's involved each time the terms *circumcised* and *uncircumcised* are used there. What's involved is in no way localized, far from it, in that little piece of flesh that forms the object of the rite. *Of uncircumcised lips, uncircumcised hearts,* all these expressions which throughout the numerous texts are almost standard and commonplace, emphasize how the essential separation from a particular part of the body, a particular appendage, comes to symbolize for the now alienated subject a fundamental relationship with his body.

Today I'm going to be taking things up from a wider angle, a broader angle, from farther off.

As some of you know, I've just got back from a trip that afforded me a few different experiences – in any case this crucial experience of a close-up, a view, an encounter with some of these works without which the most attentive study of the texts, the letter and the doctrine, in this instance Buddhist doctrine, can only be something dry, incomplete and bereft of invigoration.

I'm going to give you some feedback on what this close-up meant to me and we shall see how it can be inserted into what forms our fundamental question this year, as the dialectic on anxiety shifts over towards the question of desire.

1

Desire is indeed the essential base, the goal, the aim, and the practice too, of everything that is being announced here, in this teaching, on the Freudian message. Something new and utterly essential passes through this message and right here lies the path along which this message wends its way. Who among you – there will be someone, or a few, I hope – will be able to pick it up?

At the point we've reached, that is to say, gaining momentum again after a long break, we really must prompt afresh what this year is all about, namely, the subtle locus, this locus that we are trying to circumscribe and define, this locus that has never before been mapped out in anything of what we might call its ultra-subjective radiance, this pivotal locus of the pure function of desire, so to speak, this locus is the one in which I want to demonstrate for you how the *a* takes shape – *a*, the object of objects.

Our vocabulary has endorsed for this object the term *objectality*, in so far as it stands in contrast to the term *objectivity*. To encapsulate this contrast in some brief formulas, we shall say that objectivity is the ultimate term in Western scientific thought, the correlate to a pure reason which, at the end of the day, is translated into – is summed up by, is spelt out in – a logical formalism. If you've been following my teaching over the last five or six years, you know that objectality is something else. To bring it out in its vital point and forge a formula that balances up with the previous one, I will say that objectality is the correlate to a pathos of the cut. But, paradoxically, this is where the same formalism, in Kant's sense of the term, meets up with its effect. This effect, misrecognized in the *Critique of Pure Reason*, nevertheless accounts for this formalism.

Even Kant, especially Kant, I will say, remains steeped in causality, remains suspended from the justification – that so far no a priori has ever managed to reduce – of this function, which is essential to the whole mechanism of the lived experience of our mental life, the function of cause. Across the board, the cause proves to be irrefutable, irreducible and almost ungraspable to critique.

What is this function? How can we justify its staying power in the face of every attempt to scale it down? One can almost say that this attempt constitutes the sustained movement of the entire critical progress in Western philosophy – a movement that has never succeeded.

Well, if this cause proves to be so irreducible, it's in so far as it is superposed, it is identical in its function to what I've been teaching you here this year to circumscribe and handle as this part of ourselves, this portion of our flesh, which necessarily remains snagged in the formal machine, without which logical formalism would amount to absolutely nothing for us.

This formalism doesn't only summon us and furnish us with the frameworks of our thinking and our transcendental aesthetics, it seizes hold of us at a particular place. We give it not only the matter, not only our Being of thought, but the corporeal morsel that is torn from us as such. This morsel is what circulates in logical formalism such as it has been constituted through our work on the use of the signifier. This portion of ourselves is what is caught in the machine, and it can never be retrieved. As a lost object, at the different levels of the bodily experience where its cut occurs, it is the underpinning, the authentic substrate, of any function of cause.

This bodily portion of ourselves is, essentially and functionally, partial. It should be remembered that this portion is a body and that we are objectal, which means that we are only objects of desire as bodies. This is a crucial point to bear in mind because calling upon something else, calling upon some substitute or other, is one of the fields that creates denegation. Desire always remains in the last instance the desire of the body, desire for the Other's body, and nothing but desire for his body.

Admittedly, people say – *I want your heart and nothing more*. By that, they mean to designate goodness knows what spiritual something or other, the essence of your Being, or even your love. But, here as always, language betrays the truth. This heart can only be a metaphor so long as we don't forget that there is nothing in metaphor that justifies the common grammar-book practice of pitting literal meaning against figurative meaning. This heart might mean a good many things, metaphorizing different things depending on different cultures and languages. For the Semites, for instance, the heart is the organ of intelligence. But I'm not trying to draw your eye to these nuances. In the formula, *I want your heart . . .*, as in any metaphor of an organ, the heart is to be taken to the letter. It functions as a part of the body, as, if I may say, part of the innards. Why has this metaphor lasted so long? We know about those places where it remains very much alive, notably in the shape of the cult of the Sacred Heart.

A little book by Édouard Dhorme reminds us just how fundamental is the metaphorical use of the names of body parts for any understanding of the living Hebraic and Akkadian literatures, though not without, most curiously, one peculiar lack. I recommend this book. You can find it because it's just been reprinted by Gallimard. Although all the different parts of the body are there with their metaphorical functions, the sexual organ, and especially the male sexual organ – even though the texts I mentioned earlier on circumcision stood to be mentioned – the male sexual organ and the foreskin have strangely been omitted and don't even feature in the list of contents.

How can we explain the metaphorical use of this part of the body, a use that is still extant, to express what in desire goes beyond appearances, if not by the fact that its cause is already housed in your innards and figured in lack? There is a dread of the causal innards.

Likewise, the whole mythical discussion about the functions of causality always refers to a bodily experience – from the most classically minded positions to those that are more or less modernized, Maine de Biran's position, for example.

Biran tries to make us feel through the sense of effort the subtle balance around which is played out the position of *that which is determined* and *that which is free*. What shall I use to make you feel what is involved in the realm of cause? I'll take my arm – my arm in so far as I isolate it, considering it as such to be the intermediary between my will and my act. If I dwell on its function, it's in so far as it has been isolated for a moment and it wants me to retrieve it in some way, whatever the cost, whereupon I have to modify the fact that, if it is an instrument, it is not, however, free. I have to protect myself, so to speak, against, not immediately the fact of its amputation, but the fact of its non-control – against the fact that someone else might seize possession of it, that I might become someone's right-hand man, or his left – or simply against the fact that I might leave it behind in the metro, like an ordinary umbrella, or those corset belts that apparently – you can still find them – used to get left there in abundance some years ago.

We analysts know what that means. The experience of the hysteric is significant enough to know that this comparison, which affords a glimpse of the fact that an arm can be forgotten, neither more nor less than a mechanical arm, is no forced metaphor. This is why I take reassurance from the function of determinism that this arm does belong to me. Even when I forget its functioning, I hold firm to the knowledge that it functions in an automatic way and I'm adamant that a lower level – with all kinds of tonic or voluntary reflexes, all manner of conditioning – should let me rest quite assured that it won't come away, even were there to be a momentary lapse of attention on my part.

Therefore, the cause always comes to the surface in correlation with the fact that something is omitted in cognition's consideration. Now, desire is precisely what animates the function of cognizance. Each time the cause is brought up, and in its most traditional register, the cause is the shadow, or the counterpart, of what stands as a blind spot in the function of cognizance. We didn't wait for Freud to bring that up. Need I mention Nietzsche, and others besides, who have called into question the desire that lies beneath the function of taking cognisance? Others still have examined Plato's slant, which makes him believe in the pivotal, originative, creative function of the Sovereign Good – Aristotle's slant, which makes him believe in the peculiar Prime Mover that takes the place of the Anaxagorian νοῦς, which can only, however, be for him a mover that is deaf and blind to what it sustains, namely, the whole cosmos. These examinations always call into question what cognizance believes itself compelled to forge as a final cause.

What does this kind of critique end up in? In a sentimental examination of what appears to be most bereft of sentiment, namely, the cognizance that is elaborated and purified in its final consequences. It veers off towards creating a myth of psychological origin. These are aspirations, instincts, needs – add the adjective *religious*, you will only take one step further and we shall be responsible for all the distractions of reason, for Kantian *Schwärmerei*, with all its inherent outlets onto fanaticism.

Is this a critique we can content ourselves with? Can't we push what's involved here a bit further, spell it out in a bolder fashion, beyond the psychological aspect that is part and parcel of the structure? There's hardly any need to say that this is exactly what we're doing.

It's not about a sentiment that requires satisfaction, but a structural necessity. The subject's relation to the signifier necessitates the structuring of desire in the fantasy and the functioning of desire implies a syncope of the function of the *a* which can be defined temporally and which necessarily fades and vanishes at such and such a phase of the fantasmatic functioning. This ἀφάνισις of the *a*, the vanishing of the object inasmuch as it structures a certain level of the fantasy, is what we have a reflection of in the function of the cause. Whenever we find ourselves faced with this final functioning of the cause, irreducible to critique, we have to seek out its foundation and its root in this hidden object, this object in syncope.

A hidden object lies behind the faith put in Aristotle's Prime Mover, which earlier I depicted for you as deaf and blind to what causes it. If the certainty that is attached to what I shall call essentialist proof – the one that is not only in Saint Anselm because you find it again in Descartes too, the one that is founded on the objective perfection of the idea in order to found there the existence of this certainty, this certainty that is so contestable and always linked to scorn, both precarious and derisory – is maintained despite all the criticism, if we are always led back to it by some means or other, it's because it is but the shadow of another certainty, and this certainty I have already named here, by its name, it is the certainty of anxiety.

I told you that anxiety has to be defined as *that which deceives not*, precisely in so far as every object eludes it. The certainty of anxiety is a grounded certainty. It is unambiguous. The certainty linked to the recourse to the first cause is merely the shadow of this fundamental certainty. Its shadowy character is what imparts it its essentially precarious aspect. This aspect is only ever genuinely overcome through the affirmative articulation that characterizes what I called the essentialist argument, but it's not a convincing argument, because this certainty, when sought out in its genuine grounding, shows itself for what it is – a displacement, a certainty that is secondary in relation to the certainty of anxiety.

What does that imply? It most certainly implies a more radical challenging of the function of cognizance than has ever been articulated in our Western philosophy.

This critique can only start to be undertaken in the most radical way if we notice that there is already cognizance in the fantasy.

2

What is the nature of this cognizance that is already there in the fantasy?

It is none other than the following – the man who speaks, the subject, once he starts to speak, is already implicated by this speech in his body. The root of cognizance is this engagement of his body.

It is not, however, about that sort of engagement that contemporary phenomenology has tried to emphasize in a fertile and evocative way by reminding us that the totality of the corporeal function and presence – Goldstein's structure of the organism, Merleau-Ponty's structure of behaviour – is engaged in any particular perception. This path, which is rich with a whole cornucopia of facts, affords us something that for a long time has struck us as very desirable, namely, the solution of mind/body dualism. It sees the body, taken at the functional level, as a kind of double, the lining, of all the functions of the mind. We should not be satisfied with this, however, because there is still some sleight of hand going on.

The philosophical reactions, of a fideist nature, that contemporary phenomenology has produced in those who serve the materialist cause are surely not groundless in so far as the body, such as it is articulated, even excluded from experience in the exploration inaugurated by contemporary phenomenology, becomes something that is irreducible to material mechanisms. After long centuries gave us a spiritualized body in the soul, contemporary phenomenology has made the body a corporealized soul.

What interests us in the question, and this is what the dialectic of the cause needs to be brought back to, is in no way the body participating in its totality. It's not about noticing how seeing necessitates more than just our eyes, but rather how our reactions are different depending on whether or not our skin is bathed in a certain atmosphere of colour, as was remarked by Goldstein who presented it by means of perfectly valid experiments. It is not this factual realm that is concerned in this reminder of the body's function, but rather the engagement of the man who speaks in the chain of the signifier, with all its consequences – with the knock-on effect, thereafter fundamental, that elective site of an ultra-subjective radiance, the foundation of desire, to spell it right out. It is not that the body would allow us to explain everything by a kind of sketching-out of a non-dualism of *Umwelt* and *Innenwelt*. It is that in the body there is always, by virtue of this engagement in the signifying dialectic, something that is separated off, something that is sacrificed, something inert, and this something is the pound of flesh.

At this stop on the way we can only marvel once again at the incredible genius that guided he whom we call Shakespeare, focusing as he did the thematic of the pound of flesh in the figure of the merchant of Venice. This thematic is just what it takes to remind us that the law of debt and donation – this *total social fact*, as Marcel Mauss has since expressed it, though this certainly wasn't a dimension that was lost sight of at the dawn of the seventeenth century – doesn't assume its weight from any element that we could consider to be a third party, in the sense of an external third party such as the exchange of women or the exchange of goods, as Lévi-Strauss calls to mind in his *Elementary Structures*. . . . Rather, what is at stake in the pact *can only be* and *is only* the pound of flesh, to be *cut off*, as the text of *The Merchant* . . . has it, *nearest the heart*.

It is most certainly not for nothing that, having animated one of his most blazing plays with this thematic – driven by a kind of divination that is nothing but the reflection of something that is always being touched on without ever being tackled in its ultimate depth – Shakespeare attributes it to the merchant, Shylock, a Jew. Indeed, no written history, no sacred book, no bible, to say the word, manages like the Hebraic Bible to bring to life for us the sacred zone in which the hour of truth is evoked, which sounds the bell of the encounter with the ruthless side of the relationship with God, with this divine malice by which the debt always has to be settled in the flesh.

This domain, which I've barely touched on for you, needs to be called by its name. The name that designates it and which for us sets the value of the different biblical texts that I've mentioned for you is correlative to what is known as anti-Semitic feeling, which so many analysts have thought themselves bound to examine, sometimes not without success, with an eye to determining its sources. They are to be found precisely in this sacred zone, which I would say is almost a forbidden zone, which is better articulated there than anywhere else, not only articulated but vivid, forever carried in the life of this people inasmuch as it endures on its own in the function that, in connection with the *a*, I have already spelt out with a noun – the noun *remainder*.

What is the remainder? It is what survives the ordeal of the division of the field of the Other through the presence of the subject. In one biblical passage, this remainder is categorically metaphorized in the image of the *stem*, of the cut rod, from which, in its living function, the new rod emerges, and in the name of Isaiah's second son, Shear-Jashub, *a remnant shall return* in the *sh'eriyth* we also find in another passage in Isaiah. The function of the remainder, the irreducible function that survives every ordeal of the encounter with the pure signifier, is the point to which I already led you at the end of my last lecture, with the passage from Jeremiah on circumcision.

I also indicated to you what the Christian solution was, I ought to say the Christian mitigation, given to this irreducible relationship to the object of the cut. It is none other than the mirage that is attached to the masochistic outcome, inasmuch as the Christian has learnt, through the dialectic of Redemption, to identify ideally with he who made himself identical with this same object, the waste object left behind out of divine retribution.

It is in so far as this solution has been lived out, orchestrated, embellished and poeticized, that I was able once again, no later than a mere forty-eight hours ago, to make the acquaintance, and how comical it was, of the-Westerner-just-back-from-the-Orient, who finds that, over there, they're hard-hearted, they're crafty, hypocritical, bargaining, even swindling – my goodness, they're in on all kinds of little schemes.

This Westerner who spoke to me was an altogether average exemplification of a man, though in his eyes he saw himself as a slightly brighter star than the rest. He thought that he had been hospitably welcomed in Japan because over there, in the host family, they derived some benefit from demonstrating that they have dealings with someone who almost won the Goncourt Prize. *Now there's something*, he told me, *that of course would never happen in my* – here, I'm censoring the name of his province, let's say, the Camargue of his birth – *because everyone knows we wear our hearts on our sleeves, we are much straighter with people, there's none of this skewed manoeuvring.*

This is the illusion of the Christian who always thinks he puts more heart into things than anyone else. And, good Lord, why ever does he think that? Without doubt, this business looks clearer when you notice that the crux of masochism, which is an attempt to provoke the Other's anxiety, here become God's anxiety, has become second nature in the Christian. The ever ludic and ambiguous part of this hypocrisy is something that we can sense in the analytic experience with respect to the perverse position.

Is this hypocrisy worth more or less than what this chap feels as Oriental hypocrisy? He's right to feel that they're not the same. The Oriental man has not been Christianized and this is precisely what we're going to try to go into now.

3

I'm not going to do a Keyserling number and explain Oriental psychology to you.

First of all, there is no Oriental psychology. These days, thank goodness, one goes straight to Japan via the North Pole, which has the advantage of making us feel that it could easily be thought of as a European peninsula. And indeed it is, I assure you, and one day you'll see, I predict, some kind of Japanese Robert Musil who will be showing you where we've got to and to what extent this relationship between the Christian and the heart is still alive, or fossilized if that turns out to be the case.

This is not the direction in which I mean to lead you today. I want to take an angle, to use an experience, to portray an encounter I had, in order to broach something of the field of what still survives of Buddhist practices, notably the Zen practices.

You can well imagine that such a brief in-and-out wouldn't allow me to bring you very much. Maybe I'll tell you, at the end of what we're about to go through now, a sentence I heard from the abbot of one of the Kamakura monasteries that I was allowed to visit. Without any solicitation on my part, I was delivered a sentence that doesn't strike me as off limits in connection with what we're trying to define here, with respect to the subject's relation to the signifier. But this is rather a field to be set aside for the future. The encounters I spoke about earlier were more modest, more accessible, easier to fit into these rapid trips to which the life we lead reduces us. I'm speaking about encounters with works of art.

It might strike you as surprising that I should qualify in this way statues that have a religious function, statues that were not in principle made with an eye to representing works of art. This, however, is incontestably what they are in their intention and their origin. They have always been received and felt to be such, independently of this function. It is not therefore irrelevant for us to take this inroad in order to get something from them that leads us, I won't say to their message, but to what they can represent of a certain relationship between the human subject and desire.

I've hastily put together a little set of three photos of the same statue, with the aim of preserving an integrity about which I'm quite adamant, a statue that is one of the most handsome that can be viewed in this zone that has no shortage of them, and which date from the tenth century. It can be found in the women's monastery, the Chūgū-ji nunnery in Nara, which was the seat of imperial power for several centuries, until the tenth century. Please handle them carefully because I'd like to get these three photos back at the end.

We are moving into Buddhism. You already know that its aim, the principles of dogmatic recourse as well as the ascetic practice that can refer to it, can be summed up with this formula that interests us most keenly – *desire is illusion*. What does that mean? Here, illusion can only be a reference to the register of truth. The truth in question can only be a final truth. Alongside illusion, the function of Being still stands to be specified. To say that desire is illusion is to say that it doesn't have any support, it doesn't have any outlet, or even any aim, on anything. Now, you've heard enough about Nirvana, even if only in Freud, to know that it cannot be identified with a sheer reduction to nothingness. The use of negation, which is common in Zen, for example, through recourse to the sign *mu*,

無

can only point us in the right direction. A very particular negation is involved, a *not having*, which, in and of itself, suffices to put us on guard.

What is involved, at least in the median step of the relation to Nirvana, is always articulated, in a way that is spread throughout each and every formulation of Buddhist truth, in the sense of a non-dualism. If there be an object of thy desire, it's nothing but thine own self. This, however, is not the original characteristic of Buddhism. *Tat tvam asi*, the *that which thou dost recognize in the other is thyself*, is already set down in the Vedānta.

I can't in any way give you a history and a criticism of Buddhism, I'm just calling it to mind in order to move, by taking the shortest routes, towards that wherewith the experience – which you're going to see is a very particular one – that I had in connection with this statue can be used by us.

Such as it tends to be established, in stages, progressively, for he who experiences it, who walks its paths in a specifically ascetic way, and this is undoubtedly rare, the Buddhist experience presupposes an eminent reference to the function of the mirror. Indeed, the metaphor is commonly employed therein. A long while ago, owing to what I knew of it, I alluded in one of my texts to this mirror without surface *in which nothing is reflected*. That was the term, the stage if you will, the phase to which I wanted to refer for the precise goal I was aiming at back then. You'll find it in my article on psychical causality. This mirror relation with the object is such a common and easily accessible reference for any gnoseology that it is just as easy to fall into the error of projection. We know how easy it is for things on the outside to take on the colouration of our soul, and even its shape, and even for them to move towards us in the form of a double.

But if we introduce the object *a* as something essential in the relationship to desire, this business of dualism and non-dualism takes on a quite different relief. If what is most me lies on the outside, not because I projected it there but because it was cut from me, the paths I shall take to retrieve it afford an altogether different variety.

To give to the mirror's function in this dialectic of recognition a meaning that does not belong to the realm of the sleight of hand, of trickery, of magic, a few remarks need to be made, the first of which, and this is not to be taken in the idealist sense, is that the eye is already a mirror.

I shall say that the eye organizes the world into space. It reflects what, in the mirror, is reflection. To the most piercing eye, however, the reflection of what it carries of the world is visible in the eye that it sees in the mirror. To spell it right out, it has no need of two mirrors standing opposite one another for the infinite reflections of a mirror palace to be created. As soon as there is an eye and a mirror, the infinite recursion of inter-reflected images is produced.

This remark is not here simply for its ingenuity, but to bring us back to the privileged point that stands at the origin and which is the very point at which the originative difficulty of arithmetic takes shape, the foundation of the One and the zero.

The one image that is formed in the eye, the image you are able to see in the pupil, requires at the outset a correlate that is in no way an image. If the surface of the mirror is in no way there to support the world, it is not because nothing reflects this world, it is not because the world fades away with the absence of the subject, it's specifically because *nothing is reflected*. This means that before space there is a One that contains multiplicity as such, that stands prior to the deployment of space as such – space which is never anything but a chosen space in which only juxtaposed things can stand, so long as there is room for them. Should this room be indefinite or infinite, that doesn't change anything.

To make you hear what I want to say about this One, which is not πᾶν but πολύ, *all* in the plural, I'm simply going to show you what you can see from this same Kamakura period. It is by the hand of a sculptor whose name is very well known, the Kamakura period dates from the end of the twelfth century, and it is a Buddha represented materially in one statue some three meters high, and materially represented by a thousand others.

That makes quite an impression, all the more so given that you file past them down a fairly narrow aisle. A thousand statues take up quite a bit of room, especially when they are lifesize, perfectly executed and individualized. This work took the sculptor and his school a hundred years. You're going to be able to have a look at it, on the one hand when seen face on, and then here's what it gives from an oblique view when you move down the aisle.

The monotheism/polytheism opposition might not be such a clear-cut thing as you habitually imagine it to be, because the thousand and one statues standing there are all identically the same Buddha. Moreover, each of you is, *de jure*, a Buddha – *de jure* because, for particular reasons, you might have been cast into this world with some handicap that will create a more or less insurmountable obstacle to this point of access.

The fact no less remains that the subjective One in its infinite multiplicity and variability is here shown to be identical with the ultimate One, having successfully gained access to non-dualism, to the beyond of any variation in pathos and any shift in the cosmos.

We ought less to take an interest in it as a phenomenon than in what it allows us to broach with regard to the relations it demonstrates, through the consequences it has had, historically and structurally, in men's thoughts.

I have to bring you a few details.

The first is that these thousand and one supports, thanks to the effects of multiplication inscribed into the multiplicity of arms, of insignia, and of a few heads that crown the central head, there are in reality thirty-three thousand, three hundred and thirty-three same essential beings. That's just one detail.

The second is that this is not, in absolute terms, the god Buddha. It's a Bodhisattva, that is, to put it rapidly, a near-Buddha. He would be completely and utterly a Buddha were he not there, but he is there, in this manifold form that took a great deal of trouble. These statues are merely the image of the trouble he takes to be there, there for you. He is a Buddha that has not yet managed to lose interest in humanity's salvation, no doubt owing to one of those obstacles to which I was just alluding. This is why, if you are Buddhist, you prostrate yourself before this opulent array. You are duty-bound to acknowledge the unity that has taken the trouble in such great number to remain in arm's reach with a view to bringing you aid. The iconography lists the different cases in which they are able to aid you.

The Bodhisattva at issue is in Sanskrit called *Avalokiteśvara*. Its name is inordinately widespread, especially these days, in the social sphere that practises yoga.

The first image of the statue that I passed round is an historical avatar of this figure. Before I took an interest in Japanese, I was fated to travel by the right paths and I analysed with my good mentor Demiéville, in those years when psychoanalysis left me more spare time, the book called *The Lotus of the True Law*, which was written into Chinese by Kumārajīva to translate a Sanskrit text. This text is more or less the historical turning point at which occurred the peculiar metamorphosis I'm going to ask you to keep in mind, namely, when Avalokiteśvara, *he who hears the world's laments*, transforms – from the time of Kumārajīva, who seems to have been somewhat responsible for it – into a female divinity.

She is called – I think you are at least slightly on the same wavelength – Guanyin, or Guanshiyin. This name is linked to the same meaning as the name Avalokiteśvara carries, it is – *she who is considerate, who goes, who accords*. Here, is *Guan*.

観

Here is the *world* I mentioned just now.

And this is its tears or its laments.

The *shi* can sometimes be effaced.

The Guanyin is a female divinity. In China, it's unambiguous, it always appears in a feminine form and this transformation is what I'm asking you to pause on for a moment. In Japan, these same words are read *Kan'on* or *Kanzeon*, depending on whether or not the *world* character is inserted.

Not all forms of Kannon are female. I would even say that the majority aren't. Since you have before your eyes the picture of the statues from the Sanjūsangen-dō, from this temple – where the same holiness or divinity – a term that has to be left up in the air – is represented in a multiple form, you can see that the figures have been given little moustaches and faintly sketched goatees. Therefore they are depicted there in a male form, which does indeed correspond to the canonical structure of what these statues represent, with the correct number of heads and arms.

This is exactly the same being as the one in the first statue whose pictures I passed round to you earlier. This statue corresponds to the form specified as a *Nyo-i-rin*, a *Kan'on* or a *Kanzeon*. *Nyo-i-rin* means, as does its Sanskrit counterpart – *like the wheel of desires*.

This then is what we are being shown.

We meet, attested in the most superlative fashion, the pre-Buddhist divinities absorbed into the different stages of the hierarchy that are thereafter articulated as levels, steps, forms of access to the ultimate realization of *Bodhi*, that is, the final awakening to the radically illusory character of all desire. Nevertheless, at the very interior of this multiplicity that converges towards a centre which is, in essence, a centre of nowhere, you can see re-emerging, in a superlatively incarnate fashion, what could be most alive, most real, most animated, most human and most pathetic in it, in a first relation with the divine world, a relation that was essentially nourished and seemingly punctuated by a whole variation of desire. Holiness with a capital H, practically the most fundamental element in the access point to Bodhi, finds itself embodied in a female form of divinity that has even been identified at the origin with nothing more nor less than the reappearance of the Indian Shakti, the feminine principle of the world, the soul of the world.

This is something that should give us a moment's pause.

I don't know if this statue I've given you in these photographs has succeeded in establishing in you this quivering, this communication that I assure you one can be quite sensitive to in its presence.

Not only was I sensitive to it, but chance had it that, accompanied by my guide – one of those Japanese folks for whom neither Maupassant nor Mérimée hold any secret, nor anything else from our literature, I'll leave out Valéry because you can get your Valéry ticket in the first railway station you come across, we hear nothing else but Valéry the whole world over, and the success of this Mallarmé to the *nouveaux riches* is one of the most disconcerting things to be met in our times, but let's keep calm – I walked into the little hall where this statue is and saw there, on bended knee, a man of thirty or thirty-five years of age, a simple tradesman type, perhaps a craftsman, already very worn by his existence. He was kneeling before this statue and clearly he was praying, which is not something we are tempted to join in. But, after praying, he went right up to the statue – because nothing stops you from touching it – to the right, to the left, and underneath, he watched it, like that, for I couldn't say how long. I didn't see the end, because truth be told this moment corresponded to my own viewing time. It was clearly an effusive gaze, of a character that was all the more extraordinary given that this was not a common man, because a man who conducts himself thus could never be that, but someone whom nothing would seem to have predestined to this kind of artistic communion, given the evident burden of his labours bearing down on his shoulders.

I'm going to give the other part of what I perceived in a different form.

You've looked at the statue, its face, you've seen the absolutely stunning expression of which it is impossible to know whether it's entirely for you or entirely inward. I didn't know then that it was a Nyo-i-rin, a Kanzeon, but I first heard about the Guanyin a long time ago. I asked, in connection with these statues and others besides – *So, is it a man or a woman?*

I'll spare you the debates, the twists and turns that opened out around this question, which carries great meaning in Japan, I repeat, given that the Kanzeon are not all univocally feminine. And that was where what I took in possesses a slight character of research, well, at the Kinsey Report level – I became certain that for this cultivated young man, steeped in Maupassant and Mérimée, as well as for a large number of his workmates that I asked, the question of whether a statue of this ilk is male or female has never arisen for them.

I believe that here lies a fact that is decisive in a different way when it comes to broaching what we might call the variety of solutions to the problem of the object. With everything I've just told you, about my first approach to this object, I think I've shown you sufficiently to what extent it is an object for desire.

If you need still more details, you may notice that there is no opening for the eyes on this statue. Now, the Buddhist statues always have eyes that one cannot call shut, but half-shut, because it's a way of poising the eyes that is only arrived at through learning, namely, a lowered eyelid that only lets show a line of the white and an edge of the pupil. All of the statues of Buddha are made like that. This statue, however, has nothing of the like. It simply has, at the level of the eyes, a kind of pronounced ridge, which means that with the reflection off the wood one always seems to be able to make out an eye. But there's nothing there in the wood. I examined the wood at length, and I made enquiries, and the solution I was offered – without being able to settle the matter of what share has to be accorded to faith, it was provided by someone who is very serious and a great specialist, Professor Kando to give him his name – is that the slit of the eye on this statue has disappeared over the centuries due to the more or less daily kneading it endures from the hands of the nuns of the convent, where it is the most precious treasure, when they think to dry the tears of this figure of archetypal divine recourse.

Moreover, the monastics handle the whole statue in the same way as they do the rim of the eyes. Its polish is something quite incredible. The photo only gives you a vague reflection of it – a reflection of what, upon this statue, is the inverse radiance to what one cannot fail to recognize as a long desire, borne throughout the centuries by these recluses unto this divinity of psychologically indeterminate sex.

It's already quite late, too late to carry my talk any further. What I've said today will allow us to shed light on the point of passage at which we've now arrived.

At the oral stage there is a certain relationship between demand and the mother's veiled desire. At the anal stage, the mother's demand comes into the picture for desire. At the stage of phallic castration, there is the minus-phallus, the entry of negativity with regard to the instrument of desire when sexual desire as such emerges in the field of the Other. But the process doesn't stop with these three stages, because at its limit we have to meet up with the structure of the *a* as something separated off.

I didn't speak to you today about a mirror just for the sake of it, not the mirror of the mirror stage, of narcissistic experience, of the image of the body in its totality, but rather the mirror inasmuch as it is the field of the Other in which there must appear for the first time, if not the *a* itself, then at least its place – in short, the radical main-spring that makes one go from the level of castration to the mirage of the object of desire.

What is the function of castration in this object, this statue, of a type that is so moving for being at once our own image and some-thing else – when, in the context of a particular culture, it appears as bearing no relation to sex? This is the strange and typical fact to which I've led you today.

8 May 1963

XVII

THE MOUTH AND THE EYE

The lips, the teeth, and the tongue
The nursling, parasite
The anxiety-point and the point of desire
Anxiety and orgasm
The scopic cancelling-out of castration

The list of objects in Freudian theory, the oral object, the anal object, the phallic object – you know that I'm doubtful about the genital object being consistent with them – needs to be completed.

Indeed, the object defined in its function by its place as *a*, the object functioning as the leftover of the subject's dialectic with the Other, still stands to be defined at other levels in the field of desire. Everything indicates this in what I've already got under way in my teaching and more especially my teaching from this year.

For example, I've already indicated enough for you to have some inkling, even a crude inkling, that the desire attached to the image is a function of a cut that arises in the field of the eye. Or something else besides and which goes further than what we are already acquainted with, which has so far appeared enigmatically in the shape of a certain imperative said to be categorical in which we meet the character of fundamental certainty already marked out by traditional philosophy and spelt out by Kant in the form of moral conscience. Approaching it from the angle of the *a* will enable us to situate it in its place.

This year I have chosen to proceed starting off from anxiety because this path reinvigorates the whole dialectic of desire and it is the only path that allows us to introduce fresh clarity with regard to the function of the object in relation to desire.

My last lesson sought to presentify for you how a whole field of human experience that puts itself forward as constituting a kind of salvation, the Buddhist experience, posited, as its grounding principle, that *desire is illusion*.

What does that mean? It is easy to smirk at the briskness of the assertion *all is nothing*. Likewise, I said that this is not what is involved in Buddhism. If, however, the assertion that desire is but illusion can carry a meaning for our experience, we need to know through which point this meaning can be introduced and, to say it all, where lies the lure.

I've been teaching you to bind desire to the function of the cut and to bring it into a certain relationship with the function of the remainder. This remainder sustains and drives desire, as we have learnt to ascertain in the analytic function of the partial object. The lack to which satisfaction is linked, however, is something else.

The gulf between lack and the function of desire in action, structured by the fantasy and by the subject's vacillation in his relation to the partial object, indicates the non-concurrence that creates anxiety, and anxiety is the only thing to target the truth of this lack. This is why, at each stage in the structuring of desire, if we want to understand what is involved in the function of desire, we must ascertain what I shall call the anxiety-point.

This is going to pull us backwards – with a movement dictated by all our experience, since everything happens as though, with Freud run aground on the dead end of the castration complex, analytic theory felt something like an ebb tide, an undertow leading it back to search out the most radical functioning of the drive at the oral level. Now, I declare this dead end to be merely an apparent one and one which has never been got through until now.

What I have to tell you today shall perhaps enable us to conclude with some affirmations concerning what was meant by Freud's running aground on the castration complex.

1

It is peculiar that psychoanalysis, which perceived in its inaugural moment the nodal function of what is specifically sexual in the shaping of desire, should have been led, through the course of its historical evolution, to seek out increasingly in the oral drive the origin of all the mishaps, anomalies and disparities that can occur at the level of the structuring of desire.

Saying that the oral drive is chronologically originative isn't the end of the story, its being structurally originative still needs to be justified. It is to this oral drive that the etiology behind all the stumbling blocks we face is to be brought back.

Likewise, I have already broached what must open up for us once again the question of this reduction to the oral drive. Such as it currently functions it is merely a metaphorical way of approaching what happens at the level of the phallic object by eluding the impasse created by the fact that Freud never resolved to the last term the functioning behind the castration complex. The oral reduction veils over this and allows people to speak about it without facing up to the impasse. Although the metaphor is correct, however, we ought to uncover at the very level of the oral drive a hint of why it is no more than metaphor here.

This is why I've already tried once to take up the function of the cut of the object relative to the level of the oral drive, along with the disjunction between the locus of satisfaction and the locus of anxiety. Now the next step has to be taken, to which I led you last time, that is, to situate the join between the *a* functioning as $(- \varphi)$, that is, the castration complex, and the level we shall call visual or spatial, depending on which side we care to picture it from, a level from which we are best able to see what the lure of desire means.

To get to this, which is today's goal, we first have to trace back our footsteps and look again at the analysis of the oral drive with a view to specifying precisely where at this level the cut lies.

The nursling and the breast. This is what all the storm clouds of analytic dramaturgy have amassed around – the origin of the first aggressive drives, of their reflection, even their retention, the source of the most fundamental hitches in the subject's development. In resuming this thematic, it oughtn't to be forgotten that it is founded upon an originative act that is essential to the subject's biological sustenance in the realm of mammals, namely sucking.

What functions in sucking? The lips, apparently.

Here we meet up with the functioning of what struck us as crucial in the structure of erogeneity, the function of a rim. The fact that the lip presents the very image of the rim, that it is the very embodiment, so to speak, of a cut, is just what it takes to make us feel that we're on steady ground.

Let's not forget that at an altogether different level, the level of the signifying articulation, at the level of the most fundamental phonemes, those most firmly bound to the cut, the consonantal elements of the phoneme, are, as regards their most basal stock, essentially modulated at the level of the lips. I might come back, if we have time, to what I have already indicated several times regarding the fundamental words and their apparent specificity. *Mama* and *papa* are labial articulations, even though we may have doubts as to whether they are distributed specifically, widely, or even universally.

On the other hand, the fact that at the level of initiatory rites the lip is always something that can be symbolically pierced or stretched, altered in countless different ways, also furnishes us with the marker that proves we are indeed in a living field that has long been acknowledged in human praxes.

Is that all? There is still behind the lip what Homer calls the *fence of teeth*, and the bite.

The existence of a dentition that is known as lacteal, the implied virtual bite that we bring into the aggressive thematic of the oral drive with the fantasmatic isolation of the tip of the breast, is what we've made the very possibility of the fantasy of the nipple's isolation revolve around. The nipple already presents itself not only as something partial but as something separate. The first fantasies of the function of fragmentation as an inaugural function stem from this. Until now we've contented ourselves with them. Is this to say that we are to maintain this position?

Already, in the lesson I gave on 6 March, I accentuated how the whole dialectic of what is called weaning, the separation from the breast, had to be taken up in accordance with its natural resonances, its natural points of impact, with everything that, in our experience, has enabled us to broaden it, up to and including the primordial separation, that of birth. We have acknowledged, with good reason, that there is an analogy in our experience between oral weaning and the severance at birth. If we embrace a little more physiology, this experience is just what we need for clarity's sake.

I told you that at birth the cut lies somewhere other than where we've been putting it. It is not conditioned by the aggression brought to bear on the mother's body. It lies within the primordial, individual unit such as it presents itself at the level of birth. The cut is made between what is going to become the individual who will be cast into the outside world and his envelopes, which are parts of himself, inasmuch as they are elements of the egg, consistent with what has been produced in the ovular development, direct extensions of his ectoderm and his endoderm alike. The separation occurs within this unity, the unit of the egg.

The emphasis I mean to give here abides by the specificity, within the organismal structure, of the organization called mammalian.

What specifies the development of the egg for nearly all mammals is the existence of the placenta and even a placenta that is utterly special, called the chorioallantois, whereby for one entire part of its development the egg in its intrauterine position presents itself in a semi-parasitic relation to the organism of the mother.

For us, it is evocative that within the class of mammals two orders can be singled out, the monotremes and the marsupials. They are the most primitive orders in the mammalian set. In the marsupials, there is another kind of placenta, not chorioallantoic but choriovitelline, though we shan't be dwelling on this nuance. I think that, from your childhoods, you've retained at least the image of these monotremes in the shape of those animals that in *Le Petit Larousse* swarm in a puddle as if they were pushing at the gate of a new Noah's ark, which means they go *two and two*, though sometimes even just one by one per species. You've got the image of the platypus and also the one that's called the echidna breed. These monotremes are mammals, but in them the egg, even though it is housed in a uterus, has no placental relation with the maternal organism. Nevertheless, the mamma is already there.

At this level we can better see what the originative function of the mamma is. It presents itself as something in between the offspring and its mother. So, we need to conceive of the cut as lying between the mamma and the maternal organism itself.

Here, before the placenta shows us that the feeding relation, at a certain level of the living organism, is extended beyond the egg's function – which, laden with all the baggage that allows for its development, will only make the child join up with his progenitors in a common experience of the search for nourishment – we clearly have a relation that I called parasitic, an ambiguous function in which the amboceptive organ of the mamma steps in.

In other words, the child's relation to the mamma is more primal than the appearance of the placenta, which allows us to say that it is homologous with his relation to the placenta. In the same way that the placenta forms a unit with the child, there stand, together, child and mamma. The mamma is in some way stuck on, implanted on the mother. This is what allows it to function structurally at the level of the *a*, which is defined as something from which the child is separated in a way that is internal to the sphere of his existence.

You're going to see the consequence that results from the binding of the oral drive to this amboceptive object.

What is the object of the oral drive? It is what we habitually call the mother's breast. At this level, where does what earlier I called the anxiety-point lie? It lies precisely beyond this sphere that unites the child and the mamma. The anxiety-point lies at the level of the mother. In the child, the anxiety of the mother's lack is the anxiety of the breast drying up. The locus of the anxiety-point does not merge with the locus at which the relation to the object of desire is established.

This is peculiarly pictured by those animals I conjured up in the shape of representatives from the monotreme order. Everything occurs as though this biological organization had been put together by some foresighted creator with a view to showing us the true oral relation with this privileged object that the mamma is.

Indeed, whether you know this or not, the echidna's puggle dwells outside the cloaca for a while after its birth, in a pouch located on the mother's belly known as the incubatorium. The puggle is still, at that point, in the envelopes of a kind of hard egg, from which it emerges by using an egg tooth, a *ruptor ovi*, along with something at the level of its upper lip that is called an *os caruncle*. These organs, which allow the foetus to get out of the egg, are not unique to the echidna. They exist, prior to the appearance of mammals, in reptiles. Snakes just have the egg tooth whilst other varieties – turtles and crocodiles – just have the caruncle.

The important thing is this. It seems that, for its function to be activated, the mamma on the mother echidna needs to be nuzzled by the reinforced pike that the puggle's snout presents. For about eight days, the puggle gives itself over to this activation, which apparently owes much more to its presence and activity than to any autonomous functioning of the mother's organism. Furthermore, it curiously gives us the image of a relation that is in some sense inverted in relation to mammiferous protuberance. The echidna's mammae are concave. The puggle's beak is inserted into these hollows. I'll draw for you the glandular elements, the milk-producing lobules, and this reinforced snout that lodges there – it is not yet hardened in the form of a beak as it will be later.

Therefore, in the mammalian organization, there are two originative points that need to be distinguished. On one hand, there is the mamma as such. The relation to the mamma will remain a structuring factor in the sustenance and subsistence of the relation to desire. Later on, the mamma will become the fantasmatic object. On the other hand, elsewhere, there is the anxiety-point, where the subject stands in relation to his lack. This point does not overlap with the mamma. He is in some sense carried off into the Other, because, at the level of the mother, he is suspended from the existence of her organism.

S	A
a	Anxiety

The anxiety-point

This, then, is what we are permitted to structure in a more articulated fashion simply by taking physiology into account. It shows us that the *a* is an object separated not from the mother's organism but from the child's organism. The relation to the mother is distinct from the organismal totality from which the *a*, misrecognized as such, is separated and isolated. The relation to the mother, the relation of lack to the mother, is located beyond the locus in which the distinction of the partial object has been played out as functioning in the relation of desire.

Of course, the relation is more complex still and we need to take into account the existence, in the function of sucking, alongside the lips, of the enigmatic organ of the tongue. It has long been marked out as such – remember if you will Aesop's fable.

The tongue allows us to bring in, from the oral level onwards, that which in the subtext of our analysis stands to feed a double homology with the phallic function and its peculiar dissymmetry. On one hand, in sucking, the tongue plays the essential role of functioning by suction, as the support of a void whose drawing power enables the function to be effective. On the other hand, it can provide us with the image, in a first form, of the secret of sucking as it emerges from its most intimate secrecy, which will remain in the state of a fantasy at the base of everything we can articulate around the phallic function – namely, the glove turning inside out, the possibility of an eversion of what lies deepest in inner secrecy.

The fact that the anxiety-point lies beyond the locus in which the fantasy is secured in its relation to the partial object is what appears in the extension of this fantasy that forms an image and remains forever more or less inherent to the credence we give to a certain pattern of oral relation – the fantasy that is expressed in the image of vampirism.

Whilst it is true that within this pattern of his relation to the mother the child is a little vampire and his organism is for a while suspended in the parasitic position, the fact remains no less that he is not this vampire either, to wit, at no moment whatsoever will he go at his mother with his teeth to search out the warm and vital source of his nourishment. As mythical as it is, however, the vampire image reveals to us through the aura of anxiety that surrounds it the truth of the oral relation to the mother. Beyond the reality of the organismal functioning, a dimension takes shape and stands out that gives to the message its most profound accentuation, that of a possibility of lack, a possibility that is realized beyond what anxiety harbours by way of virtual fears over the drying-up of the breast. It calls the mother's function into question. The relation to the mother, inasmuch as it stands out in the image of vampirism, is what allows us to distinguish between the anxiety-point and the point of desire. At the level of the oral drive, the anxiety-point lies at the level of the Other. That's where we feel it.

Freud tells us – *anatomy is destiny*. You know that at certain moments I've taken a stand against this formula over its incompleteness. It becomes true if we give the term *anatomy* its strict and, if I may, etymological meaning that emphasizes *ana-tomy*, the function of the cut. Indeed, everything we know about anatomy is linked to dissection. Destiny, that is to say, man's relation to the function called desire, only assumes its full vitality inasmuch as the fragmentation of one's own body, the cut that lies at the locus of select moments of its functioning, is conceivable.

The fundamental *separtition* – not separation but partition on the inside – is what finds itself inscribed right back at the origin, and right back at the level of the oral drive, in what will go on to be the structuring of desire.

Can we really be surprised, then, that we've gone to the oral level to find some more accessible image for what has always remained a paradox for us – and why? – in the functioning linked to copulation, namely that, there too, the image of a cut, of a separation, is prevalent?

2

We call this cut *castration* quite incorrectly, because what functions here is an image of emasculation.

It is undoubtedly not by chance, nor ill-advisedly, that we went off to hunt out in more ancient fantasies a justification for what we didn't know very well how to justify at the level of the phallic phase. It needs to be impressed, however, that at the oral level something happens that will allow us to find our bearings in the whole ensuing dialectic.

Indeed, I've just affirmed for you the topological division between desire and anxiety. The anxiety-point lies at the level of the Other, at the level of the mother's body. The functioning of desire – that is, the fantasy, the vacillation that binds the subject tightly to the *a*, whereby the subject finds himself suspended, identified with this *a* – remains forever elided and hidden, underlying any relation the subject may have with any object whatsoever, and we have to detect it there.

You can see this here on the blackboard. Here is the level S of the subject, who, in our diagram of the vase reflected in the mirror of the Other, is found just shy of this mirror. This is where the relations at the level of the oral drive are to be found. As I told you, the cut is an essential term in the field of the subject. Desire functions within a world that, albeit fragmented, bears the trace of its first closing off within what remains, at an imaginary or virtual level, of the envelope of the egg. Here we are meeting up with the Freudian notion of autoeroticism.

What will become of it at the level where the castration complex arises? There, we can see a veritable reversal of the point of desire and the locus of anxiety.

If something has been promoted by the mode, no doubt still imperfect, but laden with the full depth of a painful conquest that has been made step by step since the origin of the Freudian discovery, then it is the narrow relationship of castration, namely the fact that the relation to the object in the phallic relation implicitly contains the privation of the organ. The Other is evidently implicated at this level. Were it not for the Other – and it matters little here whether we call it the castrating mother or the father of the original prohibition – there wouldn't be any castration.

The essential relation between castration and the copulatory function has already prompted us to try – after all, following the indication of Freud, who tells us that at this level, without him justifying it any way, however, we are touching on some biological bedrock – to articulate it as lying within a particularity of the function of the copulatory organ at the human biological level.

As I remarked for you, at other levels, in other animal branches, the copulatory organ, which can be called in the most summarily analogical way the male organ, is a hook, an organ that fastens. It is crucial not to believe that an accident in the particular functioning of this copulatory organ at the level of those animal organisations that are called superior, namely, the mechanism of tumescence and detumescence, is in itself essential to orgasm.

We are certainly not going to attempt to form any idea of what the orgasm might be in copulatory relations that are structured in a different way. There are, however, plenty of impressive natural spectacles to be witnessed. You just have to take an evening's stroll along a lakeside to see the flight of tightly entwined dragonflies and this spectacle can tell you quite enough about what we might conceive of as a *long-orgasm*, if you will allow me to forge a word by adding a hyphen. Likewise, I haven't brought up the fantasmatic image of the vampire just for the sake of it. The vampire is not dreamt of in human imagination in any other way than as a mode of fusing or initial subtraction at the very life source where the assailing subject can find the wellhead of his jouissance. The very existence of the mechanism of detumescence in the copulation of those organisms that are most analogous to the human organism most certainly suffices to mark out all by itself the link between orgasm and what presents itself truly and verily as the first image, the first hint, of the cut, the separation, the bowing-out, the ἀφάνιζις, the vanishing of the function of the organ.

If we take things up from this angle, we will acknowledge that in this punctuation the anxiety-point is found in a position that is the strict inverse of the position at which it was found at the level of the oral drive. The homologue of the oral anxiety-point is orgasm itself as a subjective experience.

This is what allows us to justify what the clinic shows us very frequently, namely the fundamental equivalence between orgasm and at least certain forms of anxiety, the possibility of an orgasm occurring at the height of an anguishing situation, the possible eroticization, so we are told all over the place, of an anguishing situation that is sought out as such.

This is also what justifies something to which we have universal human testimony, brought up to date by Freud's testament. It is after all worth taking the trouble to note that someone of Freud's stature dares to attest that, when all is said and done, there is no greater satisfaction for human beings than orgasm. If this satisfaction outstrips everything that mankind may be given to experience on account of its functioning with primacy and precedence, if the function of orgasm can obtain this eminence, is it not because at the base of the achieved orgasm there lies what I called the certainty that is bound to anxiety, inasmuch as orgasm is the very realization of what anxiety indicates as the direction in which lies the locus of certainty? Of all the kinds of anxiety, orgasm is the only one that is actually concluded.

Likewise, this is why orgasm is not all that commonly reached. Although we are permitted to indicate its possible function in the sex[1] where there is only any phallic reality in the form of a shadow, it is also in this same sex that orgasm remains most enigmatic for us, most closed off, never authentically situated perhaps until now in its ultimate essence.

What does this parallel, this symmetry, this reversion established between the anxiety-point and the point of desire, indicate for us if not that in neither of the two cases does it match? And this is doubtless where we have to see the source of the enigma that has been left us by the Freudian experience.

To the extent that the location of desire – which is implied in virtual terms in our experience and which, if I may say so, weaves it entirely – is not, however, truly articulated in Freud, the end of analysis runs aground on the sign implied in the phallic relation, the (φ), inasmuch as it functions structurally as $(- \varphi)$, which makes it take this form as the essential correlate of satisfaction.

If, at the end of Freudian analysis, the patient, male or female, demands of us the phallus we owe him or her, it's because of this insufficiency, whereby desire's relation to the object is not clearly distinguished at each level as the lack that constitutes satisfaction.

Desire is illusory. Why? Because it always addresses an elsewhere, a remainder, a remnant constituted by this relation that the subject has with the Other that comes to replace it. But this leaves open the question as to where certainty is to be found. No permanent phallus, no almighty phallus, is ever likely to seal off in any conciliatory fashion the dialectic of the subject's relation to the Other, and to the real. If we are touching here on the structuring function of the lure, does this mean that we must dig in here, admit our powerlessness, our limit, and the point at which the distinction between finite analysis and indefinite analysis breaks down? I believe nothing of the sort.

This is where something comes into the picture that is harboured in the most secret mettle of what I put forward long ago in the shape of the mirror stage and which compels us to organize, within the same relation, desire, the object, and the anxiety-point – namely, the new object *a* to which the previous lesson was an introduction, the eye.

3

Of course, this partial object is not new in analysis.

I only need mention the article by the most classically minded author, the most widely admitted in analysis, Herr Fenichel, on the relations between the scoptophilic function and identification, and the homologies that he went on to uncover between this function and the oral relation. Nevertheless, everything that has been said on this subject can sound, quite rightly, inadequate.

The origin of the eye does not refer us simply to the mammals, nor even to the vertebrates, nor even to the chordates. The eye appears on the animal ladder right down at the level of organisms that have nothing in common with us. As I've already had occasion to point out, it exists at the level of the praying mantis but equally at the level of the octopus. It appears there in an extraordinarily distinct way, with an anatomical appearance that is essentially similar to that of the eye we bear.

The eye presents itself with a particularity we need to mention at the outset, to wit, it is an organ that is always twain. It functions in general through a dependency on a chiasmus, that is, it is bound to an interlaced nexus that links two symmetrical parts of the body. The eye's relation to a symmetry that is at least apparent, because no organism is fully symmetrical, must be fully taken into our consideration.

Last time's reflections pointed out the radical function of mirage, which is included in the eye's very first functioning. The fact that the eye is a mirror already implies its structure in some way. The transcendental aesthetic foundation, as it were, of a constituted space has to make way for another in its stead. When we speak about the transcendental structure of space as an irreducible given in the aesthetic perception of the world, this structure excludes just one thing – the eye itself, what it is, its function. It's a matter of finding the traces of this excluded function. It is already indicated well enough in the phenomenology of vision as a homologue of the *a* function.

Here we can only proceed with punctuations, indications and remarks.

All those who have attached themselves to what I might call the realism of desire, namely the mystics, and for whom any attempt at reaching the essential has to overcome something that tends to bog us down in an appearance that is only ever conceived of as a visual appearance, have already put us on the trail of something which all sorts of natural phenomena also bear out, namely, appearances that are called mimetic, which can be seen on the animal ladder at the very point at which the eye appears. At the level of insects – at which we may be surprised, why not, that they should have a pair of eyes akin to ours – you can see appearing the existence of a double stain that has a fascinating effect on the other party, whether predator or otherwise. And the physiologists, regardless of whether or not they are evolutionary physiologists, rack their brains over what it might be that could be conditioning this appearance.

This element that fascinates in the function of the gaze, where all subjective subsistence seems to get lost, to be absorbed, and to leave the world behind, is in itself enigmatic. We have here, however, the point of irradiation that allows us to examine what the field of vision reveals in the function of desire.

Likewise, it is striking that in all the attempts to grasp, reason out and logicize the eye's mystery with a view to elucidating this major form of the capture of human desire, the fantasy of the third eye appears. I needn't tell you that, in the pictures of the Buddha I showed you last time, the third eye is always indicated in some way.

This third eye is promulgated, promoted, and articulated in the most ancient magical religious tradition. It made its way down to Descartes, who, oddly enough, would only find its substrate in a regressive, rudimentary organ – the epiphysis. People might say that at one point on the animal ladder something appears and is realized that bears the trace of an ancient emergence of the apparatus called the third eye, but this is mere fancy, because we have nothing that attests to it, fossil or otherwise.

In this new field of the relation to desire, what appears as correlative to the *a* of the fantasy is something that we may call a zero point, whose spread over the entire field of vision is for us the wellspring of a kind of appeasement that the term *contemplation* has conveyed since time immemorial. Here, there is a suspension of the wrenching of desire – certainly a very fragile suspension, as fragile as a curtain ever about to be used once again to unmask the mystery it hides. The Buddha's image seems to carry us towards this zero point to the very extent that its lowered eyelids protect us from the fascination of the gaze while at the same time indicating it to us. This figure is, within the visible, entirely turned towards the invisible, but it spares us this invisible. To spell it right out, this figure assumes the anxiety-point fully unto itself and suspends, apparently cancelling out, the mystery of castration. This is what I wanted to indicate to you last time with my remarks and the brief enquiry I made on the apparent psychological ambiguity of those figures.

Does this mean that there might be, in any way whatsoever, some possibility of entrusting oneself to an Apollonian, noetic field of contemplation in which desire could be sustained by cancelling out its central point punctiformally, by identifying *a* with the zero-point? Most certainly not, precisely because there still remains the zero point between the two eyes, which is the sole locus of disquiet that remains in our relation to the world when this world is a spatial one. This is what prevents us from finding in the desire/illusion formula the ultimate term of experience.

Here, the point of desire and the anxiety-point coincide, but they do not merge, and they leave open this *however* to which the dialectic of our perception of the world eternally comes bouncing back, this *however* that we are always seeing emerge in our patients, this *however* that I've started looking up in Hebrew. That will amuse you.

The point of desire and the anxiety-point coincide here. *However*, desire, which here boils down to the nullification of its central object, is not without this other object that anxiety summons up. It is not without object. It is not for nothing that in this *not without* I have given you the formula of the articulation of the identification with desire.

It is beyond this *it is not without object* that the question arises for us as to where the dead end, the impasse, of the castration complex can be got through.

We're going to be broaching that next time.

15 May 1963

XVIII

THE VOICE OF YAHWEH

Reik and the use of the symbol
The sound of the shofar
May God remember
The function of the beauty spot
What regards us

Broadly speaking, to give a cursory orientation to anybody who might by chance be arriving midway through this disquisition, I would say that we've come to the point of completing the range of object relations.

Indeed, based on the experience of anxiety, we've found ourselves having to add to the oral object, the anal object and the phallic object, inasmuch as each one generates and is correlative to a type of anxiety, two further stages of the object, thus bringing them to five.

For our last two meetings, I was at the level of the eye. I'm going to take my bearings there again today, so as to lead you to the stage that needs to be broached now, that of the ear.

As I told you, this is a broad presentation of things. It would be preposterous to believe that this is how things stand, except in an esoteric or obfuscating manner. Indeed, it is a matter of ascertaining what the function of desire is at each of these levels, and none of them can be separated from the repercussions they have on each of the others. A tight solidarity unites them, which is expressed in the subject's grounding in the Other along the path of the signifier and in the advent of a remainder around which the drama of desire revolves, a drama that would remain opaque for us were anxiety not there to enable us to reveal its meaning.

This often leads us to erudite jaunts in which some see goodness knows what charm that is proved or reproved in my teaching. Please believe that I don't advance in it without reticence. One day, the method by which I proceed in the teaching I impart to you will be studied. It's surely not up to me to spell out its rigour for you. The day they seek out its principle in the texts that might survive, that might be transmittable, that might still be understood, of what I'm giving you here, they will notice that in sum and substance this method is not distinct from the object that is being approached.

This method is born of a necessity. The truth of psychoanalysis, at the very least in part, is only accessible to a psychoanalyst's experience. The very principle of a public teaching sets off from the idea that this experience can nevertheless be communicated elsewhere. Having posited that, nothing is resolved, since psychoanalytic experience must itself be oriented, failing which it errs. It errs when it is partialized and, as we have unflaggingly pointed out since the start of this teaching, it has been partialized at various points along the way of the analytic movement, notably in what, far from being a consolidation of or a complement to the indications of Freud's late doctrine in the exploration of the ego's mainsprings and status, far from being a continuation of his work, is strictly speaking a deviation, a reduction, a veritable aberration of the field of experience, doubtless dictated by a kind of build-up that occurred in the field of the first analytic exploration, the exploration that was characterized by a style of illumination, a kind of brilliance that remains attached to the early decades of the dissemination of the Freudian teaching and the shape that the research of the first generation took.

Today I'm going to bring in one of them, who is still alive today, I believe, Theodor Reik, and precisely, among his numerous and immense technical and clinical contributions – some of his work has been qualified quite wrongly as applied psychoanalysis – his writings on the ritual.

Here it is specifically the article published in *Imago*, the eighth year or thereabouts – I didn't bring it along today because it slipped my mind – and which is devoted to something whose name you can see written on the board in Hebraic letters, the *shofar* – שופר.

1

This study by Reik has a sparkle, a brilliance, a fecundity of which it may be said that the style, the promise and the characteristics of the era of which it was part found themselves snuffed out in one fell swoop.

Nothing equivalent to what was produced in that period has been kept up and the reasons for this break deserve to be examined.

Nevertheless, if you read this article, you will see appear to the utmost, in spite of the praise I might shower on its penetration and high signification, a source of confusion, a deep lack of grounding, the most tangible form of which lies in what I shall call a purely analogical use of the symbol.

First of all, I need to shed some light on what this shofar is, as unsure as I am that all of you know what it designates. It is an object, and one which is going to be serving me as a fulcrum to give substance to what I understand of the *a* function at this level, the final level, at which we are permitted to reveal the sustentation function that binds desire to anxiety in its ultimate tying-in. You will understand why, rather than naming straightaway what the *a* is at this level – it exceeds the level of the occultation of anxiety in the desire linked to the Other – I'm approaching it through the handling of an object, a ritual object.

What is the shofar? It's a horn. It's a horn one blows into to make a sound. Those of you who've never heard it, I can only tell to go to the synagogue during the ritual of the Jewish festivities that follow the Jewish New Year, which is called *Rosh Hashanah* and which end on the Day of Great Atonement, the *Yom Kippur*, to treat themselves to the sound, thrice repeated, of the shofar.

This horn is generally, though not always, a ram's horn, in German *Widderhorn*, in Hebrew *Qeren hayyôbēl*. Three examples are reproduced in Reik's article, particularly precious and famed examples belonging to the London and Amsterdam synagogues. They share much the same general profile. Classically speaking, they look like this.

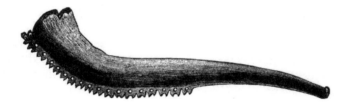

This one gives a pretty good idea of what it is.

The Jewish authors who have turned their attention to this object have drawn up a catalogue of its various forms, noting that there is one made from the horn of a wild goat. Certainly, an object that looks like this must far more probably be a result of some processing, alteration, reduction – who knows? it's an object of considerable length, larger than the one I've put on the blackboard for you – some utilization of ram horn.

Those who've treated themselves to this experience, or who are going to, will bear witness, I think – let's say, to remain within confines that are not overly lyrical – to the deeply moving, stirring character of these sounds. Independently of the atmosphere of reverence, of faith, even of repentance, in which these sounds blast out and resound, an unusual emotion emerges along the mysterious paths of a specifically auricular affect that cannot fail to touch, to a truly uncommon degree, all those who come within earshot of them.

When you read this study, you can only be struck by the pertinence, subtlety, and depth that were characteristic of the era to which it belongs and the reflections it is teeming with. It is not simply dotted with such reflections, it really gives the impression that they have been called forth from goodness knows what centre of intuition and flair. I know not what endless iteration, and worn-out method too, have since blunted us to what comes to the surface in these early pieces of work. But compared to everything that was being done at the time by way of erudite work – I can bear witness to this, trust me, you know that everything I bring you here is fed by enquiries on my part that often verge on what looks to be superfluous – Reik's specific way of examining the biblical texts, those in which the shofar is named as correlative to the major circumstances of the revelation made to Israel, was of an altogether different scope. Whilst Reik sets off from a position that, at the very least in principle, repudiates any traditional attachment, or even takes on the poise of an almost radical stance of critique, not to mention scepticism, one can only be struck by how much deeper he goes than any of the other apparently more respectful, more reverent commentators, those keener to preserve the crux of a message. He goes straight to what seems to be the truth of the historical advent reported by these biblical passages that I've been evoking and on which they focus.

It is no less striking to see how far he lapses in the end into an inextricable muddle, certainly for want of any of those theoretical touchstones that allow a pattern of study to lay down its own limits. Presenting the shofar and the voice that it supports as analogies of the phallic function is not adequate for us. And why not, indeed? But how, and at what level? This is where the question begins. This is also where people stop. At a certain limit, this intuitive and analogical handling of the symbol leaves the interpreter bereft of any criteria, and then everything overlaps, you lapse into an unspeakable mix-up. I'll just mention a few points, to give you some idea.

The ram's horn is certainly indicative of the correlation, and why not also say the conflict, with the entire totemic social structure into the midst of which the whole historical venture of Israel has been plunged. But how can it be that no barrier comes to halt Reik in his analysis, to stop him in the end from identifying Yahweh himself with the Golden Calf?

Making his way back down from Sinai, radiating the sublimity of the Father's love, Moses has already killed Him, the proof being that he becomes the out-and-out furious creature who will destroy the Golden Calf and powder it up for the Hebrews to consume. You will recognize here the dimension of the totemic meal. The oddest thing is that, the necessities of the demonstration only being able to go via Yahweh's identification, not with a calf, but with a bull, the calf in question will therefore necessarily be the representative of a son-divinity alongside a father-divinity. The calf has only been spoken about for the sake of throwing us off the scent, leaving us ignorant of the fact that there was a bull there too. Therefore, since Moses is the Father's murderous son, what does Moses destroy in the calf? Through the string of all these displacements pursued in a way that leaves us without any compass by which to take our bearings, he destroys his own emblem. Everything is consumed in a full-scale self-destruction.

I'm just giving you a certain number of points here, which show you the extremity that a certain form of analysis can reach in its immoderation. As for us, we're going to see what seems to deserve to be retrieved from this, in accordance with what we are seeking.

Our research compels us not to give up on the principles that feature in a certain text that is none other than the founding text of a psychoanalytic *Société*, the one to which I belong, the one that is the reason why I'm here, poised to deliver this teaching. This text stipulates that psychoanalysis can only be correctly situated among the sciences by submitting its technique to the examination of what it supposes and carries out in truth.

I have every right to recall how I had to defend this text and impose it when some folk who let themselves get drawn into this *Société* perhaps saw nothing but empty words therein. This text strikes me as fundamental, because what this technique supposes and carries out in truth is our touchstone, and any ruling, even a structural one, on what we have to deploy must be centred upon it. If we fail to acknowledge that what is involved in our technique is a handling, an interference, even bordering on a rectification, of desire, but which leaves the notion of desire entirely open and in abeyance and necessitates its perpetual re-examination, we can only wander off into the infinite network of the signifier, or else fall onto the most ordinary paths of traditional psychology.

This is how it is for Reik in what he uncovers in the course of this study and which he cannot turn to good account for want of knowing where to put the result of his discovery.

To go back over his analysis of the biblical texts, I'll just list those that claim to refer back to a revealing historical event. First there is

Exodus, Chapters 19 and 20, respectively verses 16 to 19 for Chapter 19, and verse 18 for Chapter 20.

First reference. The sound of the shofar is mentioned in the thunderous dialogue between Moses and the Lord, very enigmatically followed by a sort of enormous uproar, a veritable storm of noise.

One part of these verses also indicates that, even though it is strictly forbidden, not only to all men but to any living beast, to go up to the circle bounded with thunders and lightnings where this dialogue takes place, the people shall come up there when they hear the voice of the shofar. This point is so contradictory and enigmatic that in the translation they bend the meaning and say that *some* may go up. Who might that be? The business remains cloaked in obscurity.

The shofar is expressly mentioned once more in the ensuing dialogue, because it is said that the people who are supposed to have gathered around this major event hear the sound of the shofar.

To justify his analysis, Reik finds nothing else with which to qualify it than to say that an analytic exploration consists in looking for the truth in the details. This characteristic is neither false nor beside the point, but it is merely an external criterion, the assurance of a style, and not the guarantee of critical discernment which consists in knowing which detail is to be held onto. Most certainly, we have always known that the detail that guides us is the very one that seems to escape the author's design and remains opaque, shut off, with respect to the intention it preaches, but it is no less necessary to find, amidst the details, a criterion if not of hierarchy then at least of order and precedence. Be that as it may, we can only feel that his demonstration does touch on something legitimate.

Let's go back to the biblical texts. To the passages from Exodus are added those from Samuel, Chapter 6 of the second book, and those from the first book of Chronicles, Chapter 13, which make mention of the function of the shofar each time it is a matter of renewing the covenant with God in some fresh start, whether it be recurring or historical.

These texts also mention other occasions when the instrument is employed. There are first of all the uses that are carried on in the yearly celebrations, inasmuch as they refer to the recurrence and remembrance of the Covenant. Then there are those exceptional occasions like the ceremony of excommunication, under which, on 27 July 1656, as you know, Spinoza fell. He was excluded from the Hebraic community in every shape and form, which included, along with the words of malediction spoken by the high priest, the sounding of the shofar.

In this light, which is supplemented by the comparison of various occasions on which it is indicated and effectively made to function, it appears that this shofar is truly and verily, Reik tells us, the voice of Yahweh, the voice of God himself.

2

On a quick reading, this formula doubtless seems none too likely to be exploitable for analysis, but in fact it assumes importance for us in the perspective I'm training you in here.

Indeed, introducing a criterion that is more or less well marked out is something quite different from constituting, for these criteria, in their novelty and the efficiency they entail, what is called *une formation*, a training, and which is first and foremost *une reformation* of the mind in its power.

As far as we are concerned, such a formula can only hold our attention inasmuch as it makes us see what completes the subject's relation to the signifier in what might be called, in a first assimilation, his *passage à l'acte*.

There is someone here, on the far left-hand side of the audience, who cannot fail to be interested in this reference, and that is our friend Conrad Stein. I shall take this opportunity to say what satisfaction I felt on seeing that his analysis of *Totem and Taboo* led him to speak about what he calls primordial signifiers, which he cannot unfasten from what he too calls an act, namely, from what happens when the signifier is not only articulated, which merely presupposes its nexus, its coherence in a chain with others, but is uttered and voiced. For my part, I have some reservations over the term *act* being introduced here without further commentary. I want simply for the time being to pause over the fact that this brings us into a certain form, not of the act, but of the object *a*.

That which underlies the *a* needs to be fully unfastened from phonemization. Linguistics has accustomed us to noticing that it is nothing other than a system of oppositions, along with what that introduces by way of possibilities of substitution and displacement, metaphors and metonymies. This system is supported by any matter that is capable of organizing itself into oppositions that are distinctive for one and all. When something from this system passes into an utterance, a new dimension is involved, an isolated dimension, a dimension unto itself, the specifically vocal dimension.

In bodily terms, into what does the possibility of this utterable dimension plunge? You will understand, if you haven't already guessed, that introducing this exemplary object that on this occasion I've taken up in the shofar assumes its full value here – you can well imagine that this is not the only example I might have made use of – because it's within your reach, because it stands, if it actually is what we say it is, at a source-point from which our tradition gets rolling, because one of our forerunners in analytic enunciation has already dealt with it and highlighted it. But there are also the tuba, the trumpet, and other instruments besides, because it doesn't have to be a wind instrument, though it can't be just any old instrument. In the Abyssinian tradition, it's the drum. Had I gone on relating my trip to Japan, I would have reported on the place a certain type of drumming holds in Japanese theatre, in its most typical form, that of Noh, inasmuch as through its form and style this drumming has a very particular function of hastening on the main node of interest and linking it up. I might equally have gone about calling to mind, by referring to the ethnographic field, as does Reik, the function of the bullroarer, an instrument that is very close to a spinning top, though they are put together quite differently, which in the ceremonies of certain Australian tribes sound out a kind of bellowing that the instrument's name likens to nothing less than the roaring low of a bull. Reik's study compares it to the sound of the shofar because it is also put on the same level as what other passages of biblical text call *the roar of God*.

The exceptional interest of this object lies in how it presents the voice to us in an exemplary form where it stands, in a certain sense potentially, in a separated form. This is what will allow us to air a certain number of questions that are barely ever raised. What voice is at issue here? Let's not be too hasty. We're going to see its meaning and its locus by taking our bearings from the topography of the relation to the big Other.

The function of the shofar comes into action at certain periodic moments that initially present themselves as renewals of the pact of the Covenant. The shofar does not articulate its fundamental principles, the Commandments, and yet it is very clearly presented as having the function of harking back to this pact, right down to the dogmatic articulation made in this respect. This function – *Zachor*, remembrance, זָכוֹר – is even inscribed into the common name for the moment at which it comes into play – a medial moment in the three solemn blasts of the shofar at the end of the fast days of Rosh Hashanah – which is called *Zikkaron*, whilst the kind of quaver specific to a certain way of sounding the shofar is called *Zikhron Teruah*. Let's say that the sound of the shofar, the *Zichronot*, is the part of remembrance tied to this sound. Without doubt this remembrance is a remembrance of what has been meditated over in the moments that precede it, the *Akedah*, which is the precise moment in Abraham's sacrifice when God halts Abraham's willing hand so as to substitute, in the stead of the victim Isaac, the ram that you know about, or you think you know about.

Does this mean, however, that the very moment of the pact is fully included in the sound of the shofar? Is it the memory of the sound of the shofar, or the sound of the shofar as support to the memory? Who has to remember? Why would we think that it is the worshippers, because they've just spent a certain moment of reverence focused on this memory?

The question is of very great importance because it leads us onto ground where, in Freud's mind, in its most searing form, the function of repetition was traced out. Is the function of repetition simply automatic and linked to the return, the necessary carrying-over, of the battery of the signifier, or does it have another dimension? Meeting this other dimension in our experience, if this has a meaning, strikes me as inevitable. This dimension is what gives the interrogation borne by the locus of the Other its meaning. To spell it right out, isn't the one whose memory is to be awakened, the one who is to be made to remember, God himself?

This is the point to which we are brought, I won't say by this very simple instrument – because, truth be told, we can only feel at the very least a deep sense of quandary faced with the existence of such a piece of apparatus – but by its having crossed our path.

What we need to know now is where this separated object is inserted, to which domain it is to be attached – not within the inside/outside contrast, whose inadequacy you get a clear inkling of here, but within the reference to the Other and the stages of the emergence and progressive establishment for the subject of this field of riddles that the subject's Other is. At what moment can this kind of object come into the picture, with its face finally unveiled in its separable form?

What object is at issue here? This object is the one that is called the voice.

We are well acquainted with it, we think we are well acquainted with it, on the pretext that we are acquainted with its waste scraps, its dead leaves, in the form of the straying voices of psychosis, and its parasitic character in the form of the broken off imperatives of the superego.

This is where we have to mark out the place of this new object that, rightly or wrongly, with my intention of laying it out, I thought I should first present to you in a form that is not unwieldy and is even, indeed, exemplary.

To find our bearings, we have to locate what is new in what it introduces with respect to the previously articulated level, which had to do with the function of the eye in the structure of desire.

Everything that is revealed in this new dimension initially seems to be masked over at the previous level, which we need to come back to for a moment, the better to bring out what is new in the level at which there appears the form of the *a* known as the voice.

3

Let's come back to the level of the eye, which is also the level of space.

The space involved here is not the space that we can examine in the form of a category of transcendental aesthetics – even though the reference to Kant's contribution on this terrain is, if not very useful, at the very least extremely convenient for us – but space in what it presents as typical in its relation to desire.

The base of the function of desire is, in a style and a form that have to be specified each and every time, this pivotal object *a* inasmuch as it stands, not only separated, but always eluded, somewhere other than where it sustains desire, and yet in a profound relation to it. This character of elusion is nowhere more tangible than at the level of the function of the eye. It is in this respect that the most satisfying support of the function of desire, namely, the fantasy, is always marked by a kinship with the visual models in which it commonly functions, so to speak, and which set the tone of our desiring life.

In space, however – and the whole scope of this remark lies in this *however* – nothing in appearance is separated. Space is homogeneous. When we think in terms of space, even this body we have, our body, has a function. This is not idealism. It is not because space is a function of the mind that it might justify any Berkeleyism. Space is not an idea. It bears a certain relation, not to the mind, but to the eye.

The body's function is to be appended. As soon as we think about space, we have in some way to neutralize the body by localizing it. Think of the way in which, on the blackboard, the physicist makes mention of the function of a body in space. A body is anything and nothing – it's a point. But it's all the same something that is localized in space by something foreign to the dimensions of space, without producing those insoluble questions of the problem of individuation over which you have already heard me express my scorn on more than one occasion.

A body in space is at the very least something that presents itself as impenetrable. A certain realism of space is untenable. I'm not going to go back over the antinomies here, but the very use of the function of space suggests the undividable and punctiform unit, both necessary and untenable, that is known as an atom – which, of course, is not what this term refers to in physics and which has nothing atomic about it in the sense that it is in no way undividable.

Space only holds any interest given the presupposition of this ultimate resistance to the section, since it only possesses any real use if it is discontinuous, that is, if the unit at issue there cannot be at two different points at once. What does this mean for us? It means that this spatial unit, the point, can only be recognized as inalienable. It means that it can in no way be the a.

What is meant by what I'm telling you? I'm hurrying to make you fall back into the nets of what has already been understood. It means that through the form $i(a)$, my image, my presence in the Other has no remainder. I cannot see what I lose there. This is the meaning of the mirror stage.

The diagram on the blackboard is designed to ground the function of the ideal ego and the Ego Ideal, and to show you how the subject's relation to the Other functions when the specular relation is dominant there, a relation that on this occasion is being called the mirror of the big Other.

The image in its form $i(a)$, the specular image, is the object that typifies the mirror stage. It has more than one means of seduction, linked not only to the structure of each subject, but also to the function of cognition. This image is one of closure, it is gestaltian, that is, marked by the predominance of a *Prägnanz*, which should warn us against what this Gestalt function, in so far as it is founded on the experience characteristic of this field, that of *Prägnanz*, contains by way of pitfalls.

To reveal what is mere appearance in the satisfying character of form as such, even in the idea in so far as it is rooted in the visual εἶδος, to see what is mere illusion being torn away, all it takes is for a stain to be brought into the visual field and you can see where the point of desire is truly tethered. If you will allow me to employ the equivocal use of a common term, so as to lend support to what I want to make you hear, I shall say that a stain is all it takes to function as a beauty spot.

Beauty's grain and middlings – you'll permit me to pursue the equivocation[1] – show the place of the a, here reduced to the zero-point whose function I mentioned last time. Over and above the form it stains, the beauty spot regards me.[2] It attracts me so paradoxically because it's gazing at me, sometimes more deservedly than my partner's gaze, because this gaze reflects me and, inasmuch as it reflects me, it is but my reflection, an imaginary blur. The crystalline lens doesn't need to be thickened by a cataract to make vision blind – at least blind to castration which is always elided at the level of desire when it is projected into the image.

What gazes at us? The white glaze of the blind man's eyes, for example. Or, to take another image, one you will remember, I hope, even though it harks back to another year – think of the *gaudenti* in *La Dolce Vita*, at the film's final ghostly moment, when they make their way forward, skipping from shadow to shadow out from the pines and onto the beach, and see the dead-still eye of the marine creature the fishermen are hauling ashore. This is what regards us over and above anything else, and shows how anxiety emerges in vision at the locus of the desire that the *a* controls.

This is also the virtue of tattoos. I needn't remind you of the admirable passage in Lévi-Strauss when he evokes the flood of desire in thirsty colonists as they arrive in one zone of Paraná State to find women covered from head to toe with a shimmering of inter-woven designs in the widest variety of colours and shapes.

At the other end of the scale, I might mention the occurrence of the visual apparatus itself – for me, the reference to the emer-gence of forms is stamped with a style that is more creationist than evolutionist – which, at the level of the fringe cells of the lamel-libranchia begins with a pigmented patch, the first appearance of a distinct organ in the sense of a sensitivity that is already specifically visual. And, of course, nothing is more blind than a patch. To the silk *mouche* from earlier, shall I add the *Muscae volitantes* that, when one reaches one's fifties, or thereabouts, give a first warning of organic dangers?

It is through zero of *a* that visual desire masks over the anxiety of what desire essentially lacks. It is what condemns you never to be able to grasp any living being in the pure field of the visual signal except as what ethology calls a *dummy*, a puppet, an appearance.

The object *a* is what lacks, it is non-specular, it cannot be grasped in the image. I pointed out the blind man's white-eye as the image, at once revealed and irretrievably concealed, of scoptophillic desire. The eye of the voyeur himself appears to the Other for what it is – impotent. This is precisely what allows our civilization to take what it sustains and shut it away in a box, in various forms that are per-fectly consistent with the bank reserves and dividends it controls.

The reciprocal relationship between desire and anxiety presents itself at this specific level in a radically masked form, linked to the superlatively luring functions of the structure of desire. Now we have to pit this against the opening made for it by the distinct func-tion that today I have introduced with the accessory of the shofar, which is not, however, an accidental accessory.

Our most elementary tradition, the one that sets off from Freud's first steps, compels us to single out this other dimension. Once again, I shall pay homage to our friend Stein for having spelt it out so well in his disquisition. *If desire*, he says – and I subscribe to this formula, because I find it to be more than brilliant – *were primordial, if the mother's desire were what brought the original crime onto the stage, we would be in the realms of vaudeville.*

Freud tells us in the most categorical way that the origin – forget this and the whole chain comes undone, and it's on account of not having secured this first link in the chain that analysis, in theory and practice alike, seems to undergo a kind of dispersion wherewith one may sometimes wonder what is likely to go on holding it together – is the murder of the father and everything it dictates.

According to what one dares hope is only a metaphor in Reik's mouth, it is his *bellowing of a bull*, a felled bull, that is to be heard in the sound of the shofar. Let's say more simply that it's the originative fact written into the myth of the father's murder that sets rolling what we now have to grasp in its function within the economy of desire, namely, that what constitutes originative desire, in its most fundamental form, is forbidden, as impossible to transgress. It is, however, secondary in relation to a dimension that we have to tackle here, the relation to this essential object that acts as *a*, the voice, and what its function brings by way of new dimensions in the relationship between desire and anxiety.

This is the bend in the road where the functions of desire, the object, and anxiety, will be assuming their value once more, across all the stages right down to the original one.

So as not to fail to pre-empt your questions, and perhaps to tell those who've been asking themselves such questions that I'm not overlooking the furrows I have dug into this field in the interests of completeness, I shall note, as you may have noticed, that I haven't reported, at least since the resumption of our discussions this year, on either the anal object or the anal stage.

This is because it is also strictly speaking unthinkable, unless it is taken up completely from scratch in the function of desire, starting from this point which, for having been announced here as the final one, is the most originative, the object of the voice.

I'll be taking it up next time.

22 May 1963

XIX

THE EVANESCENT PHALLUS

From castration anxiety to orgasm

The pedagogy of castration
Jouissance in the fantasy
The Wolf Man's defecation
Always too soon
The dead ends of desire

Reading latterly a few recently published works on the relations between language and thought, I was led to re-presentify for myself what, after all, I might well from one moment to the next call into question for myself, namely, the place and the nature of the angle from which I've been trying to get to grips with something here – something which, either way, can only be an inevitable and necessary limit to your understanding.

Otherwise, what would I have to say to you?

1

The obstacle at issue doesn't present any particular difficulty at its objective core, the entire progress of a science bearing as much and more on the phasic revision of its concepts as on the extension of its hold. But that which does nevertheless constitute an obstacle here, I mean in the psychoanalytic field, warrants particular reflection.

This cannot be resolved as easily as the obstacles that arise when going from one conceptual system to another, for instance from the Copernican system to the Einsteinian system, a passage that for sufficiently developed minds, minds sufficiently open to mathematics, didn't prove difficult for long. It imposed itself fairly rapidly given that Einstein's equations abide by, include, those that went before.

They situate them as particular cases and therefore resolve them entirely. This doesn't mean that there shan't be a moment's resistance, as history has borne out, but it's short-lived.

In analysis, in analytic technique in so far as we are implicated in it – to a greater or lesser extent, you're already somewhat implicated in it when you start to take a bit of interest in analysis – we ought to meet in the development of the concepts the same obstacle that has been recognized as constituting the limits of analytic experience – namely, castration anxiety.

Lending an ear to my voice as it comes back at me from various distances – and not always necessarily in answer to what I've said, but certainly in response, a response coming from a particular zone – everything happens as though at certain moments certain technical positions were hardening up, positions that are strictly correlative in this matter of analysis to what I may call the limitations of understanding. Likewise, everything happens as though, in order to overcome these limits, I had chosen the path defined by a pedagogical school that ostensibly had its own way of posing the problem of school education with respect to the maturation of the child's thinking, and as though I subscribed to this.

I do indeed subscribe to a pedagogical style of procedure, which I am now going to spell out and define. When you take a close look at the pedagogical debate, the schools of thought are a long way from being in agreement on this score, as those of you who have been required more than the rest to turn your attention to pedagogical procedures will be able to note.

For one school – let's designate one, for example, in William Stern's theories, even though a fair number of you have never opened the works of this nonetheless widely renowned psychologist – everything is determined by an autonomous maturing of intelligence, one simply follows the school age. For another school, let's take Piaget's one, there is a gap, a rift, between what children's thinking is capable of forming and what can be brought to them by the scientific path. If you take a closer look, in both cases this amounts to reducing the efficacy of teaching to zero.

Now, teaching does exist.

Although many minds in the scientific sphere may fail to acknowledge this, what belongs strictly to the realm of teaching – in the sense I'm about to specify – can be taken to be something that can be elided once one has gained access to the scientific field. When one has got through a certain stage of mathematical understanding, once that's been done, it's done for good and there's no need to go on seeking out its paths. One can access it without the slightest trouble so long as one belongs to the generation that benefited from being taught in this form, in this primary formalization. Concepts that might once have seemed extremely complicated at a previous stage of mathematics are now immediately accessible to very young minds. No intermediary is required.

It is certain that at school age this is not so. The whole point of schooling lies in grasping this vital fact and in anticipating what one may call the child's mental capacities with problems that lie just slightly beyond them. In helping the child to tackle these problems, I'm only saying *helping*, one does something that doesn't only have a pre-maturing effect, a hastening effect on mental maturation, but which, at certain periods that are termed *sensitive* – those of you who know a thing or two on this topic can perfectly well follow me where I'm heading, because the important thing is my disquisition and not my references, which you might not be acquainted with – enables one to obtain true opening effects, even unleashing effects. In some domains, certain activities that are designed to afford a grasp of something have effects of fecundity that are really very special.

It seems to me that this is exactly what can be obtained in the domain we are moving into here. Given the specificity of the field concerned, something is involved that one day the pedagogues would do well to map out.

There are already hints of it in work from authors whose testimony it is all the more interesting to keep in mind on account of their having no notion of what we are able to do with their experiments. I'm speaking of those experimenters who are unfamiliar with analysis and have no wish to familiarize themselves with it. The fact that one pedagogue of this ilk should have formulated that there is only any true access to concepts from the age of puberty onwards warrants us casting an eye over it, having a sniff around. There are hundreds of tangible traces of the fact that the moment at which the functioning of the concept truly begins, and which the authors on this occasion name, exploiting a homonymy of sheer encounter with the term *complex* that we make use of, the *complexual limit-moment*, could be furnished with a very different mapping, contingent upon a link to be established in reference to the maturation of the object *a*, such as I define it, at the said age of puberty.

2

The position of the *a* at the moment of its passage through what I symbolize with the formula $(- \varphi)$ is one of the goals of our explanation this year.

The moment qualified by the notation (– φ), which is castration anxiety, can only be transmitted to you in a valuable way, your ears can only take it on board, by an approach that here can only be a roundabout path.

It was because this anxiety cannot be presentified as such, but only ascertained by a concentric path, that last time you saw me oscillating between the oral stage and something which is the voice, which I supported through its evocation in a separated form, materialized in an object, the shofar. You'll permit me to lay this object aside for a short while in order to come back to the pivotal point I've been evoking by speaking of castration.

What actually is anxiety's relation to castration? Knowing that it is experienced as such in some phase, said to be terminal – or non-terminal – of analysis is not enough for us actually to know what it is.

To set things out straightaway as they will be articulated at the next step, I shall say that the function of the phallus as imaginary functions everywhere, across all the levels that I qualified as a certain relationship between the subject and the *a*. The phallus functions across the board, in a mediating function, except where we expect it to, namely, at the phallic stage. It is this shortcoming of the phallus, which moreover is present and ascertainable everywhere, often to our great astonishment, it is this fading of the phallic function at the level where the phallus is expected to function, that lies behind the principle of castration anxiety. Hence the notation (– φ) which denotes this, so to speak, positive shortcoming. Never having been formulated in this form, it has not given rise to any of its lessons being learnt.

To make the truth of this formula more appreciable for you, I'm going to be taking various paths in a roundabout way. And since I reminded you last time of the structure that is specific to the visual field, the simultaneous sustentation and occultation of the object *a* in this field, I can do no less than come back to it, when this is the field in which the phallic presence is first approached, and in a way we know to be traumatic. This is what is known as the primal scene.

Everyone knows, in spite of the phallus being present and visible here in the form of the functioning of the penis, that what is striking in the evocation of the reality of the fantasized form of the primal scene is always some ambiguity with respect to this presence. How often can one read precisely that it is not to be seen in its place? Sometimes even the nub of the scene's traumatic effect is due to the forms beneath which it disappears, beneath which it makes itself scarce. Moreover, I will only need to bring up the mode of

apparition of this primal scene in its exemplary form, along with the
anxiety that comes with it, in the Wolf Man's story.

We heard somewhere that there was apparently something obsessional in the way we keep coming back to the original examples of
the Freudian discovery. These examples are more than supports,
even more than metaphors, they bring us to put our finger on the
very substance of what we are dealing with.

In the revelation of what appears to the Wolf Man through
the gap and the frame – pre-figuring what I turned into a function –
of the open window, and which can be identified in its form with the
function of the fantasy in its most anxiety-provoking mode, where
lies the crux? Clearly it doesn't lie in the fact of knowing where the
phallus is. It is, as it were, everywhere – identical to what I could
call the catatonia of the image of the tree and the perched wolves
that – see if you will the echo of what I spelt out last time – hold
the subject in their gaze. There's no need to go looking for it in the
five furry tails of the five animals. It is there in the very reflection of
the image, which it supports with a catatonia that is nothing but the
subject's own, the child turned to stone by what he sees, paralysed
by this fascination to the point that one may conceive of what gazes
back at him in the scene, and which is invisible on account of being
everywhere, as nothing but the transposition of the arrested state of
his own body, here transformed into a tree, *L'arbre couvert de loups*,
we might say, to echo a famous book title.

That something is at issue here that echoes the lived pole we have
defined as the pole of jouissance strikes me as incontestable. This
jouissance – akin to what Freud elsewhere called the Rat Man's
horror at a jouissance of which he was ignorant, a jouissance that
exceeds any possible marking-out by the subject – is here presentified in this erect form. The subject is no more than an erection in this
grip that makes him a phallus, that freezes him from head to toe,
that arborifies him.

Something then occurs at the level of the symptomatic development of the scene's effects. Freud tells us that this element has only
been reconstructed, but it is so essential that the analysis Freud
gives would not hold together were we not to accept it. This element
remains the only one, right to the very end, that the subject doesn't
integrate and it presentifies for us on this occasion what Freud
would later articulate concerning reconstruction per se. This element
is that the subject responds to the primal scene by defecating.

The first time, or thereabouts, at least the first time Freud reports
on the appearance of the excremental object at a critical moment, he
articulates it in a function to which we can give no other word but
the one that we thought we would be having to give as typifying the

genital stage, namely, the function of oblativity. We are told that it's a gift. Everyone knows that Freud underlined at an early stage of his work the character of an offering that marks those occasions when the infant produces an untimely release of his intestinal content. In passing, and without further commentary on such occasions, if you remember the bearings I've laid out, you will permit me to call them occasions of *passage à l'acte*.

In the text of *The Wolf Man*, things go even further, restoring its true meaning which we've been drowning out under a sneaking moralizing supposition by talking about oblativity. Freud speaks of sacrifice in this connection. Given that he was well-read, that, for example, he had read Robertson Smith, when he spoke about sacrifice he wasn't sprouting idle words with some vague moral analogy. If Freud speaks of sacrifice in connection with the appearance of the excremental object in this field, it must all the same actually mean something.

This is where we're going to take things up at the level, if you will, of the normal act, which gets qualified, rightly or wrongly, as mature.

3

In my penultimate lesson, I articulated orgasm in its equivalence to anxiety.

I situated it in the subject's inner field, whilst provisionally leaving castration with just this one mark $(-\varphi)$. It is quite clear that its sign cannot be detached from the Other's intervention, this characteristic having always been assigned to the Other, from the start, in the guise of castration threats.

I remarked in this regard that in making orgasm and anxiety equivalent I was joining up with what I'd previously said about anxiety as a reference point, a signal, of the sole relation that does not deceive, and that here we could find the reason behind the satisfying aspect of orgasm. We can understand the function of orgasm, and more specifically the satisfaction it brings, on the basis of something that occurs in the aim that gives confirmation of the fact that anxiety is not without object.

I thought I could say that and no more and be understood, but echoes have come back to me, let's say to put it mildly, of some bafflement, the terms of which were exchanged between two people whom I believe I've trained particularly well and whose discussion over what I meant by satisfaction on that occasion is all the more astonishing. Is it a matter, they wondered, of jouissance? Would this amount to a return to that cockeyed absolute that some seek to place in what is claimed to be a genital fusing? And then, the anxiety-point was at issue – place in this point all the ambiguity you will. Now, there is no more anxiety if orgasm comes to cover it back over. As for the point of desire, which is marked by the absence of the object *a* in the form (– φ), what about this relation in women?

Here's the reply. In no way did I say that the satisfaction of orgasm was to be identified with what I defined, in the Seminar on ethics, with regard to the locus of jouissance. It even seems wry to underline the trifling satisfaction, albeit sufficient, that is brought by orgasm. Why would it be the same and why would it occur at the same point as this other trifle that is offered to women in copulation, even successful copulation? This is what needs to be spelt out in the most precise fashion.

Saying vaguely that the satisfaction of orgasm is comparable to what I called, on the oral plane, the crushing of demand under the satisfaction of need, is not enough. At the oral level, distinguishing need from demand is easily sustainable, but elsewhere is not so in the least, without posing us the problem of where the drive is located. Although, through some wile or other, people might mince their words over what there is that is originative in demand's footing in the drive at the oral level, we have no right to do so at the genital level. Precisely there, where it would seem that we are dealing with the most primal instinct, the sexual instinct, we mustn't fail to refer, more than elsewhere, to the structure of the drive as supported by the formula ($ ◊ D), that is, by the relationship between desire and demand.

What is asked at the genital level, and of whom?

That inter-human copulation should be something transcendental in relation to individual existence is such a common fact of experience that, faced with the evidence, people end up no longer noticing the depth it carries. We had to take a detour via a biology that is already fairly advanced in order to notice the strict correlation between the appearance of bisexuality – the appearance of two sexes – and the emergence of the function of individual death. But in the end, it had always been sensed, right from the start – in this act, to which what we ought to call *the survival of the species* ties in closely, something is conjoined that cannot fail to concern, if the words have a meaning, what we marked out as an ultimate term with *the death drive*.

After all, why refuse to see what is immediately tangible in facts which we are altogether familiar with and which are signified in the most common uses of a language? What we ask – of whom, I haven't said yet, but in the end, since we have to ask it of someone, it happens to be our partner, is it sure that the partner is the one? That remains to be seen in a second phase – what do we ask exactly? We ask for the satisfaction of a demand that bears a certain relation to death. It doesn't go very far. What we ask for – it's *la petite mort* – but in the end it's clear that this is what we ask and that the drive is tightly entwined with the demand of lovemaking, to *faire l'amour* – if you will, *faire l'àmourir*, to do it to death, it's even *à mourir de rire*, to die laughing – I'm not accentuating the side of love that partakes of what I call a comical mood just for the sake of it. In any case, this is precisely where the restful side of post-orgasm resides. If this demand for death is what gets satisfied, well, good gracious, it's lightly satisfied, because one gets off lightly.

The advantage of this conception is that it accounts for what is involved in the appearance of anxiety in a certain number of ways of reaching orgasm. Anxiety appears – Freud had a first grasp of it in *coitus interruptus* – to the extent that orgasm is uncoupled from the field of what is asked of the Other. It appears, if I may say so, in the leeway of a loss of signification, but as such it continues to designate what is targeted in a certain relation to the Other.

I'm not telling you that castration anxiety is death anxiety. It's an anxiety that refers back to the field in which death ties in closely with the renewal of life. That analysis should have located it in this point of castration really allows us to understand how it may equally be interpreted as the reason why it is given to us in Freud's late conception as the signal of a threat to the status of the defended *I*. Castration anxiety refers back to the beyond of this defended *I*, to this foretoken of a jouissance that exceeds our limits, in so far as the Other here is strictly speaking called forth in the register of the real whereby a certain form of life is transmitted and sustained.

Call it what you will, God or some such demigod – I think I've already indicated sufficiently in my talks that this doesn't lead us towards any metaphysical heights. An aspect of the real is at issue here, something that maintains what Freud articulated at the level of his Nirvana principle as life's property of having to pass, in order to get to death, by way of forms that reproduce those that gave individual form the opportunity of occurring through the conjunction of two sexual cells.

What does that mean? What does that mean with regard to what happens at the level of the object, if not that, all in all, this result, or what I just called a lightly won result, is only carried through in such a satisfying way in the course of a certain automatic cycle, which remains to be defined, and precisely because of the fact that the organ is never likely to hold up very far on the road along which jouissance does its bidding? With regard to this aim of jouissance and with regard to reaching the final point, which would be tragic, targeted in the Other's bidding, the amboceptive organ can be said to yield, each and every time, prematurely. When the time comes at which it could be the sacrificial object, so to speak, well, let's say that, in the ordinary case, it had ducked out a long while before. It's no more than a scrap, it is no longer there for the partner save as a keepsake, a souvenir of tenderness.

This is what the castration complex is all about. In other words, it only becomes a drama in so far as the calling into question of desire is stirred and nudged in a certain direction, the direction that puts every confidence in genital consummation.

If we let go of this ideal of genital fulfilment by taking note of what is structurally and happily gulling about it, there is no reason for the anxiety bound to castration not to appear to us in a far more flexible correlation with its symbolic object and therefore in a very different opening with objects from another level. Furthermore, this was implied from the start by the premises of Freudian theory which places desire, as far as its structuring is concerned, in a completely different relation from a purely and simply natural one with the partner who is said to be natural.

To give a better sense of what's at issue, I'd like all the same to call to mind what's involved in those, as it were, initially uncouth dealings between man and woman. After all, in conformity with what I put forward on the relation between anxiety and the desire of the Other, a woman doesn't know who she's dealing with, she doesn't stand before a man without a certain uneasiness as to how far the path of desire is going to lead her. Once the man, my goodness, has made love like everyone else does and lies uncocked, if it so happens that the woman has not derived any, I'll say, tangible profit from it, which, as you know, is quite conceivable, she has at any rate gained the following – she can now be quite easy in her mind as to her partner's intentions.

In the same section of *The Waste Land* in which T. S. Eliot gives voice to Tiresias, to whom I thought one day back in March I should refer so as to compare our experience with the age-old theory of women's superiority on the plane of jouissance, we find these lines of verse whose irony has always struck me as something that should one day find its place in our disquisition.[1] When the *young man carbuncular*, the dandyish *small house agent's clerk*, has had his way with the typist, whose surroundings are depicted at length, Eliot expresses himself thus –

When lovely woman stoops to folly and
Paces about her room again, alone,

She smoothes her hair with automatic hand,
And puts a record on the gramophone.

When lovely woman stoops to folly, that's untranslatable. It's a
song from *The Vicar of Wakefield.* Let's say, *Quand une jolie femme
s'abandonne à la folie – stoops* is not even *s'abandonne,* it's *s'abaisse
– pour enfin se trouver seule, elle arpente la chambre en lissant ses
cheveux d'une main automatique, et change de disque.* This comes by
way of reply to the question my pupils were asking each other as to
what is involved in a woman's desire.

Woman's desire is determined by the question, for her too, of
her jouissance. Analytic theory has been telling us from the start
that she is not only far closer to jouissance than men are, but also
doubly determined. That the locus of this jouissance is not linked
to the enigmatic, unplaceable character of her orgasm, is what our
analyses have pushed quite far enough for us to be able to say that
this locus is a point that is archaic enough to precede the present
partitioning of the cloaca. This was perfectly marked out, from a
certain analytic perspective, by an analyst, and one of the feminine
sex. That desire, which is not jouissance, should in woman be naturally right where it ought to be according to nature, that is, tubal, is
perfectly designated by those women known as hysterics. The fact
that we have to classify these subjects as hysterics doesn't change
anything of the fact that desire placed in this way lies in the realm of
the true, the organically true.

Since man will never bring the leading edge of his desire this far,
one is able to say that man's jouissance and woman's jouissance will
never conjoin organically. To the extent that man's desire miscar-
ries, woman is led, if I may say, normally, to the idea of having the
man's organ, inasmuch as it would be a genuine amboceptor, and
this is what is called the phallus. It's because the phallus doesn't
achieve any matching of the desires, save in its evanescence, that it
becomes the common-place of anxiety.

What woman asks of the analyst at the end of an analysis con-
ducted in accordance with Freud's indications, is without doubt
a penis, *Penisneid,* but so that she might do better than the man.
There is something, there are a good many things, there are hundreds of things, that confirm all this. Without analysis, how might
woman overcome her *Penisneid,* if we deem it to be always inherent?
We are very familiar with how. It's the most ordinary pattern of
seduction between the sexes – it is to offer man's desire the object
behind the phallic claims, the non-detumescent object to sustain his
desire, namely, to make her feminine attributes the signs of man's
almightiness.

This is what I thought it necessary to develop a long while back – I ask you to refer to my former Seminars – by underlining, after Joan Riviere, the specific function of what she calls the womanly masquerade. Simply put, woman has to take her jouissance down a peg. If we leave her in some way on this path, we endorse the renewal of these phallic claims, which become, I wouldn't say the compensation, but something like the price to be paid for what is asked of her, all in all, for being saddled with the Other's miscarriage.

These are the paths along which genital realization presents itself, inasmuch as it would supposedly put an end to what we might call the dead ends of desire, were it not for the opening of anxiety.

Starting off from the point to which I've brought you today, next time we'll be seeing how all analytic experience shows us that the phallus, to the extent that it is summoned as an object of propitiation in a dead-end conjunction, and turns out to be missing, constitutes castration itself as a point that it is impossible to circumvent in the subject's relation to the Other, and as a resoluble point as far as its function of anxiety is concerned.

29 May 1963

XX

WHAT COMES IN THROUGH THE EAR

Deceptive phallic might
The infant's monologue
Isakower's prawn
The incorporation of the voice
The Gods ensnared in desire

What I told you last time concluded, significantly I believe, in the silence that greeted my comments, nobody it seems having maintained the composure to crown it with a little applause.

Either I'm mistaken, or else it wouldn't be overmuch to see in this the result of what I expressly announced when opening the topic, that is, that it wasn't possible to approach castration anxiety head on without provoking a few ripples.

After all, this is not an excessive claim since what I said to you is, all in all, something that might be qualified as not very heartening as regards the union between man and woman, a problem that at any rate has always been present, and rightly so, in the preoccupations of psychoanalysts. I hope it still enters into them.

Jones circled for a long while around this problem, embodied by what is reckoned to be implied by the phallocentric perspective, namely, the primordial ignorance, not just the man's but woman's too, concerning the locus of conjunction, namely, the vagina. The roundabout paths, in part fruitful, albeit inconclusive, that Jones took on this route show their design in the invocation to which he turns, the famous *male and female created He them*, which is moreover so ambiguous.

After all, Jones didn't do his pondering over verse 27 of the first chapter of Genesis in reference to the Hebrew text.

1

Be that as it may, let's try to lend support to what I said last time with my little diagram which has been put together on the model of the Eulerian circle.

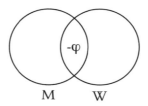

The lack of mediation

The field covered by man and by woman in what might be called, in the biblical sense, their knowledge of one another, only intersects in that the zone to which their desires lead them with an eye to reaching each other, and in which they would effectively be able to overlap, is qualified by the lack of what would otherwise constitute their medium. The phallus is what, for everybody, when it is reached, precisely alienates one from the other.

Woman can most certainly be the man's symbol in his desire for phallic almightiness, but precisely inasmuch as she is no longer woman. As for her, it is quite clear from everything we have uncovered under the term *Penisneid* that she can only take the phallus for what it isn't – either as *a*, the object, or as her own over-small *phi*, which only gives her an approximate jouissance in relation to what she imagines of the Other's jouissance, in which doubtless she can share through a kind of mental fantasy, but only by straying from her own specific jouissance. In other words, she can only enjoy (φ) because it's not in its place, in the place of her jouissance, in the place where her jouissance might be realized.

I'm going to give you a little illustration of this, rather a hot one, not in the least run of the mill, but topical.

In an audience such as this, how many times have we seen, to the extent that it's becoming a constant in our practice, women wanting to be analysed like their husbands, and often by the same psychoanalyst? What does this mean if not that they aspire to share in the supposedly rewarded desire of their husbands? The minus minus-phi, − (− φ), the re-positivizing of the *phi* they reckon to be operating in the psychoanalytic field, is what they aspire to gain access to.

The fact that the phallus is not to be found where it's expected, where it's demanded, namely, on the plane of genital mediation, is what explains how anxiety is the truth of sexuality, that is, what appears each time its ebb tide washes back and lets show the sand beneath. Castration is the price of this structure, it comes in the stead of this truth. But in actual fact, this is an illusory game. There is no castration because, at the locus at which it occurs, there is no object to castrate. The phallus would have to have been there for that. Now, it is only there so that there won't be any anxiety. The phallus, where it is expected as something sexual, only ever appears as a lack, and this is its link with anxiety.

All this means that the phallus is called upon to function as an instrument of might.[1] When we speak of might in analysis, we do so in a way that wavers because we are forever referring to almightiness, though this is not actually what's involved. Almightiness is already a slide, a sidestep, with respect to the point at which all might falters. We don't ask might to be everywhere, we ask it to be where it is present, precisely because when it falters where it is expected, we start to foment almightiness. In other words, the phallus is present, it is present *wherever it is not* on the spur of the moment.

This is the facet that allows us to pierce through the illusion that lies behind the claims generated by castration inasmuch as it covers over the anxiety presentified by each actualization of jouissance. This illusion is owing to a confusion between jouissance and the instruments of might. With the progress of institutions, human inability finds itself better off than its fundamental state of misery. It forms a profession. I mean profession in every sense of the word, from the profession of faith through to the professional ideal. Everything that shelters behind the dignity of a profession always boils down to this central lack that inability is. Inability dooms man not to be able to enjoy save in his relation to the support of $(+ \varphi)$, that is, a deceptive might.

I'm reminding you that this structure only comes along as the ensuing part of what I articulated last time so that now I can bring you to a few remarkable facts that govern the structure thus articulated.

The homosexuality that is placed at the root of social adhesion in our theory, Freudian theory, is the male's privilege. We may observe that Freud always marked it out thus and never cast the slightest doubt on it. This libidinal adhesion of the social bond, in so far as it only occurs in the community of males, is linked to the side of sexual miscarriage that is especially allotted to the male due to the fact of castration.

On the other hand, what is called female homosexuality might hold great cultural importance, but it has no value as a social function because it pertains to the field specific to sexual rivalry, that is, right where it would appear to have the least chance of success, were the subjects who carry the advantage in this field not precisely those who haven't got the phallus. Almightiness, the greatest vivacity of desire, occurs at the level of the love that is called Uranian and whose very radical affinity with female homosexuality I believe I've marked out in its place.

Idealistic love presentifies mediation by the phallus as $(-\varphi)$. In both sexes, the (φ) is what I desire, but also what I can only have as $(-\varphi)$. This minus turns out to be the universal medium in the field of sexual conjunction.

This minus, dear Reboul, is not in the least bit Hegelian, not in the least bit reciprocal. It constitutes the field of the Other as a lack and I only gain access to it in so far as I take this very path, and I become attached to the fact that the play of the minus leads me to disappear. I only find myself again in what Hegel did see, of course, but whose grounding he specifies without including this interval, namely, in a generalized *a*, in the idea of the minus inasmuch as it is everywhere, that is, it is nowhere.

Desire's support is not cut out for sexual union because, being all-pervasive, it no longer specifies me as man *or* woman, but as one *and* the other. The function of the field described on the diagram as the field of sexual union sets out for each of the two sexes the alternative – either the Other, or the phallus, in the sense of exclusion. This field here is empty. But if I make this field positive, the *or* takes on a different meaning and then means that one can be replaced by the other at any moment.

This was why I introduced the field of the eye that lies hidden behind all spatial universe, employing a reference to those image-beings which, when met, enable a certain pathway of salvation to be teased out, namely, the Buddhist path. The more Guanyin, or Avalokiteśvara, in his complete sexual ambiguity, presentifies himself as male, the more he takes on female aspects. If that amuses you, I'll show you some other day a few images of Tibetan statues or paintings, they are aplenty, where the feature I'm designating glares out at you.

Today, it's a matter of grasping how the alternative between desire and jouissance can find its point of passage.

The difference that lies between dialectical thought and our experience lies in the fact that we do not believe in synthesis. If there exists a point of passage where the antinomy closes, then it's because it was already there before the antinomy was formed.

2

For the object *a*, which embodies the dead end of desire's access to the Thing, to reveal the point of passage, we have to go back to its beginning.

Were nothing to have readied this passage prior to the capture of desire in specular space, there wouldn't be any way out.

Indeed, let's not overlook the fact that the possibility of this dead end is itself linked to a moment that anticipates and conditions what comes to be marked in sexual miscarriage for man. This is the moment, such an early moment, at which the field of insight is so very profoundly eroticized when specular tension comes into play.

We know, since Köhler and Yerkes, what starts to take shape in anthropoids as the guiding characteristic of this field now that the observation of apes has shown us that they are not devoid of intelligence inasmuch as they can do many things, but on the condition that they are able to see what is to be reached. Yesterday evening I alluded to the fact that everything is laid out there, not that primates are any more incapable than we are of speaking, but because they can't bring their speech into this operative field.

This is not the only difference. There is another, which has to do with the fact that animals don't have a mirror stage, therefore there isn't any narcissism, in so far as this term indicates a certain omnipresent subtraction of libido and its injection into the field of insight, whose form is given by specularized vision. But this form hides from us the phenomenon of the occultation of the eye, which thereafter will gaze on us from everywhere, will place us under the universality of seeing.

We know that this can occur. This is what is called *unheimlich*, but it requires very particular circumstances. Usually, what is satisfying in specular form is precisely that it masks over the possibility of this apparition. In other words, the eye institutes the fundamental relationship of the *desirable* inasmuch as it always tends, in the relation to the Other, to lead one to misrecognize how beneath the *desirable* there is a *desirer*.

Reflect if you will on the scope of this formula, which I'm giving as the most comprehensive formula for the emergence of the *Unheimliche*. Imagine that you're dealing with the most restful *desirable*, in its most soothing form, a divine statue that is just divine – what could be more *unheimlich* than to see it come to life, that is, to show itself as a *desirer*?

Now, the structuring hypothesis that we posit at the genesis of the *a* is that it is born elsewhere and prior to the capture that conceals it.

This hypothesis is founded on our practice and it is from there that I'm introducing it.

Either our praxis is inaccurate, I mean inaccurate with respect to itself, or it presupposes our field, the field of desire, to be generated by the relation of S to A. We can but meet up with this relation in our praxis, in so far as we reproduce its terms. Our praxis generates this universe, symbolized in the ultimate terms provided by the famous division that has been guiding us for a while now through the three phases in which the S, a still unknown subject, has to be constituted in the Other, where the *a* appears as the remainder of the operation.

In passing, I'll tell you that the alternative *either our praxis is inaccurate or it presupposes the above*, is not an exclusive one. Our practice can allow itself to be partially inaccurate with respect to itself and for there to be a residue, since this is precisely what is foreseen. We may therefore presume – it's a big presumption – that we risk very little in committing ourselves to a formalization that goes on to establish itself as something necessary. But it needs to be said that the relation of S to A far outstrips in its complexity – which is, however, so straightforward and inaugural – what those who've bequeathed us the definition of the signifier believe they are duty-bound to posit at the root of the interplay they marshal, namely, the notion of communication.

Communication as such is not what is primordial, because at the origin, S has got nothing to communicate for the reason that all the instruments of communication lie on the other side, in the field of the Other, and it is from the Other that S stands to receive them. As I've been saying from the start, the result of this is that at root the subject receives his own message from the Other. The first emergence, the one that is set down in the table, is simply an unconscious, since it is unformulable, *What am I?*, to which corresponds, before it is actually formulated, a *Thou art*. In other words, the subject first receives his own message in an inverted form.

I've been saying this for a long time. Today, I'm adding, if you care to lend an ear, that he first receives it in an initially broken-off form. First of all he hears a *Thou art* without any attributive. As broken-off as this message is, however, and therefore insufficient, it is never unformed, because language exists in the real, it is afoot, in circulation, and many things with respect to this S, in its presumed primordial questioning, have already been settled in this language.

Now, to take up my sentence from earlier, if I define the relation between S and A as I do, it's not only by hypothesis, because it's a hypothesis that I said was founded in our praxis, because I identified it with this praxis, up to and including its limits. What's more, the observable fact – and why is it so poorly observed? – confirms the autonomous play of speech such as it is supposed in this table. I think there are enough mothers unafflicted with deafness here to know that young toddlers, at an age when the mirror phase is far from having brought its work to a close, monologue before falling asleep as soon as they possess a few words. Time will prevent me from reading you today a long page where one such monologue has been transcribed. I can promise you some satisfaction when I do manage to do so.

Good fortune had it that, after my friend Roman Jakobson had for ten years enjoined all his expecting pupils to put an audio tape recorder in the nursery, two or three years ago this was eventually done, thanks to which we finally have the publication of one of these primordial monologues. I'm making you wait a bit because this is the right moment to show a fair number of other things besides what I have to delineate today.

My having to bring in like this references from far afield, without really knowing what you might already be familiar with, shows in and of itself to what extent we're fated to shift over into a sphere in which your being educated is nothing less than guaranteed, regardless of what people may think and regardless of what might have been spent on lessons and lectures.

Either way, some of you might remember what Piaget calls egocentric language and what is involved in this denomination, which may perhaps be tenable but is conducive to all kinds of misunderstandings. Indeed, this expression designates those sorts of monologue that a child engages in aloud when placed alongside a few playmates in a common task. Such monologues, which are very clearly turned in upon the child himself, can only occur, however, in a certain community. This is not an objection to this being qualified as egocentric, so long as its meaning is specified. Moreover, since we're speaking of egocentrism, it can seem striking that the subject of the statement is so often elided.

I'm calling this reference to mind to encourage you perhaps to renew contact with this phenomenon in Piaget's texts, for whatever purpose it may serve as a future reference, but above all to have you note that the problem arises of where to situate in relation to this display the hypnopompic monologue recorded by Jakobson's student, which emerges at a much earlier stage.

I shall say right away that the famous graph that's been badgering you so much over the years shows its worth in connection with these problems of genesis and development. Be that as it may, the toddler's monologue I'm talking about never occurs when someone else is there. The presence of a younger sibling, another babe in the bedroom, is all it takes for it not to happen. A fair number of other factors indicate that what is going on at this level, and which is such an astonishing revelation of just how early on these tensions in the unconscious that are called primordial are produced, is in every respect analogous to the function of the dream. Everything is happening on the Other stage, with the stress I've given to this term.

Oughtn't we to be guided here by the little door – it's never a bad way in – through which I've been introducing you to the problem, namely, the constitution of the *a* as a remainder? In every case, if its conditions really are those I've been telling you, we've only got this phenomenon in the state of a remainder, that is, on the tape reel. Otherwise, at the very most we have merely the far-off murmur which might break off at any moment should we appear. Doesn't this introduce us to the consideration that a path is being offered us here, by which to grasp that, for the subject in the making, we really ought to seek out the remainder on the side of a voice unfastened from its support.

Be very careful here. We really mustn't move too fast.

3

The ordinary experience is that everything the subject receives from the Other in terms of language is received in a vocal form. The experience of cases that are not so rare, though people always bring up striking cases like that of Helen Keller, show that there are other pathways besides the vocal path by which to receive language. Language is not vocalization. Take a look at the deaf.

I think, however, that we can venture to say that a relation that is more than just a random one binds language to sonority. And we shall perhaps even venture down the right path by trying to spell things out carefully in qualifying this sonority as instrumental, for instance. There's no doubt about it that physiology is what's opening up the path for us here.

We don't know everything about how our ears function, but all the same we know that the cochlea is a resonator. It's a complex resonator or, if you like, a composite one. Well, in the end, a resonator, even a composite one, breaks down into a composition of elementary resonators. This leads us onto a path that tells us that what is specific to resonance is the dominance of the apparatus. The apparatus is what resonates and it doesn't resonate at just anything. If you will, not to overcomplicate matters, it only resonates at its own note, its own frequency.

In the organization of the sensorial apparatus in question – our ear – we are dealing, concretely, with a resonator that isn't put together any old how, but a tubular resonator. The return path of the vibration, which is always brought in through the round window and along the scala tympani to the scala vestibuli, seems to be strictly linked to the length of the space travelled in a closed pipe that works in the way of a tube, any kind of tube, be it flute or organ. Clearly it's a complicated thing, this apparatus doesn't look like any other musical instrument whatsoever. It's a tube that would be, so to speak, a pipe with keys, in the sense that, so it seems, the cells which are poised in the position of strings, but which don't function as strings, are implicated at the site where the sound wave makes its return, and they see to connoting each resonance involved.

I apologize all the more for this detour because it's quite certain that this is not the direction in which we're going to find the last word on this score. But this reminder is designed to actualize the fact that something in the organic form strikes us as bearing a certain resemblance to those primary, trans-spatial, topological givens that led us to take an interest in the most elementary shape of the formation – which is both created and creative – of a void, the one that we embodied with an apologue in the story of the pot, because a pot is also a tube, and it can resonate.

We said that ten pots utterly alike will prove to be individually different, but that the question can arise as to whether, when you put one in the place of the other, the void that is put successively in the heart of each of them is always the same. Now, the void at the heart of the acoustic tube imposes a command on anything of this reality that might come to resonate therein – a reality that opens onto a subsequent step on our path and which is not so straightforwardly defined, namely, what is known as a breath. Thus, a flute titillated at the level of one of its openings imposes the same vibration on any possible suspiration. Although this command is not a law in our eyes, it is nevertheless indicated here that the *a* in question is functioning in a real function of mediation.

Well, let's not give in to this illusion. All this only holds any interest as a metaphor. If the voice in the sense we understand it holds some importance, it's not on account of resonating in any spatial void. The simplest intrusion of the voice in what in linguistic terms is called its phatic function – which is thought to lie at the level of simply making contact, when actually something very different is involved – resonates in a void that is the void of the Other as such, properly speaking *ex-nihilo*. The voice responds to what is said, but it cannot answer for it. In other words, for it to respond, we must incorporate the voice as the otherness of what is said.

It is precisely for this reason and no other that, detached from us, our voice appears to us with a foreign sound. It is proper to the structure of the Other to constitute a certain void, the void of its lack of guarantee. Truth comes into the world with the signifier, prior to any control. This truth is felt, it is reflected back only by echoes in the real. Now, the voice resonates in this void as a voice that is distinct from sonorities. It is not a modulated voice, but an articulated one. The voice at issue here is the voice as an imperative, a voice that demands obedience or conviction. It is not situated in relation to music, but in relation to speech.

With regard to the well-known misrecognition of the recorded voice, it would be interesting to see the distance that might lie between the singer's experience and the orator's. I propose to those who might like to volunteer as interviewers to go ahead and do so, because I haven't had time to do this myself.

I believe that this is where we put our finger on the form of identification that I wasn't able to broach last year and whose first model at least is provided by the identification of the voice. Indeed, in certain cases, we are not speaking about the same identification as in other cases, we are speaking about *Einverleibung*, incorporation. The psychoanalysts of *la bonne génération* noticed this and a certain Mr Isakower wrote, in the twentieth year of the *International Journal*, a quite remarkable article which, in my opinion, is only interesting for the need that impressed itself upon him to provide a striking image of what is distinct in this type of identification.

He searches out this image in something that stands peculiarly far away from the identificatory phenomenon at issue. Indeed, he turns his attention to tiny animals called – if memory serves, because I haven't had chance to check – daphnia.[1] They're not prawns, but picture them if you will as bearing a palpable resemblance to prawns. Be that as it may, at one moment in their metamorphoses, these animals, which live in saline waters, have the curious habit of filling up with minute grains of sand that they introduce into a thing they have, a small apparatus termed statoacoustic, in other words its utriculus, which doesn't benefit from our prodigious cochlea. Once these bits of sand have been introduced from the outside, because the prawn doesn't produce them itself in any shape or form, the utriculus closes up again and the animal will possess the little bells that are necessary for its balance and which it has had to fetch in from outside.

You have to admit that this relation is a long way from the constitution of the superego. Nevertheless, what interests me is that Isakower didn't think it necessary to look any further for a better comparison than to refer to the following operation, which all the same you must have thought of if you heard any echoes of physiology stirring within you. This operation, which was carried out by some mischievous experimenters, consists in replacing the grains of sand with iron dust, as a way of having a little fun with the daphnia and a magnet.

A voice, therefore, is not assimilated, but incorporated. This is what can give it a function of modelling our void. We're meeting up with my instrument from the other day, the shofar of the synagogue, and its music. But is this basic fifth, this interval of the fifth that is specific to it, actually music? Isn't it rather what gives its meaning to the moment's possibility that it might be a substitute for speech, wrenching our ear powerfully away from all its customary harmonies? It models the locus of our anxiety, but observe if you will that this only happens after the desire of the Other has taken the form of a command. This is why it can play its eminent function of bringing anxiety its point of resolution, which gets called guilt or atonement, by introducing a different order.

Desire is lack and we shall say that this flaw lies at the root of desire, in the sense of something that is missing. Change the sense of this flaw by giving it content in articulation – of what? let's leave that in abeyance – and you've got the explanation for the dawning of guilt and its relation to anxiety.

To know what can be done with it, I have to lead you onto a field that is not this year's field, but which I do have to bite into a bit. I said that I didn't know what, in the shofar – let's say, in the clamour of guilt – is articulated, on account of the Other that covers over anxiety. If our formula is right, something like the desire of the Other must be concerned here.

I'll give myself another three minutes to introduce something that readies the paths that will enable us to take our next step.

What stands most favourably ready to light the way and, similarly, to be lit up, is the notion of sacrifice.

A fair number of others besides myself have had a go at tackling what is at issue in sacrifice. I'll quickly tell you that the sacrifice is not at all intended to be an offering, nor a gift, both of which are propagated in a quite different dimension, but the capture of the Other in the web of desire.

The thing would already be perceptible if we looked at what it boils down to for us on the ethical plane. Common experience shows that we don't live our lives, whoever we are, without tirelessly offering to goodness knows what unknown divinity the sacrifice of some little mutilation, whether valid or not, that we impose upon ourselves in the field of our desires.

Not all the underpinnings of the operation are visible. There can be no doubt that this involves something that refers back to the *a* as the pole of our desire. But you'll have to wait till next time for me to show you that it takes something more and notably that this *a* is a thing that is already consecrated, which cannot be conceived of save by taking up in its original form what is at issue in the sacrifice. I do hope that for this appointment I shall have a good friary of obsessionals.

Doubtless we have lost our gods in the great civilizing bedlam, but a fairly lengthy period that stands at the origin of all peoples shows that they used to have brushes with them just as with real persons. They were not almighty gods, but mighty gods there where they stood. The whole question was one of knowing whether these mighty gods desired something. Sacrifice consisted in carrying on as though they desired in the same way as we do, and if they desire as we do, then the *a* possesses the same structure. This doesn't mean that they're going to gobble down what we sacrifice, nor even that it might be of any use to them, the important thing is that they desire it and, I shall say further, that it doesn't cause them anxiety.

There is one feature whose problem has never been resolved by anyone in a satisfying way – the victims always had to be spotless.

Now, remember what I told you about the stain at the level of the visual field. With the stain there appears, or there is prepared, the possibility of the resurgence, within the field of desire, of what lies behind, overshadowed, on this occasion the eye whose relation to this field must necessarily be elided so that desire can remain there, with this ubiquitous, even roaming possibility that allows it to evade anxiety.

When the gods are being tamed in the snare of desire, it is crucial not to awaken their anxiety.

Given the time, I'll have to end here. You're going to see that, as lyrical as this last jaunt may seem, it will serve us as a guide through the far more day-to-day realities of our experience.

5 June 1963

XXI

PIAGET'S TAP

The category of cause
Forming the symptom
A matter of understanding
Water and desires
The five levels in the constitution of the *a*

Anxiety resides in the subject's fundamental relationship with what thus far I've been calling the desire of the Other.

Analysis has always had, and maintains, as its object the uncovering of a desire. It is, you will admit, for a structural reason that I've been led this year to articulate this along a path that is, let's say, algebraic, an articulation in which the function appears in a kind of gap, a kind of residue, of the signifying function. But I've also done it by edging carefully forward, employing examples. This is the path I'm going to be taking today.

In any advent of the *a* as such, anxiety appears in accordance with its relation to the desire of the Other, but what is its relation to the subject's desire? It can be situated with the formula I put forward in its time, when I told you that the *a* is not the object of desire that we seek to reveal in analysis, it is its cause.

This feature is essential. If anxiety marks the dependency of any constitution of the subject with regard to A, the subject's desire finds itself appended to this relation by the intermediary of the prior constitution of *a*. Hence the interest in reminding you how the presence of the *a* as cause of desire was being heralded right back in the first analytic research data. It is heralded, in a more or less covert fashion, in the function of cause.

This function can be spotted in the first data from the field to which the research was committed, namely, the field of the symptom. In every symptom, inasmuch as an element that goes by this name interests us, this dimension is evident. I'm going to try to tease this out for you today.

1

To give you a sense of this, I'll be starting off from a symptom that possesses an exemplary function, and not for nothing – you'll be able to see this afterwards – to wit, the obsessional's symptom.

I'll indicate right off the bat that I'm putting this forward because it allows us to move into the mapping of the *a* function in so far as it is unveiled as functioning, with the very first data on the symptom, in the dimension of cause.

What does the obsessional present us with in the pathognomonic form of his position? Well, an obsession, or a compulsion, articulated or not as a motivation in his inner language – *Go do this or that, Go check the door's locked*, or *the tap's turned off*. We might be taking a look at this tap later. What happens if he doesn't act on it? Not acting on it awakens anxiety. Thus, the very phenomenon of the symptom indicates to us that we're at the most favourable level to link the position of the *a* as much to relations of anxiety as to relations of desire.

Anxiety appears prior to desire. Historically speaking, before the Freudian research, as before the analysis in our praxis, desire is hidden and we know the trouble it takes to unmask it, if ever we do.

One given of our experience deserves to be highlighted here, which appears in Freud's very first observations and which, even if it hasn't been spotted as such, constitutes perhaps the most essential step in our advance with respect to obsessional neurosis. What Freud recognized, what we can recognize every day, is that the analytic approach does not start off from the symptom's statement such as I have just described it, that is, in conformity with its most classically minded wording as it has always been defined since the start, compulsion together with the anxious struggle that accompanies it, but rather from the recognition that *that's how it works*.

The subject has to realize that *that's how it works*. This recognition is not an effect that stands apart from the functioning of the symptom, it's not epiphenomenal. The symptom is only constituted when the subject notices it, because we know from experience that there are forms of obsessional behaviour in which it's not simply the case that the subject hasn't ascertained his obsessions, it's that he hasn't constituted them as such. In such a case, the first step of the analysis – the passages in Freud on this topic are quite famous – is for the symptom to be constituted in its classic form, failing which there's really no way through, not simply because there's no way to speak about it, but because there's no way of grabbing the symptom by the ears. What is the ear in question? It's what we might call the unassimilated side of the symptom, unassimilated by the subject.

For the symptom to leave behind its state of an unspoken riddle, the step that has to be taken is not to formulate it, but for something in the subject to be sketched out in such a way that he has some inkling that *there's a cause behind this*.

This is the original dimension. It is being taken up here in the form of the phenomenon. I'll be showing you where else it can be found. Only here can the subject's implication in his conduct be broken off and this break is the necessary complementation for us to tackle the symptom. This sign doesn't constitute a step in what I might call the intelligence of the situation, it is something more, there's a reason why this step is essential in the treatment of obsessionals.

It is impossible to articulate this if we don't bring out the radical relation of the *a* function, the cause of desire, with regard to the mental dimension of cause. I've already indicated this as an aside to my disquisition and I wrote it up in a point that you can find in the article *Kant with Sade* that came out in the April issue of *Critique*. It's from this article that I want to tease out the main part of my disquisition today.

You can already see the point of giving a plausible account of how the dimension of cause is alone in indicating the emergence, in what is laid out at the start in the analysis of obsessionals, of the *a* around which any analysis of the transference must revolve so as not to be compelled to turn round in circles. Certainly, a circle is not a negligible thing, because the circuit is travelled. But there's a problem of the end of analysis – I'm not the one who stated that – which has to do with the irreducible transference neurosis. Is the transference neurosis in analysis the same or not as the one that could be detected at the start? Sometimes it appears to us to be a dead-end transference neurosis, sometimes it ends up in a total stagnation of the patient's dealings with the analyst, but by and large, its only difference in relation to what might have been evinced in an analogous way at the start is that it is fully together, fully present.

One enters analysis through an enigmatic door, because transference neurosis is there in every single one of us, even in a creature as free as Alcibiades. Agathon is the one he loves. That's where the transference is, the obvious transference, what we too often call lateral transference – though this love is indeed a real love. What's surprising is that one enters analysis in spite of everything that holds us in the transference that is functioning as real.

But the true subject of surprise in connection with the circuit of analysis is how, entering it in spite of transference neurosis, one can obtain transference neurosis itself on the way out. Doubtless this is because there are a few misunderstandings over the analysis of transference. Otherwise, we wouldn't see any evidence of a satisfaction I've sometimes heard being expressed, that, having given shape to the transference neurosis, *it might not be perfect, but all the same it's a result.* It's true. All the same, it's a result, a fairly bewildering one at that.

When I state that the path passes via *a*, which is the sole object that can be proposed to the analysis of transference, this doesn't mean that all the problems are thereby resolved. It leaves open another problem, as you're going to see. It is precisely in this subtraction that the essential dimension may emerge of a question that has always been posed, but certainly not resolved, because the insufficiency of the answers is glaring to any eye each time you pose it – the question of the analyst's desire.

Now that I've said this so as to show you the point of what's at stake here, with this brief reminder over, let's come back to the *a*.

The *a* is the cause, the cause of desire. I indicated that coming back to the riddle offered us by the functioning of the category of cause is not a bad way of understanding it, because it's quite clear that whatever critique, whatever effort of cutting down to size that we apply to it, phenomenological or otherwise, this category does function and not as a merely archaic stage in our development. I mean to transfer this category from the domain that I shall call, with Kant, transcendental aesthetics, over to what I shall call, if you care to endorse this, my transcendental ethics.

Here I'm moving onto ground whose sidelines I'm forced simply to sweep over with a searchlight, without being able to insist. I will say that philosophers ought to do their work and dare to formulate something that would allow you truly to locate in its stead the operation I'm indicating to you in saying that I extract the function of cause from the field of transcendental aesthetics, Kant's transcendental aesthetics. Others ought to be able to indicate to you that this is but an entirely pedagogical extraction, because there are a fair number of other things that still ought to be extracted from this transcendental aesthetics.

Here I need at least to indicate what I managed to evade last time with a sleight of hand when I was speaking to you about the scopic field of desire. I can't get out of it, I really need to explain, right now as I'm about to go further, what was implied in what I was saying to you in connection with space, namely, that it is not at all an a priori category of sensible intuition.

It's very surprising that at the point we've reached in the advance of science, nobody has yet set about directly formulating the fact to which everything draws us, namely, that space is not a feature of our subjective constitution beyond which the thing-in-itself would find, so to speak, a free field – but rather that space is part of the real.

In the topological shapes I drew up for you here last year, some of you could already sense this touch. The topological dimension, whose symbolic handling transcends space, evoked for many of you a fair number of shapes that are presentified for us by the diagrams of the embryo's development. These shapes are peculiar due to the common and singular Gestalt that is specific to them and which takes us far, far away from *Prägnanz*. With an impressionistic observation, I shall say that this shape which is reproduced everywhere is tangible in the kind of twisting to which the organization of life seems to be compelled in order to lodge itself in real space.

The thing is present across the board in what I explained to you last year, and this year too. Indeed, it's precisely at these twisting points that the breaking points are also produced whose incidence I've been trying to show you in more than one case in our topology, that of the S, the A, and the small *a*, in a way that would be more efficient, truer, and in greater conformity with the play of functions than is any of what is ascertained in Freud's doctrine, whose wavering is already in itself indicative of the necessity of what I'm doing here. I'm speaking of the wavering that is linked for example to his ambiguity over the relations between ego and non-ego, container and contained, the ego and the outer world. It's glaringly obvious that these divisions do not overlap each other, and why don't they? To answer this, one needs to have grasped what is involved in topology and to have found other markers in the subjective topology we've been exploring.

I'm coming to the end of this observation, whose import some of you I know are well aware of now that you've lent me an ear. It's crucial to grasp the nature of the reality of space as a three-dimensional space if we are to define the form that the presence of desire takes on at the scopic level, namely, as a fantasy. The function of the frame, the window frame I mean, which I tried to define in the structure of the fantasy, is not a metaphor. If the frame exists, it's because space is real.

With regard to the cause, let's try to get a sense of what stands as the common undergrowth of these forms of knowledge, bequeathed us by a certain hubbub of discussions, by passing via a class that goes by the name of philosophy.

A clue as to the origin of the function of cause is very clearly provided by the history of the criticism of this function. This criticism consists in noting that the cause is ungraspable, that the *propter hoc* is always necessarily at least a *post hoc* – and what else would it have to be to be equal to this incomprehensible *propter hoc*? – without which we can't even begin to articulate anything. This doesn't prevent this criticism from having its own fecundity, as can be seen in history. The more the cause was criticized, the more the requirements of what might be called determinism were imposed on thought. The less the cause is graspable, the more everything seems *caused* – right up to the final term, the one called *the meaning of history*.

We can say nothing else about it than that *everything is caused*, save that everything that happens in it always stems at the start from a *sufficiently caused*, in whose name a beginning is reproduced in history that I wouldn't dare call absolute, but which was certainly unexpected and which has traditionally cut out so much work for those *nachträglich* prophets whom we meet in the professional *interpreters* of *the meaning of history*.

So, let's say without further ado how we envisage this function of cause.

I shall say first of all, to make myself understood, that we envisage this function, which is present everywhere in our thought, as the shadow cast, or better still, the metaphor of the primordial cause – the substance of this function of cause – that the *a* is inasmuch as it precedes any phenomenology, the *a* that we've defined as the remainder left over from the constitution of the subject in the locus of the Other in so far as the subject has to be constituted as a barred subject.

If the symptom is what we say it is, that is, fully implicated in the process of the constitution of the subject in so far as he has to build himself in the locus of the Other, the implication of the cause is a legitimate part of the symptomatic advent I spoke of earlier. This means that the cause implicated in the question of the symptom is literally, if you will, a question, but whereof the symptom is not the effect. It is the result thereof. The effect is desire. But it's a unique effect and an utterly strange one inasmuch as it is going to explain to us, or at the very least make us hear, all the difficulties that lie in linking up the common relation, which forces itself on the mind, between cause and effect. The primordial effect of this cause, *a*, this effect called desire, is an effect that has nothing effectuated about it.

From this perspective, desire is indeed located as a lack of effect. Thus, if cause is constituted as presupposing effects, then it is based on the fact that primordially its effect is missing. You will meet this in any phenomenology of cause. The gap between cause and effect, to the extent that it gets filled in – and this is precisely what is called, from a certain perspective, the progress of science – makes the function of cause fade away, I mean, wherever the gap gets filled in.

Likewise, the explanation of just about anything winds up, to the extent that it does draw to a close, only leaving behind signifying connections, making what animated it at root, and which drove you to seek out what you didn't understand, vanish into thin air, namely, the effective gap. There is no such thing as a cause that does not imply this gap.

All this might strike you as quite superfluous. It's nonetheless what allows us to grasp what I shall call the naivety of certain research projects carried out by psychologists, notably Piaget's.

2

The paths along which I've been leading you this year have taken in a certain evocation of what Piaget calls egocentric language. As he acknowledges himself, his idea of the egocentrism of a certain discourse that children engage in starts off from the supposition that they don't understand each other, that they speak for themselves. He thinks he has demonstrated this.

I won't say that the world of suppositions that lies beneath this is unfathomable, because the bulk of it can be specified. That speech is made for communicating is an excessively widespread supposition. It's not true. Piaget is unable to grasp the gap that he nevertheless designates and the entire interest of his labours lies there.

I beseech you to get hold of *The Language and Thought of the Child*, which is an admirable book, all told. It illustrates from one instant to the next that what Piaget gathers up by way of facts in this approach, which is aberrant in its principle, is demonstrative of something utterly different from what he thinks. Naturally, since he's far from being a simple-minded fellow, it so happens that his own remarks go down this road.

Let's take for instance the problem of why the subject's language, which is essentially made for himself, is never produced in a group. I ask you to read these pages, because I can't go through them with you. You will see how, from one instant to the next, his thinking slides and adheres to a poising of the question that is precisely the one that veils over the phenomenon, which is otherwise palpable in the most traditional way. The nub of the error is to believe that the essential effect of speech is to communicate, when in fact the effect of the signifier is to call forth in the subject the dimension of the signified. I'll come back to this again, if necessary.

In the name of the socialization of language, the relation to the other party is depicted as the key to the turning point between egocentric language and language carried through to its function. This turning point is not a point of effect, of effective impact, it can be named as the desire to communicate. Moreover, it's precisely because this desire doesn't live up to expectations that Piaget's entire pedagogy comes to set up its apparatuses and phantoms. All in all, as tight-lipped as children are in his eyes, only half-understanding him, he adds that they don't even understand each other. But is that really the question?

One can see very well in his text that the question doesn't lie there. One can see it from the way he articulates what he calls *understanding between children*.

This is how he proceeds. He begins by taking an image that will be the support of his explanations – the diagram of a tap. It gives something more or less like this.

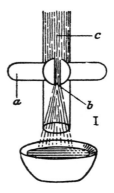

With that, the child is told, as many times as it takes – *You see the little pipe here, it's blocked, which means that the water here can't pass through to run out here,* &c. He explains.

Here's the diagram, if you want to check. Moreover, he thought it necessary to finish it off with the presence of a basin, which in the

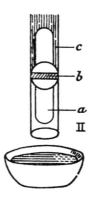

seven points of explanation given to the child never once comes in. He was struck by the fact that the child repeats all the different terms to him very well. It goes without saying that for him, Piaget, this means that the child has understood. I'm not saying he's wrong, I'm saying he doesn't even ask himself the question.

Next, he goes on to use this first child as an explainer for another child, whom he will call, rather oddly, the *reproducer*. Now, he is forced to note, not without some astonishment, that what the child has so accurately repeated to him, Piaget, in the test he's carried out, is in no way identical to what this first child will then explain to the second child. There, Piaget makes the very fair remark that the child elides in his explanations what he has understood – without realizing what this remark would imply, namely, that in giving these explanations, the child doesn't actually explain anything whatsoever, if it's true that he has really understood everything as Piaget maintains. Of course, it's not true that he's understood everything, no more than it would be for anyone.

Alongside these examples, which fall under the heading of what Piaget calls *the field of explanations*, there is the field that he calls *the field of stories*.

For the stories, things function differently. But what does Piaget call stories? He has a way of transcribing the story of Niobe that is perfectly scandalous, because it doesn't seem to occur to him that there's a myth here, that there might be a dimension that is specific to myth, which is evinced whenever one puts forward the proper name Niobe, and that by transforming it into insipid dishwater – I ask you to refer to the text, which is quite simply incredible – one might be offering the child something that's not simply within his reach, but also something that signals a profound deficit on the side of the experimenter, Piaget himself, with regard to the functions of language. If a myth is really going to be set out, then let it be one, and not this muzzy little story – *Once upon a time there was a lady who was called Niobe, and who had twelve sons and twelve daughters. Then she met a fairy who had only one son and no daughter. Then the lady laughed at the fairy because the fairy only had one boy. Then the fairy was very angry and fastened the lady to a rock. The lady cried for ten years. In the end she turned into a rock, and her tears made a stream which still runs today.*

The only thing remotely like that are the two other stories that Piaget offers, the story of the *little nigger boy* who breaks his shortbread on the way and lets the pat of butter melt on the way back, and the other one, worse still, of children changed into swans, who spend their whole lives separated from their parents by this evil spell, but who, when they do come back, not only find their parents dead but, changing back into their original forms, have nevertheless got older. I don't know whether there exists a single myth that lets the ageing run on during the transformation. To say it all, the stories invented by Piaget have one thing in common with those of Binet, which is that they reflect the deep malice of any pedagogical position.

Please pardon me for having allowed myself to stray off into this parenthesis. At least you will have acquired the dimension, noted by Piaget, of the entropy of understanding, an understanding which necessarily dissipates by dint of the verbal necessity of explanation. Piaget himself observes, to his great surprise, that there is an enormous contrast between the explanations and the 'stories', a term I'm putting in inverted commas. It is very likely that if the stories confirm his theory of the entropy of understanding, it's precisely because they are not stories, and if they were stories, genuine myths, there probably wouldn't be any of this dissipation.

In any case, I'm going to put forward a little sign. When one of these children has to repeat the story of Niobe, at the point when Piaget tells us that the lady has been attached, *attachée*, to a rock – never, in any shape or form, has the myth of Niobe detailed such a moment – the child calls forth the dimension of a rock that bears a stain, *une tache*, restoring the characteristic I brought out in a previous lesson as essential to the victim of the sacrifice, the characteristic of being spotless. *Of course*, I hear you say, *it's easy, you're exploiting a mishearing, some play of words*. All right, but why that one? Let's leave it aside. It's not proof, of course, but merely suggestion.

I'll come back to my own explanations and to Piaget's remark that, in spite of the fact that the explainer explains poorly, the one to whom he is explaining understands far better than the explainer has. The insufficiency of his explanations bears this out. Of course, here we're told – *he's redoing the work himself*. Because how does Piaget define the level of understanding among the children?

$$\frac{\text{what the reproducer has understood}}{\text{what the explainer had understood}}$$

I don't know whether you've noticed that there is one thing that never gets spoken about, and that is – what Piaget has understood. This is crucial, however, because we're not leaving the children to spontaneous language, that is, to see what they understand when one of them does something instead of another.

Now, what Piaget doesn't seem to have seen is that his explanation, from the point of view of anyone, any third party, cannot be understood at all. If the little pipe, which here is blocked, is then adjusted, thanks to something to which Piaget attaches all its importance, through the operation of the fingers that turn the tap in such a way that the water can run through, does that mean that it does indeed run through? Piaget doesn't give the slightest detail on this. Of course, he knows that if there isn't any pressure, the tap won't let out anything when you turn it, but he thinks he can omit this because he's poising himself at the level of the so-called mind of the child.

Let me continue. All this sounds quite daft, but you're going to see. The meaning of the whole venture does not spring up from my speculations, but from the experiment. It comes out of this remark that I'm putting to you, and which I don't claim to have exhaustively understood.

One thing is certain and this is that, regarding the tap as cause, when you just say that a tap is sometimes on and sometimes off, the explanation hasn't been well delivered. A tap is designed to be turned off. It only takes one occasion, when the water has been cut off and you don't know when the pressure will be back on, for you to know that if you happen to have left the tap open then that entails a few snags, and so therefore a tap should be turned off, even when there's no pressure.

Now, what is marked in what occurs in the transmission from the explainer to the reproducer? Something that Piaget bemoans. It's that the child who is supposedly in the role of reproducer no longer takes the faintest interest in what's involved with respect to the two branches, the turning operation, and everything that ensues. Piaget observes, however, that the first child has nevertheless transmitted a part of it. The dissipation in understanding strikes him as considerable. But I assure you that if you read the explanations of this young third party, this little reproducer, young Riv in the text in question, you will see that he stresses two things – the effect of the tap as something that turns off and the result, namely that, thanks to a tap, you can fill up a basin without it overflowing. In a word, the tap's dimension as cause emerges here.

Why does Piaget miss so entirely the phenomenon that is produced? Because he completely misrecognizes that what is interesting for a child in a tap as cause are the desires that the tap arouses in him, namely that, for instance, it makes him want to wee, like whenever one is in the presence of water, whenever one is a communicating vessel in relation to this water. I didn't select this metaphor to speak about libido and what happens between the subject and his specular image just for the sake of it. If people did have any tendency to forget that in the presence of water they are like communicating vessels, there exists in most people's childhoods the enema bag to jog their memory.

290 The Five Forms of the Object *a*

In a child of the age of those that Piaget designates, an irresistible kind of acting-out occurs in the presence of a tap which consists in doing something that stands every chance of taking the thing apart. In view of which, the tap finds itself once again in its place of cause, this time at the level of the phallic relation. Indeed, as the story of Hans shows, the little tap is necessarily introduced as something that pertains in some way to the plumber, something that one can unscrew, take to pieces, replace, and so forth. In short, the $(-\varphi)$.

What I mean to underline is that Piaget omits these elements of experience, and likewise, being very well informed of things analytic – he is not unaware of them – that he doesn't see the relationship between those dealings we call complexual and the whole originative constitution of this function of cause that he claims to be examining.

We'll be going back over the language of the child.

Last time I indicated that original pieces of work, which we may be surprised not to have seen before now, are allowing us truly to grasp *in statu nascendi* the first play of the signifier in the hypnopompic monologues of really very young children, around two years of age, and to grasp in a fascinating form the Oedipus complex itself, already articulated, thereby furnishing the experiential proof for the idea that I've been putting forward here since the beginning, namely, that the unconscious is essentially the effect of the signifier.

To come to an end on the psychologists' position, I'll tell you that the crucial piece of work to which I'm alluding is foreworded by a psychologist, on first approach a very nice one, in the sense that he admits that it has never before occurred that a psychologist should truly take an interest in these functions, due to the supposition, he tells us, in an avowal from the psychologist, that nothing is noteworthy about language coming into play in the subject, except at the level of education.

Indeed, language is something you learn. But it took a suggestion from a linguist, Jakobson, for people to start taking an interest in what language does outside the field of learning.

We might believe the psychologist to be laying down his arms here, because he certainly points out this deficit in psychological research with some humour. Well, he isn't at all. At the end of his foreword, he makes two remarks that show to what extent his psychologist's attitude is truly dyed-in-the-wool.

Since this volume is some three hundred pages long and weighs heavy, since it has gathered a month's worth of these monologues, since a complete chronological list of them has been made, at this rate, what a lot of time and effort it would take to investigate. That's his first remark.

His second is stronger still. *It's very interesting to note down everything the child voices, but it seems to me,* says this psychologist who goes by the name of George Miller, *that the only interesting thing would be to find out what the child knows about the language he speaks.*

Now, precisely, the question is that he doesn't know what he's saying, and it's very important to note that he says it all the same. He's already saying what he will or won't know later, namely the elements of the Oedipus complex.

3

It's ten past two. I'd like nonetheless to give you a little diagram of what I'm going to be advancing into with respect to the obsessional. In five minutes, here's how the question presents itself, in a few provisional formulas.

There are five levels, if I can put it like that, in the constitution of the *a* in the relation between S and A. They can be defined in the way I'm about to tell you, which makes itself felt well enough based on what I put forward step by step in the previous lessons.

Its first operation can be seen here.

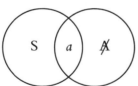

The second phase of the operation is not entirely beyond the realms of your understanding, starting off from the division that I've already added on as the Other's division. This division is still remote from the transformation of the subject S into $ when it passes from the left portion of the first diagram to the shared portion of the second. Clearly, the function of the Euler circle still stands in need of some clarification.

At the level of the relation to the oral object, let's say today, to be clear, there is, not need *of* the other – this ambiguity is rich and we certainly don't shy away from making use of it – but need *in* the Other, at the level of the Other. It's in accordance with the dependence on the maternal being that the disjunction between subject and *a*, the breast, is produced, whose true scope you can only glimpse if you see that the breast is part of the subject's inner world and not part of the mother's body.

At the second level, the level of the anal object, you've got *demand*

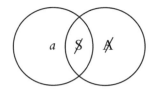

in the Other. This is educative demand par excellence, in so far as it refers back to the anal object. There's no way of grasping the function of this anal object if you don't have some inkling that it is the remainder in the Other's demand, which here I'm calling, to make myself clearly understood, *demand in the Other*.

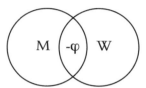

The third level is the phallus. Here you will find the entire dialectic I taught you to recognize in the function of the (– φ), a unique function in relation to all the other functions of the *a* inasmuch as it is defined by a lack, the lack of an object. This lack is evinced here as such, it is pivotal in this relationship, and this is what justifies all axiation of the analysis on sexuality. Here we'll call it *jouissance in the Other*. The relationship of this *jouissance in the Other* to the missing instrument that (– φ) designates is an inverted relationship. This is what I spelt out in my last two lessons and this is what makes for the base, the solid axis, of any fairly efficient situating of what we call castration anxiety.

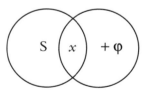

At the scopic level, which is strictly the level of the fantasy, we are dealing with *might in the Other*, which is the mirage of human desire. In what amounts to the major form of any contemplative possession, the subject is doomed to misrecognize how this is merely a mirage of might.

You see, I'm going very fast. We'll flesh it out afterwards. What stands at the fifth and final level?

We'll say provisionally that this is where the *desire of the Other* has to emerge, in a pure form. What signals it for us in the example we started off from, namely the obsessional, is the apparent dominance of anxiety in the phenomenology. The structural fact that we alone catch sight of is that, up to a certain moment of analysis, whatever he does, whatever nicety his fantasies and practices wind up at through being constructed, what the obsessional grasps from this is always the *desire in the Other*. Check if you will the scope of this formula. To the degree that this desire returns in the Other, inasmuch as for the obsessional it is essentially repressed, everything is determined in his symptomatology and notably in the symptoms where the dimension of cause is glimpsed as *Angst*.

This solution is familiar to us in the phenomenon too. To cover over the *desire of the Other*, the obsessional has one path, and that is his recourse to demand. Observe an obsessional in his biographical conduct, in what I called earlier his attempts at passing through at the place of desire. These attempts at meeting their goal, in all their audacity, complication, refinement, luxuriance, and perversity, are always stamped with an originative condemnation. He always has to get someone to authorize him in these attempts. The Other has to ask him.

This is the mainspring of what occurs at a certain turning point in any analysis of an obsessional. To the full extent to which analysis sustains a dimension that is the analogue of the dimension of demand, something endures up to a very advanced point – can it be surpassed? – in the obsessional's way of dodging. In so far as the obsessional's shunning functions as a cover on the *desire of the Other* by means of *demand in the Other*, we see that *a*, the object of his cause, comes to be situated right where demand dominates, that is, at the anal level, where *a* is not pure and simple excrement, but excrement in so far as it is asked for.

Now, nothing has ever been analysed of the relation to the anal object in these coordinates, which are genuine coordinates, as a way of understanding the source of what may be called anal anxiety, the anxiety that emerges from the analysis of an obsessional pursued this far, which almost never happens. In a point that has to be situated as a final term, anxiety appears with a certain character of dominance, as an irreducible kernel, and it is almost uncontrollable in certain cases.

This is what we are going to have to mark out next time and which entailed spelling out what results from the relation between the anal object and the demand that asks for it, a demand that has nothing to do with the mode of desire that is determined by this cause.

12 June 1963

XXII

FROM ANAL TO IDEAL

The object's circular constitution
The origin of the cause
Jones and the Immaculate Conception
To love beyond the phallus
The desire of the gods

The definition of the function of the object *a* that I've been pursuing before you this year tends, as someone remarked to me after my last talk, to contrast with the Abrahamic conception – I'm referring to Abraham the psychoanalyst – which binds the object and its variations to stages.

Indeed, this definition puts forward, as it were, a circular constitution of the object.

Across all the levels of this constitution, the object clasps to itself as object *a*. In the various forms in which it is evinced, the same function is always involved, and it's a matter of knowing how it's linked to the constitution of the subject in the locus of the Other and how it represents him.

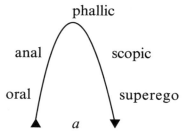

The forms of the object in stages

At the level of the phallic stage, which is pivotal in relation to the various stages of the object, and which by convention we call the third level, the *a* function is represented by a lack, namely, the missing phallus that constitutes the disjunction that joins desire to jouissance.

This stage is poised at one extreme. The fourth and fifth stages are in a return position that brings them back into correlation with the first and second stages respectively.

Everyone knows, and this little diagram is simply designed to remind you, about the links between the oral stage and its object and the primary manifestations of the superego. In calling to mind its obvious connection with this form of the object *a* that the voice is, I indicated that there cannot be any valid analytic conception of the superego that loses sight of the fact that, in its deepest phase, it is one of the forms of the object *a*. On the other hand, the connection between the anal stage and scoptophilia has long been indicated.

Despite the first and second stages being fully conjoined with the fourth and fifth, the fact no less remains that as a whole they are oriented in accordance with this arrow that rises then falls. This arrow expresses what dictates, in each analytic phase of the reconstitution of the data of repressed desire, that in a regression there is a progressive side. It also expresses that, in any progressive accessing of the stage that is posited as lying higher up on the diagram on the board here, there is a regressive side.

Now that these indications have been recalled so that they will be present in your minds throughout today's talk, I'll move on.

1

As I said last time, it's a matter of explaining the function, in the constitution of anal desire, of a certain object that is, if you will, the turd, to call a spade a spade.

After all, it is the privilege of analysis in the history of thought to have brought out the decisive function of this unpleasant object in the economy of desire.

Last time I remarked that, with respect to desire, the object *a* always presents itself in the function of cause and that it is possibly for us, if you follow me, the root-point at which the very function of cause is elaborated in the subject. The primordial form of the cause is the cause of a desire.

To endure in its mental function, the cause always necessitates the existence of a gap between itself and its effect. This gap is so necessary that, for us to be able to go on thinking about cause right where it runs the risk of being filled in, we need to keep the veil drawn over the strict determinism, the connections, through which the cause acts. This is what I illustrated last time with the example of the tap.

Who was it that allowed us to see the essence of the tap's cause-function being revealed, that is, as a concept of the tap? It was the child who flagged at the level of what Piaget calls understanding, or who dispensed with it, and who we were told neglected, on that occasion, on account of not having understood, the narrow mechanism that was drawn out for him in the shape of a cross-section of a tap.

The necessity that binds the endurance of the cause to a gap has its origin in the fact that the cause in its initial form is the cause of desire, that is, the cause of something that is essentially non-effectuated. This is precisely why we absolutely cannot mix up anal desire with what mothers, as much as the proponents of cleansing, would on this occasion call an effect, in the sense of, *has it had an effect?* Excrement doesn't play the role of the effect of what we are situating as anal desire, it is the cause of this desire.

If we are going to pause over this peculiar object, it's undoubtedly because of the importance of its function, which is always recalled to our attention and especially so, as you know, in the analysis of the obsessional, though truth be told, it's just as much down to the fact that this object once more illustrates for us how we really should conceive of the object *a* as enduring in various modes.

Indeed, on first approach, the anal stands slightly apart from the other modes.

All those anatomical facts, the mammalian constitution, the phallic functioning of the copulatory organ, the plasticity of the human larynx to the phonematic imprint, and others besides, from the anticipatory value of the specular image to the neonatal pre-maturation of the nervous system, which latterly I've been calling to your minds, one after the next, is to show you in what way they conjoin with the *a* function, and just listing them lets you see how far their place is distributed across the tree of organismal determinations – well, in mankind they only take on their value as destiny, as Freud says, so that a key place can be occupied on a chess board whose squares are structured by the subjectifying constitution, such as it results from the dominance of the subject who speaks over the subject who understands, that is, the subject of insight.

We are familiar with the limits of this subject in the form of the chimpanzee. Regardless of the presumed superiority of man's capacities over the chimpanzee's, the fact that he goes further in praxis is linked to the dominance in mankind of the subject who speaks. By virtue of speaking, he believes he can reach the concept, that is, he believes he can grasp the real by way of a signifier that controls this real in accordance with his inner causation.

The field of intersubjective relations, which doesn't seem to pose much of a problem for psychologists, does to some extent for us. Although we claim to account for the way the function of the signifier works its way into this relation at the outset, the difficulties are such that they lead us to a fresh critique of reason, and it would be stupidity, very much a schoolboy stupidity, to see in this any recession of the conquering movement of the said reason. Indeed, this critique leans towards ascertaining how this reason is already woven at the level of the subject's most opaque dynamism, right where what he feels as need is modified into the forms of desire, forms that are always more or less paradoxical with regard to their presumed naturality.

Thus the fresh critique of reason I've been speaking about rears its head in what I showed you to be the cause of desire. Are we paying too dearly in having to conjoin to this revelation the notion that the cause reveals its point of origin here? Does this amount to psychologism, with all the absurd consequences this entails concerning the legitimacy of reason? No, that's not what we're doing, because the subjectification involved here is neither psychological nor developmental. To those accidents of development that I just listed, to those anatomical particularities involved in humankind, there is always conjoined the effect of a signifier whose transcendence is thereafter evident with regard to the said development.

I said *transcendence*. And then what? There's no need for alarm. This transcendence is no more nor less marked at this level than is any other incidence of the real, the real that is called *Umwelt* in biology, as a way of taming it. But, precisely, the existence of anxiety in animals perfectly repudiates the spiritualist imputations that can in no way rear their heads in my purview on the pretext that I'm positing the location of the signifier to be a transcendental location. Indeed, in animal anxiety it's very much a question of something beyond the said *Umwelt*. It's the fact that when something comes and shakes this *Umwelt* to its foundations, animals show themselves to be forewarned, when they get into a flap, of an earthquake for example, or some other meteoric mishap.

Once again, this confirms that anxiety is *that which doesn't deceive*. The proof is that when you see animals becoming agitated in this way, in those parts of the world where such incidents can occur, you would do well to take this into account as a way of being forewarned of what is in the offing. For them like us, this is a manifestation of a locus of the Other. An Other thing is evinced as such.

This doesn't mean, and with good reason, that there's nowhere for this Other to be housed outside of real space, as I reiterated last time.

2

Now we're going to move into the particularity of the case that dictates how excrement can come to function at this point, this point that is determined by the subject's necessity of constituting himself first and foremost in the signifier.

The question is important because here, perhaps more than elsewhere, a shadow of confusion prevails.

In dealing with the anal, people think they're getting closer to the matter, quite literally, to the concrete underpinnings. They think they are demonstrating that we know how to take into account even life's more disagreeable aspects. They compliment themselves on having sought out the domain of causes here and not in the empyrean realm. This whole thematic can be very amusingly grasped in Jones's introductory remarks to an article from the collection of his *Selected Papers*. I cannot recommend you too strongly to read this text, it is worth a thousand others.

The title of the article is *The Madonna's Conception Through the Ear*. The Protestant mischief of this Welshman absolutely cannot be ruled out as underlying his readiness to treat this subject. The text was written in 1914, when Jones was just emerging from his first perceptions, which were really very enlightening for him, of the prevalence of the anal function in the first few severe obsessionals who came into his hands, just like that, a few years after Freud came into contact with his. I looked up Jones's observations in the original text, published in the two issues of the *Jahrbuch* that precede the original publication of the article on the Madonna. These are clearly sensational cases, though we have indeed seen more of the like since then.

In the article on the Madonna, Jones tackles the subject right away by telling us that the fertilizing breath is a very lovely thing, that we find its trace across myth, legend and poetry, that nothing could be more beautiful than the awakening of Being with the *Ruach*, the passing breath of the Eternal, but that he, Jones, knows a bit more about it. It's true that his science is still young, but in the end, he's very enthusiastic about it. He's going to tell us what sort of wind is involved here. It's anal wind.

As Jones tells us, experience proves the interest – this interest is presumed to be a lively interest, a biological interest – that the subject, such as he discovers himself in analysis, shows in his excrement, in the shit he produces, and that this interest is infinitely more present, more evident, more dominant, than any preoccupation the subject would have every reason to have with his breathing, which seems, going by what Jones says, not to interest him. And why not? Because breathing is automatic.

This argument is a feeble one. The argument is feeble in a discipline which didn't fail thereafter to note the importance of suffocation and respiratory difficulties in the original establishing of the function of anxiety. Saying that the living subject, even the human subject, is not aware of the importance of this function is a surprising opening argument, all the more so given that at the time they'd already discovered something that was quite apt to highlight the possible relation between the respiratory function and the productive moment in sexual intercourse. Breathing, in the form of the mother or the father's panting, was very much part of the first phenomenology of the traumatic scene, to the point of entering quite legitimately the sphere of what could emerge from it for the child as a sexual theory.

I'm not saying that what Jones goes on to unfold is to be gainsaid, because it's a fact that the road he is taking here finds hundreds of correlates that remind us how opportune it is, across a mass of anthropological domains, across all manner of references from mythological literature. He notes, for example, the function of down-breathing in the *Upanishads* where it will be specified, using the term *Apana*, that Brahma created mankind with the downward breathings of his back part. In truth, if you consult this article, you will see that the very extension of references on this particular subject goes as far as diffluence, which shows well enough at the end that he is not entirely convincing, far from it.

For us, however, this is only further stimulation to make us ask ourselves why the function of excrement can play this privileged role in the mode of subjective constitution that we qualify as anal desire. This question can only be settled by bringing in, in a more structural fashion, in keeping with the spirit of our research, the why and wherefore behind the place of the *a* that excrement can occupy.

With respect to the different accidents I mentioned earlier, from the anatomical place of the mammary gland to the plasticity of the human larynx, with, in between, the specular image of castration, linked to the particular physical structure of the copulatory organ at a fairly high level on the animal ladder, excrement is there from the start, even prior to the differentiation between mouth and anus. We can already see it functioning at the level of the blastopore.

According to the biological idea that we have of the living being's relationships with its surroundings, however, an idea which admittedly is always insufficient, it seems all the same that excrement is typified as a waste product and that consequently it is put in the flow of everything the living being tends not to be interested in. What interests the living being is what goes in. As for what comes out, the structure seems to imply that it would tend not to hold onto it. It seems therefore to be indicated, based on these biological considerations, that one should ask oneself exactly by what paths excrement comes to take on its subjectified importance at the level of the human being.

At the level of what might be called living economy, it can of course be seen that excrement continues to have its importance in the surroundings. Sometimes, given certain conditions, there comes to be a glut of it in the surroundings, to the point of making them incompatible with life. At other times, for other organisms, it assumes the function of a support in the outer surroundings. There is a whole economy of the function of excrement, an intra-living and inter-living economy.

Nor is this absent from the human field. I searched in vain in my library to show you here, to put you on the path – it's been lost, like excrement – an admirable little book, like many others by my friend Aldous Huxley, called *Adonis & The Alphabet*. In the collection that bears this promising title you will find a superb article on a sewage treatment plant, at the level of urban planning, in a city on the west coast of the US.

This only has value as an example, because the like occurs in many other places besides industrial America. You can't imagine the cornucopia that can be assembled from the mere excrement of a mass of humanity.

Moreover, it's not off limits to call to mind in this connection what a certain progress in inter-human dealings, in human relations – which have been so much in vogue since the last war – did during the said war regarding the reduction of entire masses of humanity to the function of excrement. Transforming countless individuals from a people selected precisely as a chosen people amongst others, by means of a crematorium furnace, into the state of something that was ultimately distributed, so it would seem, across *Mitteleuropa* in the form of little cakes of soap, is also something that shows us that, in the inter-human economic circuit, targeting man as a thing that can be reduced to excrement is by no means absent.

But we analysts stick to the question of subjectification.

3

By what path does excrement enter subjectification?

Well, it enters by the intermediary of the Other's demand, represented on this occasion by the mother. This is altogether clear in the analytic references, or at least seems so on first approach.

When we've figured that out, we're quite content, we've fallen in line with the observational data, the educational data, of what is called potty training, which instructs the child to hold in. That doesn't go without saying. We're acquainted with the familiar scenes, fundamental, ordinary scenes, there's no need to criticize, nor to curb, and especially not, heavens above, to make so many educative recommendations. Educating the parents, which is always being put on the agenda, only wreaks havoc across all these domains.

The child is asked to hold in. He is made to hold in too long, to start to introduce excrement into the realm of what belongs to his body, and he starts to make it a part of his body, which is considered, at least for a while, as something not to be lost. Then, after that, he is told to let it out, again on demand. Demand has a decisive role here. This part, which all the same the subject has some apprehension over losing, now finds a moment's acknowledgment. It is raised to a very special worth. It is at least given the value of providing the Other's demand with its satisfaction, in addition to being accompanied by all the care and attention with which we are familiar. Not only does the Other approve and pay attention, but it tacks on all these additional dimensions I needn't mention – in other realms, this makes for funny physics – the sniffing, the approval, even the wiping, whose erogenous effects everyone knows to be incontestable. They become that much more evident when it so happens that a mother goes on wiping her son's bottom into his twelfth year. Such things can be seen day in day out.

All this seems to indicate that my initial question is not so important and that we can see very well how poo easily assumes the function of what I have called, my goodness, ἄγαλμα. That this ἄγαλμα should have passed over into the register of the foul-smelling is merely the effect of discipline of which it is an integral part. Nevertheless, none of this allows you to ascertain satisfactorily the scale of the effects that are attached to the mother's agalmatic relationship to her child's excrement if we don't bring these facts into connection with the other forms of the a. The ἄγαλμα is only conceivable in its relation to the phallus, to its absence, and to phallic anxiety as such.

In other terms, the excremental a has come within the scope of our attention inasmuch as it symbolizes castration.

I profess that we can't understand anything about the phenomenology of obsession, which is so fundamental for all our speculation, if we don't grasp in a far more intimate, grounded and regular way than we are used to, excrement's link not only with the $(-\varphi)$ of the phallus but with the other forms of the a noted on the blackboard in the classification of what we are calling their stages.

Let's take things up regressively, with the proviso I made at the outset that this regressive vector necessarily possesses a progressive side.

At the level of the oral stage, where the object *a* is the breast, the nipple, what you will, the nub of what's at issue is as follows. The subject, constituting himself at the origin as well as completing himself in the commandment of the voice, doesn't know and cannot know to what extent he himself is this being that is stuck onto the mother's chest in the shape of the mammary gland, after having also been the parasite that plunged its villi into the uterine mucous membrane in the form of the placenta. He doesn't know, he cannot know, that the breast, the placenta, is the reality of himself, *a*, with respect to the Other. He believes that *a* is the Other and that in dealing with the *a* he is dealing with the Other, the big Other, the mother.

On the other hand, at the anal level he has the first opportunity of recognizing himself in an object. But let's not move too quickly here.

Something in this object switches. The mother's demand is involved. This demand switches – *Keep it in / Give it out – And if I give it out, where does it go?* For those of you here who have the slightest analytic experience I don't need to call to mind the decisive importance of the two phases of demand. As for the rest of you, my goodness, who only read about it, you'll see what it's all about if you open what I've called elsewhere the *psycho-analytical dunghill*, namely the analytic literature. A dunghill is a little pile of shit.

What makes these two phases important? The little pile of shit in question is obtained on demand and it is admired – *What a fine poo!* But the second phase of this demand implies that it is, as it were, foresworn, because all the same the child is taught not to get too close to this fine poo, except by the well-trodden path that analysis has also mapped out, of sublimatory satisfactions. If he smears it over himself – everyone knows that this is what it's done with – one prefers all the same to tell him that it would be better to do it with something else, with the little plastic gloves and aprons used by child analysts, or with nice colours that don't smell so bad. In this first relation with the Other's demand, we thus find ourselves at the level of an ambiguous recognition. What is there is both him and not him, and even further, it doesn't come from him.

We're progressing, the satisfactions are taking shape, and we could see this as the origin of obsessional ambivalence. We could inscribe it in a formula, $(a \lozenge \$)$, where *a* is the cause of this ambivalence, of this yea-and-nay. *This symptom comes from me, but nevertheless it doesn't come from me. I point out to you the negative thoughts I have about you, my analyst, but in the end, it's not really true that I think of you as a piece of shit.* In short, we can see a whole order of causality taking shape.

All the same, we can't ratify it straightaway as the causality of desire, but in the end it's a result, as I said last time when speaking about the symptom in a general way. At this level, a structure is taking shape that seems immediately to be giving us the structure of the symptom in its function as a result. Only, I would remark that this structure founded on demand leaves out of the loop what ought to interest us if the theory I'm outlining is correct, namely the link to desire. One might, therefore, think that introducing a different, external, foreign dimension, the dimension of desire, and notably sexual desire, would push to the rear, would sweep away, what we've got here regarding a certain relationship in which the subject is constituted as divided and ambivalent with respect to the Other's demand. As a matter of fact, it wouldn't.

We already know why sexual desire doesn't sweep it away, why it does something very different. Through its very duplicity, the object comes to be able to symbolize wonderfully, at least in one of its phases, what is going to be involved at the advent of the phallic stage. The phallus qua its vanishing, its ἀφάνισις, to employ Jones's term, which he applies to desire and which only applies to the phallus, is in mankind the medium of the relations between the sexes. The evacuation of the result of the anal function, inasmuch as it is done on command, will take on its full import at the phallic level as providing an image for the loss of the phallus.

Of course, all of this is only valid within the confines of what I said before. Thinking simply that some of you might have been away and not heard me, I feel I ought to remind you once more what the crux of the $(-\varphi)$ phase is. It holds a central place on the following chart.

5	voice	a	desire of the Other
4	image	the Other's might	
3	desire	anxiety $(-\varphi)$	the Other's jouissance
2	trace	the Other's demand	
1	anxiety	a	desire x of the Other

The $(-\varphi)$ chart

I ask you to make a note of these formulas.

Due to the $(-\varphi)$, the moment of the advance of the Other's jouissance, which is also the move towards the Other's jouissance, entails the constitution of castration as the surety of their meeting.

In other words, the fact that male desire meets its downfall *before* entering the jouissance of the female partner, and even the fact that the woman's jouissance is crushed, to take up a term borrowed from the phenomenology of breast and nursling, crushed under phallic longing, implies that woman is thenceforth required, and I would almost say condemned, to love the male Other only at a point situated beyond what halts her, her too, as desire, and which is the phallus.

This beyond is targeted in love. It is, let's put it as well as we can, either transverberated by castration or transfigured in terms of potency. The male Other is not the Other qua the Other with whom it would be a matter of uniting. The woman's jouissance is within her. She doesn't conjoin it to the Other.

You can call this pivotal function an obstacle if you like, but it is no way an obstacle, it is the locus of anxiety, anxiety over the organ's caducity, its deciduosity, inasmuch as it accounts, in a different way on each side, for what one might call the insatiability of desire.

Only through this reminder can we see the necessity behind the symbolizations that appear in this respect on the hysterical side or the obsessional side. Today we're on the second of these two sides.

By dint of the structure I've outlined here, man is only in woman through the delegation of his presence, in the form of this deciduous organ, this organ of which he is fundamentally castrated *in* sexual intercourse and *by* sexual intercourse.

To speak of gift here is mere metaphor. It is only too obvious that the male doesn't give anything. Nor does the woman. And yet, the symbol of the gift is essential to the relationship with the Other. The gift is the supreme social act, so it's been said, and even the *total social act*.

A long while ago, our experience led us to put our finger on the fact that the metaphor of the gift was borrowed from the anal realm. It has long since been spotted that the scybalum, to start using more polite language, is for the child the essential gift, the gift of love. A good many other things were spotted here too, up to and including what is called, when the burglar has passed by, the *signature*, which every police force and forensic medicine textbook are well acquainted with, namely, the bizarre fact that the fellow who comes wielding a jemmy to open your cupboards invariably has a sudden bowel movement right then and there.

From this angle, we quickly find ourselves at the level of mammalian conditionings.

It's at the level of mammals that we note, at least from what we know of animal ethology, the function of the faecal trace, more precisely faeces as a trace. And here too the trace is deeply bound to the place that the organismal subject assures for himself, a place of possession in the world, of territory, and simultaneously of safety for sexual union. A few publications have now given ample space to the phenomenon that makes the hippopotamus, certainly, or even, because this extends beyond the mammals, the robin redbreast, feel invincible within the limits of their territory, but once outside it there is a sudden about-turn and they become curiously timid. The relationship between this limit-point and the faecal trace was spotted way back in mammals and we cannot fail to see here what pre-figures in these biological underpinnings the function that the object *a* holds as a representative of the subject, in so far as it is *le fruit anal*, the anal fruit.

Are we going to make do with that? Is this all we can draw from the questions we are levelling at the *a* function in its relation to a certain kind of desire, the obsessional's desire?

So far, we've grounded nothing but the subject set in, or not, within his limits, and who, within these limits, is more or less divided.

With these limits, the subject finds himself at the level of sexual union, and these limits are peculiarly repressed in mankind. But even the access they afford him to the symbolic function doesn't tell us anything else about what's involved, and which we are demanding, which is to know in what way this concealing of the object comes to ground the function of desire. Experience is what furnishes us with the trace of this.

This is where we have to take the next step, which is also the crucial step.

4

So far, nothing has explained the obsessional's very particular dealings with his desire.

Precisely because up to this level everything has been symbolized, the divided subject and the impossible union alike, it appears all the more striking that one thing has not, and that is desire itself.

The subject's necessity of concluding his position as desire is precisely what will lead him to conclude it in the category of *might*, that is, at the level of the fourth storey. The relationship between the specular reflection, the narcissistic underpinning of self-mastery, and the locus of the Other, is where the link lies.

You're already acquainted with it and to explain it again would mean retreading a path that's already been cleared. This is why I want now to point out the originality of what the facts reveal to us. To set off from the thick of it, let's take a case, the second case that Jones draws on, in the fifth volume of the aforementioned *Jahrbuch*, for his phenomenology of the anal function in the obsessional. I could cite hundreds of other examples in the literature.

This case illustrates the following, which I've called to mind a thousand times. Although ordinarily the fantasies of the obsessional subject, whatever level of luxuriance they may reach, are never executed, it does happen all the same that, through all sorts of conditions that postpone their enactment more or less indefinitely, he realizes his desire. Better still, it does sometimes happen that others may clear the obstacle out of the way for him. It can happen that a subject who develops, and very early on, as a magnificent obsessional belongs to a family of quite dissolute folk. This case is one of those.

All the sisters – and there are a number of them, not to mention the mother, the aunt, the mother's different lovers, and even, I believe, Lord forgive me, the grandmother – had their way with this little kid when he was about five years of age. He's no less of an obsessional for it, a sound obsessional, with desires in the only mode in which they can be constituted in the register of might, namely, impossible desires, in the sense that, whatever he may do to realize them, he doesn't get there. In this register, the obsessional never gets to the bottom of his search for satisfaction.

The question I'm asking you, which is as vivid and brilliant in this observation as it is in a good many others, can be recognized in this article in the form, which is likewise vivid and brilliant, of the image that is mentioned of a little fish. This Ichthys – ἰχθύς – which I find here in arm's reach, as it were, and for good reason, you will meet at every turn in the field of the obsessional, if he's from our cultural sphere, and we don't really know any others – it's Jesus Christ himself. One could speculate a great deal over the kind of blasphemous necessity – which until now, I must say, has never been justified as such – which makes such a subject, like many other obsessionals, unable to give himself over to one or other of his more or less atypical acts in which his sexual research is exerted without immediately fantasizing Christ in association with them. Even though the fact has been present in our eyes for a long time, I think the last word has yet to be said.

If this fantasy is blasphemous, it's because clearly on this occasion Christ is a god. In truth, he's a god for many people and even for so many people that it's rather difficult to chase him out of this place, even with all the various operations of historical criticism, and then of psychologism. But in the end, he's not just any god. Permit me to cast some doubt over whether obsessionals in the time of Theophrastus, the Theophrastus of *The Characters*, amused themselves by having Apollo participate mentally in their turpitudes.

The faint outline of an explanation that I set out in passing a while back takes on its importance here – the gods are an element of the real, whether we like it or not, even if we no longer have anything more to do with them. This implies that, if they're still there, it's quite clear that they go about incognito. But one thing is quite sure, and this is that a god's relation to the object of desire is different from ours.

I've just mentioned Apollo. Neither before nor after is Apollo castrated. Afterwards, something else happens to him. We are told that Daphne is the one who is transformed into a tree. Something's being concealed from you there. It's concealed from you – this is very surprising – because it's not concealed from you. After the transformation, the laurel is not Daphne but Apollo. What's specific to a god is that, once satisfied, he transforms himself into the object of his desire, even if he must thereby be petrified therein. In other terms, a god, if he is real, furnishes, in his relation to the object of his desire, the image of his might. His might is right where he is.

This is true of all gods, even of Elohim, even of Yahweh, who is one of them, though his place is a very particular one. Only, something has stepped in here that had a different origin. For this occasion, let's call this something – it's true historically, but doubtless the historical truth goes a tad further – by the name of Plato.

Plato only told us things that remain very easy to handle within the ethics of jouissance because they have allowed us to trace out the barrier that the Beautiful constitutes at the place of the supreme Good. Except that, once mixed in with the emerging Christianity, this produced something that people believe has always been there, and has always been there in the Bible, but this is moot and no doubt we're going to have to come back to this next year, if all of us are still here. This thing is the fantasy of an almighty God, which means a mighty God everywhere at the same time, and a mighty God for everything, as a whole, because this is precisely what we're bound to come back to. If the world is as it is, it's because of the might of God, which is exerted in all directions at once.

Now, the correlation between this almightiness and, as it were, omnivoyance, signals for us well enough what is involved. It's a matter of what takes shape in a field beyond the mirage of might. It's a matter of the projection of the subject into the field of the ideal, which is split into two strands, on one hand, the specular alter ego, the ideal ego, and on the other hand, which lies beyond, the Ego Ideal.

At the level at which anxiety is covered over, the Ego Ideal takes the form of the Almighty. This is where the obsessional seeks and finds the complement of what is necessary for him when it comes to constituting himself in desire, namely, the fantasy of ubiquity, which is also the support upon which the multiplicity of his desires, which are always being pushed farther off, skit back and forth.

Within what I might call the heated circles of analysis, those in which the impulse of one first inspiration still lives on, a question has been raised as to whether the analyst ought to be an atheist or not, and whether the subject, at the end of analysis, can consider his analysis over if he still believes in God. This is a question that I won't be settling today, but on the path of a question such as this, I'll tell you that, regardless of what an obsessional bears out in his words, if he hasn't been divested of his obsessional structure, you can be sure that, as an obsessional, he believes in God. I mean that he believes in the God that everyone, or nearly everyone, in our cultural sphere abides by, this means the God in whom everyone believes without believing, namely, the universal eye that watches down on all our actions.

This dimension is there, as firmly in its frame as the window of the fantasy I was speaking about the other day. Simply, part of its necessity, I mean, even for the strongest believers, is also not to believe. Firstly, because if they did believe, it would be visible. If they did believe as strongly as all that, the consequences of that belief wouldn't go unnoticed, when in actual fact this belief remains strictly invisible.

This is the true dimension of atheism. The atheist would be he who has succeeded in doing away with the fantasy of the Almighty.

Well, one gentleman by the name of Voltaire, who all the same knew something about the anti-religious revolt, held steadfast to his deism, which means the existence of the Almighty. Diderot thought him incoherent and for that Voltaire thought that Diderot was mad. It's not so certain that Diderot was really an atheist and his life's work seems to me, this is my take on it, to vouch for this, given the way he teases out the inter-subject at the level of the Other in his principal dialogues, *Le Neveu de Rameau* and *Jacques le fataliste*. He can only do so, however, in the style of derision.

The existence of an atheist, in the true sense, can only indeed be conceived of at the limit of an asceticism, which strikes us as only being able to be a psychoanalytic asceticism. I'm speaking of atheism conceived of as the negation of the dimension of a presence of almightiness at the base of the world.

This doesn't mean that the existence of the atheist doesn't have its historical guarantor, but this guarantor is of an altogether different nature. Its affirmation is directed precisely to the side of the existence of the gods as real. It doesn't deny it, nor does it affirm it, it is directed towards this. The atheist of *The Atheists Tragedie* – I'm alluding to the Elizabethan[1] tragedy of this title – the atheist as a combatant and as a revolutionary is not one who denies God in his function of almightiness, he is one who affirms himself as not serving any god. And that is the essential dramatic worth that has always lent its passion to the question of atheism.

I apologize for this short digression, which as you can well imagine is just a preparatory one.

You can see where today's circuit has brought us. It has brought us to the fundamental link between these two stages, the second and the fourth, framing the fundamental impossibility, the impossibility that divides desire and jouissance at the sexual level.

The obsessional's way of circling both tightly and widely at a tangent, the impossible seat he gives to his desire, has allowed us, in the course of our analysis today, to see a first outline of how the subject's relation to a lost object of the most distasteful sort shows a necessary nexus with the highest idealistic production.

This circuit is not yet complete, however. We can clearly see how desire appends to the structure of the object – we still have to indicate what the middle part of the chart, which I hope you've all copied down, indicates as the next field of our disquisition – the relationship between the obsessional's fantasy, posited as the structure of his desire, and the anxiety that determines it.

19 June 1963

XXIII

ON A CIRCLE THAT IS IRREDUCIBLE TO A POINT

On the yieldable object
On defence-desire
On the act and deeds
On the phallic hole and its stand-ins
Love and desire in the obsessional

So as to try to move forward today in our topic I'm going to resume with the constitution of desire in the obsessional and its relation to anxiety. To do so, I shall first be coming back to the double-entry chart, the matrix I gave you in the very first lesson of this year's Seminar and which I completed later on. Its form has been copied up here, framed by a white line and written out in pink.

This chart corresponded to my intention back then to offset and stagger the three terms Freud arrived at, inhibition, symptom and anxiety, and which he set into the title of his article. Around these three terms I punctuated a number of moments that can be defined in the terms you can see here. By referring each term to its column heading at the top and to its row heading on the left, one finds a correlation which can be offered up to examination and which can prove, when put to the test, to be open to confirmation or disconfirmation in its structural function.

Still, these terms were given to you at the time in a certain incompleteness and included a few enigmatic suspensions. For example, in spite of the etymological references I gave, the distinction between *emotion* and *émoi, turmoil*, might all the same have been matter for an examination that it wasn't entirely possible for you to resolve with your own means.

What I shall be bringing you today seems to me to be fit to afford some precision that I have little doubt will be fresh and even unexpected for most if not all of you.

1

To begin with, let's take a look at this *émoi*, whose origin is quite distinct from the origin of *emotion*.

It's not an outward motion, it's not a movement out of the adapted field of motor action, which is what *emotion* certainly indicates etymologically, and I'm not saying that the etymology is something we can put our full trust in here. The etymology of *émoi* is to be sought out somewhere quite different, in an *esmayer*, the *mayer* referring to an altogether primal Germanic root, *mögen*, *magan*. It's a matter of something that is poised outside. Outside what? Outside the principle of power. There is, therefore, an enigma around a term that is not unrelated to might.

Considering the form this word has taken in French, I would even say that this is perhaps something which belongs to the realm of the *hors de moi*, the *beside myself* or *beside oneself*. Here one almost has to refer to the pun, *et moi*, an approach which is of no less importance.

To go straight to the heart of the matter, I can tell you quite plainly, bluntly, at the point we've reached – and also because the phenomenology of the obsessional immediately illustrates this in a very tangible fashion – that the *émoi* involved, the *turmoil*, is none other than the *a* itself, at least in the correlations we're trying to explore, to specify, and to tie in today, namely, the relations between desire and anxiety.

Throughout this year's disquisition I've taught you to get a much firmer grip on the conjuncture between anxiety and its uncanny ambiguity. This elaboration allows us to formulate what is striking in its phenomenology, what we can get from it, and what other authors have slid over and mistaken – anxiety is without cause, but not without object.

This is the distinction I'm introducing and upon which I'm grounding my efforts in order to situate anxiety. Not only is it not without object, but it very likely designates the most, as it were, profound object, the ultimate object, the Thing. It's in this sense, as I've taught you to say, that anxiety is that which doesn't deceive. As for the characteristic of being without cause, which is so evident in its phenomenon, this is better clarified from the angle from which I tried to situate where the notion of cause begins.

Thereafter, although it's linked to *turmoil*, anxiety doesn't depend on it. On the contrary, it determines it. Anxiety is to be found suspended between, on the one hand, the pre-existent form, so to speak, of the relation to the cause – the *What is there?* which will go on to be formulated as cause, namely *embarrassment* – and, on the other hand, the *turmoil* that cannot get a hold on this cause because, primordially, anxiety literally produced it.

Something illustrates this in an abject way, and which is all the more striking for it, something that I placed at the origin of my explanation of the obsessional in the Wolf Man's anguished confrontation with his major recurring dream, something that appears as a monstration of his ultimate reality. This is something that occurs but which never comes into his consciousness, to such an extent that it can only be reconstructed as a link in the chain of the entire subsequent determination. To call it by its name and its product, it is anal turmoil.

This is the first form in which the emergence of the object *a* comes into the picture for the obsessional, and which lies at the origin of everything that will uncoil from this in the mode of effect. Here, the object *a* is found to be given in an originative moment in which it plays a certain function that we're going to be pausing over now so as to specify its value, its scope, and its first coordinates, those that stand prior to the rest that are added on later. It is because the *a* is this, in its originative production, that it can subsequently function in a dialectic of desire that is the specific dialectic of the obsessional.

Turmoil is thus coordinated with the moment at which the *a* appears, a moment of traumatic unveiling whereby anxiety reveals itself for what it is – *that which deceives not* – a moment at which the field of the Other, as it were, splits open and exposes its rock bottom. What is this *a*? What is its function with respect to the subject?

If we are able to grasp it here, in some sense in a pure way, it is precisely in so far as, in his radical, traumatic confrontation, the subject yields to the situation. But what does it mean, at this level, at this moment, to *yield*? How is this to be understood?

It's not that the subject wavers, or that he flags. Think if you will of the attitude set out by the subject's fascination faced with the open window looking onto the wolf-covered tree. In a situation whose fixity puts right before our very eyes its primitively inexpressible character, and by which he will remain marked forever, what occurred is something that gives its true meaning to the subject's *yield* – it's literally a cession.

The object's yieldable character is such an important characteristic of the *a* that I'll ask you now to follow me through a brief inspection to see whether this characteristic marks all the forms of the *a* that we've listed. Here it appears that the libido's points of fixation are always poised around one of the moments that nature offers to the potential structure of subjective cession.

The first moment of anxiety, the one towards which analytic experience progressively edged at the level of birth trauma, thereafter allowed us, along the inroad afforded by this remark, to accentuate and articulate it better than what was first roughly broached in the form of frustration. The most decisive moment in the anxiety at issue, the anxiety of weaning, is not so much when the breast falls short of the subject's need, it's rather that the infant yields the breast to which he is appended as a portion of himself. Let's not forget what I depicted for you and which I'm not the only one to have noticed – I'm referring here specifically to Bergler – namely, during breastfeeding the breast is part of the individual who is being fed. It is merely *stuck onto* the mother, as I put it in a colourful expression.

The most primordial moment of surprise occurs in the fact that he can either hold onto or leave go of this breast, and this can some-times be grasped in the newborn's expression, in which, for the first time, there passes the reflection – in relation to the abandonment of this organ that is much more than an object, which is the subject himself – of something that furnishes the support, the root, for what in another register has been called dereliction.

Thence, do we have any other plain means of monitoring this besides the accent that I'm laying, as for all the objects *a*, on the possibility of replacing the natural object? The natural object can be replaced by a mechanical object, if I can express myself thus to designate the possible replacement of this object by any other object one may meet. It might be another partner, the wetnurse, which was such a big question for the first advocate of natural upbringing – see Rousseau's theme of nursing by the mother. Beyond that we have something else, good gracious, which hasn't always existed and which we owe to the progress of culture – the feeding bottle. With respect to this *a*, this sets the possibility of having it in store, in stock, of retail circulation, and also of its being sealed away in sterilized tubes.

What I'm calling the cession of the object *a* is therefore translated by the appearance, in the chain of human manufacture, of yieldable objects that can be the equivalents of natural objects. This reminder is not beside the point here because from this angle I mean to make a direct link with the function on which I've long been laying the accent, the function of the transitional object, to use the term, whether it is proper or not, but now accepted, pinned to it by its creator, the one who caught sight of it, namely, Winnicott.

One can clearly see what constitutes the object he calls transi-tional in the object function that I'm calling the yieldable object. It's a little piece torn off something, more often than not a swathe, and one can clearly see the support the subject finds in it. He doesn't dissolve into it, he takes comfort from it. He takes comfort from it in his utterly originative function of a subject in a position of falling away with respect to the signifying confrontation. This is not an investment in the *a*, this is, so to speak, investiture.

Here the *a* stands in for the subject – it's a stand-in in the position of precedent. The primordial, mythical subject, posited at the outset as having to be constituted in the signifying confrontation, can never be grasped by us, and for good reason, because the *a* preceded it and it has to re-emerge secondarily, beyond its vanishing, marked by this initial substitution.

The function of the yieldable object as a piece that can be primordially separated off conveys something of the body's identity, antecedent to the body itself with respect to the constitution of the subject.

Since I've been speaking about events in the history of human production that for us can hold the value of confirmation or revelation, I won't possibly be able to avoid a moment's mention, as the term that lies at the furthest extremity of these events, of the problems that are going to be posed for us, right up to the subject's most radical essentiality, by the imminent, likely extension, which is already under way – more than common consciousness and even more than the consciousness of practitioners such as ourselves might be aware of – of organ transplants. They are developing at a galloping rate, which is certainly surprising and which is just what it takes to suspend thinking on I know not what question of how far we shall or should consent to them.

The mine, the resource, of these astonishing possibilities could soon be allowing for certain subjects to be artificially maintained in a state that we would no longer know how to qualify as life or death. As you know, Ångström's methods allow a subject's tissues to be kept alive when everything indicates that his central nervous system cannot be brought back – brain waves flatlining, mydriasis, zero reflex response beyond the point of no return. What are we doing when we take an organ from a subject in this state? Surely you can sense something emerging in the real that is likely to stir up, in terms that are utterly new, the question of the person's essentiality and what it is attached to. On all of this, which does occasionally give rise to legalism, the doctrinal authorities will surely be solicited in order to appreciate just how far, this time in practice, the question of knowing whether the subject is a body or a soul can stretch.

I won't go any farther down this road today because these doctrinal authorities seem to have already given some highly singular replies, which ought to be studied closely to appreciate their coherence with respect to certain positions that have been taken for a long while now. For instance, identifying the person with something immortal known as the soul is radically distinct, on the very plane of

relation, from a doctrine that spells out in its practices what is most
contrary to the Platonic tradition, namely, that there cannot be any
other resurrection besides that of the body.

Likewise, the domain being evoked here is not so tightly linked
to the industrial advance in such peculiar possibilities as not to
have been evoked by visionary fantasizing since way back. I need
only send you back to the *unheimlich* function of the eyes that are
handled, to fetch them from a living being to his automaton, by the
character – incarnated by Hoffmann and whom Freud placed at the
centre of his article on the *Unheimliche* – of Coppelius. He scoops
out the sockets to seek out in their root, somewhere, the object that
it is crucial, essential to endue himself with as the beyond, and the
most anguishing beyond, of the desire that constitutes it, namely,
the eye itself.

I've said enough in passing about the same function in the voice
and how to us it appears – and how to us it will doubtless appear
ever more so, given the many technological improvements – to be
capable of belonging to the realm of yieldable objects, those objects
that can be lined up on the shelves of a library in the form of gramophone records or reels of tape. It is not indispensable to mention
such an episode here, old or new, to know what peculiar relation
this can occasionally have with the emergence of anxiety in such a
conjunction.

Let's simply add what is connoted – when it emerges for the first
time in cultural spheres that we have no reason to call primitive – by
the possibility of detaching the image from the body, the specular
image, I say, the image of the body, and of reducing it to a yieldable state in the shape of photographs or even drawings – namely,
the conflict, the revulsion, even the horror that such objects can
provoke in the sensibility of those who see them emerging quite suddenly in a form that is both indefinitely reproducible and capable of
being spread all over the place – with the refusal to let this image be
taken, when God knows, make no mistake, where it might end up
next.

The anal object comes into play in the function of desire with this
function of a yieldable object. This function is by and large the most
natural one, but this naturalness cannot be explained away as its
having taken on this function. We've still got to grasp precisely in
what way the object comes into play at this level.

Let's not forget to put to the test here the guide rope furnished by
our formula that the object *a* is not the end, the goal, of desire, but
its cause. It is the cause of desire inasmuch as desire is itself something non-effective, a kind of effect founded and constituted upon
the function of lack, which only appears as an effect at the exact spot

where the notion of cause is located, that is, only at the level of the signifying chain, to which desire lends that coherence whereby the subject is essentially constituted as metonymy.

How are we to qualify this desire at the anal level, where we grasp its incidence in the constitution of the subject? It's doubtless the desire to hold back, but is it the contingent fact, the forced fact of toilet training, that lends it the function of holding back? No, it isn't, this is not what gives anal desire its fundamental structure.

A more general form is involved in the desire to hold back and this is what we have to grasp.

2

In its polar relation to anxiety, desire is to be located where I've put it, matched up with the foregoing matrix, namely, at the level of *inhibition*. This is why desire can assume the function of what is called a defence.

Let's go step by step to see how this might happen.

What is inhibition for us in our experience? It is not enough to have had this experience or to have dealt with it as such to spell out its function correctly. What is inhibition if not the introduction into a function – in his article Freud takes the example of the motor function, but it can't be just any function – of another desire besides the one that the function satisfies naturally?

After all, we know this, and I'm not claiming to be uncovering anything new here, but I think that in spelling it out like this I'm introducing a new formulation, without which the deductions that stem from it would elude us.

The correlations that this matrix indicates invite us to acknowledge the locus of inhibition as the locus at which, strictly speaking, desire is exerted and at which we grasp one of the roots of what analysis designates as *Urverdrängung*. The structural concealment of desire behind inhibition is what makes us say together that, if Mr So-and-So has got writer's cramp, it's because he eroticizes the function of his hand. I think everyone can find their feet here. This is what prompts us to bring into the picture at the same locus the following three terms, the first two I've already named – *inhibition* and *desire*, the third being the *act*.

When it comes to defining what the act is, this being the sole pole that is correlative to the locus of anxiety, we can only do so by situating it where it stands in this matrix, at the locus of *inhibition*.

Neither for us nor for anyone else can the act be defined as something that only happens, as it were, in the field of the real, in the sense that motivity defines it, the motor response. Without doubt, there always remains some involvement of a motor effect in the field of the real, but it translates into it in such a way that another field makes its impact felt. It's not only the field of sensory stimulation, for example, as it is articulated by simply considering the reflex arc, and this is not to be articulated as the field of the realization of the subject either.

Articulating the act in the field of subjective realization whilst evading the precedence of the *a* is a personalist myth. The *a* opens the field of the subject's realization and conserves thereafter its privilege therein in a way that the subject as such can only be realized in the objects that belong to the same series as the *a*, to the same locus in this matrix. They are always yieldable objects and they are what for a long time have been called *deeds*, with all the meaning that this term carries, up to and including in the field of moral theology.

So, what happens in the other field I'm speaking about and whose incidence, whose insistence, whose persistence in the real connotes an action as an act? How are we to define the act? Is it simply by its polar relation to anxiety, by what happens in terms of a surmounting of anxiety, if I may put it like that?

Let's say, using formulas that can merely approach what an act is, that we're speaking about an act when an action has the character of a signifying manifestation where what may be called the gap of desire is written into it. An act is an action in that the very desire that would have been designed to inhibit it makes itself felt therein. Only in this grounding of the notion of act in its relation to inhibition can a justification be found for calling things *acts* that in principle look so little like what may be called an act in the full, ethical sense of the word – the sexual act on one hand, or the testamentary act on the other.

Well, with regard to the relationship between the *a* and the constitution of a desire, and with regard to what it reveals to us about desire's relationship to the natural function, the obsessional has the most exemplary value for us. We're forever putting our finger on the characteristic, whose enigmatic aspect can only be effaced for us by habit, that in him desires are always evinced in a dimension that just now I went so far as to call the function of defence.

I said it in a slightly anticipatory way, because why does the incidence of desire in inhibition warrant being called defence? Well, it is solely in so far as the effect of desire thus signalled by inhibition can be introduced into an action that is already caught in the induction of another desire.

This is also a fact of common experience for us. But without going into the fact that we're always dealing with something of this order, let's observe, to stick with our obsessional, that this is already the position of anal desire, defined by the desire to hold back, inasmuch as it is focused on a primordial object to which it will impart its value. The desire to hold back only carries meaning for us in the economy of libido, that is, in its nexus with sexual desire.

This is where Saint Augustine's *inter urinas et faeces nascimur* deserves to be called to mind. What is important here is not so much that we are born betwixt urine and faeces, but, at least for us analysts, that betwixt urine and faeces is where we make love. We piss beforehand and we shit afterwards, or vice versa.

This is yet another correlation to which we pay too little heed in the phenomenology we allow to come into analysis. We saw it in connection with that element in the Wolf Man's story that is so barely perceived as to go unmentioned – his little primordial gift. This is why one really has to listen out and ascertain, in those cases in which it rears its head, the relation that binds the sexual act to something that, of course, doesn't sound like it carries great importance, but which becomes important as something indicative of the relation I'm speaking about, namely, the usual fomentation of the little turd, whose successive evacuation doubtless doesn't carry the same signification in all subjects, depending on whether they stand on the obsessional side or another one.

3

Let's take up our path at the spot where I left you.

What about the point I'm directing you towards now concerning the desire underlying desire? And how are we to form a conception of what, on this path, leads us towards the elucidation of its meaning – leads us, I mean, not simply in the fact of it, but in its necessity?

We have interpreted desire as defence and we have said that it defends against another desire. Now we are going to be able to conceive of how we are led to this, if I may say so, quite naturally by what leads the obsessional to commit himself in a recursive movement of the process of desire, a movement wherein he tends to take up its steps afresh. This movement is generated by the implicit effort of subjectification that is already in his symptoms, to the extent that he does have symptoms.

What is meant by the double correlation, which I've written into the matrix, with *impediment* and *emotion*? This is what is designated for us by the titles I've put hereunder.

desire	*not being able*	cause
not knowing		
a		anxiety

Reformulation of the anxiety chart

I've just explained why *desire* is in the stead of *inhibition* here.

In the stead of *impediment* there is *not being able*. Indeed, impediment – a term had to be chosen – which comes from *impedicare*, ensnaring, is not the duplication of inhibition here. What is it? The subject is very much impeded from abiding by his desire to hold back and this is what emerges in the obsessional as compulsion. He cannot hold himself back.

In the stead of *emotion* there is *not knowing*. The word *emotion* is borrowed from an adaptational psychology of the catastrophic reaction, which is not ours. This word also comes into play here in an altogether different way from its traditional and usual definition. The emotion at issue here is the emotion highlighted by experiences that are grounded in the confrontation with a task, when the subject doesn't know how to go about responding. This merges with our own *not knowing*.

He didn't know it was that, and this is why, at the level of the point at which *he can't impede himself*, he lets things go, namely, the to and fro of the signifier that posits and effaces by turns. But these movements all travel the same path, which is likewise unknown, the path towards re-finding the primal trace. What the obsessional subject seeks in what I called its recursion – and you can see why that word was chosen – in the process of desire is well and truly to re-find the authentic cause of the whole process. And since this cause is nothing but the ultimate object, the abject and paltry object, he keeps seeking out the object, with its phases of abeyance, its wrong turns, its false trails, its sidelong drifting, which make the search turn endlessly around and around. All of this, which emerges at the level of acting-out, also emerges in the fundamental symptom of doubt which, for this subject, strikes at the value of all the objects of substitution.

Here, *not being able* is not being able to what? To impede oneself. Here, compulsion is the compulsion to doubt. It pertains to these doubtful objects by dint of which the moment when the ultimate object would be accessed is driven back, the object that would be the *end* in the full sense of the word, namely, the subject's loss on the road onto which he is always capable of falling via the path of *embarrassment* – the embarrassment where the question of the *cause* as such is introduced, which is where he enters the transference.

Have we clasped, or even so much as broached, the question of how the incidence of another desire steps in, which would play the role of defence with respect to the first? Clearly we haven't, not yet. I've only traced out the road back to the first object, with its correlation of anxiety, because this is indeed the reason for the escalating emergence of anxiety.

To the extent that the analysis of an obsessional is pushed farther on towards its terminal point – when the analysis is only directed along this road – the question remains open, if it's not a question of what I meant, because I think you've been able to glimpse it, but rather a question of the incidence of desire as defence, defence against a first desire. It's an active defence, whose action extends very far so as to drive back the deadline that I've just sketched out as the due date of the return to the object. How is that possible? We can only form a conception of this by giving, as I did earlier, a pivotal position to sexual desire, which is called genital desire.

In mankind, this desire, in accordance with its specific structuring around the intermediary of an object, is posited as harbouring anxiety at its core, which separates desire from jouissance. At the level of genital desire the function of the *a* is symbolized analogically, analogically to its predominance, its ascendancy, in the economy of desire, by the $(- \varphi)$ which appears as a subjective residue at the level of copulation. The copula is everywhere, but it only unites precisely by being missing right where it would be specifically copulatory. This central hole gives its privileged value to castration anxiety, the only level at which anxiety is produced at the very locus of the lack of the object.

It is precisely because of this that another desire comes into play in the obsessional. This other desire gives its seat to the outlying position I've just been trying to describe for you of the obsessional's desire with respect to genital desire.

Indeed, the obsessional's desire cannot be conceived of in its insistence or its mechanism unless through the fact that it is situated as a stand-in for what it is impossible to stand in for elsewhere, that is, at its locus. To spell it right out, the obsessional, like any neurotic, has already gained access to the phallic stage, but given his impossibility of satisfying at the level of this stage, his own object comes along, the excremental *a*, the *a* cause of the desire to hold back. If I really wanted to conjoin its function with everything I said about desire's relations with inhibition, I would much rather label this *a* as a stopper.

It is in relation to this function that this object will go on to assume its values, which I could call developed values. And this is where we pierce through to the origin of what I could call the analytic fantasy of oblativity.

I've already reiterated how oblativity is an obsessional's fantasy. Of course, everyone would like genital union to be a gift – *I give myself, you give yourself, we give ourselves.* Unfortunately, there's no trace of a gift in a genital, copulatory act, however successful one might imagine it to be. There is only any gift precisely right where it's always been perfectly well spotted, at the anal level. At the anal level, something stands out, something looms up, which arrests the subject upon the realization of the gap, the central hole, which at the genital level stops him from grasping anything that could function as an object of the gift, an object designed to satisfy.

Since I've spoken about the stopper, you can recognize here the most primitive form of the tap, which we introduced in the discussion on the function of the cause. Well, how might we illustrate the function of the stopper-object or the tap, along with its consequence, the desire to turn it off? How might the different elements of our matrix be situated here?

What is the relation to the cause? What can one do with a tap? Observing the child's experience indicates that this is truly and verily the initial point at which the attraction of this fundamental sort of object comes into the picture, contrary to what happens for any other little animal. *Not being able* to do anything with it, along with *not knowing*, are signposted well enough here, and in their distinction.

What is a symptom? It's a leaking tap.

The *passage à l'acte* is to turn it on, but to turn it on without knowing what one is doing. Something happens where a cause is liberated by one of these means that have nothing to do with this cause, because, as I told you, the tap only fulfils its function of cause inasmuch as everything that can come out of it comes from elsewhere. That which can occur at the level of the anal comes into play and assumes its meaning by dint of being drawn into the phallic hole at the centre of the genital dimension.

As for acting-out, if we want to situate it in relation to the tap metaphor, it's not the fact of turning on the tap, it's simply the presence, or not, of the spurt of water. Acting-out is the spurt, that is, what always happens owing to a fact that comes from somewhere other than the cause on which one has just acted. Our experience indicates this. Acting-out is not provoked by us when we intervene, by an inexact interpretation on the anal plane, for instance, rather it's that, when the interpretation is brought to bear on one spot, it makes way for something that comes from elsewhere. In other words, the cause of desire is not to be bothered without due consideration.

Here, therefore, on this ground – on which the fate of the obsessional's desire is played out, the fate of his symptoms and his sublimations – the possibility is introduced of something else coming in to function that will take on its meaning as what circumvents the central gap of phallic desire. This is what happens at the scopic level. Everything we've just said about the function of the *a* as the object of an analogous gift designed to hold the subject back on the edge of the hole of castration can be transposed to the image. The specular image comes into function analogically because it stands in a correlative position with respect to the phallic stage.

And this is precisely where, in the obsessional subject, the ambiguity of the function of love steps in, as is underlined in all the different observations.

What is this idealized love that we find in the Rat Man as well as the Wolf Man, and in any observation on an obsessional that has been pushed fairly far? What is the word for this enigma, an enigma of the function given to the Other, the woman on this occasion, who is the exalted object that no one waited for us, neither you nor me, nor the teaching imparted here, to know what it furtively represents by way of the negation of his desire? In any case, women make no mistake about it.

What would distinguish this type of love from an erotomaniacal love, were it not for what the obsessional engages of himself in love and which we have to seek out? If it really is, as I've told you, the last object that his analysis can reveal along a certain road of recursion, namely, the object of excrement, isn't this the divinatory wellspring whence the obsessional finds himself to be the loveable object?

I'm asking you to take out your flashlights to try to shed some light on what's involved in the obsessional's position in this regard.

Doubt is not what dominates here, it's rather that the subject prefers not even to look into it. You will always meet this prudence in the obsessional. And still, love assumes for him the forms of an exalted bond. What he expects to be loved is a certain image of himself. He gives this image to the other. He gives it so entirely that he imagines the other party would no longer know what to do should this image of him go missing. This is the fundament behind what elsewhere I've called the altruistic dimension of this mythical love, which is founded on a mythical oblativity.

Maintaining this image of himself is what chains the obsessional to maintaining a remote distance from himself, which is precisely what it is so hard to reduce in the analysis. Of course this is where one person, who had much experience with such patients, but not the apparatus with which to formulate it, for reasons that remain to be fathomed, got the illusory idea of laying the entire accent on the notion of distance. But the distance involved is the distance between the subject and himself whereby everything he does is only ever, for him, when he is without analysis and left to his solitude, something he perceives in the end as a game, which when all is said and done will only have benefited the other I'm speaking about, the image of himself.

This relation to the image is commonly highlighted as the narcissistic dimension in which everything is developed that, in the obsessional, is not central, i.e., symptomatic, but behavioural or lived. But what he has to do, and this will furnish him with his true seat, is to realize at the very least the first phase of the fact that his desire is never allowed to appear in an act. His desire is sustained by doing the rounds of all the possibilities that determine the impossible at the phallic and genital level. When I say that the obsessional sustains his desire as impossible, I mean that he sustains his desire at the level of the impossibilities of desire.

If the image of the hole impresses itself here and if I've long insisted on this reference, it's because the circle of the obsessional's desire is precisely one of those circles that can never be reduced to a point owing to their topological place on the torus. It's because, from the oral to the anal, from the anal to the phallic, from the phallic to the scopic, and from the scopic to the vociferated, it never loops back upon itself, except by going back via its point of departure.

This example is sufficiently demonstrative to be elaborated as such and it can be transposed into other structures, notably the hysteric.

Next time, in reference to these structures, I'll be giving the conclusive formulation to what will allow us to situate, in the ultimate term, the position and the function of anxiety.

26 June 1963

XXIV

FROM THE *a* TO THE NAMES-OF-THE-FATHER

The scopic masking of the object *a*
Birth as an intrusion of the Other
To separate and to hold back
Mourning, mania, and melancholia
The voice, the father, the name, and love

Today, I'm going to be concluding with what I'd intended to tell you this year about anxiety.

I'm going to be marking out its limit and its function, thereby indicating where I intend certain positions to be upheld, positions that allow us, will allow us if possible, to reach a conclusion on what is involved in our role as analysts.

1

At the end of his life's work Freud designated anxiety as a signal. He designated it as a signal that is distinct from the effect of the traumatic situation, a signal linked to what he calls danger, a term that for him refers back to the notion of vital danger, which it has to be said is not clarified.

What is original in what I will have articulated for you this year is a detail regarding what danger is. In conformity with the Freudian notion, but more precisely articulated, I say that the danger in question is bound to the characteristic of cession specific to the constitutive moment of the object *a*.

In what way, at this point in our elaboration, must anxiety now be considered to be a signal? Once again, we are going to link up in a different way from Freud the moment at which the function of anxiety is brought into play.

I situate this moment as standing prior to the cession of the object, just as the necessity of Freud's articulation forces him to situate something else, something more primal than the danger-situation. Indeed, experience forbids us from not doing so.

As I announced back in the Seminar of two years hence, anxiety makes itself tangibly felt as referring back in a complex way to the desire of the Other. Back in this first approach, I indicated that the anguishing function of the desire of the Other was linked to the fact that I don't know which object *a* I am for this desire.

What I will be accentuating today is the following. Only at the level that I designated on the blackboard as the fourth level – amongst the five that can be defined as characteristic of the subject's constitution in his relation to the Other, in so far as we can articulate it as being centred around the function of anxiety – is this specific form fully articulated, does it take on an exemplary form, which is fully fleshed out, this specific form whereby human desire is the function of the desire of the Other.

I told you that anxiety is bound to the fact that I don't know which object *a* I am for the desire of the Other, but at the end of the day this is only valid at the scopic level. It's at this level that I can give you the exemplary fable in which the Other would be radically an Other, the praying mantis with its voracious desire, to which I am linked by no common factor whatsoever. Quite contrary to this, I am linked to the human Other by something which is my quality of being his *semblable* and the result is that what remains of the anguishing *I don't know what object I am*, is, fundamentally, *misrecognition*. There is a misrecognition of what the *a* is in the economy of my human desire and this is why the aforesaid fourth level, the level of scopic desire, is the level at which the structure of desire is the most fully developed in its fundamental alienation. It is also, paradoxically, the level at which the object *a* is most fully masked and at which, by virtue of this fact, the subject is most assured in relation to anxiety.

This is precisely what makes it necessary for us to look elsewhere for the trace of the *a* with respect to the moment of its constitution.

Indeed, whilst it is true that in sum and substance the Other is always there in its full reality, and therefore, in so far as it takes on a subjective presence, this reality is always likely to make itself felt through one of its prominent edges, it's nonetheless clear that development doesn't afford even access to the Other's reality.

At the first level, the Other's reality is presentified by need, as is very clear-cut in the original powerlessness of the nursling. It's only at the second level, with the incidence of the Other's demand, that something is detached properly speaking, which allows us to articulate in a more complete fashion the constitution of the *a* with respect to the function of the Other as the locus of the signifying chain.

Today, however, I don't want to move away from the first level, the level we term the oral level, without first carefully pointing out that anxiety already appears there, prior to any articulation of the Other's demand as such. Oddly enough, this manifestation of anxiety coincides with the very emergence in the world of he who is going to be the subject. This manifestation is his cry.

Now, I have long situated the function of the cry as a relation, not an originative one but a terminal one, to what we must consider to be the very heart of this Other inasmuch as it is completed for us at a certain moment in the form of our neighbour. I ask you to pause a short while over the paradox that here conjoins the point of departure of this first effect of cession, which is the anxiety effect, with what at the end will be something like its point of arrival. The difference is that the nursling can't do anything about the cry that slips out of him. He has yielded something and nothing will ever conjoin him to it again.

Am I the first to accentuate this originative anxiety? All the authors have done so. They have accentuated its character in a certain dramatic relation that the organism, the human organism on this occasion, has with the world in which it is going to live. What can we get from the many confused notions they give us about this emergence, and which can only possess certain contradictory features? Can we, for example, endorse Ferenczi's indication as a valuable one, namely, that there is an emergence, for ontogenesis itself, from out of goodness knows what primitive aqueous environment that would be homologous with the marine environment? Would amniotic liquid bear a relation to this primitive water?

For the living animal in an environment such as this, exchanging the inside for the outside happens at the level of the gill, whereas certainly, never, at any moment of the embryo's development, does the human gill function. Not everything that is indicated to us, however, in this psychoanalytic speculation, which is often a confused speculation, should be considered meaningless, and it should even be considered as potentially lying on the path of something significant. It skips past it, it lags behind it, but sometimes this speculation illuminates it. Moreover, since they make a point of mentioning phylogeny here, I would ask you to remember the following.

In the most basal scheme of the vital exchange between an organism and its environment, the organism possesses a limit across which a certain number of choice points of exchange are distributed. This wall ensures the osmosis between the outer environment and the inner environment, between which there is thus a common factor. Stop and consider, then, this incredible fact – the strangeness of the leap by which living beings left behind their primitive environment and moved over into air.

An organ is necessary for this – I ask you to consult the books on embryology – and one cannot fail to be struck by its, as it were, arbitrary neo-formative character in development. It intrudes inside the organism and mobilizes the entire adaptation of the nervous system, which takes a fair while to get used to this apparatus before it can function as a good pump. One might say that there is as much strangeness in the leap that the appearance of this organ constitutes as there is in the fact that at a certain moment in human history we saw humans breathing in an iron lung, or even going off into what is improperly called the cosmos with something around them that is essentially no different from what I'm evoking here as a stock of air for their vital function.

Freud indicates that anxiety was in some sense chosen to be the signal of something. Shouldn't we recognize here in this *something* the essential feature, in this radical intrusion, of something that is as Other to the living human being as the fact of passing over into the atmosphere? By emerging into this world where he must breathe, first and foremost he is literally choked, suffocated. This is what has been called trauma – there is no other – the trauma of birth, which is not separation from the mother but the inhalation, into oneself, of a fundamentally Other environment.

Of course, the link between this moment and what one can call the separation of weaning doesn't appear clearly. I ask you, however, to gather up the elements of your experience, your experience as analysts and as observers of children, unhesitatingly, to reconstruct everything that proves to be necessary when it comes to giving meaning to the term *weaning*. Let's say that the relationship between weaning and this first moment isn't a straightforward relationship, it's not a relationship of phenomena that overlap, but rather a relationship of contemporaneity.

In the main, it's not true that the child is weaned. He weans *himself*. He detaches himself from the breast, he plays. After the first experience of cession, whose already subjectified character makes itself tangibly felt with the first signs that flash across his face as he starts, nothing more, to form the expression of surprise, he plays at detaching himself from the breast and taking it up again. If there weren't already present something active enough for us to be able to articulate it in the sense of a desire for weaning, how could we even conceive of the very primitive facts, which are quite primordial in their appearance, of the refusal of the breast, the first forms of anorexia whose correlations at the level of the Other our experience teaches us to seek out right away?

To function authentically as what it is said to be in the classical theory, namely, the object involved in the breaking of the bond with the Other, this first object that we call the breast stands short of a full bond with the Other. This is why I've been strongly accentuating how this bond lies closer to the neo-natal subject. The breast doesn't belong to the Other, it is not the bond that has to be broken with the Other, at the very most it is the first sign of this bond. This is why it bears a relation to anxiety, but this is also why it is the first form of the transitional object in Winnicott's sense, the form that makes its function possible. Likewise, it is not, at this level defined by the *a*, the only object that is on offer to fulfil this function.

If, later on, another object, the anal object, is going to come and fulfil this function in a more clear-cut fashion when the Other itself elaborates its own function in the form of demand, one may recall the wisdom of those women who watch over the human animal's entry into the world, the midwives, who have always come to a halt faced with the peculiar little object that accompanies the child's appearance – the meconium.

Since I spent a long while on it last time, I won't be going over the articulation today, a much more typical articulation, of the function of the object *a* that the anal object allows us to make, inasmuch as it is found to be the first underpinning of subjectification in the relation to the Other, I mean that wherein, or whereby, the subject is first required by the Other to show himself as a subject, a fully fledged subject.

At this level, the subject already has to give *what he is* – in so far as *what he is* cannot enter the world except as a remainder, as something irreducible with respect to what is imposed upon him as a symbolic imprint. That which is going to identify desire, primordially, with the desire to hold back is appended to this object as a causal object. The first progressive form of desire is, therefore, as such, akin to the realm of inhibition. When desire appears for the first time as formed – at the second level – it stands in opposition to the very act by which its origination of desire was introduced at the previous stage. The second form of desire, the form that clarifies the function of cause that I give to the object, makes itself felt in turning against the pre-existing function that introduces the object *a* as such.

Indeed, it's clear that the first form of desire really is appended to the object, the form that we've elaborated as the desire for separation. As I reminded you earlier, the object is there, of course. It has already been laid out, produced, primordially produced. It is already there as a product of anxiety. So, as something pre-existent, it is made available to the function that is determined by the introduction of demand.

Therefore, what is at stake here is neither the object in itself nor the subject who would make himself autonomous in some vague and confused priority of totality. From the very first approach, it has to do with an object that has been chosen for its quality of being especially yieldable, of being originally a ceded object, and it has to do with a subject who is to be constituted in his function of being represented by *a*, a function that shall remain essential to the end.

Here we find the level by which we must abide if we truly want to consider what is at stake in our technical function.

2

Now it's a matter of realizing that the respective positions of anxiety and what amounts to *a* are interchangeable. On one side, there is the primordial point at which desire is inserted, constituted by the conjunction that includes *a* and the capital D of demand in the same brackets, and, on the other side, anxiety.

So, here we have anxiety.

We have long known it to be staved off, hidden, in what we call the obsessional's ambivalent relationship, the relationship that we simplify, that we abbreviate, that we evade when we confine it to the relationship of aggressiveness when it's actually a matter of something else. The object that the subject cannot impede himself from holding back as the asset that gets him noticed is thus merely his ejecta, his evacuations. These are the two faces by which the object determines the subject himself as compulsion and doubt.

Upon this oscillation between these two extreme points depends the subject's possible, momentary passage through this zero-point where he ultimately finds himself entirely at the mercy of the other, here in the dyadic sense of the little other.

This is why, back in my second lesson, I pointed out that the structure of desire's relation to the desire of the Other, in the sense I've been teaching it to you, stands in opposition to the structure wherein it is articulated, defined, even algebraized, in Hegelian dialectic.

I told you that the point at which these two desires partially overlap is the very same point that allows us to define this relationship as a relationship of aggressiveness. I've already written out the formula that defines this relation at the point we equate the *moment* of this desire – I mean *moment* in the sense that this word carries in physics – with zero. It is the formula $d(a): 0 > d(0)$, which is to be read – desire of *a*, in other words, desire as determined by the first characteristically yieldable object. In this point, one may say that the subject effectively finds himself faced with what Hegelian phenomenology translates as the impossibility of coexistent self-consciousnesses, and which is but the subject's impossibility of finding his cause within himself at the level of desire.

You should be able to see that what coordinates the causal function of the notion of *causa sui* is already taking shape here, a fantasy where thinking is confronted with the existence, somewhere, of a being to whom his cause would not be foreign, to which human speculation is in some way forced to come back as a compensation, as an arbitrary surmounting of a fact of our condition, the fact that the human being is first submitted to producing the cause of his desire in a danger of which he is unaware.

To this is linked the supreme and magisterial tone that resounds and goes on resounding at the heart of sacred Scripture, in spite of its blasphemous aspect, the *heh'bel* or *hab-ale*, the *all is vanity* from the text called Ecclesiastes. What we translate as *vanity* is this in the Hebrew text, whose three radical letters I've written up here, הֶבֶל, and which means wind, or even breath, if you like, vapour, a thing that fades away – which brings us back to an ambiguity that I think it's more legitimate to mention here, in connection with what can be most abject about breath, than all of what Jones thought he had to elaborate with respect to the Madonna's conception through the ear. This thematic of vanity is precisely the one that furnishes its abiding resonance and scope to the Hegelian definition of the original fruitful struggle from which the *Phänomenologie des Geistes* starts off, the struggle to death called the *struggle for pure prestige*, which really does carry the overtone of meaning the struggle for nothing.

To make the obsessional's treatment revolve around aggressiveness is to introduce into its principle – in a patent fashion and, if I may say so, an affirmed fashion, even if it hasn't been deliberated – the subduction of the subject's desire to the analyst's desire. Like any desire, this desire, although it has a reference that is internal to *a*, is articulated elsewhere. Here, it is identified with the ideal of the position that the analyst has obtained or believes he has obtained at the place of reality, the ideal to which the patient's desire will be obliged to stoop.

Now, the *a* at issue, marked out as the cause of desire, is neither this vanity nor this piece of waste. Although in its function it really is what I've been spelling out, namely, the object defined as a remainder that is irreducible to the symbolization that occurs at the locus of the Other, it nevertheless depends on this Other because how else would it be constituted?

Although the *a* is the sole remainder of existence to the extent that existence makes itself known, it is not, therefore, contrary to what has been said, existence as a forced fact. Indeed, this forced fact could only be situated through its reference to a professed mythical and noetic necessity, itself posited as a first reference. But there is no forced fact in the remainder *a* because the desire that will succeed, more or less, in culminating in existence takes root here.

The more or less thorough severity of its reduction, namely, what makes it irreducible, and in which everyone can recognize the exact level to which it has risen in the locus of the Other, is what gets defined in the dialogue that is played out on a stage. The principle of this desire is that, after having got up there, the object will have to fall back down again through the ordeal of what it will have left upon it in a relation of tragedy, or more often than not of comedy.

It is played out there, of course, as a role, but the role is not what matters. We all know this from inner experience and certitude. What matters is the remainder beyond the role. It's undoubtedly a precarious and exposed remainder because, as everyone knows these days, I am forever this yieldable object, this object of exchange, and this object is the principle that makes me desire, that makes me desirous of a lack – a lack which is not the subject's lack, but a failing that strikes the jouissance situated at the level of the Other.

It is in this respect that each function of the *a* simply refers to the central gap that separates, at the sexual level, desire from the locus of jouissance and condemns us to the necessity which means that for us jouissance is not inherently destined to desire. Desire can only set out to meet it and, in order to meet it, it must not only comprehend but overcome the very fantasy that supports and constructs it.

We discovered this at the point of running aground that we call castration anxiety, but why not call it castration desire because a desire is also suspended from the central lack that disjoins desire from jouissance? Its threat for each and every subject is only fashioned from having recognized it in the desire of the Other. In the end, the Other, whoever it is, appears in the fantasy as the castrator, the agent of castration.

Certainly the positions are different in men and in women. For women, the position is more comfortable because what's done is done. This is also what makes for her much more special bond with the desire of the Other. Kierkegaard's peculiar remark, that women are more anxious than men, is, I believe, profoundly correct. How would this be possible if, at the pivotal, phallic level, anxiety were not fashioned precisely from the relation to the desire of the Other?

Desire, inasmuch as at its core it is desire for desire, that is, temptation, leads us back to this anxiety in its most originative function. At the level of castration, anxiety represents the Other, if the encounter with the bowing-out of the apparatus here gives us the object in the form of a shortcoming.

Need I call to mind what, in the analytic tradition, confirms what I'm spelling out here? Who is it that gives us the first example of the castration that is beckoned, assumed, and desired as such, if not Oedipus?

Oedipus is not first and foremost the father. This is what I've meant for a long time by wryly pointing out that Oedipus couldn't have had an Oedipus complex. Oedipus is he who wants to pass authentically, and mythically too, to the fourth level, which I really have to broach via its exemplary path – he who wants to violate the prohibition on the conjunction between the *a*, here $(-\varphi)$, and anxiety – he who wants to see what lies beyond the satisfaction of his desire, a satisfaction that has been met. The sin of Oedipus is *cupido sciendi*. He wants to know, and this is paid for by the horror I described – what in the end he sees are his own eyes, *a*, cast to the ground.

Does this mean that this is the structure of the fourth level and that this bloody rite of blinding always has to be present somewhere? No, it doesn't. They have been given eyes *that they should not see*. They don't need to tear them out.

This is precisely why the human drama is not tragedy, but comedy.

Anxiety is sufficiently staved off and misrecognized in the mere capture of the specular image, *i(a)*. The best one may wish for is for it to be reflected in the eyes of the Other – but there's no need for this since we have the mirror.

3

Let's see now what the fourth-level articulation is by using our inhibition-symptom-anxiety reference chart.

Here is how I shall describe this articulation.

I	desire not to see	powerlessness	concept of anxiety
S	misrecognition	almightiness	suicide
A	ideal	mourning	anxiety

The scopic level

In the stead of *inhibition* stands the *desire not to see*. Given the arrangement of the phenomena, it scarcely needs to be argued out, everything accommodates it.

Misrecognition, being structural at the level of *not wanting to know*, stands there in the second row.

In the third row, as *turmoil*, stands the *ideal*. It's the Ego Ideal, that is, that part of the Other that it is most convenient to introject, as they say. The term introjection is being brought in with good reason, but I would nonetheless ask you to take it on board reservedly because the ambiguity that remains between introjection and projection indicates well enough that another level will have to be brought in here to give the term introjection its full meaning.

At the heart of the fourth level, at the central place of the *symptom* such as it is incarnated specifically at the level of the obsessional, I've already designated the obsessional's fantasy of *almightiness*. This fantasy is correlative to the fundamental *powerlessness* to sustain the *desire not to see*.

What we are going to place at the level of *acting-out* is the function of *mourning* in so far as in a moment I'll be asking you to recognize here what in a previous year I taught you to see in terms of a fundamental structure of the constitution of desire.

At the level of the *passage à l'acte* stands the fantasy of *suicide*, whose character and authenticity stand to be reappraised in an essential way within this dialectic.

At the bottom right still stands *anxiety*, here masked.

At the level of *embarrassment* stands what we shall legitimately call the *concept of anxiety*. I don't know if Kierkegaard's audacity in bringing in this term has really been taken account of. What can it mean other than that there is *either* the function of the concept as Hegel would have it, that is, the symbolic hold over the real, *or* the hold that we have, the one anxiety gives us, the sole final perception and as such the perception of all reality – and that between the two, one has to choose?

The concept of anxiety only emerges as such at the limit and from a meditation that everything suggests runs aground fairly quickly. But what matters to us is simply that we're meeting fresh confirmation of the truths that we've already tackled from another angle.

Now, as announced, I'm going to go back over the function of mourning.

At the end of his speculation on anxiety, Freud wonders in what way everything he has put forward on the relationships between anxiety and object-loss is distinct from mourning. The entire addenda, the entire appendix to *Inhibitions, Symptoms and Anxiety* marks the most extreme awkwardness when it comes to defining the way in which one can understand how the two functions for which he provides the same reference give rise to such divergent manifestations.

I think I need to call to mind here what led us to our examination when we looked at the eminent dramatic character Hamlet, who marks the emergence of a new relation of the subject to his desire at the dawn of modern ethics.

I pointed out that it's strictly speaking his mother's absence of mourning that makes any possible impetus of a desire in him fade away, recede, and crumble in the extreme, even though this being is also presented to us in a way that allowed a certain Salvador de Madariaga, for instance, to recognize in him the specific style of the heroes of the Renaissance. Hamlet is a character of whom the least one can say – need I remind you? – is that he doesn't draw back when faced with something and he's not easily fazed. The only thing he can't do is precisely the act he's cut out for and that is because the desire is wanting.

The desire is wanting because the Ideal has crumbled. Indeed, Hamlet mentions his father's past reverence for a creature before whom, to our astonishment, this supreme king, Old Hamlet, literally bowed down to pay homage, stooped in his loving allegiance. What could be more doubtful than the kind of idolatrous relationship Hamlet's words sketch out? Do we not have here the signs of an overly forced, overly exalted sentiment, which even belong to the realm of a unique, mythical love, akin to the style of courtly love? Now, when courtly love appears outside the field of strictly cultural and ritualistic references, where clearly it is addressed to something other than the Lady, it is on the contrary the sign of some shortcoming, some shirking, faced with the difficult paths that gaining access to a true love implies.

Patently, to his father's overvaluation of the conjugal Gertrude, such as this attitude is presented in Hamlet's memories, there corresponds dialectically his own animalistic evasion of the maternal Gertrude. When the Ideal is contradicted, when it crumbles, we can see that the result is that Hamlet's power of desire vanishes. As I showed you, this power will only be restored with the vision, on the outside, of a bereavement, a true one, whose fray he enters, that of Laertes for his sister, whom for Hamlet is the loved object from which he was suddenly separated due to the shortcoming of his desire.

Doesn't this unlock the door for us, doesn't it furnish us with the key that enables us to articulate, better than Freud does but following the same line of his examination, what a bereavement signifies?

Freud tells us that the bereaved subject is faced with a task of consummating for a second time the loss of the beloved object that has been occasioned by the fateful mishap. And goodness knows how much he insists, and rightly so, on the piecemeal, painstaking aspect of the remembrance of everything that was lived out in the bond with the beloved object.

As for us, the work of mourning strikes us, in a light that is at once identical and contrary, as a labour that is carried out to maintain and sustain all these painstaking links with the aim of restoring the bond with the true object of relation, the masked object, the object *a* – for which thereafter a substitute can be given that will ultimately have no more scope than the one that initially occupied this place. As one of our circle told me, light-heartedly, in connection with the fling depicted for us in the film *Hiroshima mon amour*, it's a story that shows us very well how any old *irreplaceable German* can immediately find a perfectly valid substitute in the first Japanese man she comes across.

The problem of mourning is the problem of maintaining, at the scopic level, the bonds whereby desire is suspended, not from the object *a*, but from *i(a)*, by which all love is narcissistically structured in so far as the term love implies the idealized dimension I spoke about. This is what makes for the difference between what occurs in mourning and what occurs in melancholia and mania.

Unless we distinguish between the object *a* and the *i(a)*, we cannot form a conception of the radical difference that lies between melancholia and mourning, which Freud recalls and articulates powerfully in the note I've just cited, as well as in the well-known article on *Mourning and Melancholia*. Do I need to read you the passage to jog your memory? After having gone into the notion of the reversion of the professed object libido onto the subject's own ego, Freud affirms – he's the one who says this – that, in melancholia, this process clearly doesn't come to a conclusion because the object takes the helm. The object triumphs.

Something other than the mechanism of libido's return in mourning is involved in melancholia and, by dint of this, the whole dialectic is built up differently. Freud tells us that the subject – I won't be trying to see why today – has to have it out with the object. But the fact that it's an object *a* and that at the fourth level this object is usually masked beneath the *i(a)* of narcissism and mis-recognized in its essence, means that the melancholiac necessarily passes through, as it were, his own image. Initially he attacks this image so as to reach, within it, the object *a* that transcends him, whose control escapes him – and whose collapse will drag him into the suicide-rush, with the automatism, the mechanism, the necessary and fundamentally alienated character with which, as you know, these suicides of melancholiacs are committed. And they are committed in not just any setting. That this occurs so often at the window, or even *through* the window, is not by chance. It marks a recourse to a structure that is none other than the fantasy.

We can only grasp that which distinguishes what belongs to the cycle of mania/melancholia from everything that belongs to the ideal cycle related to mourning and desire by accentuating the functional difference between, on one hand, the relationship between *a* and *i(a)* in mourning, and, on the other, in the other cycle, the radical reference to the *a*, which roots the subject more than does any other relation, but which is also fundamentally misrecognized and alienated in the narcissistic relation.

Let's specify right away that what is at issue in mania is the non-function of *a* and not simply its misrecognition. No *a* comes to ballast the subject and this delivers him, in a way without any possibility of freedom, to the sheer infinite and ludic metonymy of the signifying chain.

Doubtless I've missed out a fair few things here, but this is going to allow us to conclude at the level at which I wanted to leave you this year.

4

Desire in its most alienated character, its most fundamentally fantasmatic character, is what characterizes the fourth level. I went a little way into the structure of the fifth level and indicated sufficiently that at this level the *a* is recast, openly alienated this time, as the support of the desire of the Other that, this time, can be named – you might note that this is also to tell you why this year I'll be stopping on this term.

Indeed, the entire dialectic of what happens at the fifth level implies a much more fastidious articulation than has ever been given with what I designated earlier as introjection – which as such implies the auditory dimension, and which implies the paternal function too.

If everything happens next year in a way that will allow me to pursue my Seminar in accordance with the path foreseen, I'll be making you an appointment with not only the Name, but the Names-of-the-Father. And this is not for nothing.

In the Freudian myth, the father intervenes in the most evidently mythical fashion as the one whose desire submerges, crushes, forces itself upon all the others. Isn't there a plain contradiction here with the fact clearly afforded by the experience that, on his path, something very different is operating, namely, the normalization of desire on the pathways of the law?

Is that all? Doesn't the very necessity of keeping up this myth alongside what is traced out for us here and made tangible by experience, right down to facts that we have weighed up time and again regarding the shortcoming of the father function, draw our attention to the fact that when his desire is evinced, the father knows to what *a* this desire refers?

Contrary to what religious myth states, the father is not a *causa sui*, but a subject who has gone far enough into the realization of his desire to be able to integrate it back into its cause, whatever that may be, back into what is irreducible in the function of the *a*. This is what allows us to link in with the very principle of our research, without eluding it in any way, the fact that there is no human subject who does not have to posit himself as an object, a finite object, to which his finite desires are appended, desires which only look like they are infinite inasmuch as, in each getting farther away from their centre, they carry the subject farther away from any authentic realization.

Now, the misrecognition of the *a* leaves one door unlocked. We have always known this, there wasn't even any need of analysis to show it because I believe I've been able to show it you in one of Plato's dialogues, *The Symposium*. The sole path on which desire can furnish us with that wherein we shall have to recognize ourselves as object *a* – in so far as, at the end-point, an end-point that is doubtless never reached, it is our most radical existence – only opens up by situating the *a* as such in the field of the Other. And not only is it to be situated there, but it gets situated there by every single one of us. This is none other than the possibility of transference.

The interpretation we give always bears on the greater or lesser dependence of desires in relation to one another, but this does not mean that anxiety is being contended with. Anxiety is only ever surmounted when the Other has been named. There is only ever any love when there is a name, as everyone knows from experience. The moment the name of he or she to whom we address our love is uttered, we know very well that this is a threshold of the utmost importance.

This is just a trace, a trace of that something that stretches from the existence of the *a* to its passage into history. What makes a psychoanalysis a unique adventure is the search for the ἄγαλμα in the field of the Other.

I have questioned you on several occasions about what the analyst's desire ought to be for the work to be possible, right where we are trying to push things, beyond the limit of anxiety.

The analyst certainly ought to be the one who, however little, from some angle, from some line of approach, has merged his desire back into this irreducible *a* sufficiently to offer the question of the concept of anxiety a real guarantee.

3 July 1963

Note to the Text

Establishing the text of this Seminar has benefited from the exist-ence of an exceptional typescript. Lacan sent each lesson to his daughter Judith, who at the time was absent from Paris, and added to the typescript his handwritten annotations, which I have used.

The reader will have noticed that in the first chapter Lacan calls out to his audience to confirm whether the word *smagare* exists in Italian and the reply he receives leads him to conclude that some doubt remains. On the typescript copy addressed to his daughter, bearing a dedication dated 16 November 1962, thus two days after the first lesson, the following detail features in the margin: 'Here, I called out to Piera – who suggested this doubt to me – but since then I've checked things out and *smagare* does indeed carry the meaning that B. & W. give it.'

An annotation in the margin identifies the author of the article Lacan had been expecting: 'This refers to a piece of work by Green on *The Savage Mind*'. André Green's review of Lévi-Strauss's book subsequently appeared in the journal *Critique*.

J.-A. M.

Notes

All notes below have been provided by the translator.

Chapter I Anxiety in the Net of Signifiers

1 The personal pronoun *on*, and not the *Un*.
2 The French edition of the *Seminar* reproduces Lacan's hand-drawn illustration, from which these arrows are missing.
3 The French *embarras* carries a far wider range of signification than the English 'embarrassment', encompassing discomfiture, nuisance, confusion and situations of annoyance and quandary. The idioms 'to be in a bind', or 'to be in a pickle' convey to some extent this range of meaning.
4 The English word 'turmoil', of uncertain origin, is by no means a completely satisfying rendering of the French *émoi*, although one etymological hypothesis, that 'turmoil' is the condensation of 'turn + moil', parallels to some extent Lacan's discussion below. The English word 'commotion' is another candidate (in the French language, *commotion* refers rather to the condition of concussion). Dennis Porter opts for 'excitement' in his translation of *Seminar VII*, p. 249. 'Dismay', while inviting interesting points of etymological contrast, is too far removed semantically.
5 Bloch and von Wartburg erroneously set down the modal auxiliary as an infinitive. Lacan reproduces their error in his *Seminar*, which we have permitted ourselves to correct here.

Chapter V That Which Deceives

1 'Making unhappened' is the literal rendering proposed by Strachey in the footnote on page 274 of his translation, *Inhibitions, Symptoms and Anxiety*, in *Penguin Freud Library, Vol. X, On Psychopathology*, 1993.

Chapter VI That Which Deceives Not

1 *Prendre des vessies pour des lanternes* is a French idiom, dating back at least to the fourteenth century, used to denote someone's credulity. A common English language equivalent is, 'to think the moon is made of green cheese'.

Chapter IX *Passage à l'acte* and Acting-out

1 Cary F. Baynes gives 'gentleness that is adaptable', in his translation of Richard Wilhelm's *The I Ching or Book of Changes*, Princeton University Press, 1950, p. 205.

Chapter X On a Lack that is Irreducible to the Signifier

1 It was in fact in the first year of the Seminar.
2 *La vie est faite de frustrations* is a common phrase in French.

Chapter XIII Aphorisms on Love

1 The second sentence that Kaufmann brings corresponds to the fourth line of Russian text on the first page of this chapter (p. 170).
2 *Bête comme chou* is an idiomatic French expression to mean 'easy as pie' or 'simplicity itself'. It is left un-Englished here given the ensuing reference to the *Satyricon*.

Chapter XIV Woman, Truer and More Real

1 An allusion to Proust's expression in *Swann's Way* which has passed into common French usage: *S'en soucier comme un poisson d'une pomme*, 'to care as little for something as a fish does for an apple'.

Chapter XV Men's Business

1 The author of *She Stoops to Conquer* is in fact Sheridan's contemporary, Goldsmith.
2 In English translation as 'Outline of a Psychodynamic Theory of Masochism', in *The Psychoanalytic Quarterly* 25: 193–214.

Chapter XVII The Mouth and the Eye

1 *Le sexe* could also be understood as 'the sexual organ' here.

Chapter XVIII The Voice of Yahweh

1 *Grains et issues*, as in the title of Tzara's collection of poems, is the French term that groups together, on one hand, freshly milled grain, or flour, with, on the other, the 'tail of the mill': the wheat bran particles that are its by-product. A beauty spot is *un grain de beauté*. An *issue* is also a solution or an outcome.
2 *Ça me regarde*, is quite literally 'it regards me': both 'it's looking at me' and 'it concerns me', 'it's my business'.

Chapter XIX The Evanescent Phallus

1 Extract from 'The Fire Sermon' taken from The Waste Land © Estate of T. S. Eliot and reprinted by permission of Faber and Faber Ltd.

Chapter XX What Comes in Through the Ear

1 The trio *puissance, toute-puissance* and *impuissance*, we have rendered here and hereafter as 'might', 'almightiness' and 'powerlessness'. The reader may, however, entertain the alternative trio: 'potency', 'omnipotence' and 'impotence'.
2 The genus in question in Kreidl's experiment was in fact a different member of the Crustacea subspecies, the brackish-water palaemonetes, and not the freshwater daphnia.

Chapter XXII From Anal to Ideal

1 Cyril Tourneur's play is actually slightly later, first published in 1611.

Index